Privatization, Restructuring, and Regulation of Network Utilities

Privatization, Restructuring, and Regulation of Network Utilities

The Walras-Pareto Lectures

David M. Newbery

The MIT Press
Cambridge, Massachusetts
London, England

Third printing, 2001
©1999 Massachusetts Institute of Technology

This book was set in Palatino by Best-set Typesetter Ltd., Hong Kong
Printed and bound in the United States of America.

Library of Congress Cataloging-in-Publication Data

Newbery, David M. G.
    Privatization, restructuring, and regulation of network utilities / David M. Newbery.
        p.   cm.—(The Walras-Pareto lectures ; 2)
    Includes bibliographical references and index.
    ISBN 0-262-14068-3 (hardcover : alk. paper)
    1. Public utilities. 2. Privatization. 3. Public utilities--Government policy. I. Title.
II. Series.

HD2763 .N48   2000
363.6—dc21   99-052764

Contents

Preface

This book is the direct response to the invitation to give the Walras-Pareto Lectures in Lausanne in November 1995. Then it was rather more than a century since Pareto succeeded Walras to a chair at Lausanne, and 86 years since the University honored Walras as the first economist to establish the conditions of general equilibrium and thus as the founder of the School of Lausanne. As I am not a general equilibrium theorist, I searched in *The New Palgrave* to see whether my interests overlapped those of the distinguished Lausanne economists that the lectures commemorated. I found that Walras had strong "scientific socialist" views on natural monopolies, which he believed should be nationalized. Railways were the quintessential nineteenth-century example of a network utility, and Pareto's first writings appear to have been on the advantages and drawbacks of public and private ownership of railways. He rapidly abandoned his early plans to become a railway engineer, and his support for free trade led in due course to his exposition of social optimality, a guiding principle for the continental approach to public utility pricing. I therefore take some comfort that these lectures are on a fit subject to honor both Walras and Pareto.

The invitation to give the lectures allowed me to reflect on the continued excitement of studying policy toward network industries and, more generally, on the boundaries between the market economy and the state. Thirty years ago, at the start of my career, I was absorbed by developments in optimal tax theory and social cost–benefit analysis. These gave clear insights into what should be done and how to evaluate the merits of policy choices. They indicated clearly that what should be done was frequently not done. Why that was has been an absorbing topic ever since. The simplest explanation was that agents were not provided with the right incentives. The same techniques of optimal tax theory could be applied to examine the problems of motivating agents to act in the interests of the principal, and they led directly to modern theories of regulation. These were fine if there was no choice of market structure, but if network services could be made competitive, the problems of information, incentives, and transferring the gains to consumers appeared to be there for the taking. The last fifteen years have demonstrated the truth and limits of that insight.

Interest groups might be more concerned with private gain than the social good, and they compete to control the regulatory institutions. Competition over networks differs from conventional market competition in a variety of ways, while managing the interface between the regulated and competitive sectors remains key to successful liberalisation. Just how important the institutions of capitalism for regulating market behavior has been underlined by events in transitional economies since the fall of the Berlin Wall just a decade ago.

This has been an exciting time to be an applied economist. I feel privileged to have worked in areas of such great intellectual fascination and practical importance. I was able to follow the British electricity experiment from the start, at the same time as working with colleagues here and abroad on Central Europe's transition to the market economy. As so often, the historical accidents of time and place played a large part, but I have been fortunate in my colleagues and in the intellectual support of Churchill College and the University of Cambridge.

I am of course also indebted to the University of Lausanne for the invitation that prompted this book, and for the warmth of their hospitality during a very pleasant brief stay presenting the lectures. Much of my work of network utilities has been supported by the British Economic and Social Research Council under a series of projects (000231811, 000233766, and 000236828) on privatizing and regulating network utilities. I am indebted to my colleagues who worked on these projects: Richard Green, Christopher Doyle, Maria Maher, Michael Pollitt, and Tanga McDaniel. Collaborative work with Rich Gilbert on the credibility of regulatory regimes, published in *The Rand Journal of Economics*, 1994, appears in chapter 2. The University of California commissioned joint work with Richard Green that appears as Newbery and Green (1996), which features extensively especially in chapter 4. Chapter 6 draws on Green and Newbery (1992), Newbery and Pollitt (1997), and parts of my recent articles listed in the bibliography appear with varying degrees of modification throughout the book. I am indebted to Richard Gilbert, Richard Green, and Michael Pollitt for permission to reproduce collaborative work.

Claude Henry has been supportive and remarkably patient in dealing with a manuscript whose first draft was available in December 1995, but whose redrafting to reflect the rapid developments of the last few years has had to be fitted into brief intervals between the normal pressures of academic life and the administrative responsibility of running the Department of Applied Economics, whose support has nevertheless been invaluable. Sharon Swann has provided secretarial support, while seminar and lecture invitations around the world have provided invaluable feedback, as well as welcome distractions from completing the task.

Cambridge, England
August 1999

Abbreviation and Units

AGR	advanced gas-cooled reactors
ATM	asynchronous transfer mode
bcm	billion cubic meter
BG(C)	British Gas (Corporation)
BT	the incumbent British Telecoms company
CATV	cable television
CCA	current cost accounting
CCGT	combined cycle gas turbine
CfD	contract for differences
CEE	Central and Eastern Europe
CEB	Central Electricity Board
CEGB	Central Electricity Generating Board
cm	cubic meter
CO_2	carbon dioxide
CPS	carrier preselection
CPUC	California Public Utilities Commission
CV	coefficient of variation = SD/mean
DEA	data envelopment analysis
DGES	Director General of Electricity Supply
DGFT	Director General of Fair Trading
DGSS	Director General of Gas Supply
DGT	Director General of Telecommunications
DTI	Department of Trade and Industry
EC	European Commission
ECNZ	Electricity Corporation of New Zealand
EdF	Electricité de France
EFA	Electricity Forward Agreement
ESI	electricity supply industry
EU	European Union

FCC	Federal Communications Commission
FERC	Federal Energy Regulatory Commission
FFL	fossil fuel levy
FGD	flue gas desulphurisation
GATS	General Agreement of Trade in Services
GATT	General Agreement of Trade and Tariffs
GCV	gross calorific value
GDP	gross domestic product
GNP	gross national product
GOAL	Generator Ordering and Loading (program for scheduling generation)
HFO	heavy fuel oil
HSHC	Hungarian State Holding Company
ICOR	incremental capital output ratio
IMF	International Monetary Fund
IONU	investor-owned network utility
IP	Internet protocol
IPP	independent power producer
ISO	independent system operator
JTC	Jamaica Telephone Company
LD	long distance
LDC	local distribution company (usually of gas)
LNG	liquified natural gas
LOLP	loss of load probability
LRMC	long-run marginal cost
LTI	long-term interruptible (gas contract)
MAR	market to assets ratio
MFJ	modified final judgement
MIT	Ministry of Industry and Trade
MJ	MegaJoule (heat unit)
MMC	Monopolies and Mergers Commission
MTS	message telephone service
MVM	Magya Villamos Muvek (the Hungarian power company)
NBP	national balancing point
NCV	net calorific value
NFFO	nonfossil fuel obligation
NFPE	nonfinancial public enterprise
NGC	National Grid Company Plc
NIE	Northern Ireland Electricity Plc
NO_x	nitrogen oxides

NOPR	Notice of Proposed Rulemaking
NTS	national transmission system
OECD	Organization for Economic Cooperation and Development
OFT	Office of Fair Trading
PE	public enterprise
PGT	public gas transporter
PJM	Pennsylvania–New Jersey–Maryland interconnection
PNU	public network utility
PPA	power purchase agreement
PPP	pool purchase price
PSP	pool selling price
PSTN	public switched telephone network
PUC	Public Utilities Commission
PWR	pressurized water reactor
PX	power exchange
R&P	restructuring and privatization
RAB	regulatory asset base
RBOC	Regional Bell Operating Company
REC	regional electricity company
ROR	rate of return
RPI	retail price index
SB(M)	single buyer (model)
SD	standard deviation
SMP	system marginal price
SRMC	short-run marginal cost
SO$_2$	sulfur dioxide
SOE	state-owned enterprise
SPA	State Property Agency
TCC	transmission congestion contract
TELRIC	total element long-run incremental cost
TFP	total factor productivity
TO	transmission operator
TPA	third-party access
UUROR	used and useful rate of return
VAT	value-added tax
VOLL	value of lost load
WEM	wholesale electricity market
WTO	World Trade Organization

Units

kW	kilowatt
MW	megawatt = 1,000 kW
GW	gigawatt = 1,000 MW
kWh	kilowatt hour
MWh	megawatt hour = 1,000 kWh
GWh	gigawatt hour = 1,000 MWh
TWh	terrawatt hour = 1,000 GWh
kbs	kilobits = 1,000 bits per second
Mbs	megabits = 1,000 kbs
BTU	British thermal unit
MBTU	million BTU
therm	100,000 BTU

Privatization, Restructuring, and Regulation of Network Utilities

1   Introduction

Network utilities are public utilities that require a fixed network to deliver their services, and include gas, electricity, water, rail, and fixed link telephony. They are economically of high importance—the value added of the privatized U.K. network utilities in 1995 was 5 percent of GDP, with a market value of 15 percent of GDP. The networks of these utilities are classic natural monopolies; they create rents that are fought over. The networks are durable and fixed, so the rents persist. The capital of the network of the utility is large and sunk, so once created the balance of bargaining advantage shifts from investor to consumer. Finally the networks of gas, water, electricity, and telecoms are directly linked to the consumer, giving their owner potentially large exploitative power. These consumers are numerous, are politically important, and have no choice of network. In the telling phrase of Albert Hirschman, they cannot exit and so will use their voice.

The problem facing investors and consumers is to devise an institution that will balance these interests and powers. The tension between the investor and consumer can be side-stepped by state ownership, which has the coercive power to finance the sunk capital without requiring the assurance of a future return from the utility. Alternatively, it can attempt to reconcile private ownership with consumers' political power through regulation. Either way, network utilities operate under terms set by the state.

Economists since Adam Smith have argued that competition not only provides incentives for firms to minimize production costs but also restrains prices and ensures that consumers will satisfy their wants at least cost. This claim fails for natural monopolies. They either face no effective competition and hence are under little pressure to cut costs or keep prices low or, if competitors enter, wastefully duplicate facilities, raising costs and prices. Either way, the market will fail to satisfy consumer needs at least cost. The conventional analysis of network utilities starts from this market failure, which justifies regulation or public ownership to restrain prices and restrictions on entry to avoid costly duplication. The task is then to devise rules for setting prices and meeting demand that encourage efficiency.

This book takes a rather different approach. It argues that designing price-setting rules is only a part of the policy agenda for network utilities. Network utilities pose special problems of ownership and regulation whose solution is constrained by the institutional endowment of the country. Public policy toward these utilities will inevitably reflect deeper political and cultural features of society, as will the institutions that evolve in response to these factors. How these utilities should be regulated, structured, and even owned, may vary over time in response to changing circumstances. Utility policy may respond to changes—in the balance of political power, in the relative power of competing interest groups, in technology, in risks (e.g., of supply disruptions), in international competitive pressure, or in investment needs. Most of the time the balance of forces will be such that the existing governance structures of these utilities will be in equilibrium, but occasionally the balance is disturbed sufficiently that change becomes possible or likely. The growth slowdown and loss of confidence after the oil shocks of the 1970s ushered in one such period of disturbance, eventually opening the prospect of fundamental reforms in utility governance.

The post–oil-shock period has witnessed a sea-change in our view of the legitimate role of the state in economic activity. The boundaries of the state started to shift with privatization in Chile and Britain, and they changed dramatically with the transition from state socialism to the market economy in Eastern Europe. Legitimacy is not just about public versus private ownership, but about control—whether the state should exercise control directly though ownership or indirectly through regulation, or whether economic activity should be guided by the market, subject only to general competition policy. The wave of deregulation that started in 1978 in the United States showed that markets were better than regulators at reducing prices and increasing efficiency, and this cast doubt on the social value of regulation. Economists learned that the information they had assumed to be costlessly available for directing utility policy was sadly incomplete. Regulation was therefore unavoidably inefficient, and regulatory failure had to be balanced against the costs of market failure.

This book argues that societies have to evolve satisfactory regulatory institutions to deal with the special problems of network utilities. The most basic requirement is that these utilities should be able to finance their investment and meet the demands made upon them. Economies with different institutional endowments have evolved different solutions, notably in the form of ownership, and some have been considerably more successful than others. The simplest way to ensure an adequate supply of investible funds is to give the utility a protected franchise monopoly or to give it access to the tax powers of the government.

The next problem is ensuring efficiency in operation, and responsiveness to new technological possibilities. Here competition is more effective than regulation, but it is in apparent conflict with the protected franchise, and the associated tendency to vertical integration that this encouraged. The great innovation of the post–oil-shock period was not so much privatization as liberalization and/or restructuring. If regulation could be confined to the core natural monopoly network, and competition introduced for the services supplied over the network, then efficiency and innovation could be encouraged.

From this perspective the most important problem to address is to choose the right structure for the utility that will limit the need for necessarily inefficient regulation. The evidence presented below suggests that there may be little difference in efficiency between state-owned network utilities and vertically integrated private network utilities subject to cost-of-service regulation. The key innovation that makes a difference to performance is to introduce competition into the services supplied over the network. This may be done either by vertical separation or liberalizing access to the network. Vertical separation has the advantage that given adequate competition, regulation can be confined to the network. Liberalization requires more complex regulation to prevent the network owner from exploiting his incumbency advantage. Apparently quite modest reforms that allow entry and remove the protected franchise can precipitate far-reaching changes in the whole system of regulation, with further consequential changes for the structure of the utility. The traditional concerns of utility regulation of ensuring efficient pricing and operations remain for the core network, but the appropriate choice of regulatory instruments and institutions has been transformed by liberalization and restructuring.

Not all network utilities lend themselves to liberalization and competition. The costs of moving water any significant distance through pipes is so high compared to its value that there is unlikely to be much competition in water supply. Britain, and the EU through its Railway Directive, would like to promote competition between different train-operating companies using the same rail track, but time-tabling problems have so far prevented much progress. This book therefore concentrates on the three utilities where there is good evidence of the possibility of vigorous competition: telecoms, electricity, and gas. Of these, telecoms are the most popular choice for privatization, for reasons that will become clear in chapter 2, though it raises complex regulatory issues. Electricity privatization and liberalization are well on track in the Americas and Europe. Gas liberalization is lagging outside North America and Britain, but is set to start in Europe with potentially large benefits.

Competition is difficult to sustain in government-owned utilities (though it may be possible where municipally owned utilities can compete on a national market, as with Norwegian electricity), and so there is a natural complementarity between privatization and competition. In that sense privatization seems to be a necessary but not sufficient step to achieving the benefits of competition. Britain was somewhat slow to appreciate the distinction between privatization and liberalization for network utilities. British Telecom (later BT) was privatized in 1984 as a vertically integrated monopoly (owning the entire existing network), though Mercury was granted a time-limited franchise as its sole licensed competitor with access to its network. British Gas was also privatized as a vertically integrated monopoly, and although it was no longer protected against entry, entrants had to negotiate for the right to transport gas over its pipelines and were at an obvious competitive disadvantage.

It soon became clear that privatized monopolies had many of the drawbacks of public monopolies, with the added disadvantage that the government no longer had the power to order their reorganization and restructuring. Regulation was left with the difficult task of encouraging competition to develop. This was clearly easier to do before the utility was privatized, a lesson that was taken to heart by the time it was decided to privatize the electricity industry. But private ownership did not necessarily protect vertically integrated utilities from the pressures to introduce competition. In 1984, the United States liberalized access to gas pipelines and dismantled AT&T, making long-distance calls competitive. In due course, the now privatized British Gas was forced to liberalize access to its pipelines and eventually chose to break up its business in 1997. The duopoly telephone restriction was lifted in

1991 and entry liberalized, and in 1996 BT was required to introduce accounting separation. The United States is now encouraging vertical separation when electricity markets are liberalized, at a pace to be determined by each state. In Britain the combination of private ownership, liberalized access and regulation that had a duty to foster competition eventually induced a degree of postprivatization restructuring, arguably at considerably higher cost than if it been done before privatization.

Privatization raised new regulatory questions that did not arise where utilities had always been under private ownership, and where regulation had evolved organically. Rate-of-return regulation evolved through a series of landmark court cases in the United States to provide procedural fairness in the allocation of rents accruing to franchise monopoly investor-owned utilities. Economists have increasingly criticized it for its inefficiency. Price regulation was designed in the United Kingdom to create an efficient system of regulation to enable publicly owned utilities to be transferred to private ownership. Instead of competitive firms making it unprofitable to raise prices above the market level, the regulator sets a cap which is intended to reflect the efficient (i.e., competitive) price. Initially this form of regulation was proposed as a stopgap for BT until the market became adequately competitive, but because BT was privatized with such a dominant market position, it will not be until 2001 that retail price control is removed. Price-cap regulation was adopted for all subsequently privatized U.K. utilities, and has been adopted for regulating AT&T in the United States and in a number of other countries. Politicians and the public have criticized price regulation for its lack of fairness in the distribution of rents between consumers, shareholders, and managers. Price-cap regulation may not be sustainable in some countries, and public ownership of the network remains a serious option, though the case for privatizing the network services remains strong.

The emphasis in this book is on structural reform and comparative institutional economics, to see how far it is possible in practice to improve performance by reducing costs while sustaining investment, rather than on the traditional topics of pricing and short-run allocative efficiency. Even for that important topic it remains important to ask whether regulatory institutions can be designed and sustained to deliver the promised benefits of intelligent price setting.

Many of the examples presented below have been taken from the British experience, mainly because the experience of privatization has served as a model for many other countries but also because the system of regulation differs sharply from the standard U.S. model. It is important to see how relevant the British model is for other countries with their possibly very different cultures, politics, and institutions. The United States provides excellent evidence on restructuring under regulatory pressure, as well as providing the contrast between traditional rate-of-return regulation and the price regulation introduced in Britain. Most developed and many developing countries are transforming telecoms regulation, in response to technical change, to secure a competitive advantage, or under international pressure. Others are privatizing water, gas, and electric utilities. It is now more than fifteen years after the first British utility privatization, and a decade since the most dramatic restructuring of a network utility—that of British electricity. As the United States wrestles with a similar restructuring, now is a good time to take stock of what has become an increasingly international movement to reform and restructure network utilities.

Although the evidence suggests that the market can bring efficiency gains, we observe that the early network utilities started life in the free market, but they were rapidly captured by regulatory institutions. One of the lessons of history is the remarkable underlying similarity in the mature form of these institutions under both public and private ownership. This raises obvious questions, some of which may require more time to elapse before we are confident with the answer. Will the forces that caused convergence to regulated vertical integration in the past reassert themselves? Are we just witnessing a transient historical episode of liberalization, or can the benefits of competition be protected against the pressure to reintegrate? Will different utilities diverge in their form and structure, with technology facilitating competition in some (telecoms, electricity, gas) but not in others (water, rail)? Would a large increase in the price of gas undermine the advantages of competition in electricity generation and shift the balance back toward vertical integration? Can fast-growing developing countries sustain sufficient rates of investment in privatized and liberalized utilities? These questions are important, and a fuller understanding of the forces shaping regulatory institutions should help to answer them.

1.1   Privatization in Britain

Privatization in Britain marked such a decisive change of policy that it is worth asking why it happened. It is true that Chile had re-privatized companies that had been taken into state ownership by the Allende government not very long before, but that hardly marked a decisive change of policy, merely a restoration of the previous status quo. Privatization in Britain was different, in that it gradually emerged as the decisive instrument to achieve the objectives of the Conservative government under Margaret Thatcher. More than anything else it signaled a clear change in direction of economic philosophy. Political memoirs are, of course, written with the benefit of hindsight and with the intention of securing a place in history. Provided that this is recognized, they can nevertheless shed light on one of the defining features of the Thatcher government. They need to be placed in the wider economic context, for the problems that Britain was facing were not unique, though perhaps more severe than elsewhere, and hence more in need of a radical solution.

Figure 1.1 shows the dramatic change in trend rate of growth that occurred at the time of the first oil shock in 1973. The gross domestic product (GDP) of the United Kingdom had been growing at 2.9 percent each year in real terms since 1960, while the other continental member countries of the present European Union (described in the figure as EU14) had been growing at an impressive 4.5 percent each year. In figure 1.1 the index numbers of GDP are plotted on a logarithmic scale; the lines of constant slope represent constant proportional growth, and the dashed lines indicate constant growth at the various trend rates identified. From 1979 to 1995 the fitted trend rate of growth for the United Kingdom was 2.3 percent each year, which is slightly below its former trend, but instead of lagging far behind the rest of Europe, Britain now had exactly the same trend growth rates as the remaining EU member countries. The gap between the earlier and later trends gives an idea of the loss in output relative to the earlier (unsustainable) rate of growth, which for EU14 is equal to two-thirds of the actual level of output by 1995. The figure shows the greater instability of post–oil-shock growth and the severe recessions in the United Kingdom in 1974–75 and 1980–81.

The impact of the oil shock on public finance was more dramatic than on output as expenditure continued to rise, initially along past trends. If anything, the divergence was amplified by the rise in payments to the rapidly rising numbers of unemployed, while tax receipts fell with the collapse in profits. Figure 1.2 shows the total expenditure of government as a percent of GDP for the OECD-Europe economies (as "OECD Exp"), and the current revenue of government ("OECD Rev"), also as a percentage of GDP.[1] It shows that while expenditure and

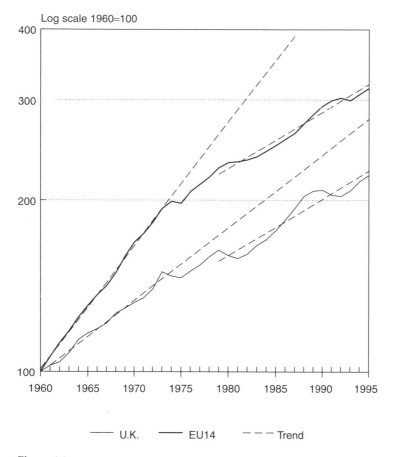

Figure 1.1
Growth in GDP in Britain and Europe real GDP, 1960 to 1995.
Source: OECD (1996b).

revenue tracked each other closely before 1973, thereafter revenue lagged behind. Europe appears to have experienced a series of upward steps in the share of expenditure, with revenue gradually rising, while Britain (whose expenditure and revenue are shown in figure 1.2 as lines) has managed to resist a trend rise in revenue despite expenditure that stabilized at a higher level after the step change in the oil shock.

With little room for cutting current expenditures on health and social security, the ax fell heavily on public sector investment. Worse still, the fourfold rise in oil prices created an inflationary surge, and as part of its counterinflation strategy, the government held down the prices of

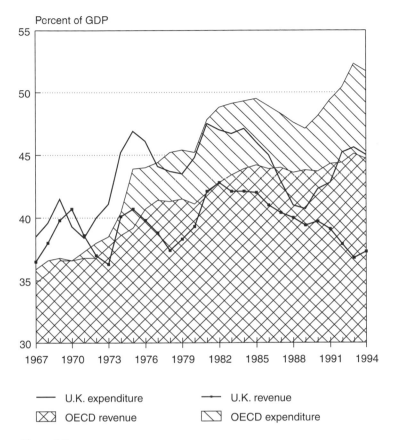

Figure 1.2
OECD-Europe government revenue and expenditure as share of GDP, 1967 to 1994.
Source: OECD (1996a).

public utilities, causing them a cash-flow problem and a fall in their investment as well. Figure 1.3 shows the collapse of net investment in local government (mainly housing) and in public corporations. This was the background to the run-up to the 1979 election.

Margaret Thatcher begins her story in *The Downing Street Years* with the vote of no-confidence in the Labour government in 1979, shortly before the election that began eighteen years of unbroken Conservative government. Her diagnosis was that Britain's relative decline in the world could be directly attributed to a "socialist ratchet" in which Labour governments moved Britain toward more statism, which the Conservatives failed to resist. Her primary objective for the Conservative Party Manifesto was to reverse Britain's economic decline, without

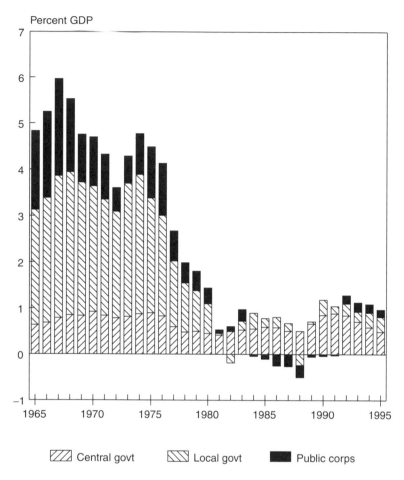

Figure 1.3
Net public sector capital formation as share of GDP.
Source: CSO (1996).

which her other objectives stood little chance of success. The means to
this end were on the economic side, to limit the role of government and
put its faith in free markets, and on the political side to put faith in
freedom, strongly defended. When the polls closed on May 3, 1979, the
Conservatives had won an overall majority in the House of Commons
of 44 seats. The speech in which she set out the agenda for the new parliament called for legislation to enable state assets to be privatized and
council houses to be bought at heavily discounted prices by their
tenants (Thatcher 1993, p. 39). One of the points that attracted most

attention, however, was the promise of trade union reform, and in the coming years a considerable part of the attraction of privatization, particularly of large public utilities, was the impact it had on the power of organized labor.

The fiscal constraints facing the new government (and illustrated in figure 1.2) were severe in the extreme—heavy deficits, a world recession, and manifesto commitments to increase spending on defense, pensions, the police, and not to cut spending in the National Health Service. At this point privatization emerged as an appealing solution from the fiscal as well as the ideological perspective. The government-owned shares in British Petroleum could be sold at once, but other state-owned companies required legislation to set them up in a form suitable for sale.

The next few years of industrial strife and heavy losses by the publicly owned industries made it clear to the harder-headed members of the cabinet that the public sector was overmanned and unable to finance its activities. Despite this, the unions had considerable power to cause widespread economic damage if their wage demands were not met. The case of the British Steel Corporation (BSC) illustrates this most clearly—labor productivity was half that of its major European competitors, and it had absorbed over £3 billion of public money over the previous five years. Faced with BSC's demand to cut 52,000 jobs, the steel workers went on strike in January 1980, but this time failed to deflect the government from its purpose.

British Leyland had been taken into public ownership to prevent the collapse of volume car production in the United Kingdom, and the government was clearly anxious to transfer it to private ownership, if necessary with a dowry to ensure its survival. In the event, the prospects of immediate sale were so poor that the government itself undertook the very substantial costs (£990 million) of restructuring. The National Coal Board was in even worse financial shape, and the miners, whose strike had caused the collapse of the Conservative government of 1974, were even more militant. Faced with the prospect of another strike in January 1981, for which the government had not had time to prepare, they increased the amount of agreed public funding from £800 million in 1981–82 to well over £1 billion. Margaret Thatcher drew the lesson that the government had to take steps to avoid being held to ransom in the future by the miners, and in due course electricity privatization became a part of that strategy.

The first period of office had been a salutary reminder of the power of the unions, the inefficiency and overmanning of the public sector, and the great difficulty of cutting public expenditure while not damaging the investment and modernization needed in these publicly owned enterprises. Buoyed by the successful outcome to a small war in the South Atlantic, the Conservatives dissolved Parliament in 1983 to seek re-election. Margaret Thatcher's diagnosis of Britain's problems, tempered by experience of office, remained firm. They were attributable to a pervasive mentality of socialism, its hold over institutions, and the power of the trades unions, which still covered nearly half the employed workforce. She saw privatization not just as fundamental to improving Britain's economic performance but as central to reversing the "corrosive and corrupting effects of Socialism" (Thatcher 1993, p. 676). If nationalization was the way in which socialists gained control to advance their vision of society, then privatization was seen as the cornerstone of recreating individual freedom.

The manifesto pledged to "continue our programme to expose state-owned firms to real competition" and to "transfer more state-owned businesses to independent ownership. Our aim is that British Telecom—where we will sell 51 percent of the shares to the private sector—Rolls Royce, British Airways and substantial parts of British Steel, of British Shipbuilders and of British Leyland, and as many as possible of Britain's airports, shall become private sector companies." (*The Conservative Manifesto 1983*, p. 16). Whereas the 1979 manifesto had only promised to sell back industries that had been taken into public ownership recently to rescue them from bankruptcy, the 1983 manifesto was both revolutionary in spirit and ambitious in scope. The Conservatives had started by wishing to reverse recent nationalizations, much as in Chile. They gradually realized that privatization had considerably greater political attractions, in curbing the power of the public sector unions, as well as an economic logic. The latter was more fully appreciated and at an earlier date by Nigel Lawson, an economist who had enjoyed a successful earlier career as a journalist at the *Financial Times*. Speaking as energy secretary at the Conservative Party conference in November 1981, he said "The Conservative Party has never believed that the business of government is the government of business" (Lawson 1992, p. 199). He went on to argue that the only industries that should remain state-owned were those for which there was an overwhelming case for public ownership (Lawson 1992, p. 211). Margaret Thatcher echoed these sentiments, further arguing that state ownership effectively removed the disciplining effect of the threat of bankruptcy (Thatcher 1993, p. 677).

1.2   U.K. Privatization Program

Between 1979 and 1992, some 39 U.K. companies were privatized by shares sales (see the appendix to this chapter) and between 1985 and 1989, of the £23.6 billion raised by listed share sales, £16.6 billion or 70 percent were privatizations (Jenkinson and Trundell 1991). Over the period 1979 to 1992 the government raised more than £40 billion by share sales (Bishop and Green 1995). In July 1992 the top 100 quoted U.K. companies included seventeen privatized companies with a share valuation of £80 billion (Jenkinson and Mayer 1994; Bishop, Kay, and Mayer 1994). In addition a large number of local government-owned council houses were sold at discounted prices to their tenants— arguably the largest single privatization of all.

The costs of sales were considerable (3 to 5 percent of receipts, which was about average for smaller new issues), and at 25 percent the degree of underpricing was also substantial, resulting in a loss of sales revenue of £2.5 billion relative to a normal underpricing on new shares of 10 percent (Jenkinson and Mayer 1994, p. 295). This encouraged wide initial public subscription, and the experience of past underpricing doubtless encouraged bids for later sales, though many small share- holders sold out—4.4 million bought British Gas shares initially, but fewer than 2 million held them by 1994 (Bishop and Green 1995).

Figures 1.4 to 1.6 show just how dramatic the effect of privatization has been on the pattern of ownership and control over production, investment, and capital, especially after 1983. Figure 1.4 charts the share of output of public and private corporations in GDP since 1976 (the latter are restricted to industrial and commercial corporations), while figure 1.5 shows the shares of public and private corporate gross investment in GDP. Figure 1.6 charts the ownership of public and private net capital stock in industrial and commercial enterprises as a share of GDP. All three figures show the share of the public corpora- tions in the total corporate sector as a continuous line on the right-hand scale. Between 1979 and 1991 public corporate capital fell from 40 percent to just over 10 percent, or by three-quarters (and has fallen further after 1995 with the privatizations of rail and nuclear energy). Figures 1.4 and 1.5 show similar falls in the share of output and invest- ment up to 1991. This was not lost on Margaret Thatcher who claimed

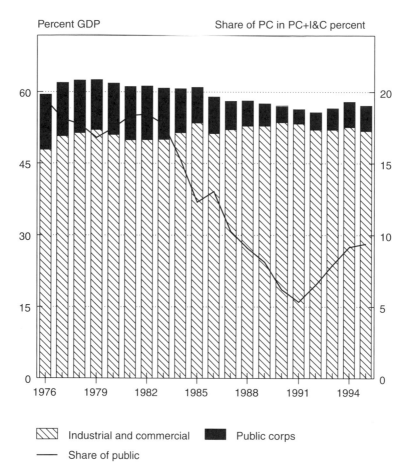

Percent GDP   Share of PC in PC+I&C percent

Figure 1.4
Shares in GDP at current factor cost U.K. public and private sectors.
Source: CSO (1996).

credit for the greatest transfer of assets and power from the state to private individuals outside the former communist bloc, reducing state ownership in industry by some 60 percent and transferring 600,000 jobs to the private sector. (Thatcher 1993, p. 687).

Figure 1.7 shows the impact of these sales on the net worth of the public sector, updating work by Hills (1989). The net worth of each sector is defined as the value of tangible assets, as far as possible measured at market prices, *plus* the value of financial assets, *less* the value of financial liabilities.[2] If the public enterprises to be privatized had been sold at their market value, and had the proceeds been used to

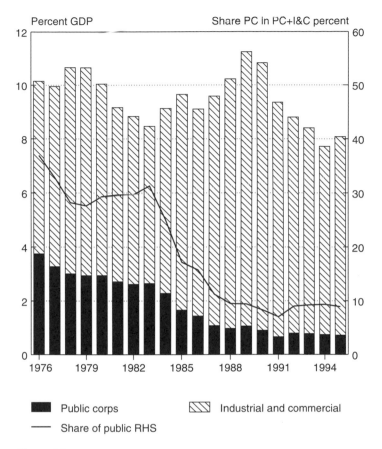

Figure 1.5
Gross domestic capital formation U.K. public and private sector.
Source: CSO (1996).

decrease the national debt, then the net worth of the public sector should not have been adversely affected. As it is, public enterprise were sold at a discount of about 25 percent, and council houses sold to tenants were also discounted (though they were already shown in the accounts as having a below-market value as they lacked vacant possession). The impression given by figure 1.7 is that sales of public enterprises financed consumption, not capital formation. Figure 1.7 also demonstrates the weakness of the Maastricht conditions on public debt as a measure of the creditworthiness of the country. A proper public sector balance sheet should record the assets of the public sector as well as the liabilities, and may tell a very different story if public debt is reduced by privatization.

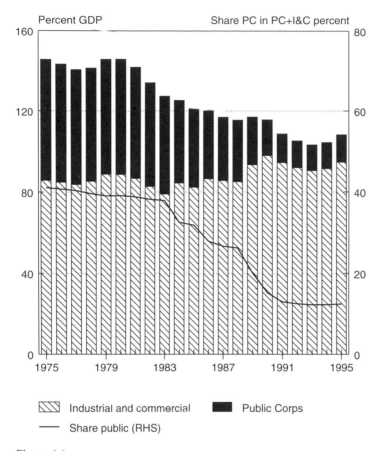

Figure 1.6
U.K. public and private net capital stock fixed assets as share of GDP.
Source: CSO (1996).

The case for privatizing British Airways, British Steel, British Aerospace, holdings in oil companies, and other industries exposed to local and international competition was clear, and it needs little defense. But the privatization program did not confine itself to selling industries whose market power can be handled by normal competition policy. A large part of the program consisted in selling network utilities that inevitably raise problems of market failure, where the claim that "the business of government is (never) the government of business" necessarily fails. This book is addressed to the problems raised by network utilities, the remedies that have been proposed, and the place of privatization among those remedies.

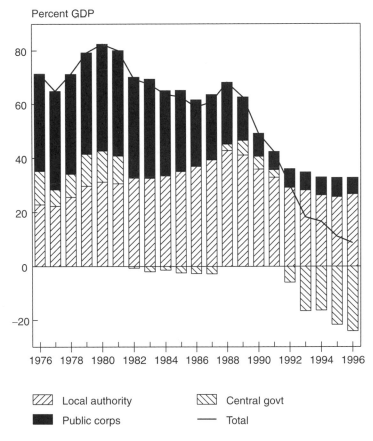

Figure 1.7
Net worth of the public sector as percent of GDP.
Source: CSO (1996).

1.3   Property Rights, Structure, and Efficiency

Policy toward network utilities must address three levels of question. The first and most fundamental is how to ensure that the large amounts of specific sunk capital are financed, and specifically, how property rights in this capital are to be defined, allocated, and protected. This question underlies the issue of ownership and hence privatization, and it depends critically on the form of the regulatory contract between the owner and society's agent. The second question is what is the right structure of the utility, both vertically and horizontally. Should the industry be de-integrated with the potentially competitive parts under separate ownership from the network? How should the industry be structured to take best advantage of network economies? The issues here are of market structure, access, coordination, entry, expansion—ensuring the efficient choice of location and type of new investment.

The first two questions have to do with intrinsically forward-looking or dynamic issues. The final question is how best to secure the efficient use of the existing network, and it is the main focus of the classic static questions of public utility regulation and pricing. While important, this question is arguably the least critical of the three levels, though failure at this level may precipitate important changes at the deeper levels of ownership, the regulatory regime, and industry structure.

Until recently, economists tended to assume that the first two questions had already been answered, or could not be re-opened, so the theory of regulation concentrated on how best to achieve efficient outcomes for each utility. The British experience, increasingly replicated elsewhere, is that questions of ownership, regulatory regime, and industrial structure need to be examined afresh, and they offer prospects of larger benefits than minor adjustments to the pricing of utility output.

1.4 Ownership and the Boundaries of the State

Historically, in Britain and many other early industrializing countries, the first network utilities were created by private entrepreneurs. By the middle of the twentieth century, private ownership of network utilities was unusual even in developed market countries with little public ownership of manufacturing (Short 1984). Why? What is special about network utilities that predisposes public ownership, and what difficulties do these features create for private ownership? These are clearly critical questions to address before considering privatization.

In nineteenth-century Britain, private property rights were upheld in law and by the political power structure, which was virtually coincident with the propertied classes. Workers were in excess supply, were poorly organized, and did not have the vote unless they owned property. Wealth was concentrated so that a small number of financiers could raise sufficient funds for many ventures. Where this was not possible, the reputation of leading financiers could be used to borrow additional funds, in turn encouraging the development of an effective financial system able to finance profitable ventures (as well as various fraudulent schemes). In such an environment manufacturing investments and trade could be financed and, in due course, so could the early network utilities. The United States was equally sympathetic to private enterprise, but the circumstances differed in various obvious ways—with an open frontier the population was more mobile, labor was scarce, but wealth still concentrated in the rapidly growing towns.

Regulation historically arose as part of the contract between municipalities, who granted rights of way in exchange for quality standards and curbs on prices. It is instructive to contrast the experiences of the United Kingdom and United States in the nineteenth and early twentieth centuries. Coal gas derived from distilling coal was the first of the modern network utilities, though piped water began to be developed on a large scale in the same period. Coal gas was first supplied to Lee's factory in Britain in 1806 to replace tallow candles. Gas light was less than one-third the cost of the candles it replaced (Falkus 1982). Municipalities were as anxious as factory owners to find cheaper street lighting, and granted the right to lay pipes and disturb roads in exchange for concessional street lighting, though the main commercial demand came from factories, shops, and other public places.

Economies of scale gave monopoly power to the first entrant, and with it high profits. Early attempts to regulate prices were ineffective, and profits could only be restrained by entry, which created obvious inefficiencies—by 1850 London had fourteen gas companies (Foreman-Peck and Millward 1994, p. 30). In such a competitive environment, quality suffered, often with lethal consequences, making municipal ownership look increasingly attractive in Britain. This step required a number of developments—the municipalities had to be given authority, incentive, and opportunity. Before 1870, municipalities required a parliamentary bill to set up a utility, which could be contested by private interests. After the 1870 Gas and Water Facilities Act, this could be achieved by a simpler administrative decision. The incentive to municipal ownership in water came with the 1875 Public Health Act, which made local authorities responsible for ensuring adequate and satisfactory water supplies. Municipalities could therefore take over private water companies on public health grounds, though it was harder to make that case for gas. It was, however, now easier for municipalities to set up their own gas companies, and between 1851 and 1881 nearly one-third of new gas companies were public. (Foreman-Peck and Millward 1994, p. 171).

Municipal ownership has several attractions. It provided local political support by keeping prices at reasonable levels while generating profits to finance local public goods and reduce the burden of local taxes. This political-economic equilibrium gave the consumers political voice, the politicians economic power, while the profits benefited both. It was an attractive alternative to the unsatisfactory regulation of private utilities, and thereafter Parliament typically granted limited life franchises to any privately owned network utility, which the local municipality then had the right to buy, typically after twenty-one years. Limiting the life of franchises completed the set of conditions for public ownership by providing the opportunity to take over private utilities. By 1907, 33 percent of net output of gas companies was public, as were 57 percent of trams, 64 percent of electricity, and 81 percent of water companies (Foreman-Peck and Millward 1994, tab. 1.3).

Water and gas are local utilities, naturally regulated or owned at the local level, but rail, telegraph, and trunk telephone are regional or countrywide utilities. A countrywide rail or telegraph network requires a degree of coordination and planning if it is to be developed efficiently, which competitive and decentralized markets were poorly equipped to provide. Three solutions were tried in different countries. Coordination could be achieved by central state ownership as with Belgium railways, which by 1838 were pricing at half the British level (Foreman-Peck and Millward 1994, p. 21). Monopolization or cartel agreements might be able to achieve sufficient economies of scale to prevent inefficient duplication. In the United States, Western Union emerged as the dominant telegraph company, buying up rivals to achieve network economies. The third solution was monopolistic competition, the norm in Britain, where private companies failed to achieve efficient scale either by voluntary agreement or takeover.

This third solution was eventually unsustainable—in the case of rail, cartellization was imposed after the network had already reached its final inefficient configuration (Foster 1992), while in 1868, all the telegraph companies were nationalized and transferred to their competitor, the Post Office. The result was that prices were cut, new offices opened, and the network gaps filled such that traffic doubled in the following four years. Telephones followed suit, with the long-distance company nationalized in 1896 and local companies in 1911. Compared to countries with exclusive state ownership or those with private ownership, Britain had an inferior telephone system with low penetration and poor quality.

Electricity differed in that it evolved its regulatory equilibrium at the local level, with mixed private and municipal ownership, but this blocked the larger-scale integration achieved on the continent and in the United States. The First World War made Britain's backwardness painfully apparent, but the intense hostility of private capital to public ownership delayed the creation of the publicly owned Central Electricity Board, charged with building a national grid, until 1926. Thereafter the Board was highly successful, maintaining technical excellence and commercial independence. It created a profitable system of centrally dispatched efficient scale power stations delivering power over the national grid to local distribution companies, both public and private, without any compulsory public acquisition of assets. After the end of the Second World War, the remainder of the electricity industry fell under central government ownership almost by default—the alternative was a demonstrably inferior pattern of municipal ownership as the private franchises expired. Other utilities were nationalized by the postwar Labour government at the same time.

The experience of the United States with these same utilities has interesting similarities but lead to a different institutional solution to dividing the rents. Initially most cities offered a contractual franchise, starting with the introduction of gas in New York in the 1820s (Priest 1993). These contracts typically provided for access to public rights of way and a franchise monopoly in return for restraints on prices, concessional terms for supplying the municipality, and occasionally other benefits valued by politicians, such as union membership for utility employees. The contracts had to be long enough to enable the utility to recover the large capital investments, and they typically ran for 20, 30, or even 50 years. Inevitably they encountered the problem of bounded rationality (Williamson 1985)—the contracts would have to be renegotiated in response to changes in circumstances, such as changes in costs. The contracts often explicitly made provisions for renegotiation, subject to arbitration, or reference to an independent committee, who later might assume responsibility for monitoring service quality. Power to renegotiate contracts shifted to municipalities as sunk costs increased, and the threat of permitting further entry or not renewing the franchise became more costly to the utility. The power of regulatory committees grew, and with them their concern over fair pricing. These arbitration committees evolved in due course into state public utility commissions.

As time passed and technical progress introduced new services (electricity, telephony) and dramatically lowered production costs, each public service moved from being a luxury to a necessity, increasingly recognized as part of the essential infrastructure of a modern economy.

With the growing power of the emerging working class, with or without democracy, came demands for access to these services at "fair" prices—prices that the mass of the population could afford. Political concerns moved on from health and safety to equity and efficiency, and a strong political concern over the terms on which these services would be provided. Once it became clear that the network utility was not completely free to enter the market, set prices, determine quality, and offer services in the same unfettered fashion as the butcher, the baker, and the candlestick maker, the genie was out of the bottle. The political process, either local or central, was inevitably involved in regulating these utilities. The real problems emerged when the political process was captured by those who saw that the need to regulate network utilities provided the opportunity to redistribute income or patronage.

We will return to explore the dynamics of regulation in chapter 4, but it is worth noting the contrasts in the experiences of the early local public utilities of gas and water compared with the later utilities of electricity, telephones, and gas, whose natural boundaries were no longer those of the municipality. The end of the fundamental patents for Bell Telephone in 1894 led to a rush of new entrants and a period of aggressive competition as Bell attempted to restrict entry by denying interconnection. Competition was waged via political lobbying to secure protection against entry or to force interconnection. Eventually the head of Bell, Theodore N. Vail, decided that rather than fighting over a luxury market, it was preferable to accept regulation in exchange for protection against entry; on this basis he went on to build a monopoly for a mass market founded on high technology. With the passage of the Willis-Graham Act of 1921, Bell was free to acquire the independent companies to gain 79 percent of the market by 1930 (Vietor 1994). Electricity companies facing competition similarly sought regulatory protection, particularly since under interstate holding companies they could avoid the full weight of state-level regulation. The same was true of interstate gas holding companies, and in due course federal-level regulation had to be developed to resolve state-level conflicts.

What is striking about the U.S. experience is that with the notable exception of water, this process of increasing regulatory oversight was less likely to lead to public ownership; it instead led to improvements in the system of regulation. Only 8 percent of electrical utilities and less than 1 percent of trams were public by 1902, though more than half of the water companies were (Priest 1993, p. 317).[3] It is interesting to speculate on the causes of this difference in institutional solutions, which was to influence the next century of utility development in each country. Perhaps the higher rate of growth in the United States, and the availability of an open frontier, meant that the balance of advantage lay more with the utility and less with the municipality, providing greater incentive to reach a satisfactory solution that respected private ownership. Perhaps the political debate was less polarized between capital and laboring consumers with a greater willingness to compromise. Perhaps the division of political power among municipality, state, and federal government, each limited in its jurisdiction, made private ownership the natural default option. Perhaps the democratic origins of the country, its Constitutional protection of liberty and property against over-mighty central power, was better able to sustain private ownership. Whatever the reason, the embryonic form of cost-of-service regulation in exchange for a monopoly franchise was rapidly evolved, and sustained at the state level, later subject to federal oversight. It was consolidated in the wave of regulatory reform prompted by the social dislocation of the Great Depression. Congress passed the Public Utilities Holding Company Act of 1935 and the Natural Gas Act of 1938 to restrain vertical, horizontal, and geographic integration and to ensure that utilities were not able to evade state-level regulation. This anti-capitalist response froze the form of the industry until the deregulation movement starting in the mid-1970s finally lifted the defenses built by incumbents against competition.

The British experience shows that the failure to develop a viable regulatory compact for private ownership made public ownership ultimately irresistible. Regulating monopoly profits by entry and duplication, as in the railways, was inefficient. Local franchises typically failed to achieve adequate economies of scale, as in electricity, while competition with an incumbent public monopoly like the Post Office lead that monopoly to disadvantage and eventually take over its rivals. The final form of nationalized utilities was the logical outcome of earlier failures at the local level.

Across Europe, nationalized utilities have emerged where local failures of coordination and scale were demonstrably costly, except where a federal system protected state-level interests. Several countries were able to sustain municipally owned electric utilities. In Scandinavia, this was based on hydro power, where scale is unimportant. In Denmark; it came from developing town-scale combined heat and power systems, while cooperating in regional transmission systems. France, like Britain, nationalized its electricity system after the second world war, but unlike Britain, it created a single, very powerful vertically integrated utility, EdF. Germany has retained essentially the same mixed public and private structure that emerged in the interwar period, protected by state-level interests against federal restructuring.

This brief history of the evolution of governance structures for public utilities suggests that a number of factors influence whether the utility will fall into public ownership, or whether and how it will be regulated if it remains in private ownership. The next chapter looks more closely at the conditions needed to sustain private ownership, to see when these might be lacking, with public ownership as the default, and what is needed to successfully privatize publicly owned utilities.

Appendix: Enterprises Privatized, 1979 to 1994

Enterprise	Sale (%)	Gross proceeds (million £)	Activity
Competitive industries			
Amersham International (1982)	100	63	Isotopes for research/ medicine
Associated British Ports (1983)	51	22	Ports, property
Associated British Ports (1984)	49	270	
British Aerospace (1981)	?	149	Aircraft, weapons
British Aerospace (1985)	?	550	
British Airports (1987)	100	919	Airports
British Airways (1987)	100	900	Airline
British Coal Corp (1994)	100	700	Coal mines
British Petroleum (1979)	?	290	Oil
British Petroleum (1983)	?	565	
British Rail (various)			Some non-rail assets
British Shipbuilders (various)			Shipbuilding yards
British Steel (1988)	100	2,500	Steelmaking
Britoil (1982)	51	548	Oil
Britoil (1985)	49	450	
Cable and Wireless (1981)	50	224	Telecoms
Cable and Wireless (1985)	50	602	
Enterprise Oil (1984)	100	393	Oil
Jaguar (1984)	100	294	Cars
Leyland Bus, Leyland Trucks (various)			Vehicles
National Bus Corps (various)			Local and intercity bus/coach

Enterprise	Sale (%)	Gross proceeds (million £)	Activity
National Freight Corp (1982)			Road freight transport, property
National Transcommunications Ltd			Terrestrial TV signal relay
Rolls-Royce (1987)	100	1,363	Aero engines
Rover Group (1988)			Car-making
Royal Ordnance (1987)			Weapons, ammunition
Trustee Savings Bank (1986)	100[a]	1,360	Banking
Wytch Farm oilfield (1984)			Oil
Utilities			
British Telecom (1984)	52	3,916	Telecoms
British Telecom (1991, 1993)	26, 21	5,241; 5,202	
British Gas (1986)	100	5,434	Gas
Electricity:			
Generators NP + PG (1991)	60	2,100	Generation
Generators NP + PG (1995)	40	3,590	
12 RECs (incl NGC)	100	5,100	Transmission, distribution
Scottish Cos (1991)	100	2,900	Gen + trans + dist
Northern Ireland Electricity (NIE) (1992)	100	362	Gen + trans + dist
10 Water cos (1989)	100	5,200	Water

Sources: Vickers and Yarrow (1988, p. 175); Bishop and Green (1995).
a. Owned by depositors.

2   The Problem of Regulatory Commitment

Networks are capital-intensive, durable, long-lived and immovable. Network utilities make up a large fraction of the economy's productive capital. Foreman-Peck and Millward (1994, p. 3) show that between 1850 and 1960 network utilities[1] accounted for between 18 and 30 percent of the total net fixed assets in the United Kingdom, always larger than the share of manufacturing industry. The value added of the privatized U.K. network utilities in 1995 was 5 percent of GDP, employment was 422,000, fixed assets at historic cost were 13 percent of GDP, and the stock market value of shares on September 10, 1995, was £90 billion, or 15 percent of GDP. These numbers would be even larger if rail and nuclear power, privatized in 1996, were included. In the United States in 1992, the gross capital stock of telecoms alone was $525 billion, or 11 percent of GDP, and the net capital stock was $301 billion (Crandall 1993, p. 49). The book value of the assets of the electricity utilities was estimated at $298 billion in 1995 by Moody's (White 1996).

Network utilities are thus significant in size as well as function. They also provide the clearest example of natural monopolies, that is, cases where a single firm can satisfy the entire market demand for the range of goods or services at lower total cost than any other combination of firms.[2] Ware (1986) defines a natural monopoly in terms of social surplus maximization rather than cost minimization—not necessarily the same. On this criterion, a natural monopoly arises where the social surplus in a market is maximized by a single firm, which avoids any ambiguity about the scale at which costs are to be compared. Markets are often spatially limited, so it is completely possible that a network utility has a local natural monopoly but not a national natural monopoly—electricity and gas distribution companies are good examples.

Most surveys of natural monopoly[3] cite Farrer's (1902) catalog of
typical characteristics of natural monopolies:

1. Economies of scale
2. Capital-intensity
3. Nonstorability with fluctuating demand
4. Locational specificity generating location rents
5. Producing necessities or essential for the community
6. Involving direct connections to customers

They usually go on to argue that the modern definition of natural
monopoly is restricted to the first characteristic. Network utilities fit
Farrer's catalog perfectly and suggest a richer set of reasons for public
concern over the activities of these utilities. The network itself is an
obvious case where duplication raises the total costs of supplying a
market; it hence meets the modern definition of a natural monopoly. If
demand fluctuates, and the product or service cannot be stored, then
capacity will need to be sized to peak demand, or demand rationed. At
other times capacity acts more like a public good, precipitating market
failure or inducing what earlier economists described as "wasteful
competition."

Locational advantage suggests that one firm will obtain at least a
local monopoly, and different firms may enter to exploit different locations. In this case competition will not necessarily duplicate facilities
but may fail to secure the benefits of coordination, interconnection, and
system standardization. These potential market failures may not be
readily soluble by contracts or negotiation where there are many different local monopolies. Network externalities arise where the benefit
to one user depends on the number of other users connected to the
network, telecoms providing the leading example. These externalities
may lead to market failures such as inadequate interconnection and a
failure to achieve efficient network expansion. Finally, and crucially, the
combination of necessity and direct connection implies large potential
exploitative power by the producer, ensuring that regulation or public
ownership is politically inevitable.

The political demands for access and "fair" or nonexploitative prices
means that investors must expect that after they have sunk their capital,
they will be limited in the prices they can charge and subject to possibly onerous obligations to supply, to guarantee security, stability, and

safety. If these investors are to be induced to invest, they need the reassurance that future prices will be set at a sufficiently remunerative level to justify the investment. Once the capital has been sunk, the risk is that the balance of advantage will shift toward those arguing for lower and possibly unremunerative prices. In Britain in the nineteenth century, real utility costs fell, and there was no general inflation; this allowed owners to benefit even if prices were held constant. In the inflationary times of the twentieth century such inertia would lead to bankruptcy.

The problem can be posed more sharply. What would be needed to persuade investors to sink their money into an asset that cannot be moved and that may not pay for itself for many years? The investors would have to be confident that they had secure title to future returns and that the returns would be sufficiently attractive. Durable investments thus require the rule of law, and specifically the law of property, which is a public good provided by the state. If the state exists primarily to enforce the rights of property owners, then there is no problem. However, by the second half of the nineteenth century, the state represented a wider range of interests and needed to balance the claims of property against those of workers, voters, and consumers. The resulting tensions weakened property rights, for the coercive power of the state could be used not only to enforce laws but also to regulate economic activity, impose taxes, and even to expropriate property.

If public utilities are to be successfully privately financed, then regulation must credibly satisfy the demands both of consumers and investors. If consumers are unhappy, they cannot "exit" or choose an alternative supplier but must use their "voice" through the political process to secure their demands, to use Hirschman's (1970) illuminating terminology. If investors are fearful for the security of future returns, they will not finance the needed investment. This can be seen clearly in the British historical record. The 1870 Tramway Act allowed municipalities to purchase the tram companies at written-down cost at the end of the twenty-one-year franchise. Trams that should have been electrified in 1890s were near the end of their franchise, but no private company was willing to incur the considerable cost required, and instead electrification was delayed until after municipalization. The National Telephone Company refused to invest unless provided with compensation guarantees after 1908 as it neared the end of its franchise in 1911 (Foreman-Peck and Millward 1990, pp. 107, 167).

Spiller (1993, nn. 13, 14) observes that in 1962 the Jamaican government informed Jamaica Telephone Co. that it wished to renegotiate the terms of its license upon its expiry in 1966. JTC stopped all investment, and eventually sold out to another company. More recently, in Bolivia the municipality of La Paz started negotiations in 1984 over the renewal of the license of the electricity company, due to expire in 1990. The company suspended all investment activity after 1984, and the license was still not satisfactorily renewed by 1991. Suspending investment is a completely rational act for a utility suddenly faced with uncertainty over its future regulatory regime. The question we now wish to explore is whether or when that threat is sufficient to persuade the regulatory agency to protect investors' as well as consumers' interests, whether additional constitutional protection to private property is needed and under what circumstances private ownership is viable.

2.1   Modeling the Regulatory Compact as a Game

The interests of the community and those of the utility owner are partly in accord and partly in conflict. Both parties need to cooperate to realize the investment—the community has the power to grant exclusive access rights, while the utility has the expertise and finance to undertake the investment and to subsequently operate the utility. The potential conflict arises over the distribution of the rents, that is, the excess of the value of the service over the avoidable costs of continuing to operate the utility. The two players—the utility and the representative of the community, whom we will call the regulator—are locked in a game of conflict and cooperation, which can be studied using the techniques of modern game theory.[4]

Game theory has attractions and limitations as an approach to understanding economic interactions, where the possible actions of one player affect the outcome and hence the choices that will be made by the other. It is appealing because it offers a way of predicting how rational agents will behave once they understand the choices open to each other and their impact on the payoffs each will receive. It is limited because the game must be precisely defined to predict the outcome, and it is hard to be sure that all the relevant features of the problem have been included. Nevertheless, the approach offers insights that can be checked against history and evidence. The account given here is necessarily informal, and it is an abbreviated account of the more rigorous arguments presented in Gilbert and Newbery (1988, 1994).

The full description of a game includes a list of the players, the set of actions from which they can choose, the information they have at the time of choosing an action, the set of strategies, or rules that tell them what action to select given the information they have, the payoffs they can expect given the strategies chosen by all the players, and an equilibrium concept that determines the outcome or outcomes of the game.[5] Modeling any economic situation, such as the regulatory regime under which the utility will operate, requires us to specify each of these elements of the game precisely while matching them up with relevant features of the economy in question. This is not an easy task, but it is needed in any kind of modeling.

In the present case, to keep things simple, we suppose there are just two players: the utility and the regulator who represents the interests of the community. Of course, there may be a number of players whose actions can affect the utility's payoff, ranging from suppliers (the coal mines for electricity generators, gas producers supplying gas utilities), unions representing the workers in the utility, the judiciary, politicians (both those in power and those in opposition who may be returned in future), consumer and environmental groups—any group that believes that its interests are affected by the utility's actions and that has some means of affecting the utility's payoff. Later we will see that increasing the number of players is important for understanding the efficiency of the regulatory compact. For the moment the aim is to keep things simple and concentrate on the issue of trust as it affects investment decisions. The basic problem and its possible resolution arise even in the simplest two-player game.

The most troublesome step in modeling regulation as a game is delimiting the set of actions open to the players. It is reasonably simple to describe those open to the utility: It can operate existing plant up to the limit of its capacity, and it can invest varying amounts to add to capacity, but it cannot recover the value of existing capacity. It is harder to define the set of actions open to the regulator, and how they might be circumscribed. The approach taken by Gilbert and Newbery (1994) was to suppose that the regulator operates under a stable predetermined regulatory regime. This regulatory regime, together with other fair trading or antitrust laws that apply to the utility, lays down the rules of the game and the actions legally available to the regulator. In the United States, the Constitution provides investors with various safeguards, and these restrictions on the regulator have been clarified in a series of test cases heard in the courts. Over time the players become increasingly confident that they know which actions by the other player will be upheld as legal, and which can be successfully contested, though there may be a gray area of actions that, if contested, might be either upheld or overruled.

In Britain, the Acts under which the various utilities were privatized specify the duties and powers of the regulator (and the roles of other parties such as the Minister, the Office of Fair Trading, the Monopolies and Mergers Commission, and other regulatory agencies such as Her Majesties' Inspectorate of Pollution and the Health and Safety Executive). These powers have also been tested and clarified in various disputes and rulings, though over a shorter period. In some European countries, the regulatory regime was rather poorly defined and was still evolving at the time utilities came to be privatized, though there is a growing body of European Union law, particularly articles 81 and 82 (formerly articles 85 and 86) and directives that applies to an increasing number of utilities. In some transitional countries of Eastern Europe, the whole corpus of commercial and competition law is still relatively untried, and hence the actions open to the players are less clearly delimited. We will be concerned to see whether, and if so, how this lack of effective regulatory restraint affects the outcome.

We also need to specify the sequence in which the players choose their actions, and what they know at the time they make these choices. The natural sequence is that the community or government initially spells out in greater or lesser detail the regulatory rules of the game and empowers a regulator to act as its agent. The utility then chooses a level of capital to install, based on a prediction of what revenue the regulator will allow the utility to enjoy over the lifetime of the investment and what the future level of demand for service will be. To capture the idea that it is difficult to predict all the events that might occur, suppose that the future level of demand is not known with certainty at the time the investment is made; it might be either low (L) or high (H) with known probabilities (P and $1 - P$). Demand is inelastic; that is, it does not depend on the price that the utility charges over the relevant range of prices, again, to keep things simple. The level of low demand is $1 - \sigma$ and that of high demand is 1 (so expected demand is $1 - \sigma P$).

After the utility has invested, both the regulator and the utility learn the actual level of demand. The regulator then announces a formula that will determine the amount of revenue that the utility can earn or the price it can charge. The regulator might allow the utility to earn a prespecified return on all of its capacity, or on that part of the capacity that is actually needed. It might set a price cap, which may or may not depend on the level of demand, and the choice of the formula may affect the utility's behavior. The utility then sets its price and decides how much to produce, and at that point the players can calculate their payoffs for the period.

The payoff to the utility is just the profit from operating, equal to the revenue less operating costs and the cost of financing the investment. The payoff to the regulator is less well defined; it will depend on whose interests the regulator represents. Again, to keep things simple, suppose that the only beneficiaries are (undifferentiated) consumers and the shareholders of the utility who receive the profits. If the government has a share of the profits (through taxes or dividends), or if the government represents the interests of the capitalist class, including those who invest in the utility, then the regulator may place some weight on profits. If regulators reflect the median voter's concerns (as they would in some theories of representative democracy), then they will heavily discount any utility profits (which will be small compared to expenditure on the utility's service for the median voter), and regulators will be primarily concerned with consumer benefits. In the short run, higher utility revenue increases utility profits and increases consumer costs, reducing their benefits, so the weights of each in the regulator's payoff function matters.

The natural formulation is that the regulator's payoff in period t is $U_t + \theta \pi_t$, $\theta < 1$, where U_t is consumer surplus, π_t is profit, both at date t, and θ is the weight on profits relative to consumer benefits. In an extreme case $\theta = 0$ when the regulator is solely concerned with consumers' interests. The assumption that $\theta < 1$ emphasizes that the regulator can behave opportunistically with respect to sunk investments. There would be no efficiency problem if the regulator were indifferent to the distribution of income between consumers and the utility (or its shareholders), that is, if $\theta = 1$. One reason that has been advanced for $\theta < 1$ is that regulators are more concerned with serving the interests of their local citizenry, and while consumers are local, not all owners are (Baron 1989, p. 1362). This takes an extreme form when owners are foreign companies. Consumers are also more numerous and have more votes than owners.

The costs of the utility are made up of variable costs, b per unit, and capital costs, r per unit of output, the amount needed to finance a unit of capacity (interest and amortization of the loan). If the utility produces less than is demanded, the consumers face a higher cost c per unit for their unsatisfied demand. This higher cost may come from having to use an imperfect substitute (candles instead of gaslight, kerosene for lighting instead of electricity, post instead of telephone) or from the costs of disruption (power shortages, obtaining and operating portable generator sets), or from the extra costs involved in replacing the service by public supply, with shortages and delays during the transition period. Thus, if consumers demand D_t units, while the utility supplies Q_t units ($Q_t \leq D_t$) for a total charge of R_t, then consumer benefits will be $U_t = cQ_t - R_t$. This will then form part of the regulator's payoff.

The sequence of moves for the utility and the regulator is shown in figure 2.1, which defines a "basic game" that repeats in every period $t = 1, 2, \ldots, \infty$. The utility moves first, choosing its capital stock, K_t. As shown, there are only three sensible choices: 0, $1 - \sigma$, which would meet demand in the low demand state but not in the high demand state, and 1, which would be sufficient to meet demand whatever the state. "Nature" moves second, determining the level of demand, D_t. The regulator moves third, and determines the allowable revenues payable to the utility, R_t, with full information about the capacity installed, K_t, possibly conditioned on output. (The simplest example would be to set a price, p_t, so that $R_t = p_t Q_t$). Finally the utility produces $Q_t \leq \min(K_t, D_t)$ and payoffs for period t are realized. At the end of the period, the capital is assumed to have deteriorated; it will need

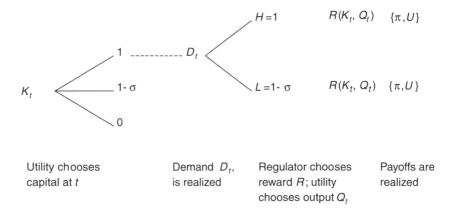

Figure 2.1
Basic regulation game.

replacing the next period, so the next period problem looks just like the previous one.[6]

2.2   Playing the Game: Commitment, Credibility, and Repetition

Our game is a simple noncooperative game in that each player is concerned solely with its own payoff. The normal method to solve such games is to look for a Nash equilibrium. A Nash equilibrium is a list of strategies for each player such that no player will wish to change his strategy, given the choice of strategies of the other players. That is, each player chooses the strategy that gives him the highest payoff, given the other player's choice of strategies, so no single player will wish to deviate from the equilibrium. In the present game the regulator has a range of legal revenue functions that it is free to impose, and otherwise cannot credibly precommit to restrict its choice of future behavior. The utility must predict what will be in the interest of the regulator to do after the capital has been sunk. Suppose, for the moment, that the regulator is free to set any price ceiling on the utility, though it cannot take control of the utility, nor can it force the utility to do anything it does not wish to, and specifically cannot tax the utility.

   If the game only lasts one round, and if the regulator is not restricted by the regulatory constitution in his choice of revenue function, then the outcome is predictably pessimistic. Figure 2.2 illustrates the game in extensive form for the special case in which variable cost $b = 1$, fixed cost $r = 1$ (so the average cost is 2), alternative cost $c = 3$ (so consumers gain 1 if the utility operates, $\theta = 0$, since the regulator is only concerned with consumer welfare), and $\sigma = \frac{1}{4}$ (so demand in H is 1, and in L it is $\frac{3}{4}$). The payoffs are listed with the utility's on top, the regulator's below, and ε is a small positive amount representing the difference between the utility's return and the cost of borrowing, which is sufficient (if certain) to ensure that the utility will invest.

   Since the regulator can freely choose whether to pay the return r or not ("cheat") when it reaches any node R (for regulator), and since the payoff to the regulator is always higher if it cheats (and would be for any value of $\theta < 1$), the utility confidently predicts that if it invests, it will make a loss, and hence does not invest. In the language of game theory, the "one-shot" game conditional on the choice of investment has a unique Nash equilibrium in which the regulator sets price equal

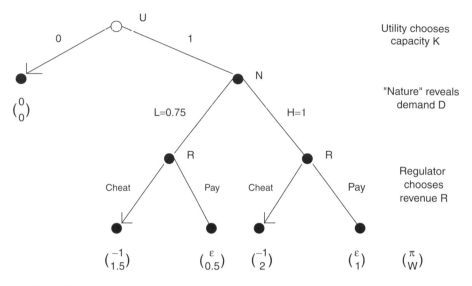

Figure 2.2
Game in extensive form.

to variable cost and the utility does not invest. There is little problem
with the notion of equilibrium in this case, both because it is unique
(and thus avoids difficult questions to do with how to choose between
alternative equilibria) and because the inability to commit and the
sequencing of decisions makes each player take the other's strategy as
beyond its influence, and hence given.

The solution becomes more interesting and more problematic if the
game is repeated. Also, since we are interested in the possibility of sustaining private regulated ownership, a repeated game is the natural formulation. The idea behind the Nash equilibrium—that neither player
can influence the choice of the other, and hence takes it as given—needs
extending when players can respond to the choices of their opponents
in the next iteration, punishing deviant behavior and rewarding cooperative outcomes. Such threats and rewards must, to have an effect,
be credible; that is, once the time comes to implement the threats or
rewards, it must still be in the interest of the player to carry them out.
This idea of credibility can be illustrated from another branch of economics. Consider a market in which a monopoly sets a high price, and
a particular firm is considering whether to enter. The monopolist may
announce that if the firm enters, then it will expand its own output and
drive down the price to short-run avoidable cost. If the firm believes

this, it will not enter, since it will not recover any return on investment (assuming that it does not have a huge advantage in variable costs). If the firm enters, and indeed cannot recover its sunk capital, then it has no choice but to compete as best it can with the incumbent. The incumbent will then have to make the best of a bad job and decide what, given the presence of its rival, is its profit-maximizing price and output. This is unlikely to be to price at short-run avoidable cost. As a result the earlier threat is not credible, since it would not pay to carry it out.[7]

To return to the game of regulator and utility, we wish to know whether it is possible to support more attractive outcomes even if the regulator cannot credibly commit his future actions and has considerable discretion over the revenues he allows the utility to earn. Again, the utility has to predict what it will be in the interest of the regulator to do in each possible future state that might occur. Given that prediction of the regulator's future action, the utility can decide what best to do at the previous date and state. Returning to the game tree in figure 2.2, after demand is realized, the regulator choses between the various sensible revenue functions. This time the regulator knows that at each node at the tips of the tree, each player will receive a payoff for this stage of the game, and the utility will then makes another capacity choice. Another set of branches will sprout out of each node and the game will repeat.

The regulator now has an interest at the earlier stage in the next and subsequent capacity and output choices of the utility; he can rule out some branches of the tree by choosing to respond in one way rather than another. The rest of a game starting from a subsequent node of the game tree is a called a subgame. The appropriate equilibrium concept where agents cannot precommit their future behavior is to look for a subgame perfect Nash equilibrium, defined by Selten (1965) as a set of strategies for each player such that in any subgame the strategies for that subgame form a Nash equilibrium.

The idea is to work backward from future choices, predicting the strategies that the players would choose if they reached that node. Given these predictions, the value of choices starting from each node can be determined. At each earlier node, taking these subsequent choices and their resulting values as given, players choose the best branch to take. Strategies can now be very sophisticated, since they can depend on the history of the choices taken by the players at previous nodes, provided that it is in each player's interest to continue such strategies. If so, each player can predict the consequences of a new choice that will add to that history. This greatly increases the number of possible equilibria, and in particular allows more attractive outcomes than the pessimistic result of the one-shot game, even without constitutional restraints on what the regulator may do. The main purpose of this chapter is to see when restraints on regulatory discretion are needed to ensure desirable outcomes and when they may be less important—critical information in deciding whether a country may benefit from privatizing a utility, and which utilities it makes sense to privatize first.

The appendix derives the condition under which the best outcome is for the utility to create enough capacity to meet the high level of demand (of 1 unit) for which $K_t = 1$, namely that

$$(1 - P)(c - b) > r. \tag{2.1}$$

In this inequality, $1 - P$ is the probability of high demand, $c - b$ is the extra variable cost of not having the utility's investment, and r is the fixed or capital cost of investing in capacity. We will assume that this condition holds so that the benchmark against which we can measure investment efficiency or adequacy is that the utility is able to fully meet high demand.

2.3   Rate-of-Return Regulation

Historically, where regulation has been in response to consumer concerns about excessive profits, the natural remedy has been to allow the utility to charge a price that just covers the cost of the service and so limits profits. The best example of this is rate-of-return regulation as developed in the United States. Rate-of-return regulation suffers from a number of well-known defects. It encourages excessive capital intensity when the rate of return exceeds the cost of capital (Averch and Johnson 1962; Baumol and Klevorick 1970). It creates obvious allocative distortions that result from setting prices at average and not marginal costs, while the "cost-plus" characteristic of rate-of-return regulation provides little incentive to cut costs. These shortcomings and their possible remedies will be discussed later. For the moment the question is how well rate-of-return regulation copes with opportunistic behavior—an issue that was rather neglected in the regulatory literature when the main example of utility regulation was the United

States, but is now central to discussions of privatizing utilities in Latin America, Eastern Europe, and elsewhere.

The simplest example of rate-of-return regulation would be one in which the regulator announces his willingness to pay a rate of return r on any capital required by the utility. Notice that this is ambiguous. Does it mean any capital that the utility chooses to invest, no matter what the actual demand, for example, $K = 2$, or does it mean only up to the amount that might reasonably be required, which in this model would be $K = 1$ as is required in the high-demand state, or does it mean only capital that is actually used, which is $1 - \sigma$ in the low-demand state? We will return to these questions shortly, but for the moment suppose that capacity up to the efficient level of $K = 1$ is normally rewarded with r. The rate of return will also have to be adequate to encourage investment but no higher. Finally, in order to understand the importance of constitutional restraints on regulatory discretion, we continue to assume that the only regulatory restraints are that the regulator cannot take control of the utility and cannot levy taxes on its capacity or profit.

These constraints (respect for private property) mean that prices will have to cover variable operating costs b to ensure production and that the return paid on capital must be nonnegative. Otherwise, the regulator is free to set prices or revenues as he wishes, and in particular to fail to honor his original stated willingness to pay r per unit of capital up to $K = 1$. The situation is thus not as in the United States, but more like that in a country with a long history of public ownership, no track record of regulating private utilities, and rather slow to put in place credible restraints on the regulator—a situation all too familiar in developing and transitional economies. How will such a game be structured?

In this simple sequential game both players are assumed to have common knowledge of the strategy sets of each player. That is, they each know the choices available to themselves and the other player, they can each observe the past choices made and remember them, and they each know that the other knows all of this. The strategy set of the utility at date $t - 1$ is the level of next period's capacity, $K_t \geq 0$. The strategy set of the regulator at date t, after observing K_t and the level of demand, D_t, is to determine the revenue that the utility can earn, $R_t(\cdot)$ (the dot notation indicates that revenue may depend on a whole list of variables, including K_t, D_t, past history, etc.).

The regulator will pay the variable cost b on any capacity available and needed to ensure production (because it cannot take control of the utility and force it to operate) and it must also pay a nonnegative return on K_t (no taxation), so we can confine attention to the capacity payment. All but two choices can be ruled out as inferior, so the regulator's strategy set can be limited to either a *normal return function* R^n, in which he allows the utility to earn an unconditional return r on $K \leq 1$, but zero on any excess above 1, or an *punishment return function* R^p, in which the utility only receives variable cost and no return on any capacity. (It will be clear from what follows that it would not be sensible to pay either more than r or less than r but greater than zero, so the choices can be narrowed down to just these two.)

The utility would find it profitable to invest $K = 1$ if it were sure of earning r on all its capital, but would clearly invest no more than that. It would then cover all its costs, current and capital (and we suppose that the normal return r is just sufficiently attractive to make investing worthwhile). The utility and the regulator play this repeated game, employing strategies that determine their actions as a function of the past history of interaction. The utility's strategy will be a level of investment at date t, $S_t(\cdot)$, that will depend on the past history of regulatory actions—the utility's experience to date. The regulator's strategy will be a choice of return function depending on the past history of investment and possibly previous regulation. Imagine that the regulator announces before the game begins (i.e., before the utility is privatized) that it will pay

$$R_t(\cdot) = \begin{cases} R^n & \text{if } K_t \geq 1, \\ R^p & \text{otherwise,} \end{cases} \tag{2.2}$$

and that it expects the players to select the following strategy:

$$S_t(\cdot) = \begin{cases} 1 & \text{if } R_{t-1} \geq R^n, \\ 0 & \text{otherwise,} \end{cases} \tag{2.3}$$

The regulator announces that he will to pay the normal return R^n whenever the utility invests at least $K_t = 1$, but if the utility does not fulfill its side of the bargain, it will only receive variable cost. The utility is expected to continue to invest $K_t = 1$ if the regulator pays a normal return, but the regulator indicates that he is aware that the utility will not invest ever again if his side of the regulatory compact is not kept. Each player therefore has some power to punish the other for departing from the (verbal) undertaking. Note that the threat of no subsequent investment is stronger than just not investing for one period, and makes sense because the regulator has said that any failure to invest would be met by an expropriatory return, which makes it sensible not to risk any further investment. Can the strategies given by (2.2) and (2.3) support efficient investment as a subgame perfect equilibrium?

The utility makes a loss if it invests less than $K_t = 1$ but earns an adequate return if it does invest $K_t = 1$, assuming that the regulator follows the announced strategy. The regulator, however, may be tempted not to pay for sunk capital even if $K_t - 1$ (i.e., to deviate to the payment R^p), thus breaking the initial verbal undertaking. The immediate regulatory benefit would be a transfer of r from shareholders to consumers, which is worth $(1 - \theta)r$, where θ is the weight placed on the shareholders' loss. The cost is that consumers will forever have to pay a higher cost to obtain alternative supplies or bear the cost of going without. Figure 2.3 shows the regulatory gain, while figure 2.4 shows the cost, which is the extra cost less the saving (shown black) from not having to pay for capital that is, on average, underemployed.

The regulator will choose to deviate if the one-period gain exceeds the present value of these costs. In that case the utility would not invest in the first place, and private regulated ownership is not viable. The appendix shows that rate-of-return regulation will be credible if

$$(1 - \sigma P)(c - b) > r[1 + (1 - \theta)i], \tag{2.4}$$

where i is the rate of return used by the regulator to discount future benefits (less than r, which includes the amortization of the investment as well as the return on the investment). If condition (2.4) is satisfied, then strategies (2.2) and (2.3) are rational for the players, and the equilibrium will be efficient: The utility will invest 1 each period and receive R^p, the full rate of return on all capital. If not, the game degenerates into the one in which the regulator never rewards capital, and the utility does not invest.

These very simple conditions help to identify circumstances that are favorable to credible regulation, and those that are inimical. First, the larger is θ, and hence the more weight is placed on investor profits, the more likely (2.4) is to be satisfied, regulation to be credible, and hence private ownership viable. This was clearly the case in nineteenth-century Britain, but it was eroded with growing conflicts between labor (and the Labour party) and capital in the twentieth century, culminat-

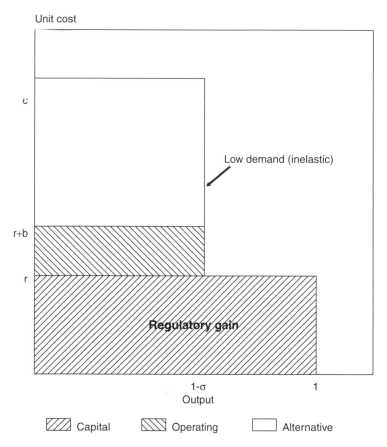

Figure 2.3
Unconstrained rate of return regulation deviation gain.

ing in the General Strike of 1926. Wherever political power has derived from populist anticapital sentiments, unconstrained regulation runs the risk of unsustainability and would benefit from further constitutional constraints, considered below.

Second, the larger is expected output next period, $1 - \sigma P$, the more likely is (2.4) to be satisfied. With some slight stretching of interpretation of this static model, rapid demand growth makes it easier to sustain the regulatory compact. Third, the greater is the comparative advantage of private over alternative (possibly public) supply, or the higher the costs of making the transition to the alternative supply, $c - b$, the easier it is to sustain private utilities as the penalties for breaking the regulatory compact become too high.

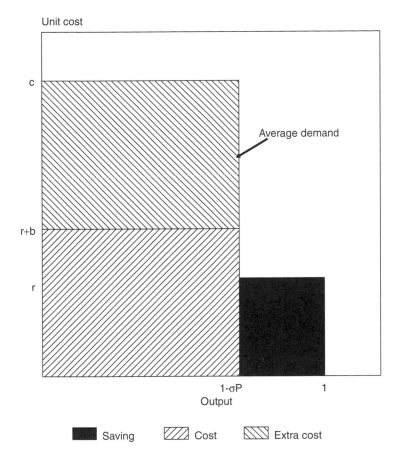

Figure 2.4
Unconstrained rate of return regulation expected deviation cost forever.

Finally, to take an extreme case in which $\theta = 0$, low values of r help sustain the compact. The size of r depends on the capital intensity of production (r/b measures the relative size of capital and variable costs per unit of output at full capacity), and also on the length of the period over which capital depreciates and needs to be replaced or augmented. If this period is long, then the regulator gains a considerable advantage for consumers before having to incur the replacement costs, but if short, then the benefits of reneging are transient, but the costs go on forever. Again, rapid growth of demand and high rates of depreciation or obsolescence help sustain the regulatory compact. In modern times, investors are likely to have more confidence in the durability and credibility of telecoms regulation in Eastern Europe, where demand growth is fast and technological change rapid, than they are to have in electricity regulation, where demand is sluggish or falling and the technology mature. Privatizing telecoms is therefore likely to be easier and to produce higher revenue per unit of capital than privatizing electricity. We return to the problem of privatizing utilities in transitional economies later in this chapter.

2.3.1 Extensions: The "Used and Useful" Doctrine

The simple model illuminates the problem of regulatory commitment in a country without an evolved history of regulatory restraints. To see how these might improve matters, and also how the simple model can be extended to deal with some of its limitations, consider the system of regulation that has evolved in the United States. The U.S. rate-of-return model derives its legitimacy from a series of judicial precedents that a regulated utility is entitled to a "fair return upon the value of that which it employs for the public convenience" (*Smythe v. Ames*, 1898). This immediately raises several questions: What is the fair return? What is the value? What is the amount employed? Naively interpreted, rate-of-return regulation appears to require that the regulator must transfer sufficient revenues in each state to ensure that the utility earns at least a normal rate of return on its invested capital. Such a policy leads to the Averch-Johnson overcapitalization problem.

Courts, however, have resisted this interpretation. In its most decisive opinion on the scope of utility regulation (*FPC v. Hope Natural Gas*), the U.S. Supreme Court concluded that "rates which are adequate to attract capital for growth . . . are not unreasonable," but the Court did not say that regulators are obligated to provide at least a normal rate of return at all times. Subsequent Courts have resisted the view that a normal return should be paid on any invested capital, and as a result actual returns earned by utilities have varied widely. In the postwar history of utility regulation in the United States, utilities frequently earned rates of return that exceeded their capital costs (Joskow 1973).[8] In the 1980s regulators have disallowed compensation for investments that were considered to be either "not used or useful" or "imprudent." Typically the first case has involved expenditures on discontinued or unnecessary plants, and the second expenditures on nuclear and supercritical coal plants that have experienced large cost overruns. In either case the net effect is to reduce actual earned rates of return below a normal return on investment in special circumstances.[9] Returns have therefore varied with demand growth and costs.

Let us define the term "used and useful" rate-of-return (UUROR) regulation as requiring the regulator to pay at least a normal return on utilized capital (equal to realized demand in the model), but allowing noncompensatory rates when there is excess capacity. Suppose that the regulator pays a gross return s_b on base-load capital up to $1 - \sigma$, (i.e., up to that level of capacity that will always be utilized) and thereafter s_j in the demand state $j = \{H, L\}$ on the additional capital, up to the level of high demand, 1. Legally permissible rates of return under UUROR are defined by the state-contingent rates of return $\{s_b \geq r; s_H \geq r; s_L \geq 0\}$, where the first entry is the return on base-load capacity, and the second and third are the returns on any additional capacity in the high- and low-demand states, respectively.

The equilibria that can be sustained depend on the punishments that the injured party can impose on the other party for defecting from announced strategies. The maximum punishment that the regulator can legally impose on the utility is to pay a return of zero on any excess capacity, or to choose the state-contingent returns $(r, r, 0)$. The maximum punishment the utility can impose is not to invest ever again, though it is worth considering what happens if it responds in a less extreme manner.

As before, the regulator's strategy set is one of two alternative levels of capacity payment on top of variable costs. The *normal return function* is defined by the vector of returns $\mathbf{R}^n = (r, s_H, s_L)$ with $s_H \geq r, s_L \geq 0$ (where s_H, s_L are chosen to minimize the incentive to deviate), and the *punishment return function* is given by $\mathbf{R}^p = (r, r, 0)$. The utility chooses a level of investment from a strategy $S_t(\cdot)$ which, since the regulator has only two alternatives, needs only to consist of two alternatives. Given the regulator's punishment strategy, the utility earns zero expected profits with any level of capacity up to $1 - \sigma$ and negative expected profits with any larger capacity. We assume that the utility responds to a deviation by the regulator from his announced strategy by reverting to the strategy of investing $K = 1 - k$ forever for some $\sigma \leq k \leq 1$. Thus, if $k = \sigma$, the utility invests just enough to meet low demand and thus avoids future shortfalls in return, but if $k > \sigma$, it will not even be able to satisfy the low demand. When $k = 1$, no private utility will invest. As before, we wish to see if the game will sustain an equilibrium with the following strategy pairs:

$$R_t(\cdot) = \begin{cases} R^n & \text{if } K_t \geq 1, \\ R^p & \text{otherwise,} \end{cases} \tag{2.5}$$

$$S_t(\cdot) = \begin{cases} 1 & \text{if } R_{t-1} \geq R^n, \\ 1-k & \text{otherwise, where } \sigma \leq k \leq 1. \end{cases} \tag{2.6}$$

The main difference from the earlier game is that the regulator cannot expropriate the returns on any used capacity, and as a result the utility can be assured that a minimal level of capacity will be adequately rewarded. Failure to reward currently unused capacity makes investing above $1 - \sigma$ unwise, but to deter deviation, the utility might in addition retaliate by cutting capacity below the minimum level always needed. The regulator knows that any deviation from the normal reward will cause the utility to underinvest forever. Once again the regulator will be deterred from deviating if the present value of the costs outweigh the short-run gains. Figure 2.5 shows the one-period regulatory gain of deviating in the high demand state, which will depend on the level of s_H. Figure 2.6 shows the regulatory gain of deviating in state L, which depends on s_L. Figure 2.7 shows the continuing costs of deviating, again equal to the extra cost less the saving. The extra cost can be made larger by increasing k.

Appendix A shows how the costs and benefits of deviating vary with the demand state in which the regulator deviates, and that the most favorable case for equilibrium has a zero expected profit for the utility and equal incentives for deviation in both states (otherwise, the incentive to deviate in the more vulnerable state could be decreased at no cost). This can be satisfied if

$$(c-b) \geq \frac{r[k+(1-\theta)iP\sigma]}{k-\sigma P} \tag{2.7}$$

Condition (2.7) can be compared with (2.3) to judge the effects of constitutional (legal) constraints on the actions of the regulator. First, note that the higher is k, the lower will be the right-hand side and the more likely the inequality will be satisfied; that is to say, the more the utility underinvests in response to regulatory deviations, the less likely such deviations are. The extreme case is $k = 1$; in this case the term $1 - \sigma P$ in (2.4) and (2.3) are the same while the numerator of (2.4) is unambiguously less than right-hand side of (2.3), making the regulatory compact more durable. Figures 2.2 to 2.8 also show that while the regulatory gain is smaller under UUROR, the costs can be made just as large.

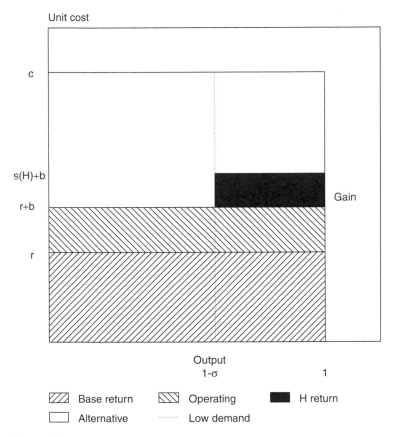

Figure 2.5
"Used and useful" rate-of-return returns in high-demand state.

Thus constitutional limits on regulatory discretion can reduce the risk of regulatory failure provided that the utility responds as vigorously as before to any deviation. Whether this is plausible is an interesting question. With no restrictions on regulatory discretion, zero investment (abandoning the industry) made sense for the utility. In the present case some limited protection is available, and so less drastic responses by the utility are to be expected. It is one of the apparent paradoxes of this kind of game that the regulator would prefer to be able to make credible commitments and thus increase the costs of regulatory deviation. Institutions that allow the utility to appeal against decisions in ways that are costly to the regulator may have this property, and it is possible to devise more complex strategies to encourage

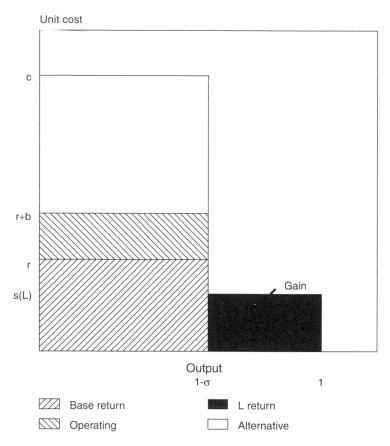

Figure 2.6
"Used and useful" rate-of-return returns in low-demand state.

the utility to respond with zero investment (see Gilbert and Newbery 1994). Even if extreme responses are ruled out for various reasons (mainly to do with the costs of mistakes), and the utility makes only a minimal response (just investing to meet minimal demand on which a return is legally assured), provided that capital is adequately durable, the rate of return not too high and that the downside risks (σ) are not too large, then UUROR improves on unrestricted rate-of-return regulation.

The difference between UUROR and rate-of-return regulation unsupported by constitutional restraints is that the regulator can underreward capacity in low-demand states in return for allowing above-normal returns in high-demand states, effectively sharing the

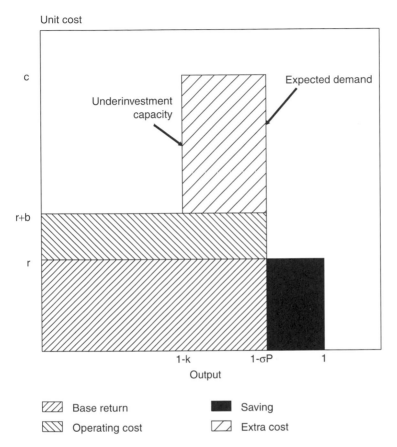

Figure 2.7
"Used and useful" rate-of-return costs of deviating forever.

fixed costs during periods of low demand (when average unit costs are higher) between the utility and customers in exchange for a premium in high-demand (lower-average-cost) states. This is the reason why the regulator is less likely to be tempted to renege on the regulatory compact when average costs are high and there is evident excess capacity. It shifts some investment risk from consumers to investors but, perhaps paradoxically, may reduce regulatory risk. UUROR has the additional effect of providing better incentives for avoiding excessive investment, which may be underremunerated. The disadvantage is that giving the regulator more discretion may weaken the clarity of the regulatory compact. It suggests a different way of looking at properties of the regulatory regime, in terms of credibility, and robustness against different kinds of shocks and risks. If a regulatory regime is not credible and robust against plausible shocks, then its possible incentive effects may be irrelevant. With that in mind, how do other systems of regulation compare?

2.4   Price Regulation

Rate-of-return regulation can support an adequate level of investment provided that it is credible and hence sustainable. Sustainability depends on the particular legislative framework, with "used and useful" rate-of-return regulation more likely to be sustainable than unconstrained rate-of-return regulation. Legislative constraints are therefore valuable as are institutions that raise the cost to the regulator of breaking the implicit regulatory compact. The main problem of rate-of-return regulation is that linking revenues to costs reduces the incentive to cut costs. Economists have therefore argued for systems of regulation that give better incentives. When it was decided to privatize British Telecommunications (BT), the initial proposal was for rate-of-return regulation. Alan Walters, the prime minister's advisor, strongly criticized this as being effectively a 100 percent profits tax, with poor incentives for efficiency and a tendency to encourage excessive capital intensity. Walters proposed an output-related profits levy where the rate of profits tax decreased with increased output. Stephen Littlechild was commissioned to advise on regulation, and recommended a local tariff reduction scheme, rapidly renamed RPI − X. His idea, set out in Littlechild (1983), was to confine regulation to the noncompetitive core (local service) and leave competition to restrain other prices, thus providing incentives and avoiding the complexity of the U.S. system of regulation. The same system of price control was adopted for all subsequently privatized U.K. utilities.

The difference between the two systems of regulation can be described in various ways. Rate-of-return regulation *evolved* through a series of landmark court cases in the United States to provide procedural fairness in the allocation of rents accruing to franchise monopoly investor-owned utilities, but it has been criticized for its inefficiency. Price regulation was *designed* in the United Kingdom to create an efficient system of regulation to enable publicly owned utilities to be transferred to private ownership, but it has been criticized for its lack of fairness. Fairness and regulatory credibility are closely linked, as the following argument demonstrates. The simple model under discussion is not set up to deal with incentive issues; it can examine whether these advantages come at the expense of adequate capital investment. Can price regulation do as well as rate-of-return regulation in terms of the level of investment and cost to consumers? That is, can efficient investment paths be sustained as equilibria of the regulatory game under price regulation?

Price regulation can take various forms, but there are a number of specifications that seem natural in the present setting. The distinctive feature of price regulation is that the utility receives no return on unutilized capacity. If we restrict attention to linear price schedules, then it is sufficient to specify two state-specific prices, p_L and p_H, which have to be high enough to induce investment. If prices can be capped at different levels in each state, but must be uniform for all output in that state, then the regulator announces a *normal price-cap strategy* $p^n = \{p_H = b + r/(1 - P); p_L = b\}$ which he would pay if the utility invests at the efficient level, and a *punishment price-cap strategy*, $p^p = \{p^p_i = b, i = H, L\}$ paid otherwise—anything lower would dissuade the utility from producing from its sunk capital. The appendix shows these to be the lowest prices that lead the utility to invest $K = 1$ and in that sense are efficient.

With these prices the regulator would have no incentive to deviate in the low-demand state but would gain more from deviating in the high-demand state than under UUROR. The reason is simple. Even the state-contingent form of price regulation gives rise to more variable profits than rate-of-return regulation, and when profits are high, the temptation to expropriate them is greater. If the regulator cannot make the price cap depend on the level of demand, then there is an additional problem. If the price is kept low enough to avoid above-average returns, the utility will underinvest, but if it is high enough to induce the right level of investment, it will yield an above-normal return to the utility. Of course, this is not the end of the story. Although price regulation may give higher returns to the utility, if the incentives to cut cost are sufficiently strong, then the prices charged could be lower than under rate-of-return regulation. However, this is a feature the present model is not designed to address.

Summarizing, we can say that simple, non-state-contingent price regulation suffers doubly by allowing both excessive profits and more variable profits. More sophisticated state-contingent price regulation (where prices are adjusted or allowed to respond to reflect excess supply) may be able to mitigate the problem of excess profits. Price-cap regulation still runs into the difficulty that because profits are more variable than under cost-based regulation, the pressure to renege on the regulatory compact is greater. The policy maker faces a difficult choice: Are the legal, constitutional, and other constraints on regulatory discretion that protect the investor sufficiently strong that the regulatory compact will be robust to large swings in profit, in which case price-caps may have strong advantages? Or are these restraints weak, so that the only regulatory system that will survive populist pressure is one that holds returns down and keeps prices close to average costs? How robust are different regulatory regimes to changes in the environment—changes in the risks of overinvestment, the cost of alternatives, or the rate of growth of demand? Can one explain periodic changes in regulatory regimes by such external factors? More fundamentally, are the problems of commitment so serious in some circumstances that they can only be overcome by public ownership? Indeed, given the problems of regulatory commitment, is the obvious solution public ownership—a solution that has, after all, been adopted by a large fraction of the developed world, and most of the developing and socialist countries?

The next chapter examines the reasons for public ownership for network utilities, and the growing dissatisfaction with their performance that has led some policy makers to press for privatization. The remainder of this chapter looks more closely at the institutions that restrain regulators, and how far their powers need to be clearly limited if private owners are to invest in and operate network utilities.

2.5 Design of Regulatory Institutions

Regulatory institutions are usefully thought of as part of the "economic institutions of capitalism," to take the title of Williamson's 1985 book. North (1991) describes institutions as the set of rules, formal and informal, that organize and constrain human interactions. The *Concise Oxford Dictionary* gives as its definition of institutions "established law, custom or practice." They are supported by such a complex web of rules, norms, expectations, and sanctions that they have great inertia, and their evolution is typically incremental and history dependent. North goes on to observe that if players are few and interact in repeated games with full information, they will usually find ways of cooperating, but something more is needed to restrain opportunism where these conditions are not satisfied. The stylized regulation games just presented show the tensions even when these conditions are satisfied, and they show how additional restraints can increase the range of cooperative outcomes. Clearly, further restraints are needed to secure efficient outcomes when the game is never exactly repeated and the players lack full information.

North and Weingast (1989) provide a very appropriate example of an institutional innovation that had profound effects on the willingness of individuals to invest in seventeenth-century Britain. The problem was that the king had unlimited powers that could be exercised in arbitrary taxation or other confiscatory acts. The Glorious Revolution of 1688 forced the crown to seek parliamentary assent for any action, and hence secured property rights and protected individual wealth from confiscatory government. The reform had a very beneficial effect on investment and the development of capital markets. This example of institutional reform illustrates the importance of restraining arbitrary confiscatory actions for efficient private investment. It also cautions against assuming that just because such institutions are efficient they will therefore be immediately created to underwrite economic activity.

If institutions constrain choices, what happens to the conventional economics approach in which choices are only constrained by technology and endowments? The older school of institutional economists argued that neoclassical economics failed to adequately explain the allocation of resources, power, and wealth by ignoring institutions, and that the proper study of resource allocation would have to focus on how institutions evolved and constrained the actions of economic agents. This challenge has finally been taken up by the "new institutional economics" in which information is recognized to be incomplete and transactions costly. Once these are recognized, economic analysis can address the role of institutions in resource allocation and, more important, the forces acting to change the institutional environment.

Williamson (1985) argues that transactions, rather than tastes or technology, are the basic unit of institutional analysis, and that *transaction cost economics* is the appropriate framework for understanding why different institutions emerge to handle different kinds of transactions. The key determinant of the evolutionary success of institutions is their ability to organize transactions to economize on bounded rationality while guarding against opportunism. Williamson gives as an example of successful institutional innovation the rise of the M-form or multidivisional corporate structure replacing the centralized, functionally departmentalized or unitary (U-form) company from the 1920s. This view of institutional design stresses the importance both of *bounded rationality* or the costs of acquiring and processing information, and also *opportunism*, or the use of guile and deceit to distort outcomes to the benefit of the agent (also known as moral hazard). The third ingredient in transaction cost economics is *asset specificity*, or the extent to which the original value of assets is hard to realize after they have been committed to their chosen purpose.

The relative importance of these three features in any transaction will determine the appropriate institution for mediating these transactions. Thus, if there is bounded rationality and opportunism but no asset specificity, competitive outcomes are efficient (e.g., in the case of contestable airlines whose assets can be readily relocated). If there were no problems with bounded rationality, both opportunism and asset specificity could be handled by sophisticated contracts or plans, with every contingency carefully anticipated and dealt with. If there were no opportunism, transactions could be handled by promises or simple contracts in which agents would do as they said they would without further monitoring or enforcement. But if all three features are present, then governance structures are required that specify tasks in advance, together with mechanisms to monitor and enforce outcomes ex post. Since these cannot be adequately specified in advance, the institution that handles them becomes critical.

Regulation of network utilities has to deal with asset specificity on the part of the utility, bounded rationality on the part of the regulator (incomplete and costly information about the options open to the utility), and opportunism by both parties. It also has to protect agreements between the regulator and utility against interventions by other parties, which is something that the simple two-player games just described could conveniently ignore. The utility will attempt to deliver services that are most profitable rather than those that are most efficient, either at too high quality and cost, by "gold plating," or at too low quality and cost through skimping, depending on the incentives it faces. The regulator's opportunism is that it may take advantage of the sunk nature of the assets to renege on its original promise of adequate reward.

Williamson (1985, p. 347) describes traditional U.S. rate-of-return regulation as follows: ". . . regulation may be described contractually as a highly incomplete form of long-term contracting in which (1) the regulatee is assured an overall fair rate of return, in exchange for which

(2) adaptations to changing circumstances are successively introduced without the costly haggling that attends such changes when parties to the contract enjoy greater autonomy." Historically this is a good description of the evolution of regulation in the United States, though many would question the success with which costly haggling has been avoided. Indeed, if we look at telecommunications regulation in the United States, rate-of-return regulation requires the utility to file all the supporting information for any proposed tariff changes, which are subject to lengthy judicial hearings. As such they are ill adapted to the rapid changes of tariffs by competitors in the contestable long-distance market.

Since 1989 the FCC has switched to setting price-caps for interstate services and allowing AT&T freedom to introduce new tariffs within those caps. The change made the whole system simpler and more flexible,[10] and can be seen as an attempt to reduce the transaction costs of regulatory change. A more cynical view might be that the original regulatory institution had lost its purpose once long-distance telecoms became sufficiently competitive, and that the change reflects the attempt of the FCC to maintain its regulatory purpose in life.

For privately owned network utilities to be superior to public ownership, the society has to restrain regulatory opportunism without incurring excessive transaction costs. Spiller (1993, 1994) argues that these restraints need to operate at two levels: the regulatory agency itself needs to be restrained and its discretion limited, but the government also needs to be restrained from changing the regulatory framework. If these restraints are to be credible, they will require institutions to enforce them. Countries differ in their institutional endowment, which include the legislative, executive and judicial institutions, norms of behavior, administrative capability, and the degree of social consensus within the society. These differences will condition the kind of restraints that can be placed on regulatory opportunism, and whether regulated private ownership is viable.

In the United States, the regulatory compact is sustained by the separation of the judiciary from the legislative and executive branches of government, by the Constitution, and by a well-developed body of administrative procedures that specify how regulatory agencies must behave, how they are to reach decisions, and how they may be challenged. The case of the Bell System is instructive. The Communications Act was passed by Congress in 1934 setting up the FCC. It defined its mission to facilitate universal service "at reasonable charges," and pro-

nouncing "any unjust or unreasonable discrimination . . . to be unlaw-
ful" under the 1887 Interstate Commerce Act (Temin 1987, p. 11). The
Act is imprecise about how the FCC should achieve these objectives,
but the FCC was not given a free hand to act as it liked. The Department of Justice can intervene, and it did in the case that led to the
breakup of AT&T, as we will see in chapter 4. The independence of the
judiciary is critical in restricting the discretion of the regulatory agency.
Nevertheless, the predictability, and hence credibility, of regulation
rests heavily on established procedures enabling the regulated industry to appeal against unreasonable regulation. The system is designedly
cumbersome, though the AT&T case shows that reform and changes in
the system of regulation can be negotiated, given enough time to build
up the necessary support.

Where these established procedures are not available, or where
administrative law does not adequately restrain discretion, very specific regulatory legislation may be required, as in Chile. Chile lays
down in the legislation how regulated prices are to be set for electricity and telecommunications in very specific detail, and how the fair rate
of return is to be determined (using the capital asset pricing model),
how prices are to be indexed, and how disputes are to be resolved. This
approach requires that laws are difficult to change and will not be
reversed by a subsequent government, and also that the judiciary is
sufficiently independent to challenge regulatory deviations from the
law. Spiller (1994) argues that these conditions are satisfied in Chile
(and to some extent in Argentina) because the fragmented legislature
makes it difficult to amass sufficient support to change laws once
enacted, ensuring their stability and commitment value. The obvious
drawback is that the system is very inflexible. For electricity regulation
this may not be a problem, but for the rapidly evolving telecommunications industry there is a serious risk that the legislation may fail to
deal with new eventualities—as new forms of entry threaten the basis
of charging access, as in the United States.[11]

If legislation can be changed easily with a change in government,
then enshrining the detailed restraints on regulation in the law will not
provide much security. If in addition the country lacks a tradition of
administrative procedures and regulatory case law built up over time,
as in the United States, then it may be necessary to restrain opportunism by specifying the rights of the utility in contracts. The British
case demonstrates why this has been the preferred method of specify-

ing regulation. Britain has chosen a high-powered regulatory scheme which is potentially vulnerable to opportunism. Parliament is sovereign and can thus overrule previous legislation, making legislative commitment low. The courts are, however, independent, and well able to uphold contracts, and the main body of regulation is therefore included in the licenses granted to the utilities. The next section describes this process in some detail; the model is good provided that contracts can be enforced by an independent judiciary. If that is lacking, there may be no credible method of deterring regulatory opportunism, and public ownership is the default option, except for those cases where the regulatory compact is self-enforcing because the costs of regulatory deviation are sufficient to deter opportunism (noticeably for telecoms).

2.6 Role of Licenses in U.K. Utility Regulation

U.K. utilities have typically been privatized by the passage of primary legislation (e.g., the Telecommunications Act 1984 and the Electricity Act 1989, described in appendix B to this chapter). These specify the general framework for regulation, and also the requirement that utilities supplying services specified in the Act will need a license under the Act unless exempted by order under the Act. The bulk of the regulatory system is typically contained in the licenses, which are drawn up to suit the specific circumstances of the licensee with the agreement of the Secretary of State or the Director General of the relevant utilities (e.g., the Director General of Telecommunications for telecommunications and the Director General of Electricity Supply for the electricity industry).

If we look at licenses under the Electricity Act 1989, for example, we find that there are generation licenses for the two nonnuclear privatized generating companies formed from the former Central Electricity Generating Board (National Power and PowerGen), a somewhat different license for the state-owned Nuclear Electric (e.g., for issues of safety), individual licenses for Independent Power Producers, a transmission license for the National Grid Company (NGC), Public Electricity Supply (PES) licenses for the regional electricity companies who have a monopoly in their local area for the distribution of electricity, and Private Electricity Supply or "second-tier" licenses for others supplying (large) consumers within a PES's authorized area.

Most of the important regulations are contained in the PES and transmission licenses that cover the natural monopoly parts of the de-integrated industry created on privatization. Both licenses contain conditions that control the average level of prices, require nondiscrimination and prohibit cross-subsidy, and specify the conditions to be met to ensure security of supply. The PES license requires the licensee to acquire electricity from the most economic sources and restricts the extent of own generation to preclude vertical re-integration. The transmission license requires NGC to schedule power stations in order of lowest bids and to run a settlement system. In addition the generators, NGC, NGC Settlements Ltd., and Energy Pool Funds Administration Ltd. must sign a pooling and settlement agreement that contains the contractual obligations under which bulk electricity is dispatched and paid for.

Unless revoked though failure to meet license obligations, the licenses continue until the Secretary of State gives twenty-five years notice, which he may not do for at least ten years, ensuring that the initial license is for at least thirty-five years. The conditions of the license may be modified or amended by agreement between the licensee and the Director General of Electricity Supply, or following a reference to the Monopolies and Mergers Commission as provided for in the Electricity Act (sections 14 and 15). An example of an agreed modification is provided by the insertion of a new condition 9a in the generation licenses of National Power, PowerGen, and Nuclear Electric, authorized on July 24, 1992, which enables the director to receive information that allows him to monitor whether the generators "are restricting, distorting or preventing competition in the generation or supply of electricity." This was agreed after PowerGen had manipulated the Pool (electricity spot) price by first declaring generation capacity unavailable a day ahead of time, but then on the day redeclaring the generation stations available.[12]

Why has regulation in Britain taken this dual form, with a rather general framework in the primary legislation, and the details of regulation largely concentrated in the licenses? The answer is that in Britain, Parliament is sovereign, and each government can introduce legislation that supersedes preceding legislation. With a tradition of adversarial politics, and frequent reversals in party control under the "first past the post" system of election, there would be little guarantee of stability of the primary legislation given the considerable hostility to privatizing network utilities by the then opposition Labour party.

Licenses, however, are legally enforceable contracts that will be upheld in the courts by the independent judiciary and cannot be readily changed without the agreement of the license holder. If there is a dis- agreement, the director can refer the matter to the Monopolies and Mergers Commission (MMC), which can make recommendations either to the director or to the Secretary of State.

This last proviso is important. The problem in utility regulation is to balance two conflicting objectives. Because utilities have durable, immovable, and valuable assets, investors require a durable and stable regulatory contract in which the government and regulator are committed to uphold the original conditions. The other requirement is that regulation be adapted to changing circumstances and in the light of experience which reveals weaknesses in the original regulation. The ability of the generators to manipulate capacity payments by strategic capacity declaration, mentioned above, is a good example of an unanticipated exercise of market power that required changes to the license conditions. There must therefore also be a mechanism for changing license regulation to counter any perverse signals. The difficulty lies in reconciling the required durability and stability of regulation, on the one hand, with flexibility and adaptability, on the other.

The solution is to require that changes must be by agreement between the director and the licensee in the first instance, but encour- aged by the threat that if agreement is not forthcoming, the director can refer the matter to independent arbitration through the MMC. This process is potentially costly to both parties and the costs are inten- tional, designed to strengthen the durability and credibility of the orig- inal regulation unless the costs of inflexibility outweigh the benefits of change. The costs of a reference to the MMC for the license holder are obvious; they can be seen in the fall in share prices whenever a threat of such a reference becomes a serious possibility. Apart for the direct costs of assembling and presenting a case to the MMC, there is the obvious additional threat that the MMC may recommend changes to the license that would be costly in terms of forgone profits. The cost to the director of a reference is that he or she might lose the case, which would undermine his or her reputation for regulation. Regula- tory uncertainty undermines the confidence of investors, thereby raising the cost of capital for future investment at the expense of con- sumers. In an extreme case the utility might refuse to invest and pre- cipitate a crisis.

2.7   Privatization and Regulation in Transitional Economies

Britain is an example of a country with an independent judiciary, a competent administration, and a set of institutions to manage competition policy and resolve regulatory disputes. This institutional endowment was critically important when it came to create a new set of institutions to regulate network utilities once they were privatized. East European countries were far less well endowed with these key "economic institutions of capitalism," and therefore faced more serious problems of regulatory credibility when they attempted to privatize their network utilities.

Privatization is a key objective of the reform process in transitional economies of Central and Eastern Europe (CEE), though progress has been slower than anticipated.[13] There are powerful arguments for privatizing enterprises producing for competitive markets. Here the issues are largely practical; they have to do with sequencing legislation, re-structuring and demonopolization, deciding how and to whom to sell, and what degree of discount to provide to citizens. The network utilities do not fall into this category, yet they are frequently selected as attractive industries to privatize, mainly because their very capital intensity gives them a large book value. They are simply the most valuable commercial assets in countries often laden with heavy foreign debts.

The importance (and ultimate political necessity) of regulating privatized natural monopolies was not widely appreciated in the CEE countries. Regulation was seen as the deadening hand of socialist ownership, to be replaced by the free and unregulated market as soon as practical. Telecommunications companies were at the top of the list of utilities to be sold, but the energy utilities, particularly gas and electricity, followed shortly behind. Hungary started to look at the electricity industry as early as 1991, with a succession of foreign advisors helping to draft legislation, suggest regulatory frameworks, and propose alternative structures for the industry. Czechoslovakia valued companies for possible privatization in 1990, and found that seven of the ten largest firms were energy companies. The Czech privatization program as a whole has been remarkable for its scale and speed: 24,000 small firms were auctioned for U.S.$1 billion by the end of 1993, over 100,000 property restitution claims with an estimated value of between U.S.$2.5 to 4 billion had been settled, and over 3,500 larger firms were at least partly privatized by the end of 1995. The value of the large firms privatized in the first wave in 1993 was about U.S.$11 billion. However, most of the shares in the network utilities (with the exception of telecoms) were then still held by the Fund of National Property, pending the creation of a satisfactory regulatory framework (Mejstřík 1997).

In Poland the government started an ambitious program of privatizing large state enterprises (SEs) in 1990 aiming to privatize half of the 9,000 SEs within three years. By mid–1992 only 1,285 SEs had been privatized, mainly by liquidation, but no energy enterprises had yet been privatized; 7,735 out of 8,199 remaining SEs were still not commercialized and continued to be self-managed by their workers' councils. Only three large power plants and a few district heating enterprises had been commercialized, though the World Bank was proposing the privatization of a cogeneration company. Despite this rather slow start, Poland planned further privatizations of parts of the energy sector, with the electricity generation companies considered the best candidates. These plans were still not realized by the end of 1998.

In the case of telecoms, the arguments for privatization are simple. Huge investments in new technology are required to provide the infrastructure needed for a market economy and an efficient financial system, and this can most readily be supplied by Western companies, particularly the telecoms companies of America and Western Europe. These companies will not only supply the technical expertise but management skills and access to foreign capital, all of which are essential for rapid progress. The case for privatizing electricity is less clear-cut, and the problems of regulatory design and commitment likely to be more difficult. The arguments presented in this chapter explain why privatizing electricity satisfactorily is harder than privatizing telecoms (or indeed, airlines). Consider their attraction to a potential foreign buyer who must balance risk and return in deciding how much he is willing to pay for the utility. The return depends on the level of prices he is allowed to charge relative to both operating and purchase cost, while the risk depends on the period over which the investment is recouped and the confidence he has in his ability to charge high enough prices over the life of the investment. The prices he charges will depend on the system of regulation, the demand for the service, and the bargaining power of the investor *after* he has made the investment.

If the regulatory powers are kept within government, investors may fear that populist pressures to protect consumers during the wrenching adjustments of transition may deter the government from approving rate increases in line with inflation. Investors will have little confidence that initial or proposed tariff levels will remain cost-reflective in the future. If the regulatory body is independent, reasonably insulated from day-to-day political pressures, has a clear set of objectives and procedures for dispute resolution, and issues licenses with legally enshrined rights and obligations to the utilities, as in Britain, then investors are likely to have more confidence in the protection afforded by regulation and in its durability. How much the durability of the regulatory regime matters will depend on the characteristics of the industry, and the bargaining power of the investor.

The bargaining power of the investor after he has made his investment can be measured by the damage that he would inflict on the government or the country in the event of regulatory breakdown. What would it then be in the interest of the investor to do if the initial regulatory contract or understanding has been broken, and how costly would it be for the host country? Would this implicit threat of the consequences of regulatory breakdown be sufficient to dissuade the regulator and/or the government from breaking its original undertaking?

Consider now three potential candidates for privatization: the national airline, telecoms, and electricity. The airline raises the fewest problems, since the network is the least durable. If the regulator or government were to take arbitrary action to undermine the profitability of the routes (relative to the rest of the world), then the airline owner could overnight reallocate his capital (the airplanes) to other more profitable routes. Given this, the investments are very secure; they can be reallocated or resold for a high fraction of their value in the original use. As a result carriers can operate with a negligible capital base, leasing or renting the airplanes. Since capital is not sunk, it is not necessary to have a very durable form of regulation, and negotiations over the form of regulation or fare-setting can take place repeatedly on essentially the same terms as before the investor originally entered the industry or bought the airline. Provided that there is adequate competition (which may depend on treaties beyond the control of the country), there is little point is either state ownership or regulation.

Telecoms are very different; since the investment is highly durable and specific, the investor cannot recover his sunk cost and move elsewhere. The investment is very capital intensive, at about $2,000 per new line, and the operating costs are low relative to the capital cost.

The worry that the investor has is that once the investment has been made, the regulator or government may wish to lower prices and transfer rents from the foreign owner to domestic subscribers. Since operating costs are so low relative to total costs, this would seem to be attractive to the host country. What might deter the regulator or government from expropriatory tariffs or overtight price regulation? What credible counterthreats are open to the telecoms company?

The most immediate counterthreat is that the company will stop investing, and this would be credible if future profits are threatened. Most bids for telecoms companies in Eastern Europe (and other developing countries) are ranked both on the price paid on acquisition and a rate of investment (lines connected per year) over some time horizon, and a good contract will make that undertaking conditional on continued regulatory good behavior. The threat is that if both finance and foreign expertise are required to modernize and expand the network, then an investment strike will be very costly to the country. That is to say, if the foreign investor pulls out because of justified dissatisfaction with regulation, then other companies will be reluctant to risk a similar fate, and the country will be forced to stop telecoms investment, or will have to spend large sums acquiring the indigenous expertise for autarkic expansion.[14]

The retaliation costs will be even higher if foreign expertise is needed to operate the system on a daily basis, or if foreign cooperation is needed to interconnect with foreign networks, for then the host country loses not only future expansion but risks the whole current system. Modern telecoms systems rely heavily on software programs to manage the switches and route the calls, and the threat of erasing (or not adequately maintaining) this software would be an even more costly form of retaliation. In fact the costs to the country of alienating a major foreign telecoms investor would seem to be so large relative to the benefits that all parties should rationally be confident that it will not happen, and therefore there is little to worry about.[15] The main concerns of the parties will probably be spelled out carefully in the initial bids or contracts, specifying how tariffs are to be set and adjusted, how cross-subsidies are to be protected against competitive entry ("cherry picking" or "cream-skimming"), and how fast investment is to be undertaken. It would clearly be imprudent for a foreign investor to rely on profits from long-distance or international calls to cross-subsidize local rates, since these are unlikely to be protected effectively against subsequent entry and competition, and one would therefore expect investors to require regulatory assurances that they could set cost-recovering charges for access to the local loop.

The other advantage enjoyed by telecoms companies is that telephones are a luxury, usually in excess demand with long waiting lists, and in competition with even more expensive mobile phones (which have the advantage of lower sunk investment for the telecom operator, and more rapid coverage). Telephone charges are therefore far less of a political issue, and there is likely to be considerably less political resistance to raising rates in line with inflation. Therefore the political pressures to abrogate the original contract are lower than with necessities like electricity and gas or district heating.

Now consider the electricity industry. In most CEE countries, electricity demand fell with the fall in industrial output during the transition, and forecast demands are unlikely to put pressure on current capacity until the end of the century. Most CEE countries are so energy intensive and electric intensive that improvements in efficiency caused by sensible pricing and market responses will weaken demand growth for at least a decade. In Hungary, demand fell 17 percent between 1989 and 1994, and the reserve margin was already very high in 1989 (Dobozi 1995). In Poland, electricity demand fell 10 percent between 1989 and 1994, while in Eastern Europe as a whole demand fell 16 percent, with considerably larger declines in the former Soviet Union countries.

Foreign buyers could not therefore inflict much damage on these countries by declining to invest in additional capacity if they became dissatisfied with the way prices were being regulated. In addition these countries have a history of building and operating power stations to reasonably high standards, and so are not dependent on foreign suppliers for access to appropriate technology. In short these countries have been independent of Western technology in the past, and they could continue to be so in the future at low cost, greatly reducing the bargaining power of any foreign buyer.

It follows that any foreign buyer will have little power to damage the country by refusing to invest if it fails to earn a satisfactory return, and there will be clear political temptations to hold down electricity prices at the expense of the owner. In order to convince potential buyers that this will not happen, the regulatory system will have to be carefully designed because it will not be self-enforcing. It is interesting to contrast the experiences of Eastern Europe attempting to privatize electricity and telecoms. The following two examples are illustrative of the very different problems of regulatory commitment facing the two industries.

2.7.1 Telecommunications Privatization in the Czech Republic

The Czech Republic has been following a purposeful move to the market economy since the Velvet revolution of 1989, with the ultimate goal of joining the European Union. It has therefore followed the model of telecoms restructuring set out in the 1987 EC Green Paper on telecommunications. As a result post and telecoms were separated in 1992, and on January 1, 1994, SPT Telecom became a joint-stock company ready to participate in the second wave of voucher privatization later that year. Twenty-six percent of the stock was "sold" (i.e., exchanged for vouchers that had previously been allocated to the population), and 4 percent transferred to state-owned funds. In June 1995 the Dutch-Swiss consortium TelSource successfully bid $1.451 billion for 27 percent of SPT Telecom, leaving 51 percent in the hands of the National Property Fund. The sales proceeds were to be reinvested in SPT Telecom, and the expenditure plans required $5.19 billion to be invested to bring supply in to balance with demand by the year 2000. (Seda and Hruby 1995).

The structure of regulation was set out in the Telecommunication Act 1992 which enables demonopolization and liberalization of telecoms as well as privatization. The Act was accepted by the parliament of the new Czech Republic after the division of Czechoslovakia at the beginning of 1994, and the Ministry of Economy created the regulatory body of the Czech Telecommunication Office (CTO). The Act requires that operators hold licenses, while the CTO administers tariff regulation and grants permission to enter. Tariffs were subject to the approval of the ministry of finance, and STP Telecom has a statutory monopoly until the year 2000 for long-distance voice telephony. Although a number of operators have been licensed for the 16 local networks, they remain very small, while STP Telecom is dominant and also jointly owns the single cellular phone service Eurotel Praha (Erbenovà and Hruby 1995). The initial situation was thus similar to British Telecom at privatization in terms of market dominance.

Tariffs were realigned in 1993, but were still very unbalanced. They were not related to costs and, while well below OECD averages for local calls, were extremely high for international calls. On the other hand, the company was highly profitable with 1994 earnings of $844

million, gross profit of $281 million, and a gross return on net assets of
24 percent. Much of the expansion could therefore be financed out of
retained profits and borrowing, while the initial low productivity of the
company offered sufficient cost saving to protect profits if the company
were to lose some of its excess profits on international calls through
competition, even if it could not raise local charges.

The other noticeable contrast with electricity is that not only are
telecoms highly profitable, but the international companies clearly
have considerable bargaining strength compared to individual governments, since they operate both across Europe and in many cases
worldwide. These companies, which normally enjoy the support of
their national government, are in a position to exercise considerable
diplomatic and economic pressure through such avenues as negotiations to enter the European Union, as well as other multilateral trade
negotiations. It is therefore not surprising that even the state telecoms
companies were queuing up to bid for stakes in companies in Central
and Eastern Europe and in the developing world.

The favorable balance of power in the regulation game enjoyed by
telecom utilities does not, however, necessarily extend to other network
utilities like electricity and gas. Indeed, one of the main lessons of experience is how different the various network utilities are in their viability as private regulated companies and their regulatory requirements.

2.7.2   Preparations for Electricity Privatization in Hungary

Under the 1962 Electricity Act the state had a monopoly to produce and
distribute electricity. Between 1963 and January 1992, the electricity
supply industry was controlled by a trust, Magya Villamos Muvek
Troszt (MVMT), which acted as the accounting organ for the 22 legally
independent enterprises: 11 power and heat-generating companies, a
transmission company, 6 regional distribution companies, and 4 service
companies dealing with construction, maintenance, and installation.
In the 1960s MVMT operated under tight control from the ministry
of industry and trade (MIT) and in turn regulated the enterprises
with tight control over the allocation of funds and transfers of revenues. In the 1970s, under the New Economic Mechanism, authority
was increasingly decentralized, together with authority to invest up to
prescribed limits. MVMT negotiated with the enterprises within the
framework of the five-year and one-year plans, with the government
determining the rate of profit by controlling tariffs through the state

pricing authority and later through MIT. Tariffs to consumers were held below cost, and MVMT financed investments partly out of the profits on the resale of cheap imported electricity. As with other state enterprises, taxes were set to transfer the surplus to the center, and large investments like the nuclear power station at Paks were initially financed by the state, with the debt subsequently transferred to MVMT to be serviced and repaid.

MVMT appears to have been starved of investment resources except for those projects for which it could make a strong case on grounds of reduced energy dependence or increased demand. Investments to reduce operating costs and increase efficiency appear to have carried less priority, and the distribution network in particular appears to have suffered from underinvestment compared to generation. Relations between MVMT and the member enterprises appear to have reflected those between state enterprises and the state, in that contract prices for delivery of electricity were held close to costs in order to transfer surpluses to the Trust, and as a result different generating companies were paid different prices per unit of electricity generated. Over time there was a move to devise an internal tariff structure rewarding efficiency (heat rate, availability, etc.), in the spirit of providing more decentralized incentives, while the Trust attracted competent and loyal engineers who maintained high technical standards. The Trust thus had considerable similarities with the state-owned Central Electricity Generating Board (CEGB) in Britain and had other similarities in its heavy dependence on indigenous and rather high-cost coal, coupled with a desire to reduce its dependence on imported fuels by its nuclear construction program.

In January 1992 MVMT was reorganized in response to the requirement to corporatize under the Company Law. MVM Rt (Rt denoting a joint stock company) was established as the holding company with 15 subsidiaries: 8 for power generation, 6 for distribution, and 1 as the National Transmission Company; the 1962 Electricity Act was modified by canceling the requirement that the state had a monopoly to produce and distribute electricity. In November 1992 the Hungarian State Holding Company (HSHC, or AV Rt) was created by Law LIII of 1992 as a wholly state-owned joint-stock company to manage all companies deemed to have a long-term future in public ownership. The HSHC was allocated 99.8 percent of the share capital of MVM Rt, with the balance of 0.2 percent allocated to the municipal governments. MVM Rt in turn owned 50 percent of the subsidiary companies, the

State Property Agency (SPA) owned 48 percent of these companies, and the balance of about 2 percent was held by the municipal governments. Of the 48 percent of the companies held by SPA, 10 percent were set aside for those with restitution vouchers (compensation warrants) who may use these to buy shares, 15 to 20 percent were notionally set aside for social security funding, and the balance was available for sale by SPA. Shares in two distribution companies were offered to those holding compensation warrants (which could also be used to purchase land) in January 1993 to test market demand but at the quoted price only 2 million forints' worth (U.S.$20,000) were sold.

The objective of SPA was to privatize its assets quickly, but at a commercial price, in contrast to HSHC, which was concerned to manage and if necessary restructure assets that remain in the state sector. The rather complex ownership structure of the electricity industry meant that different owners, with their different objectives, might find it difficult to agree over strategy. SPA organized a trade sale for 15 percent of the six distribution companies, but the government decided that the tender offers were too low, and resolved the unsatisfactory ownership structure of the industry by transferring all the shares from SPA to HSHC in November 1993.

Current assets were valued at U.S.$6 billion, with negligible debts, divided between the distribution companies ($2.5 billion), generation ($2.5 billion), and the grid ($1 billion), though it is hard to judge whether these valuations were realistic. Forecast investment and refurbishment expenses were estimated at $2.5 billion up to the year 2000 so that if half the industry were sold for $3 billion (and was then responsible for its share of investment), HSHC would only need to finance $1.25 billion in future investment to 2000, much of which would be financed out of revenue and borrowing. The larger part of the sale proceeds of $3 billion would thus be available to reduce Hungarian public debt. The expectation was that the sale would be 70:30 debt to equity, so the net effect would be an increase in private debt and foreign equity equal to the reduction in public debt.

On the face of it, this would appear to substitute government-guaranteed debt for private debt at a probably higher interest rate and equity capital that would certainly require a higher real return. The net indebtedness of Hungary would not decrease, and therefore presumably its credit rating on international markets would not change. Given that Hungary could borrow to finance investment in electricity from the World Bank with little difficulty, it is therefore difficult to see the attraction of this financial maneuver if judged purely as a means of raising international capital.

The original argument for privatization was the belief that private ownership would constrain the power of the state to intervene to achieve political objectives that might be incompatible either with economic efficiency or, more generally, with the satisfactory operation of a decentralized market economy. The obvious gains from private ownership would be to remove or reduce constraints forcing the use of high-cost domestic coal or nuclear power, though these choices had been originally made in the interests of national security, now less of a problem with the end of the cold war. Between 1990 and 1992, a team of foreign advisors and Hungarian counterparts drew up a plan for restructuring the industry on the British model. They prepared a draft law with a strong regulatory framework neutral as to ownership and designed to ensure that tariffs were set to earn a reasonable rate of return on the underlying assets. The foreign advisors went to considerable lengths in presentations and seminars to stress the importance of sound regulation as the cornerstone to successful privatization.

This emphasis on regulation was resisted by the senior management of the utilities, who provided little direct support to the team, and hence were not adequately involved in the lengthy discussions about the philosophy and necessity of regulation. Management believed that the main purpose of privatization was to gain the freedom of the market, not to substitute one form of state or ministry regulation for another, possibly more tightly specified form of public utility regulation. The tension between the industry arguing for light regulation and the ministry wishing to specify the form of regulation in considerable detail was resolved at the end of 1992 by a change of the minister and secretary. The draft plan was scrapped, and a new commission more favorably inclined to the industry set up. The new commission had little overlap with the old, but worked fast and produced a draft by May 1993 that differed sharply from the first draft. The detailed specification of the powers and method of appointment of the regulatory body was deleted, and replaced by a brief description of the Hungarian Energy Office, to be established under an Act on Gas Services. The draft was submitted to Parliament in September 1993 and approved with some changes in April 1994.

The Hungarian Energy Office can issue licenses where there is a natural monopoly. The minister of industry and trades has established "a fixed price (charge) of electrical energy," though until December 31,

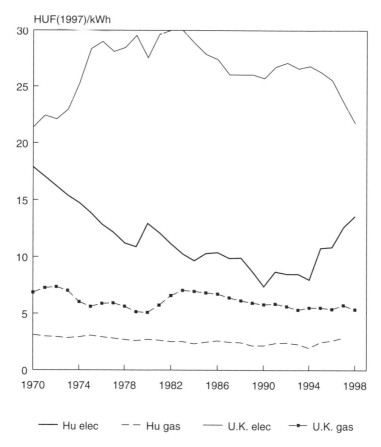

Figure 2.8
Real domestic electricity and gas prices Hungary and the United Kingdom, 1970 to 1998.

1996, the price was fixed under existing legislation. Thereafter the maximum price had to be sufficient to cover environmental costs, to provide adequate profits to finance prudent investment and ensure adequate reserve margins, and to take account of the requirements of energy and economic policy. It also required that the form of regulation should result in efficient despatch and least cost supply.

The obvious concern was that the minister continue to regulate the price, since in the past the minister was subject to strong political pressure to hold down the price to domestic consumers. Figure 2.8 shows the evolution of real domestic (tax-inclusive) prices (i.e., the price deflated by the retail price index) for electricity and gas in Hungary and the United Kingdom, computed at the exchange rates prevailing over the three years up to mid-1997 (and which are very close to the exchange rate for January 1, 1997, taken as the base of the price comparisons). The top two continuous lines are the electricity prices in HUF/kWh (200 HUF = £1 or 2 HUF = 1 p or 1.65 U.S. cents). While Britain and Hungary start from quite similar initial positions in 1970, prices in Britain are hit by the oil shocks while those in Hungary drift steadily down; by 1990 they are less than one-third the U.K. level. Competition and regulation are gradually reducing prices in Britain (but by not nearly as much as fuel costs have fallen), while adjustments of prices toward costs are gradually raising prices in Hungary (which still remain below the cost-justified level, though the change from 1994 is striking).

The problem with the inherited tariff structure (not only in Hungary but elsewhere in CEE countries) was that it was upside down, with the lowest prices to the customers that were most expensive to supply (domestic householders) and the higher prices to industry, which was supplied at higher voltages and lower cost. This reflected the general philosophy that state enterprises were mechanisms for producing surplus for allocation to investment or consumption in which questions of incentive and efficiency were largely neglected. Once this tariff structure is put in place, it creates a vocal constituency of consumers who will resist an efficient rebalancing. It is worth noting that a 1992 attempt to sell part of a gas utility failed because foreign investors lacked confidence in the regulatory framework for setting tariffs.

There was an obvious political tension over price setting for electricity that was not resolved within government before the 1994 elections. In May 1994 there was a change of government, and the new socialist-liberal coalition reaffirmed its commitment to privatize the network utilities, oil refining, broadcasting, and banking. It merged the two privatization agencies SPA and HSHC in May 1995, drafted a new privatization law setting out the necessary legal framework, and appointed expert advisers for each of the sectors. In September 1995 tenders were invited for the six distribution companies and the seven power generation companies, with commitments to invest, and for 24 percent of MVM Rt. More than thirty international companies purchased the tender documents.

Despite criticisms (particularly from English bidders about regulatory uncertainties), the distribution companies received 10 bids and were successfully sold to continental electricity companies in 1995 (who, unlike the British, were perhaps more used to the more discretionary and negotiating style of continental regulation). The average price paid amounted to \$84/MWh of sales revenue (with a range from \$64 to \$104). The generating stations received 14 bids, but only three generating companies were sold in the first wave for an average of \$170/kW. The apparent greater ease of selling distribution companies can be explained by the system of regulation and the structure of subsidies. The price that the distribution companies can charge is made up of the cost of buying high-voltage electricity and the cost of operating the local distribution service. If the main problem is that the price of bulk power is too low, then buying generation is unattractive. If, however, the distribution companies can pass on any subsequent increase in bulk power costs, then buying power does not present them with problems. Of course, they are still at some risk from price controls that fail to allow them to pass through cost increases, but these are likely to be combined with price controls on bulk power. In addition the successful purchasers were electric utilities in neighboring countries with which Hungary interconnects.[16] Some of these are state-owned, and all are powerful and would expect to exercise considerable pressure on Hungary through political channels in the event of a breach of the regulatory contract. Whilst U.S. companies have been very successful in buying British electricity distribution companies, they were not successful in Hungary, suggesting that this local political advantage may have been decisive. Of course, there is the additional possibility that state-owned electricity companies might not worry so much if they make losses in other countries.

2.8   Conclusions

If network utilities are to operate successfully under private ownership, they will need a credible system of regulation, in which the utility is confident that the regulator will allow it to earn a fair rate of return on its past investment. The argument of this chapter is that regulatory credibility is enhanced if the regulator faces high costs of deviating from this commitment to a fair rate of return or is legally restrained from deviating. The costs of breaking the regulatory compact will be higher for technologically innovative utilities serving rapidly growing and/or luxury markets like telecoms than mature technologies in stagnant and/or mass markets like electricity. The more volatile profits are, the harder it may be to sustain regulatory credibility, so regulatory systems that link revenues closely to costs are less prone to regulatory opportunism. Unfortunately, this provides poor incentives for reducing costs. Regulatory flexibility may be desirable to encourage efficiency, by retaining the right to disallow imprudent costs, but there is a fine line between flexibility and arbitrary discretion. Regulatory discretion needs to be restrained by dispute resolution mechanisms that are costly to invoke, deterring actions that undermine credibility.

If regulatory institutions are not sufficiently strong to provide adequate credibility, then private ownership may be infeasible or too costly. The costs may take the form of a high rate of return required to reward investors for the high perceived regulatory risk, which may show up as a high discount to fair asset value when the utilities are privatized, as well as the costs of monitoring and renegotiating the regulatory agreement or license. Privatization will only be socially profitable if the benefits of increased efficiency outweigh the extra costs of regulation. This next chapter therefore compares the efficiency of public and private ownership to see whether and if so when this is likely to be the case.

Appendix A: Modeling Regulation as a Dynamic Game

The utility earns profits π_t in period t:

$$\pi_t = R_t - bQ_t - rK_t, \qquad Q_t \leq \min(K_t, D_t).$$

where, as before, R_t is the revenue allowed by the regulator, Q_t is the amount produced at variable cost b, K_t is the capacity, whose total cost per period per unit is r, and D_t is demand, all in period t. Consumers benefit by avoiding purchasing Q_t from an alternative source at cost c, less the revenues paid to the utility, and enjoy benefits

$$U_t = cQ_t - R_t.$$

Both the utility and the regulator are risk neutral. The regulator wants to maximize expected welfare, and the utility will not invest unless its expected profit is nonnegative in each period:

$$\max E \sum_{t=0}^{\infty} \beta^t W_t$$

s.t. $E\pi_t \geq 0, \quad W_t = U_t + \theta\pi_t, \quad \beta = \dfrac{1}{1+i},$

where θ is the weight placed on profits ($\theta < 1$), i is the rate of interest used for discounting, and β is the discount factor; both the interest rate and the discount factor will depend on the length of the period. For example, if the annual rate of interest is 6 percent real and the period is 5 years, then $i = 34$ percent, and $\beta = 0.75$.

Note that since prices have no allocative effects in this simple model, any profits that the utility makes above zero are direct transfers from the consumers and will lower the measure of social welfare if $\theta < 1$. If the regulator could choose capital directly, the best program would generate expected consumer surplus at least cost and thus maximize

$$(c - b)[(1 - P)Q_t(H) + PQ_t(L)] - rK_t,$$

where $Q_t(H) \leq \min\{K_t, 1\}$ and $Q_t(L) \leq \min\{K_t, 1 - \sigma\}$ are outputs in the high and low demand states, whose probabilities are $1 - P$ and P, respectively. Expected costs are linear in the utility's capacity, so the efficient level of investment is $K = 0$, $1 - \sigma$, or 1. For the interesting (because more demanding) case in which the optimum choice of K is 1 (so there is always adequate capacity and never any excess demand), the marginal benefit of additional capacity must be greater than its marginal cost for $1 - \sigma < K < 1$. The marginal benefit is the expected additional savings in operating costs relative to the alternative source of supply, which occurs only in the high state of demand. The marginal cost of capital is the rental rate, r, so the condition for $K_t = 1$ is

$$(1 - P)(c - b) > r. \tag{2A.1}$$

Inequality (2A.1), which is (2.1) in the chapter, is assumed to hold in what follows.

In the first game, of unconstrained rate-of-return regulation, the regulator is tempted to deviate from its previously stated willingness to reward capacity with a return r and instead to pay just the avoidable cost, b, with no allowance for capital cost. The gain to the regulator is $(1 - \theta)r$, the value of the one-period transfer to consumers. Thereafter the utility will never supply and the regulator must secure alternative supplies. The expected extra cost per period $C = (c - b)(1 - \sigma P) - r$. The regulator would want to deviate from his announced normal reward if

$$(1 - \theta)r > \frac{C}{i} = \frac{(c - b)(1 - \sigma P) - r}{i}, \tag{2A.2}$$

where $r = i + \delta$ is the gross return including amortization δ and i is the rate of return used in discounting. It will be efficient for the utility to set $K = 1$ if (2A.1) is satisfied. Taking (2A.1) and (2A.2) together, there will be a problem of sustaining the efficient outcome if

$$\frac{r[1+(1-\theta)i]}{1-\sigma P} > (c-b) > \frac{r}{1-P}, \tag{2A.3}$$

while rate of return regulation will be credible if

$$(c-b) > \frac{r[1+(1-\theta)i]}{1-\sigma P}. \tag{2A.4}$$

which is (2.5) in the chapter.

In the next game, "used and useful" rate-of-return (UUROR) regulation, the legally permissible rates of return are

$$\{s_b \geq r; \ s_H \geq r; \ s_L \geq 0\}. \tag{2A.5}$$

Let $s_\sigma \equiv P s_L + (1 - P)s_H$, the expected rate of return on investment in excess of the assured minimum (or "base-load") level of demand $1 - \sigma$. The expected profit to the utility is, for $1 - \sigma \leq K \leq 1$,

$$E\pi = (1-\sigma)s_b + s_\sigma[K - (1-\sigma)] - rK.$$

The regulator can induce the utility to choose the efficient level of capacity ($K = 1$) with a policy that satisfies the constraints of UUROR. For example, the policy $R(\cdot) \equiv \{s_b = r, \ s_L = r - \mu, \ s_H = r + \rho\}$ with $0 < \mu \leq r$ and $\rho = P\mu/(1 - P) + \varepsilon$ for $\varepsilon > 0$ satisfies this condition. As ε tends to zero, this policy extracts all producer surplus.

The main difference from the earlier game is that the regulator cannot expropriate the returns on any used capacity, and as a result the utility can be assured that a minimal level of capacity will be adequately rewarded. Failure to reward currently unused capacity makes investing above $1 - \sigma$ unwise, but in addition the utility might retaliate by cutting capacity below the minimum level always needed in order to deter deviation. The regulator knows that any deviation from the normal reward will cause the utility to underinvest forever. The regulator would then have to find alternative supplies at a cost c in amount $k - \sigma$ if demand is low and in the amount k if demand is high. The expected excess return to the utility investing above base-load demand is $(1 - P)s_H + Ps_L - r = s_\sigma$, and this must be positive if the utility is to invest. The least-cost system of regulation will hold this to the lowest level that will still induce investment. This is the zero level by the definition of r, defining the efficient trade-off between s_H and s_L:

$$s_H = \frac{r - Ps_L}{1-P}.$$

Once again the regulator will be deterred from deviating if the present value of the costs outweigh the short-run gains. In a state of low demand, the regulator could legally pay zero instead of s_L on the excess capacity σ. The one-period gain from deviating is $(1 - \theta)s_L\sigma$. This would signal a deviation from his announced normal return policy, and the utility would respond to the deviation by underinvesting thereafter. The expected cost per period to the regulator when he reneges rather than paying the normal reward and have the utility invest, $K = 1$, is $C(k) = (c - b)(k - \sigma P) - kr$. The regulator would not want to deviate from his announced normal reward in a low-demand state if

$$(1 - \theta)s_L\sigma < \frac{C(k)}{i}, \quad \text{or} \quad s_L < \frac{C(k)}{i\sigma(1 - \theta)}. \tag{2A.6}$$

In the high-demand state the regulator could renege on his announced normal reward and legally pay a return of r rather than s_H on the utility's installed capacity. The one-period gain from deviating is $(s_H - r)\sigma$. The expected extra cost in each subsequent period is $C(k)$, and deviation will be deterred if the gain falls short of the present discounted cost; that is, if

$$(1 - \theta)(s_H - r)\sigma < \frac{C(k)}{i}, \quad \text{or} \quad s_H < r + \frac{C(k)}{i\sigma(1 - \theta)}. \tag{2A.7}$$

Figure 2.9 illustrates the nature of these constraints on returns in the two states for the extreme case in which $\theta = 0$. The gain from deviating, divided by σ, is equal to s_L in the low-demand state, and this is bounded below by zero. Deviation is deterred in low-demand states if s_L is to the left of $C(k)/\sigma i$. The normalized gain in the high-demand state is $s_H - r$, which is bounded below by zero from the UUROR constraint. Deviation is deterred in high-demand states if s_H is below $r + C(k)/\sigma i$. The zero profit line is the lower boundary of the constraint $(1 - P)s_H + Ps_L - r \geq 0$ which (s_H, s_L) must satisfy to persuade the utility to undertake efficient investment. The sustainable set of rates of returns (s_H, s_L) is contained in the region $ABCD$.

The most favorable case for a subgame perfect equilibrium has a zero expected profit for the utility and equal incentives for deviation in both states (otherwise, the incentive to deviate in the more vulnerable state could be decreased at no cost). This point corresponds to the intersection at point E of the zero profit line and the line $s_H - r = s_L$. At this

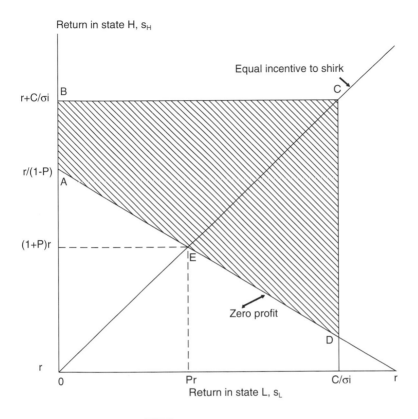

Figure 2.9
Rates of return in each state.

intersection, $s_H = (1 + P)r$ and $s_L = Pr$. Corresponding to point E in figure 2.9, a necessary and sufficient condition for existence of an efficient subgame perfect equilibrium is that

$$Pr \le \frac{C(k)}{\sigma i(1 - \theta)}$$

or

$$(c - b) \ge \frac{r[k + (1 - \theta)iP\sigma]}{k - \sigma P}, \tag{2A.8}$$

which is (2.7) in the chapter.

Appendix B: U.K. Legislative Framework for Telecoms and Electricity

Telecommunications Act of 1984

The 1984 Act set the pattern for privatizing utilities, and it had substantial similarities with later Acts, for example, the Electricity Act of 1989. It starts, in section 1, by requiring the Secretary of State to appoint a Director General of Telecommunications (DGT), and the duties of the Secretary of State and the DGT are laid down in section 3, which specifies the duty to supply unless "not reasonably practicable", public service obligations and to ensure that such services can be financed. In pursuit of these requirements, the Secretary of State and the DGT are to promote the interests of users in the United Kingdom, competition, efficiency, research and development, and various other desirable objectives. Operators must have a license, which are issued as with electricity under section 7 of the Act, and any "public telecommunications system" so designated by the Secretary of State must permit interconnection with other systems, publish charges, and act in a nondiscriminatory way. The conditions for license modification are much as with electricity and part V of the Act provides for the privatization of BT.

BT was granted a twenty-five-year license under section 7 of the Act on August 5, 1984. The Act specifies BT'S public service obligations, the crucial interconnection terms, which give the DGT power to determine the interconnection arrangements in the event of a dispute, and particular competitive activities which are subject to specific license conditions (conveniently summarized in table 1 of Gist and Meadowcroft 1986, pp. 50–51). The system of price controls is set out in condition 24 of the license as a price-cap of RPI − X, where X is 3 percent for 5 years. Price controls are applied to a basket of services which includes long distance and local calls, and business and residential rentals covering about half of the total value of BT's services. International calls were not regulated, nor were connection charges and line leasing charges.

At the same time that BT was licensed as a public telecommunications system, Mercury was licensed and granted a statutory duopoly position for seven years until 1991, but not subject to price control. By the end of this period, Mercury still only had 6 percent of the business market, 15 percent of the international market, and a negligible share of the residential market, though these shares increased after 1991.

Almost immediately, the DGT had to rule on the interconnection terms for Mercury, and proposed favorable interconnection terms that would continue until Mercury's annual interconnection payments exceeded 7 percent of BT's national call revenue. This judgment was based on the perceived desirability of increasing Mercury's market share, even if the connection charges fell short of the license entitlement that BT held under condition 13.5 to charge "the fully allocated costs attributable to the services to be provided and taking into account relevant over-heads and a reasonable rate of return on attributable assets." Subsequent modifications to the license incorporate extensive modifications to the connection condition 13, setting out the concept of an access deficit charge and allowing the DGT to waive all or part of this charge to operators on the first 10 percent of market share, provided that BT's market share exceeds 85 percent (13.5A, 13.5B, 13.5C in DTI 1991).

Electricity Act of 1989

The Act begins by requiring the Secretary of State (the elected minister holding the portfolio of the Department of Trade and Industry) to appoint the Director General of Electricity Supplies (DGES) to carry out functions assigned to him by the Act. They each have a duty to exercise the functions assigned or transferred that are specified in section 1 (3) of the Act. Section 6 (1) states that either the Secretary of State after consulting with the DGES, or the DGES with the consent of the Secretary of State, may grant a license to generate, transmit, or supply electricity. The crucial sections 11 through 15 lay down the circumstances under which licenses may be modified and the procedures to be followed.

Section 11 allows the DGES to modify the license conditions with the consent of the license holder, while section 12 (1) allows the DGES to make a reference to the Monopolies and Mergers Commission (MMC) requiring the commission to investigate matters that "operate, or may be expected to operate, against the public interest," and allows the director to serve a copy of the reference on the license holder. The director also publishes the particulars of the reference to bring it to the attention of those likely to be affected (section 12 (4)), but he must inform the Secretary of State, who may direct the MMC within 28 days not to proceed (section 12 (5)). The MMC reports to the director (section 13 (4)), who must pass it on to the license holder and to the Secretary of State, who in turn has the power to prevent publication of those parts where he holds that publication may be against the public interest. Section 14 (1) requires that if the MMC finds against the license holder, and if modifying the license would remedy the effects, then it must recommend appropriate modifications to the license, and the director must make such modifications.

Under section 15 the Secretary of State may modify the license conditions where the license holder engages in anticompetitive practices, proposes a merger, or meets the conditions for a monopoly reference under the Fair Trading Act 1973 or the Competition Act 1980. Thus it is the prime duty of the Secretary of State and the Office of Fair Trading to review proposed structural changes to the industry, but it is the responsibility of the DGES to examine the current operations of the industry.

Building a generation station of above 50 megawatts capacity requires a consent under section 36 by the Secretary of State, which may include conditions for the ownership or operation of the station. The DGES, with the consent of the Secretary of State, may prescribe performance standards under section 39, and under section 44 the DGES may from time to time fix maximum prices at which electricity may be resold.

Most of the remainder of part I of the Act describes methods of enforcement, procedures for investigating complaints, collecting information, publishing reports, holding public enquiries, and so on. Part II (sections 65–95) sets out the reorganization and privatization of the industry, while the remaining part III deals with miscellaneous and supplementary matters, followed by the schedules integrating the legislation with previous legislation.

The Act is thus primarily concerned to specify the responsibilities and powers of the two key players, the DGES and the Secretary of State, in issuing and amending licenses and in monitoring performance of the license holders to ensure that they do not act against the public interest. All of the regulatory details are contained in the detailed licenses (with their subsequent modifications).

3   Ownership of Network Utilities

Looking across a wide range of both developed and developing countries, Short (1984) finds that public ownership is common among the network utilities and for other natural monopolies such as ports and airports. We can now attempt an explanation of this pattern, based on the problems of regulatory commitment set out above. Two factors seem to have been important: the geographical spread of the utility, and the balance of power between property owners and populists.

The geographical dimension dictates the relative importance of local or national politics. Water, coal gas (revealingly called town gas in Britain), and electricity in the nineteenth century were all produced locally as they required consent from the local authority for rights of way and the right to dig up streets. Railways, telegraph, and telephone companies serve national markets and connect different localities. Economies of scale in generation and the additional security and reliability that comes from having several interconnected sources of power meant that the optimal size of each electricity market rapidly grew from local to regional and even national level. Countries with distant fuel sources (notably hydro resources, but also large coal deposits) often found it cheaper to generate near the fuel source and transmit the electricity rather than carry the fuel to a local power station. This encouraged the development of high-tension transmission systems that operated at a national rather than local level. The switch from locally produced coal gas to natural gas extracted from distant wells required national pipeline systems, though in the case of gas, electricity, and telecoms, local distribution was crucial to successful operation; it often required separate local or regional distribution companies.

3.1   Local Utilities and Municipal Ownership

Where utilities first emerged at the local level and conducted their initial bargains over access rights with local authorities, the regulatory compact was struck at the local level and could vary from place to place. Whether regulated private ownership was viable, or whether munici- pal ownership was the default, depended on two related questions— whether private or municipal ownership could deliver cheaper or better quality services, and whether municipal ownership could deliver ser- vices at the same price while generating dividends for the municipality to finance its other obligations. These two questions are not quite the same, for although private utilities might have lower costs than munic- ipal utilities, it might not be possible to secure the advantages of lower costs in lower prices under regulated private ownership. Even if it were possible, it might not be possible for the municipality to capture these cost savings for its own local financial needs (local taxes on the services might not be possible, and franchise bidding was unusual at the local level). Nevertheless, the answers to both questions depend on the dif- ference in costs under public and private ownership, that is, on $c - b - r$ in the model of chapter 2. This value in turn would depend on the scale and competence of the municipality, on the evidence of success of other municipal utilities, on the existence of a market for utility managers, and on the relative importance of consumer/rate payers and utility owners in local politics (i.e., the value of θ).

In addition the preferred British solution of creating limited life fran- chises for the utilities created its own regulatory dynamic. Its advan- tage was to secure a reasonable expectation that the utility could recoup its investment over the period of the franchise, but it gave the munic- ipality the incentive to find methods of public supply at reasonable alternative cost c by the end of the franchise. This would strengthen the hand of the municipality when it came to renegotiate the franchise but would, at the same time, undermine the durability of future regu- latory compacts. Worse still, as the franchise neared the end of its life, the incentive for the utility to deviate from its part of the bargain, and reduce quality or supply, further tipped the balance toward munici- palization, and with it the collapse of the regulatory compact.

3.2   Nationwide Network Utilities

Rather different forces operate at the national level for the intercon- nected utilities like rail, telecoms, and (later) electricity, influencing their final ownership structure. A rather subjective interpretation of history would distinguish a number of typical outcomes.

3.2.1 Capitalism and Pragmatic Nationalization

The first pattern of development, exemplified by Britain in the nineteenth century, is that of early capitalism. The network utilities were successfully established under private ownership soon after their original invention by virtue of the advantages they offered and given the availability of private finance. Entrepreneurship and private finance both require private property rights and hence the institutions of capitalism. Much then depends on the regulatory bargain that must be repeatedly struck between the utilities and the representatives of their customers. In Britain the sanctity of private property was so strong that state ownership was effectively ruled out of court, at least until the old imperial and class confidences were shaken by the First World War, the Russian Revolution, and the General Strike of 1926.

Protection of private property was so well entrenched that although attempts to directly regulate profits or prices were largely ineffective, private ownership of railways survived repeated calls for nationalization. Indeed, private franchises of local utilities were also upheld, and in the case of electricity, the original franchise period of 21 years was doubled to 42 years by Parliament in 1888 to provide the necessary security for private investment. Instead of devising better ways of regulating the utilities to secure the advantages of rapidly declining costs for the customers, the only way in which the government was willing to see profits controlled was by competition. The ideology of laissez faire encouraged Parliament to authorize further entry, which in turn led to problems of duplication, coordination, and cartellization. Profits were kept at subexploitative levels by the threat of further entry.

The evolution of such utilities then depended on wider industrial and political dynamics. In some countries, particularly on the continent, different undertakings were better able to consolidate and reap economies of scale, opening the prospect of larger and politically unsustainable profits. Some countries were able to evolve systems of self-regulation which preserved private ownership without excessive profits, some achieved this through joint public-private ownership, while others, notably the United States, evolved formal systems of profit regulation. Other countries were tempted to nationalize these profitable utilities.

In Britain the clinching argument for nationalization was not excessive profits but rather the failure of private ownership to consolidate and secure the advantages of coordination. Its early history of excess entry and inadequate scale had not been followed by rationalization but by cartelized coexistence—perhaps because the system of light regulation ensured adequate profits, while rationalization and dramatic cost cutting might only have precipitated tighter regulation. The United States may have benefited from an open frontier encouraging expansion rather than duplication, while the more corporatist continent may have encouraged cooperation rather than competition. By the end of the First World War there was widespread agreement that the British system was deeply unsatisfactory. Ultimately the only solution was restructuring under public ownership, a subject to which we will return later.

3.2.2   Public Ownership as Ideology or Default

The second pattern of development was one of ideological nationalization, which can be interpreted as a shift in the relative weight attached to consumer benefits or public control rather than private profits. In some cases this reflected the belief that the state had an overwhelming advantage in raising an investible surplus through taxation, and hence in raising the rate of growth of capacity in what were increasingly seen as vital infrastructural services. There is no doubt that the example of Soviet accumulation had a profound effect on planners in newly independent developing countries. The argument that the state had a comparative advantage in accumulation received intellectual support in the 1960s, when it was observed that the relevant comparison between public and private ownership did not just depend on the rates of return under each, but also on the rates of saving and the allocation of the profits. On this view, a country suffering from inadequate capital might do better with public enterprises generating profits which could be reinvested in the enterprise or transferred to the budget for investment elsewhere.

This kind of social cost–benefit analysis is brought out very clearly by Little and Mirrlees (1974) who draw out the logical implications of applying a utilitarian calculus in a capital-poor dual economy. Even if private ownership were more profitable, the profits might be distributed to the undeserving rich rather than reinvested, while attempts to tax profits to generate public investible funds run into the obvious problem that high rates of tax would discourage investment and undermine the process. Public capital, on this argument, avoids the discouragement effects of taxation while retaining the option of socially desirable use.

While this argument would have been considered quite persuasive in the 1970s, as handbooks of social cost–benefit analysis were being written for various international aid agencies such as the OECD (Little and Mirrlees 1969), UNIDO (Dasgupta, Marglin, and Sen 1972), and the World Bank (Squire and van der Tak 1975; Ray 1984), the mood changed in the 1980s, with growing disillusionment by welfare economists that governments pursue the objectives postulated by these rather utopian visions of the social good. The evidence mounted that governments frequently failed to invest adequately, that they often had lower rates of savings than private corporations, and that they underpriced output leading to low rates of return, lower rates of reinvestment, and higher borrowing than private enterprises. We will return to examine this evidence below.

The examples so far include a small number of countries that successfully developed a robust system of regulation to sustain private ownership of network utilities, or the larger number that found the alternative of mixed or public ownership superior (either in permitting restructuring, or in sustaining higher rates of investment, or though a lack of confidence in the distributional outcomes of regulated private ownership). Other countries (particularly the poorer developing countries) were not ideologically committed to public ownership, and might have been content with vigorous private investment delivering infrastructural services, but they lacked a credible constitutional commitment to private ownership in the sensitive areas of the economy served by network utilities. In such cases public ownership was almost inevitably the default option. Given the experience of the planned economies, the intellectual support of cost–benefit analysts, and the willingness of international organizations like the World Bank to fund state-owned network utilities and other infrastructure, there seemed no strong reason for these countries to resist the movement to public ownership. Indeed, public enterprises, though particularly prevalent in the durable network utilities, were also found in capital-intensive extractive industries (where they were defended as more efficient than taxation in capturing resource rents), and in other industrial sectors where economies of scale were large compared to the size of the market.

The next section looks at the evidence on public sector enterprises to see if they perform poorly at the macroeconomic level. Later we will look at more microeconomic evidence on performance. If publicly owned network utilities are no less efficient than privately owned utilities, then the particular historical reasons that cause the utilities to be publicly owned are not important. If public ownership is less efficient than private ownership, then it is important to explore the difficulties involved in privatizing them and creating a sustainable system of regulation capable of delivering these potential efficiency gains.

3.3 Macroeconomic Performance of Public Enterprises

Ideally we would like information on public sector utilities, but most studies on public enterprises are concerned with all state-owned production units that market their output, not just the natural monopolies which must necessarily be regulated if privately owned. Though not ideal, the evidence is nevertheless instructive. The World Bank (1995) has collected data on public enterprises in developing countries for the period 1978 to 1991, significantly updating the earlier study of Short (1984) that presented data for the late 1970s. Figure 3.1 shows the share of public enterprises (PEs) in GDP, averaged for the period 1986 to 1991, and graphed against real income per head in 1988 measured using purchasing power parities, taken from Summers and Heston (1991).[1] The graph shows the weighted average shares for the world (actually a subset of the developing countries plotted), Latin America (LA, also a subset of the larger countries), Africa, and Asia. There is no correlation between income and PE share, and the world average shown is almost identical to the average using Short's data, which also included developed countries (Newbery 1992a, fig. 2). PEs have a larger share in Africa than Asia, which exceeds that in Latin America. Developed countries (at least in the 1970s) would be similar in share to Latin America on average.

Figure 3.2 shows that PEs have a relatively larger share of total investment than they do of GDP. This implies that PE capital intensity is higher than for the private sector. The average PE capital intensity is fact twice that of the private sector, rather higher in Asia, and lower in Africa. This is partly explained by the concentration of public ownership in the capital-intensive power, telecommunications, railways, and extractive industries but possibly also by the tendency of PEs to underprice their output in many countries. This tendency to underprice can

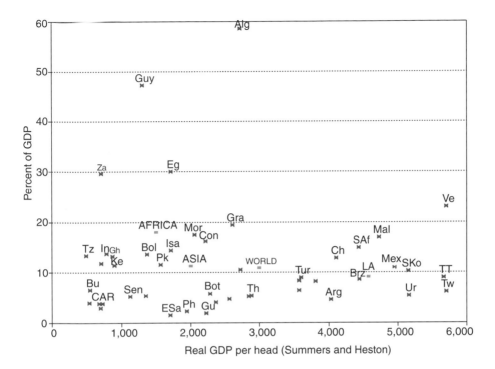

Figure 3.1
Share of public enterprise in GDP, 1986 to 1991.

be illustrated in the case of the electricity industry, which, in addition to being a key network utility, accounted for nearly one-quarter of total public investment in a sample of middle-income countries in the 1980s, or about $80 billion in developing countries (World Bank 1994a, figs. 1.1, 2; and figure 3.4 below).

Performance was frequently unimpressive, particularly in the high-inflation period after the oil shocks of the 1970s. Prices were normally below long-run marginal cost, often despite excess demand, so investment could not be adequately financed out of profits as in many developed countries. Figure 3.3 shows that average real power tariffs declined to below 4 U.S. $/kWh (1986 constant $) for a sample of 60 World Bank countries in 1989, while the rate of return on revalued net fixed assets also declined to below 4 percent for a sample of 360 actual financial rates of returns recorded for 57 World Bank countries (World Bank 1993), which is well below the 10 percent rate of return normally taken as the test discount rate by international agencies. Only 60 percent of power sector costs were covered by revenue (Besant-Jones

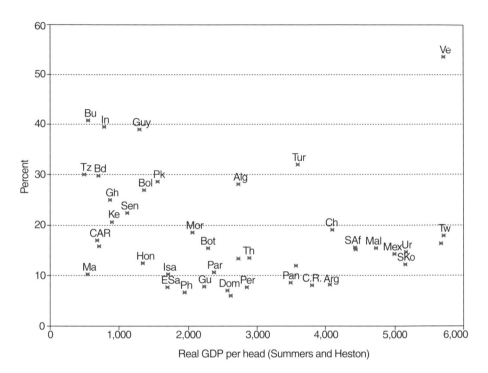

Figure 3.2
Public enterprise share in investment, 1986 to 1991.

1993), while self-financing ratios fell to only 12 percent of investment requirements in 1991 (World Bank 1993, p. 12).[2] Newbery (1993) noted similar problems for Asian countries. Figure 3.4 shows the magnitude of the problem. Underpricing electricity resulted in a heavy fiscal burden estimated at $90 billion annually or about 7 percent of total government revenues in developing countries, larger than annual power investment requirements of about $80 billion, while technical inefficiencies caused true economic losses of nearly $30 billion annually (World Bank 1994, table 6.7).

We can use World Bank's (1995) data to further investigate the contributions of PEs to the government budget. Figure 3.5 shows the weighted average PE savings and investment for 17 low-income developing countries (shown shaded) and 29 middle-income developing countries (shown as the lines) as a percent of PE value added.[3] The excess of investment over savings gives the PE savings–investment gap or balance, which is defined as the difference between the current surplus (revenues excluding transfers *less* costs excluding dividends)

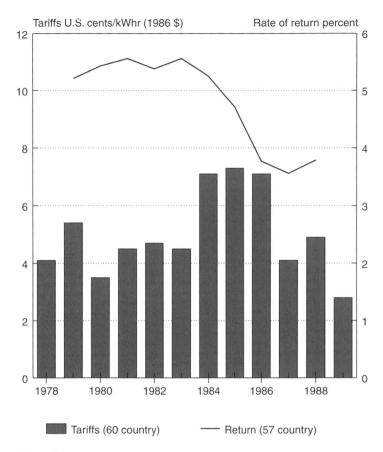

Figure 3.3
Tariffs and Returns of ESIs in World Bank countries.
Source: World Bank (1993).

and gross investment (including stock changes). The graphs shows that although investment declined slightly over the period in low-income countries, savings (i.e., the ability to finance that investment) remained systematically below that investment.

Tables 3.1 and 3.2 present data for the larger countries in the sample for which a reasonably long time-series of data were available. The first two columns of table 3.1 give the growth rates of GDP and PEs over the decade showing a correlation between the two, as would be expected. The next three columns give estimates of the capital–output ratio. The period ICOR or incremental (gross) capital–output ratio is computed as the average ratio of the share of investment in PE output

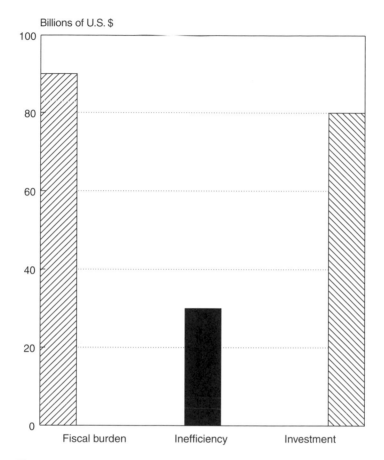

Figure 3.4
Inefficiencies in electricity in developing countries.
Source: World Bank (1994).

to the average rate of growth of PE output. An estimate of the capital stock was constructed using the perpetual inventory method of adding successive gross investments to an assumed initial capital stock and depreciating the resulting capital at 4 percent per annum. The initial capital stock was chosen to produce a smoothly varying capital–output ratio over time, and it does not have too much influence on the average for the period 1985 to 1991. The average capital–output ratio is then the average of the yearly values of the capital stock divided by the value added. The last two columns give measures of gross profitability: The average RoR is the gross rate of return, defined as gross profits divided by gross capital stock, and the resulting annual rates

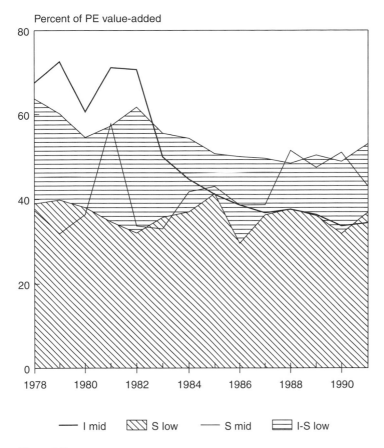

Percent of PE value-added

Figure 3.5
Public enterprise savings and investment developing countries, 1978 to 1991.
Source: World Bank (1995).

were averaged over the period. The inverse of the ICOR expressed as a percentage is a rather cruder measure of returns to additional gross investment.

Table 3.1 reveals high capital intensities and low rates of profit for most of these countries, consistent with low productivity of public enterprises and/or underpricing of the output. The incremental capital–output ratios are considerably larger than the (less-well-estimated) average capital–output ratios, reflecting the low returns to investment in terms of increased output. Further, although some of the measured gross rates of return appear high, this is more because the estimated average capital–output ratios are suspiciously low (when compared to the ICORs, or those of other countries).

Table 3.1
Growth and profit measures of public enterprises

Country	GDP growth rate % p.a. 80–90	PE growth rate % p.a. 80–90	Period ICOR 79–91	Capital-output average (ratios)		Average ROR (%)	100/ICOR (%)
				79–91	85–91		
Middle-income countries							
Argentina	-0.4	-4.0	-10.1	9.7	9.5	-5.6	-9.9
Brazil[b]	2.2	6.2	11.6	11.2	7.7	3.0	8.6
Chile	3.2	2.2	10.0	2.7	2.8	32.1	10.0
Colombia	3.4	5.2	8.0	3.9	4.4	8.8	12.6
Mexico[a]	1.6	2.2	12.4	3.8	4.3	13.5	8.1
Venezuela	1.0	2.0	20.1	5.0	5.1	17.2	5.0
Turkey[a]	4.9	10.1	9.6	1.0	0.8	33.5	10.4
Low-income countries							
Bangladesh[a]	3.7	7.9	11.8	5.4	6.4	2.8	8.5
India[a]	5.6	9.2	7.4	4.9	4.9	8.7	13.6
Indonesia[a]	5.5	2.4	9.4	3.3	3.1	3.2	10.7
Average (unweighted)	3.1	4.3	9.0	5.1	4.9	11.7	7.7

Sources: World Bank (1995); IMF database for GDP.

Notes: Shares in value added are computed from real GDP on an annual basis from shares of PE categories in GDP. The ICOR is average share of investment in PE output divided by rate of growth of PE output. The capital–output ratio is computed yearly from an estimate of PE capital stock: PE capital stock is estimated from a permanent inventory (adding successive gross investment) assuming 4 percent depreciation and sensible initial K/Y. The gross profit is from World Bank (1995, table A6) which gives PE savings less investment, to which is added investment to give savings. The savings is the PE operating surplus (gross profit excluding depreciation, plus nonoperating net revenue). The ROR is gross rate of return on capital stock, as percent, from gross profit./capital stock.

a. See country notes in World Bank (1995). The major points to note are as follows: Mexico directly controlled NFPEs only; Bangladesh 85–91 data are for 10 large PEs, 81–84 for five large PEs only; India NFPEs are owned by central state and local governments; Turkey includes PEs under privatization schemes.

b. Financial sector PEs are included.

Table 3.2
Investment and balances of public enterprises (percentages)

	Profit/value added			Investment/VA			Balance/VA			Balance/GDP
	78–85	86–91	78–91	78–85	86–91	78–91	78–85	86–91	78–91	78–91
Middle-income countries										
Argentina	-44	-21	-34	55	30	40	-99	-52	-93	-4.0
Brazil[b]	-4	57	22	117	39	72	-121	19	-32	-0.6
Chile	70	92	77	22	23	23	48	67	59	8.7
Colombia	24	51	35	42	37	42	-23	14	-6	0.1
Mexico[a]	48	48	48	55	25	27	17	23	21	2.6
Venezuela	80	80	80	42	41	40	38	39	39	9.2
Turkey[a]	24	17	21	142	81	97	-118	-64	-73	-5.4
Low-income countries										
Bangladesh[a]	7	19	13	53	120	93	-46	-101	-76	-2.2
India[a]	44	29	37	79	61	68	-35	-19	-19	-2.4
Indonesia[a]	6	18	10	26	16	22	-20	2	-11	-2.0
Average (unweighted)	25.5	39.0	31.0	63.3	47.2	52.4	-35.9	-7.2	-19.1	0.4

Sources: World Bank (1995); IMF database for GDP.
Note: Shares in value added are computed from real GDP on an annual basis from shares of PE categories in GDP.
a. See notes table 3.1.
b. Financial sector PEs are included.

Table 3.2 compares the profit, investment, and the savings-investment gap to the output (i.e., value added) of the PEs. The first three columns give gross profits as a share of value added, in most cases high, consistent with the high capital intensity of these PEs. What is perhaps more surprising is the high share of gross investment to value added which, because it exceeds the share of profits in most cases, implies the need for external financing shown in the largely negative balances. The unweighted averages are heavily influenced by Venezuela, probably because of its oil sector. Table 3.2 illustrates in more detail at the country level the evidence from middle-income countries in figure 3.5 that profits (and savings) have risen and investment has fallen to give a declining net burden on the budget. The table therefore demonstrates both the possibility of improvement and the remarkably poor performance of these enterprises in the subperiod 1978 to 1985. What is particularly surprising is the high rate of investment with low achieved rates of growth and the slightly negative relation between these two.

The evidence from at least this sample of developing countries is that far from contributing to improved economic performance, public investment in PEs appears to earn a low net rate of return and to require net transfers to these enterprises, rather than generating net contributions to the government. It should not be the case that the return on investment is less than the rate of growth of output, so it should be possible for investment to more than finance itself out of retained profits and, indeed, to provide dividends to its owner, the state. At least in the period 1978 to 1985 this was generally not the case, and despite heavy economic pressures to improve the performance of PEs, even the second half of this period suggest a precarious balance between savings and investment, with the improvement coming largely from lower investment rather than improved profitability.

The fiscal case for privatization in developing countries is the belief that it is impossible to sustain improvements in performance, pricing, and finance of these enterprises so long as they remain in public ownership, even if temporary improvements may be possible in the face of sufficiently serious crises. If so, they should be privatized to reduce the fiscal burden on the economy, and hence improve the prospects for sustained growth. Once again, the case for privatizing potentially competitive enterprises appears overwhelming. The real question is whether the arguments extend to network utilities, and here we need to look at the case studies discussed below.

3.3.1   Public Enterprise Performance in the United Kingdom

If the performance of PEs in developing countries has been unimpressive and burdensome, has this also been the case in developed market economies? It would be too large a task to properly evaluate the experience even of Western Europe, and once again the United Kingdom will have to provide a single example. Some of the dramatic consequences of the privatization program have already been presented in figures 1.4 to 1.8 of chapter 1. Recall that they showed the large impact that privatization had on the wealth and income-generating potential of the public sector.

Figure 3.6 presents data for public and private corporations (the latter restricted to industrial and commercial corporations) for their surplus and net rates of profit. The surplus is defined as the gross trading surplus *plus* rent excluding subsidies and before taxes *less* gross investment, and it is shown as a percentage of value added. This is the measure of the surplus available to the economy after investment. The net rate of return is computed as the profit net of depreciation, and excluding subsidies, before taxes, as a percentage of the net capital stock. Figure 3.6 shows that private corporations earn a net return of about 15 percent and generate a surplus of a similar amount, while public corporations essentially make a zero net rate of return and impose large deficits on the economy, though this improved somewhat between 1979 and 1988 (and has been adversely affected by the recession from 1989 to 1993, or possibly from transferring the most attractive public enterprises to the private sector). It would seem that U.K. PEs are not so different from those in developing countries.

3.4   Efficiency of Public and Privately Owned Network Utilities

Privately owned or investor-owned network utilities (IONUs) must be regulated, while public network utilities (PNUs) will operate under the oversight of the government. What are the essential differences between these two organizational forms? The modern approach (e.g., Sappington and Stiglitz 1987) is that the owner is the authority with the residual rights, that is, those rights that are not subject to contract or control. Regulation limits the actions of IONUs but cannot specify in full detail all the actions of the utility, which retains considerable discretion. In a state-owned enterprise the state may delegate day-to-day control to the management, who may report to a board that has con-

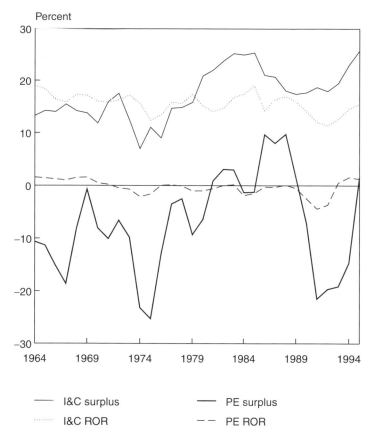

Figure 3.6
U.K. public and industrial/commercial companies: Net surpluses and rates of profit.
Source: CSO (1996).

siderable autonomy, but the state as owner retains the right to intervene directly. Sappington and Stiglitz (1987) argue "that the main difference between them (i.e., public and private ownership) involves
transaction costs the government faces when attempting to intervene
in delegated production activities. Government intervention is generally less costly under public ownership, but a promise not to intervene
is more credible under private production, and it can also have beneficial incentive effects."

Ownership affects the ability to control the behavior of the utility,
so the objectives of the owner matter. The simple assumption is that
private firms maximize profit (which they will have to do within the
constraints laid down by regulation), while nationalized firms in

Britain were instructed to pursue "the national interest," which economists normally interpreted as maximizing social welfare. Both assumptions are oversimplified. Indeed, in both public or private utilities, the managers who take operational decisions are not the owners (though managers in private utilities may have stock options that give them ownership claims). Managers may have wider objectives than maximizing profits (or social welfare), such as their own wealth, power, and prestige, whose pursuit may conflict with the efficient operation of the utility. In private firms, representatives of the owners nominate a board of directors, who in turn appoint and monitor the performance of managers, inducing them to behave in the owners' interests by incentives (promotion, stock options, salary increases) and penalties (job loss). In addition publicly quoted companies with dispersed ownership, where shareholder power over the board may be weak, are subject to the capital market disciplines of takeover, bank monitoring over debt, and bankruptcy, all of which encourage, albeit imperfectly, the pursuit of profit and discourage costly managerial discretion.

PNUs similarly have managers subject to monitoring by boards, appointed by the owner, the state, who should be better placed to exercise control as there is no free-rider problem that affects individually small shareholders. The argument can be pushed further back to ask whose interests the state represents, and specifically why the state should wish to maximize social welfare. In addition we need to know what objectives the regulator has, and how far these constrain the actions of the private utility. One plausible interpretation is that regulation represents essentially the same interest groups that influence the government in its monitoring of public utilities, and the differences between the two are more a function of the form of regulation or oversight. Obvious differences are that IONUs not only have more managerial discretion but are subject just to periodic review, and that they normally operate within a well-specified regulatory framework (e.g., license conditions, price caps, quality standards, protection against entry, universal service obligations). PNUs might have contracts specifying their obligations, rather like license conditions for IONUs, but these contracts can be renegotiated in their entirety, while the licenses of IONUs can often only be renegotiated with the agreement of the utility. The difference is thus one of the degree of commitment to future regulatory or monitoring behavior, and it can be exaggerated. For instance, some systems of regulation lack commitment, and some public utilities may be given very considerable autonomy and operate on the expectation that this will continue. Thus the Central Electricity Board set up in Britain in 1926 to construct the national grid was free to raise capital privately without government guarantee, was free to set the terms of employment of its staff and management, and was largely left free to complete its task under its very competent engineer managers.

The other obvious differences are that IONUs can reward managers with stock options, providing greater incentives to maximize profits, while PNUs cannot go bankrupt, since they lack the hard budget constraint of the private utilities. But public managers can be given performance bonuses (and this is increasingly common in Britain), while regulators are normally enjoined to ensure that the utility can finance its investment, that is, will not go bankrupt. Managers in both sectors can be sacked as well as rewarded, and in some countries, like France, the route to power and prestige can as readily be followed through the public as private sector, with easy movement between them.

The implication of this rather inconclusive comparison is that there may be less pressure to get prices right in the public sector, and specifically to keep them from going too low. While the budget can provide subsidies to PNUs, IONUs are rarely explicitly subsidized, and must therefore price to cover costs.[4] Pricing may thus be less efficient, and the pressures to cut costs weaker in the public sector (though scrutiny over current costs can be tighter in the public sector). The tendency to underpricing in public utilities takes two forms. The most obvious is that capital may be relatively underpriced compared to private utilities, either by preferential access to cheap debt finance guaranteed by the state, as in Britain and most continental countries, or by explicit tax reliefs and other advantages open to municipalities in the United States. The second, less obvious method is by rent dissipation through average rather than marginal cost pricing, when average costs lie below marginal costs. This transfers rents inefficiently as lower prices to customers rather than to the public owner (where they could reduce the burden of taxation). This does not violate the budget constraint, and so avoids scrutiny and correction.

This can be seen in publicly owned electricity utilities which have a high share of hydroelectricity, which frequently underprice electricity, both in producing a low rate of return on the high capital cost invested, and also because the average cost of existing hydro will lie below the long-run marginal cost of new hydro (since the best sites have already been developed). Bernard and Roland (1995) show that in a median voter model in which median income is less than average income and electricity expenditures as a proportion of income decrease with income (both of which invariably hold in developed countries) and in which the average cost of electricity lies below the marginal cost (quintessentially true for hydro systems), then voters will vote for average cost electricity prices rather than efficient prices that would allow the burden of taxation to be reduced. Furthermore the same voters will resist privatization, which would lead to adverse redistributional impacts via increases in electricity prices. Bernard and Roland test their model informally against the Canadian data and find their predictions upheld.

Similar rent transfers may occur for very long-lived assets like water mains, whose book values are written down by depreciation and inflation, even though their true value remains very high.[5] When the U.K. water companies were privatized, their current cost replacement value was over £100 billion, but they were sold for £6 billion, the present value of the profits they were to be allowed. Had prices been raised to the level that would have yielded an adequate rate of return on the current cost value, consumers would almost certainly have voted the government out of office at the first opportunity. The inefficiency of underpricing capital mainly arises in connecting new customers where the marginal cost may greatly exceed the apparent average cost.

Rent transfer to consumers rather than tax payers certainly does not always occur, since municipal-owned (as opposed to state-owned) utilities have often treated their utilities as attractive sources of local revenue, particularly in the nineteenth century when the local tax base was poorly developed. This is not necessarily inconsistent with the political preference model described above, for political power may have been more closely allied with property interests, and property taxes may have been the unattractive alternative to higher utility charges.

Underpricing capital in the public sector may also lead to wasteful investment, but rate-of-return regulation of private utilities has been argued by Averch and Johnson (1962) to lead to excessive capital intensity, though this would show up in higher costs and prices compared to subsidized public utilities. A potentially more important difference might be in the quality of investment, where greater future security and managerial discretion might achieve better planning and management of investment projects in the private sector. Problems of regulating commitment may reverse this claim.

How can these implications be tested? The question we are anxious to answer is whether there is any advantage to private ownership in a particular country, given the potential problems of regulatory commitment for private ownership which make public ownership the simpler default option. Why not compare the performance of utilities before and after an ownership change? Such events are not very common, and although they are informative, the problem is that ownership change is often associated with restructuring, as well as being an obvious change of the form of regulation. Often the change is prompted by an unsatisfactory state of affairs, which might have been dealt with either by a change of regulation (if previously private) or a change of monitoring/controlling (if public). The change in ownership has effects that cannot readily be disentangled from other changes, and we can see this in some of the studies reported below. It remains possible that the same improvements might have been achievable by changes in regulation or control without ownership change. For example, Britain split generation from transmission and created a spot market for bulk electricity as part of the restructuring before privatization. Norway made similar structural changes but did not change the ownership structure, and the United States is considering these reforms, again with no change in ownership. How can one allocate the very real efficiency gains in generation in Britain between the structural changes and the ownership change?

This suggests that it would be helpful to compare the long-run equilibrium performance of utilities under different ownership, holding constant the market structure and organization, to try and isolate the effects of ownership itself. Unfortunately, in most countries the utilities are monopolies, either under entirely public or private ownership. Comparisons between utilities in different countries are particularly difficult, since input and factor prices will differ as will the quality of managerial talent, the labor force, and the institutional environment. It is noticeable that in some countries both public and private enterprises are more efficient than both ownership forms elsewhere, perhaps because of the quality of the institutions and their ability to make intertemporal commitments (Newbery 1992a).

Yarrow (1988) compares the time taken to construct power stations in different countries (a major determinant of the capital cost of electric generation) and finds that Japan, West Germany, and the United States, where public ownership is less pervasive, have considerably shorter construction times than Britain and Italy with state-owned generation (Japan having less than half that of Britain); but France does well despite state ownership, and private utilities in Belgium and Holland do rather poorly. This may reflect more on the comparative efficiency of the construction industries in the various countries than the ownership of the commissioning utility. Other macroeconomic factors must also be important, for example, sustained growth and low unemployment in Japan compared to stop–go in Britain. Yarrow's finding supports the view that the quality of regulation and the quality of public sector management are key determinants of efficiency, as well as the view that it is more difficult to ensure efficient public sector management of investment than to ensure that regulation does not impede private sector incentives for efficient investment.

Comparisons between different forms of ownership of the same utility in the same country at the same time might seem to be a way to avoid these problems, but another problem is encountered. The most obvious way for a government to monitor/regulate public utilities is to benchmark their performance against that of comparable private utilities. The coexistence of both forms of ownership is probably only feasible so long as public utilities deliver about the same social benefits (in terms of prices, quality, tax revenues, etc.) as private utilities, so we should not be surprised if the differences between them are not very great when each can be readily compared with the other. The area where the most important differences might lie, in the efficiency and cost of investment, are also the most difficult to measure, as balance sheet data are notoriously unreliable measures of the capital stock, and it is rare to find the unit investment costs of contemporary plant.

What then does the evidence show? Unfortunately, most of the studies of contemporary utilities relate to the United States, as the leading example of a country where both public and private network utilities coexist, and thus compare a particular form of regulation, rate-of-return or cost-of-service regulation, with public ownership, which has rather similar incentive effects to cost-of-service regulation. Most of the relevant studies either deal with electric utilities (of which there are over 150 in the United States) or water companies, which are often municipally organized. Telecoms and rail are normally either public or private at the country level, while there do not seem to be any readily available studies comparing the recent performance of local gas distribution companies. If we are willing to use historical evidence (which may be no longer relevant, since so many institutions have changed, as has the sophistication of regulation and technology), then Britain (and other countries) provides additional useful comparisons between private (often franchised) utilities and municipal utilities.

Foreman-Peck and Millward (1994) make careful econometric comparisons for nineteenth-century Britain. They find that for gas utilities, after correcting for differences in scale (and costs are U-shaped), municipally owned utilities have unit costs 1 percent below those of private utilities, but the difference is statistically insignificant. The municipal gas utilities appeared as commercially oriented as private utilities (and were seen by the municipalities as desirable sources of dividend income to support public services). There was no evidence that they either lowered prices to favor consumer interests or maximized sales rather than profits (where their rate of return was the same as for private utilities).

In contrast, Baker (1913, 1915) published a comparison of the efficiency of some 300 private and municipal electricity undertakings, and demonstrated that municipalities sold at lower prices (in 1910–11 at 1.7d/kWh compared to 2.5d for companies) and operated with lower capital and operating costs, perhaps because their objectives were to maximize sales, and they thus moved further down the average cost curve than their profit-maximizing private rivals. Their lower prices led to 40 percent higher sales per customer than private companies. In part the municipalities were better placed than their private rivals, since they commanded the denser urban areas where distribution costs per kWh supplied would be lower; in part they obtained directors' services free, though their success must have also derived from other factors (Hannah 1979, p. 50).

This early period was one in which scale economies were still very important, so maximizing sales and keeping prices low was closer to the social optimum than private price-setting behavior—a result that would not necessarily continue as scale economies were exhausted. Foreman-Peck and Millward (1994) note that by 1925–26 the average revenue per unit sold was essentially the same in both sectors, with private undertakings charging relatively more for domestic use and less for power and traction (i.e., base-load use) than municipal undertakings, reflecting a more cost-oriented and less political view of charging. The effect of the objectives of the local generation stations on scale and hence cost became considerably less important after the Central Electricity Board (CEB) was set up to build the national grid. The CEB selected stations to connect to the grid and controlled their despatch to achieve economies in generation by running the lowest cost stations before the higher cost stations. Foreman-Peck and Millward (1994, p. 219) compare public and private generation for 1937, when the electricity grid was essentially complete, and the system was relatively mature and stable. They found that the stations selected by CEB to run were 20 percent cheaper than those not selected, and of the selected stations, the municipally owned and private were equally efficient. However, the nonselected municipals were less efficient than the nonselected private utilities. The CEB thus introduced direct competition between public and private stations, and where this continued (i.e., while they were both subject to the same rules of despatch by the CEB), it proved equally effective in achieving efficiency despite ownership differences. Where it was lacking (for nonselected stations), the public undertakings appear to have been under less pressure to minimize costs than private utilities.

Hausman and Neufeld (1991), using best-practice econometric techniques, compare 218 private (unregulated) and 97 municipally owned U.S. generating stations for 1897–98 and find that the municipals had significantly higher productive efficiency (9 percent higher) than the private undertakings, mostly because of greater scale economies. A rather more informal study by Wallace and Junk (1969) had compared 900 U.S. electric generation plants for 1964–65 and found that municipally owned plants had 74 percent higher unit operating costs than private plant because of their small size and spare capacity, which they attributed to the federal subsidies to interest payments. Since then there has been considerable consolidation, reducing the number of high-cost small plants.

Emmons (1991) studies the effectiveness of regulation in keeping electricity prices down by looking at data from 145 firms for 1930 and 152 firms for 1942. In the 1930 sample, publicly owned firms charged 28 percent less on average than private firms, of which about half could be attributed to interest rate subsidies. Emmons concluded that at least 14 to 17 percent of the price was monopoly profit. In electricity markets facing competition (usually at the borders of the territory or for new service areas), private firms charged 13 percent less than private firms in noncompetitive markets, though competition had no effect on publicly owned firms. By 1942, correcting for interest rate subsidies, public firms charged only 5 percent more than private firms, and competition had no effect on prices, suggesting that regulation after the New Deal had become as effective as competition at passing rents to consumers.

DiLorenzo and Robinson (1982) and Atkinson and Halvorsen (1986) find public and private generation equally cost efficient given the prices they face, but they also note that public utilities face lower (subsidized) prices of capital. Part of the claim that public utilities are inefficient is precisely that they have subsidized capital, and hence make inefficient choices. The problem revealed by these studies is not that the utilities do not minimize costs as they perceive them, but that the structure of public ownership is more likely to confront them with misleading market signals.

Some of these early studies suffer from various methodological shortcomings (discussed by Pollitt 1995). A more sophisticated study by Fare et al. (1985) using the same data set as Atkinson and Halvorsen (1986) found a slight but statistically insignificant advantage in the efficiency of the public over private utilities. Hjalmarsson and Veiderpass (1992a, b) examined two samples of about 290 Swedish electricity distribution utilities and failed to find any significant ownership effect on efficiency.

All of these studies (except the last) used rather old data from the 1970s. In contrast, Pollitt (1993, 1995) has subjected two recent datasets to exhaustive comparisons of efficiency. The first dataset was an international sample of 95 utilities operating in nine countries in 1986. Depending on the approach used, Pollitt found evidence for no significant difference in technical efficiency between the two ownership types, but some evidence for the superior cost efficiency of investor-owned utilities (IOUs).[6] The second dataset was an international sample of 768 power plants in 14 countries in 1989, which together produced about 40 percent of world thermal electricity. The plant-level data were divided into four subsamples on the basis of load factor and analyzed using four different methodologies for measuring efficiency. Pollitt was unable to reject the null hypothesis that there is no difference in technical efficiency between publicly owned and investor-owned generating stations on the basis of the subsamples; when all four subsamples were pooled, there was stronger evidence that investor-owned plants were more technically efficient than public plants. (Pollitt 1994). The failure to find significant differences in technical efficiency in the first (and other, earlier) studies reflects the inadequacy of their sample size for detecting rather small differences in measured technical efficiency, which reduced cost by between 1 and 3 percent.

Pollitt then measured the cost efficiency of 164 of the 213 base-load plants in the dataset for which input price data could be found. He strongly rejected the hypothesis that public utilities are as efficient as private, finding IOUs to be more efficient both in minimizing costs and overall, though the difference is quantitatively small—perhaps 5 percent higher efficiency (the difference varies with the methodology employed). Given the rather small differences in technical efficiency, his suggestion was that the lower overall efficiency under public ownership is primarily a consequence of poor technology choice rather than poor performance of given technology. The example of the British electricity industry forced to buy high-cost domestic coal is a good example that could be replicated in many other countries, though of course national energy policies can create inefficiencies even for investor-owned electricity utilities, if they are constrained in their fuel choice.

Pollitt's study looked at generation, but in a more recent study Kwoka (1995, 1996) compared the economic performance of 543 U.S. electric utilities for 1989, of which 147 were IOUs, and the balance were publicly owned. Almost all IOUs were vertically integrated (141, with a 74 percent ratio of own generation to sales), but fewer than half the public utilities were (165 out of 396), with only 17 percent of sales from own generation. IOUs were on average 15 times as large as public utilities. Kwoka estimated a three-equation system for price, quantity, and cost using instrumental variables and linear-quadratic forms. He found rising marginal costs for generation, U-shaped costs for distribution (rising in the area of observation), vertical economies (i.e., lower costs for integrated utilities), and scale economies in transmission.

Controlling for all variables other than ownership, public ownership had 2.3 percent lower costs than otherwise comparable IOUs, and this was not because of cheaper capital or differences in size, vertical integration, or fuel type. Prices under public ownership were 1.9 percent cheaper than otherwise comparable IOUs, though domestic prices were 19.6 percent lower, commercial prices 6.5 percent lower, and industrial prices 3.1 percent higher than IOUs, reflecting the different objectives of the owners. Kwoka attributed the better performance of public electric utilities to weaknesses in regulation, though one must also worry whether the quadratic specification of costs adequately reflects the technology when the scales of public and private utilities are so different.

Few of the IOUs in Pollitt's sample faced competition, and so it was difficult to judge the effect of competition on efficiency. Kwoka's sample covered 46 towns in which two electric utilities had exclusive territories, and a further 22 towns which allowed some competition between the two utilities, and he found that competition lowers prices (by nearly 8 percent). Private owners typically perform better in competitive markets, particularly where innovation is important, or least-cost solutions require careful and informed choices, and where costs need to be closely monitored. Generation is therefore a natural choice for private ownership, particularly if it is associated with open access to transmission. This is borne out by the study of the restructuring and privatization of the English electricity industry, reported in chapter 5.

Further evidence suggesting that competition is more important than ownership comes from Frantz's (1988) study of X-inefficiency. He reviews (pp. 118–132) several comparisons of the efficiency of monopolies and more competitive structures in the electricity industry. Primeaux (1977, 1978) compared public monopoly electric utilities with a matched set of public duopolies, most of which competed against a private utility, for the period 1964–68. Competition lowered costs, which Primeaux attributed to reducing X-inefficiency, particularly at smaller scales. Stevenson (1982) compared 25 gas and electric utilities with 54 single-fuel utilities (which therefore had to compete against the other fuel) and found the more competitive were less X-inefficient both statically (taking the capital stock as given) and dynamically (allowing for investment).

3.5   Effects of Ownership Changes

Methodologically sound empirical studies of the effects of ownership on performance are hardly conclusive, even if they are suggestive. Case studies of changes in ownership run the risk of confounding the many causes of subsequent changes in performance, but they offer additional insights that it would be foolish to ignore. Historically the changes have been in two directions—in the earlier period from private to public ownership through nationalization and, less frequently and more recently, from public to private ownership by privatization.

3.5.1   Nationalization

Foreman-Peck and Millward (1994) give a fascinating account of the nationalization of first the telegraph and then the telephone in Britain. The Post Office had been created as a statutory monopoly in the sixteenth century, but stagnated until William Hill realized that costs varied less with distance than density. He introduced the adhesive penny stamp, so that the sender paid rather than the recipient, drastically cut the price, and made it uniform across the country. The price cut was too drastic. The Post Office initially lost money, but demand increased so rapidly, and economies of scale were so important, that unit costs fell by 66 percent between 1839 and the adoption of postboxes in 1853. The strategy of low uniform prices eventually paid off, and created huge popular support for nationalized ownership (which was effectively mobilized to resist more recent attempts in the 1990s to privatize the Post Office).

The introduction of the telegraph in the 1840s was entirely private. Whereas in the United States, perhaps because of greater distances and lower population densities, Western Union emerged as the dominant company, buying up rivals to achieve network economies, in Britain higher densities and fragmented railway ownership encouraged fragmented ownership, accommodating rivals by cooperation in price setting rather than merger, forgoing economies of scale. The resulting cartellization, wasteful duplication, and incomplete geographic coverage gave the worst of both competitive entry and monopoly power (and provides a good example of the "excess entry theorem" that there will be excessive entry into oligopolistic industries experiencing economies of scale).[7]

For various reasons, including the desire of the politically influential newspaper companies for cheap telegraphy, all telegraph companies were nationalized in 1868 and transferred to their competitor, the Post Office. The result was that prices were cut, new offices opened, and the network gaps filled, so traffic doubled in the following four years. The telegraph workers became unionized and considerably increased wages, so costs rose, and uniform pricing was introduced, which lacked the commercial logic of the parent company's uniform postal rates. The Post Office ran telegraphy to maximize volume, and relied on cross subsidies to cover costs. The authors conclude that private and public ownership each had their different faults, and that a well-regulated dominant firm with free entry (i.e., the U.S. model) might have performed better, with lower costs and less cross-subsidy. State-owned systems appeared to do better at lower-income levels (perhaps where economies of scale were more important so that underpricing was closer to the social optimum), but private systems appeared to do better at higher income levels (perhaps because of the diseconomies of size associated with public sector union strength).

The subsequent nationalization of telephony further reveals the difficulty that Britain appears to have experienced in managing the coexistence of public and private utilities. Alexander Bell secured the British patent rights to telephones in 1876 and visited the country in 1877 to demonstrate his invention to an unimpressed Post Office. They rapidly changed their mind after Bell and Edison set up telephone exchanges in London in 1879, fearing competition with the public telegraph. When Bell and Edison merged their companies in 1880 to form the United Telephone Company, the courts declared that telephony was a form of telegraph and as such covered by the Post Office monopoly.

The Post Office granted a limited-term franchise to the company in return for 10 percent of the revenue, with the right to buy the company out at specified dates. Other companies applied for licenses, but in 1889 the principal companies merged to form the National Telephone Company. The Post Office also granted way leaves (rights of way) but, fearing competition particularly from long distance or trunk telephone routes, was very slow to issue licenses; it finally nationalized National Telephone Company's trunk routes in 1896. Relations between the private local telephone companies and the Post Office continued to be very poor, and were only resolved by almost complete nationalization in 1911.[8] Compared to countries with exclusive state ownership or those with private ownership, Britain had a very poor telephone system with low penetration and poor service quality.

The British electricity industry experienced two stages of public ownership, the first involving just the creation of the national grid. The First World War had demonstrated the relative backwardness of Britain in electricity supply. The one exception, demonstrating what was possible with visionary management, was the Newcastle-upon-Tyne Electric Supply Company (NESCo). In 1900 NESCo's distribution covered just 16 square miles, but by 1903 it started work on the largest power supply station in Europe. NESCo rapidly became the biggest integrated power system in Europe, and by 1914 it covered 1,400 square miles, having increased sales by a factor of 32 over this period (Hannah 1979).

Elsewhere the industry appeared unable to secure the economies of scale that NESCo had demonstrated could be obtained by interconnecting power stations to serve a larger area that could then be efficiently scheduled. Part of the reason perhaps lay in the mix of public and private ownership: Municipal undertakings resisted efficient mergers with rivals beyond their boundaries. These antagonisms continued to impede rationalization, and private interests opposed the use of compulsory purchase by any public body set up to coordinate generation. The Weir Committee, set up in 1925, argued for a national grid and suggested an ingenious compromise to the conflict between public and private interests. The Central Electricity Board (CEB) should build and operate the grid, while existing companies would continue to build, own, and operate stations and distribute power locally. New investment would be coordinated by the CEB, as would despatch. Such a proposal was presented to Parliament in 1926 and bitterly opposed, although no private assets were to be transferred to public ownership. It finally passed in December with Labour party support (and after the General Strike).

The CEB was a statutory corporation modeled on the BBC, acting more like a commercial enterprise than a "nationalized industry." It had considerable autonomy, paid high salaries, and was financed by fixed-interest loans that were not guaranteed by the government in a conscious decision to remain independent of the Treasury. The grid was completed in September 1933 and full grid trading over the whole country followed almost immediately. This meant that the CEB operated a "merit order" and directed the operation of all major power stations (which continued to be owned and operated by the undertakings). Running costs of the pre-existing stations were reduced as a result of merit order scheduling, and by 1938 overall grid savings from interconnection had risen to 11 percent of total payments for electricity. Reserve power capacity was cut from 40 to 10 percent, saving almost the same again on annual levelized capital costs. Hannah (1979, p. 129, n. 59) demonstrates that the grid was a socially profitable investment.

It is interesting to compare the successful integration of a national grid (also secured in a number of continental countries) with the situation in the United States, where most utilities, whether public or private, are vertically integrated regional monopolies with some interconnection. In most states, utilities buy and sell power under negotiated bilateral agreements, though in some parts of the country their are tight power pools, in which the members agree to submit stations for central despatch in merit order. White (1995) has estimated the potential gains from introducing pooling to California, to replace bilateral deals between the four major electric utilities (three private; one, the Los Angeles Department of Water and Power, is the largest municipal electric utility in the United States). The estimated cost saving of pooling would be about 4 percent of total costs or $240 million per year (and this ignores longer-run benefits of coordinated investment in generation and transmission, and possible reductions in reserve plant to achieve a given level of security).[9]

The obvious question is why the utilities cannot reach agreement (as other regional groups have) to set up a voluntary power pool to reap these large gains. White suggests that the system of regulation would capture these gains and pass them on in lower prices, removing the incentive to interconnect. Worse, if pooling reduced capital requirements by economizing on reserve capacity, profits would fall as investors lost the Averch-Johnson bonus on the now smaller capital base. White cites evidence that when the Florida Power Pool was set up in the early 1980s, the Utilities Commission required 80 percent of the cost savings to be passed on to customers. Finally pooling reduces individual utility managers' discretion and power, and might be resisted for that reason. This example confirms that either national ownership or regulatory reform might be necessary to secure the benefits of coordination that elude more decentralized organizational structures. In some cases national ownership can deliver additional advantages that might be very hard to realize by other means.

Certainly in Britain, public ownership seemed the only way to secure the cost reductions from regional integration and coordination of despatch. Other countries like Germany, with more harmonious relations between commerce and government, were able to achieve this at the regional level by cooperation rather than legislation. Although the CEB was able to improve the efficiency of large-scale generation, it had no control over the local private and municipal companies. Any hopes that the CEB's demonstration of the benefits of scale and coordination would encourage the numerous distribution companies to merge were soon dashed. Municipal and private owners remained hostile to such suggestions or even that they should better coordinate their activities. The debate was suspended during the second world war, but around this time the original 42-year franchises were maturing. The threat was that municipal ownership would be extended, and would make subsequent amalgamation and coordination even more difficult. During the war these franchises were frozen, but after the war the incoming Labour government was faced with the choice of either nationalization to impose a sensible coordinated distribution system or increased fragmentation among municipalities, which seemed incapable of rational coordination. Public ownership at the national level was thus a superior alternative to public ownership at the municipal level.

Where nationalization was successful, it seems to have been the simplest way to overcome the constraints on achieving economies of scale and coordination in public municipal ownership. Private ownership does not suffer from the natural local constraints that municipal ownership faces, but a municipal capability to organize local supply can certainly hinder rational private development. Central public ownership is clearly a better ownership form to restructure an industry than is local public ownership, though evolution under private ownership unfettered by municipal ownership may be even better. Poorly designed regulation, however, can reduce the incentives to realize these benefits of coordination, and remove the evolutionary advantages of private ownership. It is noticeable that the most successful regulated industry in the United States (and perhaps anywhere) was the Bell Telephone System, which was a nationwide integrated utility. Once the industry has been rationalized, it may or may not be better managed under private ownership, and here evidence on privatization is particularly valuable.

3.5.2   Privatization

Jones, Tandon, and Vogelsang (1990) set out a cost–benefit methodology for evaluating the privatization of public enterprises (PEs), and implement this for twelve case studies (of which five are network utilities) in Galal et al. (1994). As with all cost–benefit analysis, one first measures the quantitative impact on the world with the project (privatizing a PE) relative to the counterfactual of the world without the project (the PE remaining in public ownership), and then values the impact, breaking this down into its component parts. This impact will typically affect operating efficiency and hence costs, on the one hand, and prices (and hence allocative efficiency), on the other. The price changes will also generate distributional impacts on consumers, workers, owners, and the government (via taxes paid on profits and outputs).

Figure 3.7 illustrates some of these impacts schematically. Initially we can suppose that the public utility set price p equal to unit cost, c (which in this case is equal to the average and marginal cost and includes the normal return on capital) and sold quantity q. Privatization leads to a fall in marginal and average costs to c' and an increase in the price to p', so price is now above the efficient level and demand falls to q'. The effect of privatization is then an increase in private profits equal to the

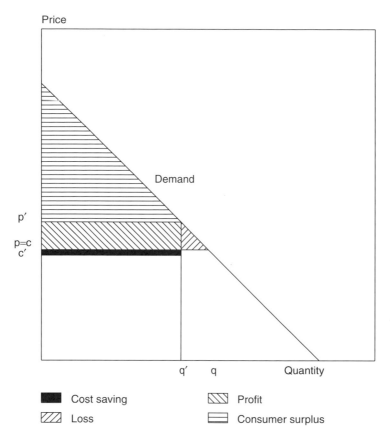

Figure 3.7
Cost–benefit analysis of privatization.

amount labeled as "profit" *plus* that labeled "cost saving." Consumers suffer a loss in consumer surplus equal to the amount labeled "profit" (excluding the cost saving) *plus* the triangle labeled "loss"—which is the deadweight loss or excess burden usually associated with taxation and caused by the distortions of inefficient pricing.

If we ignore who gains and who loses, and just add up the gains and losses, then the gain is the cost saving $q'(c—c') = q'\Delta c$, where Δc is the cost saving, and the loss is the deadweight loss, approximately $L = \frac{1}{2}(p' - p)(q - q') = -\frac{1}{2}\Delta p \cdot \Delta q$, using the same shorthand for changes in price and quantity.[10] If the elasticity of demand (as a positive number) is ε, then $\Delta q \approx -\varepsilon q \Delta p/p$, and $L \approx \frac{1}{2}\varepsilon pq(\Delta p/p)^2$. The ratio of the deadweight loss to original revenue pq is $\frac{1}{2}\varepsilon(\Delta p/p)^2$. If the cost saving is also expressed as a fraction of original revenue, pq (also equal to original total cost cq), then $q'\Delta c/(cq) \approx \Delta c/c$, which may be directly compared with the proportional loss.

For example, if the demand elasticity $\varepsilon = 0.5$, and if $\Delta p/p = 20$ percent, then the deadweight loss will be 1 percent (of revenue); if unit costs could be reduced by more than 1 percent, the net efficiency gains would be positive. If the public enterprise were underpricing, and privatization corrected the price, then deadweight losses would be reduced, not increased, and would further add to any cost reductions as part of the total efficiency gains.

The redistributional effects may also be important, as we have seen in the case of the median voter model of Canadian hydroelectricity. Higher utility prices of necessities that transfer consumer surplus to private profits will have adverse distributional effects, since the profits are likely to go to richer consumers. If the utility remains in public ownership, higher prices transfer income to the public sector, with possibly different redistributional consequences. If the utility is about to be privatized and prices are raised, the effects may lie between these two cases. Consider first what happens if higher prices create higher public sector revenues in order to see how this might be taken into account.

The distributional effects of raising utility prices to finance tax reductions is analyzed further in the appendix to this chapter, which shows that in Britain electricity and gas price rises have a very disadvantageous impact on the poor, though rather less so in Hungary. Telephone price increases have a less distributionally adverse effect in Britain, while in Hungary they are luxury goods, with price increases falling on the better off. There are two rather separate issues here. If the object is to prevent strong opposition to bringing utility prices up to their efficient level, then the prime concerns will be to protect the most vulnerable and to ensure that a majority of consumer/voters do not suffer any decrease in welfare. For essential goods like electricity, both objectives are likely to be best achieved by providing an explicit equal lump-sum transfer to consumers.[11]

If the object is to use the price increase to improve social welfare, then efficiency as well as distributional issues become important. If the underpricing of utilities is symptomatic of an inefficient system of redistribution, then it may be desirable to reduce indirect taxes on all goods by an equal proportional amount.[12] This would involve some redistribution from the poor to the better off (who consume more and therefore pay more indirect taxes), but the benefit would be a greater reduction in the deadweight losses from taxation. These increase as the *square* of the tax rate (as can be seen from the formula for the loss resulting from a price rise shown in figure 3.7, exactly the same as a tax rise, $L \approx \frac{1}{2}\varepsilon pq(\Delta p/p)^2$), so using the extra revenue from raising utility prices to efficient levels can have a large effect on tax efficiency elsewhere. Such a reform would not necessarily command majority support, however.

How one views the distributional impact of privatization depends very much on what compensating actions the government can or does take, whether the price was initially at the right level when in the public sector, and whether the criterion is social welfare (equity *and* efficiency) or just equity. If privatization leads to a price rise which generates increased private profits, as in figure 3.7, then the final effect on social welfare (taking account both of efficiency and redistribution) depends on whether the buyers pay the present value of these extra profits, whether the government receipts are used to reduce taxes (or the public debt, and hence future interest payments and future taxes) or to raise transfers, whether, at the margin, the social value of the reduced tax revenue is equal to the social value of increased transfers (as it should be if taxes are optimally set, as assumed above), and whether the original utility price was too high or too low.

Figure 3.8 shows the evolution of real consumer prices for gas, electricity, telephones, and water in Britain, that is, the price index of consumer expenditure on these utilities deflated by the consumer price index, taking 1987 = 100, and plotting them on a log scale. The slopes of the series then indicates the value of X in RPI − X used to regulate the natural monopoly parts of these utilities (but not the cost of landed gas or electricity generation). Preparations for privatization revealed that prices were too low in the case of water, needed some increases for electricity, but were about right for gas and telecoms. In the case of electricity, the distribution margins were allowed to rise after privatization to ensure the reasonable profit forecasts needed for the prospectus and hence to secure an adequate sales price for the assets.

In the case of water, the problem was not so much to secure a reasonable sales price for the assets as to ensure that the privatized companies would be able to fund the very heavy investment program required to make good a century of neglect and to meet the new water quality standards specified by the European Union. The political difficulty of raising water prices before privatization was compounded by the fact that most consumers paid a flat charge for water based on the

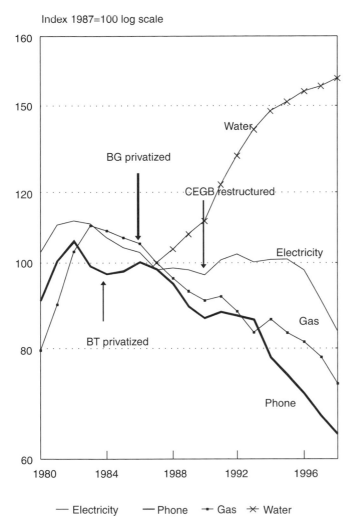

Figure 3.8
Real prices: Phone, gas, water, electric U.K. domestic customers.
Source: *CSO Monthly Digest of Statistics.*

ratable value of their house, so water charges were rather similar to local rates (taxes)—and, before privatization, were typically collected in the same way. The Conservative government had attracted huge unpopularity by reforming the system of local rates, and replacing property taxes based on value by a poll tax. This had to be almost immediately scrapped and replaced by a revised system of property taxes, but the message that large increases in taxlike water charges related to property values would be politically disastrous was readily grasped. The solution was to build subsequent real price increases for water into the system of regulation so that the companies were privatized before the consumers were aware of the gradually escalating water costs. In contrast to gas and telephones where real prices fell steadily, water prices increased rapidly, attracting considerable consumer hostility. Electricity prices stabilized after their initial rise, and would have fallen below their preprivatization level by 1996 if the government had not introduced an 8 percent VAT in 1994 (also applied to domestic gas).

On one view, privatizing the water companies was the only politically acceptable way to secure price rises to fund the investment needed. Privatization was beneficial because it corrected an inefficient price structure. The opposing view is that the investment needs were mandated by bureaucrats in Brussels, completely unjustified by any cost–benefit analysis, and would more successfully have been resisted under public ownership with the Treasury both reluctant to increase taxlike charges and to subsidize investment. Given the huge difficulty of determining willingness to pay for the public-good-like quality aspect of water supply, the matter will not readily be resolved. In the event the water companies were sold for about £6 billion, though the modern asset equivalent replacement cost of the industry was estimated at £106 billion. Shareholders who bought the shares at privatization enjoyed an appreciation of nearly 100 percent relative to the all-share index over the next five years.

Most of the privatized utilities enjoyed considerable increases in both profits and share prices, as the full extent of potential cost savings became apparent and as the generosity of the initial price caps became clear. The merchant banks advising the government on the initial share price were understandably cautious, particularly with the early flotations, since there was little experience on which to judge the demand for shares in utilities in the United Kingdom. There was no experience of the system of regulation, and the opposition Labour party was very hostile to each privatization, threatening to return the utilities to public ownership. The Conservative government was equally anxious that the early privatizations should succeed and command widespread popular support, and this was achieved by deliberately underpricing the share offer and rationing demand so that small shareholders and utility customers could, if they applied, each receive a minimum number of shares. This was a simple way of transferring some of the increase in profits back to voter/consumers and increasing the proportion of share-owning voters, who might resist or make politically costly any attempts to return the utilities to public ownership. For various under-standable reasons, then, most utility privatizations failed to secure fair market value for the state, and there was an inevitable redistribution of rents from taxpayers (to whom the state could have returned the extra value of selling the utilities) to richer shareholders—an adverse redistribution.

To summarize, in many countries network utility output is under-priced, reflecting its salience for the poor, the political pressures limit-ing price increases which in inflationary periods rapidly lead to profit erosion, and, in some cases, a reluctance to allow the utility to gener-ate funds for reinvestment—instead investment can be centrally con-trolled, managed as part of the public expenditure program, and financed by loans to the utility. Selling the utility for fair market value (i.e., the present value of future profits), regulating prices at a level not too much above the efficient level, and using the proceeds to reduce taxation or increase public expenditure optimally (i.e., using the oppor-tunity to nudge the whole structure of taxes and expenditures in a desirable direction) should increase social welfare, with any cost reduc-tions an additional bonus.

In practice, many privatizations are underpriced, so they fail to secure fair market value. The gains often go to shareholders of above-average income and hence of lower social value. The problem is not so much that prices rise to consumers (though they did for U.K. water consumers) but that the resulting profits are distributed in a less egal-itarian way than might have happened in the public sector. In Britain an attempt was made to counter this by giving preferential access to employees and customers of the utility, and to small shareholders. It had the additional advantage of compensating customers facing price rises by increased dividends.

With this preamble, we can turn to a fuller accounting of the impact of privatization:

$$\Delta W = \Delta S + \Delta G + \lambda_p (\Delta\Pi_d + \Delta C_d) + \lambda_f (\Delta\Pi_f + \Delta C_f) + \lambda_L \Delta L,$$

where ΔW is the present value (PV) of the change in welfare, ΔS is the PV of the change in consumer surplus, ΔG is the change in government net receipts, $\Delta\Pi$ is the PV of the change in private net profits of the new owners, with subscript d referring to domestic owners and subscript f to foreign owners, ΔL is the change in the PV of net benefits to workers (i.e., their extra surplus), and ΔC is the change in the PV of competitors' net benefits, again distinguished by location. Consumers and the government are both domestic and equally valued,[13] while λ_p is the social weight attached to income received by private domestic owners, presumably less than the value of government receipts whose value is taken as unity (so $\lambda_p < 1$). A purely nationalistic view of privatization would set $\lambda_f = 0$. The parameter λ_L is the social value of income received by workers, which is normally the same as that of consumers (i.e., $\lambda_L = 1$) unless they are considerably better off than the average consumer.

Galal et al. (1994) looked at 12 privatizations of public enterprises in four countries, and the results for the five network utilities (three telecommunications companies and two electricity utilities) are summarized in table 3.3. (The other privatizations were British Airways and National Freight—a British road transport business, in Malaya the Malaysian Airline System, Kelang Container Terminal, and the gambling enterprise Sports Toto Malaysia, and in Mexico the two airline companies Aeroméxico and Mexicana de Aviación.) On an unweighted adding of all the gains and losses (i.e., taking λ_p, λ_f and $\lambda_L = 1$), eleven enterprises produced a positive net gain, and only Mexicana de Aviación produced a net loss. The same was true when foreign benefits were ignored but all domestic gains included (i.e., taking λ_p and $\lambda_L = 1$ but $\lambda_f = 0$).

In table 3.3 the network utilities are evaluated taking $\lambda_p = 0.5$, $\lambda_L = 1$, and $\lambda_f = 0$. (the appendix at the end of this chapter shows how to quantify the weights). The gains are presented as an annualized perpetuity as a percent of the last predivestiture annual sales revenue. Allowing for the lower distributional benefit of transferring gains to buyers makes two of the privatizations socially unprofitable (CHILGENER and Teléfonos de México) but the remaining three profitable. Two privatizations—both Chilean electricity utilities—had an adverse impact on the budget. The full details are given in the source and are only summarized in the next few sections.

Table 3.3
Impacts on welfare of privatizing network utilities (percent of annual sales in predivestiture year)

Country/enterprise	Government	Domestic buyers[a]	Other domestic[b]	Foreign	Social welfare[c]
United Kingdom					
British Telecom	2.7	3.1	5.1	1.2	9.4
Chile					
CHILGENER (electricity)	−1.4	2.0	0.1	1.4	−0.3
ENERSIS (electricity)	−1.6	0.2	6.0	0.6	4.5
CTC (telecoms)	8.0	5.0	132.0	10.0	142.5
Mexico					
Teléfonos de México	13.3	39.7	−46.4	43.0	−13.3

Source: Galal et al. (1994, p. 528).
a. Including changes in domestic competitors' profits.
b. Consumer surplus plus worker benefits: $\Delta S + \Delta L$.
c. $\lambda_p = 0.5$, $\lambda_f = 0$, $\lambda_L = 1$.

3.5.3 Case Studies of Electricity Privatization

The British privatization of the electricity supply industry will be discussed in more detail later, but it is noteworthy that Chile undertook a radical reform of the electricity sector as early as 1978. Nationalization of Chilectra in 1970 was followed by rapid inflation, a failure to adjust tariffs, and hence serious deficits at a time when the state had assumed responsibility for all the electricity industry's investment of about $200 million per year (Covarrubias and Maia 1994, app. B 1.17). After the change of government in 1973, losses continued because of suspected inefficiencies and powerful unions, and were addressed by tariff reforms and an attempt to make the utilities behave in a more commercial fashion. The 1978 Decree–Law 2.224 created the National Energy Commission (CNE) and initiated a program of reform aimed at de-integrating the industry to introduce competition into the power market, and separating the state's commercial and regulatory functions. After the new electricity law of 1982, the two state-owned integrated companies, ENDESA and Chilectra, were divided into separate generation and local distribution companies. Thus ENDESA was divided into five separate generating companies and eight distribution companies. However, the interconnected transmission system was placed under ENDESA's umbrella, giving that generating company potentially preferential access.

A new system of regulation was put in place in 1980 and formalized by law in 1982. The system of regulation is interesting, and managed by CNE, consisting of government ministers under the office of the presidency. The system of price regulation is based on long-run marginal cost, itself determined by relatively simple computer models according to specified formulae, doubtless greatly aided by the fact that Chile is 60 percent hydro and has adequate storage hydro to buffer the price of energy over the course of the day and possibly longer. Transmission and retail prices are regulated, while large users negotiate directly. CNE lays down rules for dispatch of generation managed by the Economic Load Dispatch Center which in turn estimates marginal generation costs used for settlement. Companies are free to invest in transmission and generation, and CNE plays some coordination role. The system of regulating prices has survived financial turmoil and has encouraged adequate investment in generation, transmission, and distribution. If CNE wishes to depart from the formulaic rules, then it can only do so with the approval of the minister of economics, and then subject to judicial appeal if companies can demonstrate that the new prices are below long-run marginal costs.

The restructured companies were subsequently privatized and by 1991 there were 11 power-generating companies, 21 electricity distribution companies and two integrated companies. Galal (1994) presents a social cost–benefit analysis of the privatization of Chilgener, one of a number of competing generators, and Enersis, a monopoly distribution company, both created out of Chilectra. Chilgener had generating capacity of 597 MW at privatization in 1987, when it was sold for Ch$12.6 billion (U.S.$53 million or $90/kW of capacity)[14] or 20 percent of its net worth. (The implied value of generation is U.S.$90/kW capacity, compared to a new combined cycle gas turbine—the cheapest normal form of generation—of U.S.$600/kW.)

Chilgener increased its profits, investment, and productivity after divestiture. The improvement in profits was due to a move to marginal cost pricing and increased capacity utilization, both owing to improved regulation rather than divestiture. Surprisingly divestiture did not relax the financial constraint on investment. Galal's base estimate shows that the present value of world welfare was Ch$4 billion, 21 percent of the private value of Chilgener (the figures shown in table

3.3 are percentages of predivestiture sales revenue). Of this Ch$4b, Ch$2.7b went to foreign shareholders, Ch$3.8b went to domestic shareholders, Ch$0.1b to employees, zero (i.e., no change) to consumers, and −Ch$2.7b (i.e., a loss) to the government. On the alternative view that none of the postprivatization productivity increase was due to privatization per se, the government lost Ch$6.6b, and the country lost what the foreign shareholders gained, namely Ch$2.7b or 14 percent of the private value of the asset. Whether privatization of Chilgener was beneficial to Chile thus depends on whether one thinks that privatization was essential to achieve the productivity gains or whether these would have occurred anyway as a result of earlier regulatory reforms.

Enersis, unlike Chilgener, is not subject to competition, and its external regulatory regime did not change with privatization. Nevertheless, privatization encouraged the company to reduce losses from theft and improve returns on non-operating assets. The gainers were shareholders (Ch$42.9b, of which foreign shareholders received Ch$2.2b) and honest customers (Ch$17.5b), while the losers were nonpaying consumers (Ch$9.8b), the government (Ch$5.6b), and Chilean citizens (Ch$26.3b), who lost the opportunity to receive the shareholder gains in ENDESA (had they remained publicly owned) which were instead captured by Enersis and passed to its own shareholders. The net benefit to Chile was Ch$16.3b, and to foreigners Ch$2.2b, or together 31 percent of the private value of Enersis. Privatization was again costly to the government. Privatization resulted in considerable redistributions (some desirable, from nonpaying to paying customers), but more of the gains were captured domestically than in the case of Chilgener.

Regulatory reform was clearly the major determinant of improvements in Chile, though there were additional gains from privatization (Galal et al. 1994, p. 542). The sequencing of reform in Chile is instructive in that the reform of the regulatory system and the restructuring of state enterprises occurred first, to ensure that the new enterprises had some experience of the regulatory regime before privatization. Privatization proceeded slowly, avoiding some of the risks of underpricing with attendant larger transfers to shareholders, while wide share ownership created political support for the new system. By 1990, about 62 percent of the total electricity supply system value was in private ownership (Covarrubias and Maia 1994, app. B 4.1). Both privatizations were costly to the government, which lost out to domestic and foreign shareholders in the case of Chilgener, but to consumers in the case of Enersis.

3.5.4 Case Studies of Telecommunications Privatizations

The privatization of British Telecom in 1984 marked the start of the British government's sequence of network utility privatizations, and it clearly had a profound impact on the course of privatizations, not only in the United Kingdom but elsewhere. The logic of selling a capital-intensive utility with rapid demand growth, high-investment require-ments at the leading edge of technological development has proved persuasive in many countries, and frequently telecoms are the among the first utilities to be sold, as argued in section 2.6. The British example will be discussed further below, but the cost–benefit study reported here is useful in providing the context for the other two telecoms privatizations. The case study of British Telecom by Vogelsang and colleagues (1994) is based on data to the end of 1990, before the liber-alization set in train by the duopoly review, of which more later.[15] The authors concluded that privatization benefited the shareholders who purchased the underpriced shares, government (through the sales revenue and subsequent tax revenues) and consumers who benefited from rebalanced tariffs. Among these, business consumers did sub-stantially better than residential consumers, many of whom may have made a net loss from the divestiture. In compensation, domestic con-sumers were offered even more preferential terms for buying shares, and those that took advantage of this offer would have been net beneficiaries.

The main sources of these benefits were changes in prices, and improvements in the rate of investment once the constraints imposed by state ownership were removed. The first six years of private own-ership did not appear to change productivity compared to the experi-ence of comparable companies elsewhere, though there was a sharp improvement in 1992, after the duopoly review and subsequent entry liberalization (as can be seen from figure 7.4). Privatization relaxed the Treasury's controls over investment, and allowed the company to raise its rate of investment by almost 50 percent in real terms over the next four years. This allowed the accumulated backlog of modernization to be addressed, while allowing a rapid expansion in output, which, given the level of regulated prices, allowed it to more than double profits. Investment as a share of turnover did not rise; it fell after 1989, perhaps because of dramatic decreases in the cost of computer-based switches. Investment as a share of profit, which had considerably exceeded 100 percent before privatization, necessitating net borrowing, fell below

100 percent after privatization, since BT became well able to finance investment out of retained profits and modest borrowing.

The authors' assessment is that privatization generated annualized unweighted benefits worth an estimated 12 percent of the predivestiture annual sales, nine-tenths of which accrued to the national economy, the balance to foreigners. The initial sales value of £3.92 billion for 50 percent of a company with 20.55 m lines in 1984 translates into a value of U.S.$1,000/line at 1995 prices (£1 = $1.6). The socially weighted benefits are shown in table 3.3 as 9.4 percent of sales, also high. In social cost–benefit terms, compared to continued state ownership, they claim that privatization was a considerable success. Subsequent developments, particularly liberalization which is associated with significant improvements in productivity growth and real price declines, can be interpreted in two ways.

One view is that liberalization would have been greatly delayed had BT stayed in public ownership, as evidenced by the reluctance of continental telecoms companies to liberalize. The other view is given by Armstrong, Cowan, and Vickers (1994), who compared the particular form of privatization against an alternative in which more competition had been encouraged rather than maintaining a statutory duopoly until 1991. In their view, "the duopoly policy has been detrimental to development of competition, and its main beneficiary has been BT itself" (p. 240). "Against the background of a history of vertically integrated nation-wide monopoly, progress toward a more competitive and better regulated telecommunications industry in Britain was made during the 1980s. In important respects, however, it was a decade of lost opportunities" (pp. 240–241). Clearly much depends on the counterfactual, and whether it was plausible that the first telecoms privatization would have been able to identify and introduce the optimal industry structure at the same time as organizing the largest yet asset sale. We will return to this question in chapter 7.

The other two case studies of telecoms privatization are both in Latin America, and they took place several years after the BT privatization. The first of these was the privatization of Compañía de Teléfonos de Chile (CTC) in 1987, described by Galal and Torres (1994). As with the Chilean electricity companies, CTC was originally private (before 1970) and was privatized again in 1987. The government took control (but not ownership) in 1971, and in 1974 the state-holding company CORFO acquired the shareholding from the foreign-owned company ITT. CTC had a fifty-year concession from 1982 to supply local telephone services to 92 percent of the population, and it also supplied national long-distance services to Santiago and Valpariso. The other telephone company (ENTEL) had the remainder of the long distance service market and was privatized as a duopoly competitor with CTC at the same time. Since privatization, each company has been attempting to penetrate the market of the other. CTC's sales price for the first tranche of sales (35 percent to Bond in 1988) was approximately U.S.$700 per line in 1988, about the same as Argentina realized from its sale in 1990 (Wellenius 1994, p. 128). The subsequent sales price at which Bond sold to Telefónica in 1990 was U.S.$1,100 per line.

Since 1977 telecoms have been regulated by SUBTEL, which is part of the Ministry of Transportation and Telecommunications. Regulation is similar to electricity, and where services are not competitive, their tariffs are regulated on the basis of marginal cost adjusted to cover the average total costs of an ideal efficient firm (in this case defined to have 760,000 lines of digital, fully automated service).[16] This form of price regulation has potentially better incentive properties than the British RPI − X, by relating the price level and productivity gain X to a (hypothetical) benchmark, and severing the link between costs and the regulated price. The problem is to agree on a suitable model of the ideal efficient firm. Not surprisingly, each side hires consultants to construct models favoring their particular position.

The very large benefits shown in table 3.3, mostly to domestic consumers, derived from an increase in output caused by a large increase in investment. Profits doubled from Ch$8 billion in 1987 to Ch$15.7 billion in 1988 and doubled again by 1990. Galal and Torres argue that divestiture released the financial constraint, allowing new equity and subsequent bonds to finance the expansion needed to meet massive excess demand. Changes in tariffs played no role in the benefits as these were already set by a preexisting regulatory system. The number of installed lines was expected to increase by more than 160 percent between 1988 and 1996, and the value of gains to the domestic economy were estimated at Ch$574 billion, about five times the private value of CTC.

There may be subsequent benefits from increased competition between the two telephone companies, though whereas disputes between them when publicly owned were settled by negotiation through the Ministry, they must now be resolved in court. Wellenius (1994) noted that there were still critical regulatory issues that had not been resolved despite several years of litigation in the courts. Galal (1996) argues that the reforms since 1982 have taken advantage of

Chile's existing ability to devise and enforce credible regulatory contracts and that the incentive to devise efficient regulatory structures reflected a shift in the political constituency of phone users, from the wealthy under the period of socialism to business interests in the more commercially minded period after the fall of Allende.

Tandon and Abdala (1994) present the case study of privatizing the Mexican telephone company Teléfonos de México or Telmex. As in Chile, Telmex was originally privately owned and formed from two different companies created by ITT and Ericsson. The cost of integration proved too much for the private companies, and in 1972 the Mexican government loans were converted to stock, giving the government a majority holding (by 1990, 56 percent of equity), though it continued to be traded on the Mexican stock exchange. The capital structure was subsequently reorganized to restrict voting rights to 40 percent of the shares, and 51 percent of the voting stock (20.4 percent of total stock) was sold in December 1990. The first tranche was sold for $1.67 billion valuing the company at $8.19 billion, and subsequent tranches realized increasing amounts. The final 4.7 percent was sold for $1.4 billion, valuing the company at $30 billion.[17] By 1992 the government had sold 51.1 percent for a total of $6.2 billion. Wellenius (1994, p. 128) estimates the sales price at U.S.$1,700 per line in 1990.[18]

Telmex is regulated in a similar way to BT with a price control on a basket of services subject to RPI − X, with X set at zero from 1991 to 1996, 3 percent for the next two years, and thereafter reset every 4 years. Telmex had a monopoly on all fixed-link services until August 1996 provided that it meets agreed network expansion targets. Thereafter other firms may be licensed and Telmex must grant interconnection.

Telmex's prices had been declining in real terms until 1987, as a result of accelerating inflation, though social policy objectives appear to have dissuaded the government from a more rapid indexation of tariffs. Prices were raised significantly in 1988, in part to finance rehabilitation after the 1985 earthquake. Subsequent reforms primarily transferred taxes on telephone revenue from the government to the company to be available as company revenue flows after privatization. The 1988 price reforms relaxed the investment constraint well before privatization, and the increase in investment cannot be attributed to privatization. On the other hand, labor productivity, and with it total factor productivity, increased sharply after privatization and can be attributed to private sector reorganization.

Given the increased revenue from the tax switch and increased productivity, profits rose sharply and with it the stock market valuation, transferring most of the gains to the foreign shareholders, who held 56 percent of the company at June 1992. These foreign owners have gained U.S.$12 billion, despite the strategy of the Mexican government in selling the company in tranches at ever higher prices. Tandon and Abdala argue that initially the company was undervalued by shareholders because of its poor profit reputation and tendency for prices not be adjusted in line with inflation. Credibility of the new regulatory regime was untested and the authors argue that selling Telmex successfully was a critical part of Mexico's strategy to convince foreign shareholders of its creditworthiness and commitment to market reforms more generally. As such it played a key part in the macroeconomic stabilization exercise, and the apparently poor returns to the country from selling Telmex must be balanced against the wider gains of renegotiating its foreign debt. Nevertheless, the contrast with the careful creation of a regulatory regime before privatization in Chile, or the British approach of attempting to keep most shareholder gains within the economy, show the benefits of these alternative strategies.

3.5.5   *Lessons from the Privatization Case Studies*

In some cases the improvements in economic performance of the network utility can be traced to regulatory reform, and specifically to tariff reform which may have been prompted by the need for investment revenue, but when undertaken, they relaxed the financial constraints limiting expansion. In such cases the main benefits of privatization lay in managerial improvements introduced at privatization, such as improving labor productivity and reducing theft or losses. This evidence is consistent with the view that workers in public network utilities constitute an important interest group, and that some weight is attached to their welfare in the utility's objectives while in the public sector (together with that of consumers), placing relatively lower weight on the pursuit of profit. Privatization can change the balance of power of each interest group and thus increase the prominence of pursuing profits.

In other cases, notably the telecoms examples of BT and CTC where investment needs were both costly and more pressing, the unwillingness of the public sector to either raise tariffs to generate the investible resources, or to provide the necessary capital through loans, imposed high costs that privatization was able to relax. In the case of Telmex, the Mexican government's commitment to reform ensured that tariffs were adequate to finance investment, when coupled with the ability of the company to borrow. Perhaps Telmex was a special case, since it was already partly private.

In almost all cases the utilities were sold for less than fair market value, judged with the benefit of hindsight, reflecting problems of regulatory credibility and the fear of investors that they will not be allowed to keep any predicted large profit increases. In some cases the exchequer benefited from the extra profits tax revenue, and where expansion had previously been constrained, this could outweigh the initial sales loss. The worst case was Telmex, where regulatory uncertainty perpetuated the considerable undervaluation dating from a period of low and declining tariffs, despite the regulatory reform. On top of this, profits increased dramatically, partly because the government had reduced telephone taxes and allowed a compensating price increase to generate higher profits, but surely partly because of the very loose price regulation. Finally the overwhelming foreign ownership (common for high tech industries such as telecoms in developing and transitional countries) meant that most of these gains flowed out of the country.

The main lesson to draw is that the quality of regulation is a key determinant of performance whether the utility is public or private; regulatory reform can take place in the public sector, though the evident need for regulation under private ownership may mean that privatization prompts regulatory reform. Compared to the quality of regulation, ownership seems relatively less important, though there may be more chance of high-quality regulation under private than public ownership. Ownership changes in both directions often coincide with (and may be provoked by or induce) structural and managerial changes that can have significant effects on factor productivity, especially labor productivity (and the same is true in the private sector with takeovers), but privatizations can be fiscally costly.

We started this chapter by pointing to the poor macroeconomic performance of state-owned enterprises, especially network utilities, in developing countries. Such observations have led some observers to argue that the main argument for privatization is to solve the fiscal problems and enable utilities to finance their heavy investment needs, particularly in the capital-intensive electricity and telecoms utilities. Although there may be a strong case for privatizing such utilities, it does not rest on the financial case. In order to privatize a network utility, the buyer has to be convinced that prices can be set at cost-recovering levels and that profits are adequate to finance investment.

The best way to ensure that potential buyers are confident that the utility can set sensible prices is to raise prices to those levels before privatization; otherwise, the utility will be sold for far less than its replacement value. Once that has been done, the fiscal and financial problems have been solved, and the fiscal case for privatization disappears. The real case for privatization must be that it is easier to sustain efficient pricing under private ownership in the face of political and populist pressures, and that privatization will generate additional efficiency gains. The case for privatization is that it locks in hard-won regulatory reforms that continued state ownership would erode, while the case against hurried privatization is that it foregoes the option of future restructuring and better regulatory design.

Given the importance of regulation, both of public and private utilities, the time has come to look more closely at theories of regulation and of regulatory reform, and that task is undertaken in the next chapter.

Appendix: Evaluating Distributional Impacts

Privatization may lead to utility price increases, but so can a more commercial approach to the management of public enterprises, as New Zealand has demonstrated with its program of corporatizing its public utilities. In both cases there may be concerns about the distributional impacts of these price increases, and any social cost–benefit analysis will need to quantify these impacts, to set against any efficiency gains. They can be evaluated using the same methodology used in the theory of marginal tax reform developed by Feldstein (1972) and summarized in Newbery and Stern (1987).

Suppose that the government ranks distributional outcomes according to a utilitarian social welfare function $W(V^1, \ldots, V^h, \ldots, V^H)$, where agent h enjoys utility $V^h = V^h(m^h + g, p)$ that depends on income before transfers, m^h, government transfers, g, and the vector of consumer prices, p.[19] Consider the impact on social welfare of a change in consumer price p_i:

$$\frac{\partial W}{\partial p_i} = \sum_h \frac{\partial W}{\partial V^h} \cdot \frac{\partial V^h}{\partial p_i} = -\sum_h \beta^h q_i^h, \tag{3A.1}$$

where

$$\beta^h \equiv \frac{\partial W}{\partial V^h} \cdot \frac{\partial V^h}{\partial g}$$

is the social marginal utility of transferring \$1 to agent h, q_i^h is consumption of good i by agent h, and the last equality in equation (3A.1) makes use of Roy's identity: $q_i = -(\partial V^h/\partial p_i)/(\partial V^h/\partial m^h)$. The impact of the price change will thus depend on both the level of consumption and its distribution among the population. It is convenient to isolate these two effects by defining d_i, the *distributional characteristic* of good i:

$$d_i \equiv \frac{\sum_h \beta^h q_i^h}{\bar{\beta} Q_i}, \quad Q_i \equiv \sum_h q_i^h, \quad \bar{\beta} \equiv \frac{1}{H} \sum_h \beta^h, \tag{3A.2}$$

where Q_i is aggregate consumption of i and $\bar{\beta}$ is the average over the H agents of β^h. The distributional characteristic d_i is a measure of how concentrated the consumption of good i is on the socially deserving (those with high social marginal values of consumption, β^h). The social welfare impact of a price change is then

$$\frac{\partial W}{\partial p_i} = -\bar{\beta} d_i Q_i. \tag{3A.3}$$

In order to make this approach operational, one needs a method for calculating the social weights, β^h. The simplest and most easily parameterized such measure is given by the isoelastic utility function defined over real consumption per equivalent adult, $u^h = (c^h)^{1-v}/(1-v)$, ($v \neq 1$), $u^h = \log c^h$, ($v = 1$), where v is Atkinson's (1970) coefficient of inequality aversion. Then, for an additive (utilitarian) social welfare function, $W = \Sigma u^h$, $\beta^h = (c^h)^{-v}$. Thus, if $v = 1$, transferring \$1 to someone at double the living standard of another has a social value of only one-half that of the reference person. If $v = 2$, the transfer would only count one-quarter as much, while if $v = \frac{1}{2}$, it would count for 70 percent as much.

Newbery (1995b) presents the distributional characteristics of consumer goods for both Hungary and the United Kingdom. If we summarize distributional concerns by taking a value of $v = 1$ (and the results are robust to values of v over the range 0.5 to 2), then we can compare the different public utilities in both countries. Electricity in the United Kingdom has an average budget share ω_i of 2.3 percent, a distributional characteristic d_i of 0.954 (compared with a weighted average for all commodities, $\Sigma \omega_i d_i$, of 0.685), and is ranked seventh out of 87 goods, with only 1.7 percent of consumers' average expenditure spent on more worthy goods than electricity (i.e., those with a higher distributional weight). Electricity consumption is thus relatively a far larger share of expenditure of the poor than the better off, and more of a necessity than almost any other good. Gas appears somewhat less distributionally sensitive, with a budget share of 1.9 percent, a distributional characteristic of 0.889 (ranked 18th), and 10 percent of average consumer expenditure spent on more worthy goods. Post and telephone (unfortunately not separated) have a budget share of 1.7 percent, a value of d_i of 0.811 (rank 41), and 22 percent is spent on more worthy goods.

Hungary, as a poorer socialist country, offers an interesting contrast. Electricity has $d_i = 0.908$ (compared to a weighted average of 0.839),[20] ranked 20 out of 87, but has 24 percent spent on more worthy goods, while gas is the next in rank, with $d_i = 0.906$, and 26 percent spent on more worthy goods. Post and telephone come a long way down the list with $d_i = 0.717$, rank 74, and 86 percent of expenditure on more worthy goods. Whereas telephones are a necessity in the United Kingdom, they are a luxury in Hungary.

One way to interpret these findings is to ask whether the adverse distributional effects of raising utility i's price can be offset by an equal reduction in taxation. One natural way to do this is to increase the lump-sum transfer g to everyone. Suppose that the government's budget constraint is

$$\overline{R} = \sum_j t_j Q_j + p_i Q_i - C(Q_i) - Hg, \qquad (3A.4)$$

where t_j is the tax on good j with $t_i = 0$, $C(Q_i)$ is the cost of producing the utility's output Q_i, assumed to be in the public sector, and $\overline{R}$ is the revenue required to meet prespecified activities. We wish to know the impact on social welfare of an increase in p_i that allows g to be increased, holding all other tax rates and public expenditure constant. As in (3A.1), but remembering that g now depends on p_i, we have

$$\frac{\partial W}{\partial p_i} = \sum_h \frac{\partial W}{\partial V^h}\left(\frac{\partial V^h}{\partial p_i} + \frac{\partial V^h}{\partial g} \cdot \frac{\partial g}{\partial p_i}\right) = \overline{\beta}\left(H\frac{\partial g}{\partial p_i} - d_i Q_i\right). \qquad (3A.5)$$

The value of $\partial g/\partial p_i$ is found by totally differentiating (3A.4):

$$0 = \sum_j \frac{t_j \partial Q_j}{\partial p_i} + \left(\sum_j \frac{t_j \partial Q_j}{\partial g} - H\right)\frac{\partial g}{\partial p_i} + Q_i + (p_i - C')\frac{\partial Q_i}{\partial p_i}. \qquad (3A.6)$$

The term $\Sigma t_j \partial Q_j / \partial g$ is the extra indirect tax recovered from the extra expenditure afforded by the lump-sum transfer, which is equal to $H\tau$ if the average marginal indirect tax rate is τ as a fraction of expenditure. If we make the strong but convenient assumption that consumer demands are given by the linear expenditure system, and if the subsistence minimum quantity of the utility's service is γ_i, then $\Sigma t_j \partial Q_j / \partial p_i = -H\tau\gamma_i$.[21] Substitute this in (3A.6) to give

$$H(1-\tau)\frac{\partial g}{\partial p_i} = \left(1-\left(\frac{p_i - C_i'}{p_i}\right)\varepsilon_i\right)Q_i - H\tau\gamma_i,$$

where C_i' is the marginal cost and ε_i is the elasticity of demand for the utility's output as a positive number. This can be substituted in (3A.5) to give

$$\frac{\partial W}{\partial p_i} = \overline{\beta}\left(\frac{1-m_i\varepsilon_i - \mu_i\tau}{1-\tau} - d_i\right)Q_i, \quad \mu_i \equiv \frac{H\gamma_i}{Q_i}, \qquad (3A.7)$$

where m_i is the proportional markup of price over marginal cost for the utility and μ_i is the ratio of minimum subsistence utility consumption to average consumption.

Equation (3A.7) shows that it is a good idea to raise the utility's price if the markup m_i is low compared to the average indirect tax rate τ and/or if the elasticity of demand is low, provided that the ratio of the minimum consumption to the average is not too high and the distributional characteristic d_i is not too high. Unfortunately, the last two factors go in the same direction: high μ_i means a necessity, and hence a high value of d_i. Equation (3A.7) shows the importance of efficiency considerations (m_i relative to τ, and ε_i which affects the size of the excess burden or the distortionary cost of taxation) as well as the distributional considerations—the extent to which the utility is a necessity, μ_i and d_i.

In fact the particular simplifying assumption that demands were given by the Linear Expenditure System corresponds to a case where the optimal commodity tax is a uniform VAT on all goods, including the utility, which should also be pricing efficiently (i.e., without subsidies to capital, and at marginal cost, so that the markup of the tax-inclusive price over marginal cost is the same as the tax rate).[22] Under more general (and reasonably defensible) assumptions the optimal tax system involves an income tax, supplemented by uniform value-added taxes, and an optimal lump-sum demo-grant (i.e., a grant that depends on demographic circumstances, such as family size).[23] The tax system raises revenue efficiently, and redistribution is concentrated on the expenditure side of the budget (in the form of direct transfers like child benefit), but more broadly through publicly supplied health, education, and other social services, most of which are akin to (demographically differentiated) lump-sum transfers. Once again, network utilities in the public sector should set prices efficiently and pay the standard rate VAT. If the network still experiences economies of scale at its optimum scale, and if it is required to break even (to ensure budgetary discipline), then the pretax price would be above the marginal cost, and there would be a case for a lower rate of tax, to bring the margin between the tax-inclusive price and the marginal cost into line with the normal rate of VAT.

The same approach can be used to value price increases necessary to privatize utilities, taking care to identify who receives the extra profits—the state in the sales price, or subsequent shareholders who enjoy a windfall gain. This approach is illustrated in the social cost–benefit analysis of privatizing the British Central Electricity Generating Board presented in chapter 6.

       Theories of Regulation

In the last chapter we saw that private regulated network utilities are not necessarily more efficient than public network utilities, but subjecting utilities to competition improves their performance. Investor-owned utilities that are vertically integrated franchise monopolies operating under rate-of-return regulation appear to behave very like public utilities, whose budgetary control is rather like cost-of-service regulation. Restructuring, which is often associated with a change in ownership (nationalization or privatization), can improve efficiency and may have distributional consequences (which may be good or bad). Nationalization and subsequent restructuring may be prompted by the apparent impossibility of achieving desirable reorganizations under private ownership, and may thereby release pent-up efficiency gains, as with the creation of the British Central Electricity Board and the building of the national grid. The most obvious reason to restructure these days, though, is to prepare the industry for privatization. The Chilean electricity industry was restructured under public ownership, and the regulatory framework was clarified to give considerable improvements in performance, before the industry was finally privatized. The English Central Electricity Generating Board was restructured specifically as part of the process of privatization.

Restructuring may also be required for investor-owned network utilities as part of the process of confining regulation to the natural monopoly network and introducing competition where possible, and it will often be resisted by the incumbent vertically integrated monopoly. Such restructuring is therefore more difficult, and needs either the threat of something worse, as we will see with the Bell System, or the offer of compensation, perhaps resolving the problem of stranded assets, as in the case of the U.S. electricity industry.

If competition improves performance, then one should expect the form of regulation to also affect performance. If rate-of-return regulation is associated with monopoly provision, then price regulation appears to mimic the competitive market, and ought to give greater incentives for efficiency. This chapter argues that regulation (in the broadest sense, including the management of public utilities) is inevitably inefficient because of problems of information and commitment and, more fundamentally, because of inefficient bargaining between interest groups over potential utility rents. The choice of regulation faces a trade-off between higher efficiency on the one hand and a better (or at least politically more acceptable) distribution of the benefits on the other. Competition may offer some escape from this trade-off.

Until the late 1980s almost all network utilities were vertically integrated, with a protected franchise monopoly in some region or nationally. If regulation is inherently inefficient, then structural reforms that introduce competition become attractive. It suggests a rule for structural reform: competition where possible, regulation only where unavoidable. The reforms may take the extreme form of separating the potentially competitive network services from the natural monopoly core, or the less extreme form of liberalization—allowing competitive suppliers access to the network that remains under the ownership of a vertically integrated utility, some of whose services now face competition from new entrants. If some parts of the formerly vertically integrated public monopoly are potentially competitive, this in itself is a strong argument for privatization. It is difficult to sustain competition between state-owned companies, and logical to privatize them as the argument for public ownership based on market failure no longer applies. This does not necessarily mean that the natural monopoly network should be privatized, and there may be good arguments, considered later, for keeping, for example, the high-tension electricity grid in public ownership (as in Norway).

The reason that competition is superior to regulation is twofold: Pricing is more efficient and costs are lower. The ideal sales price is set at the efficient level (compared to other prices in the economy), and is beyond the influence of the utility, giving maximum incentive to reduce costs and innovate as the only ways to increase profits. This ideal is most closely approached in competitive industries with many noncolluding firms or contestable entry conditions, where the price is set by other firms. If competition is sufficiently intense, then the rents (the benefits of having the utility) will be entirely transferred to consumers, eliminating the inefficiency caused by attempts to capture the rents (by monopoly, or mandated cross-subsidies which make prices differ from their efficient level).

The cost of liberalizing or de-integrating the network services is a possible loss of economies of scope, that is, of the advantages of coordinating the operation and expansion of the network with the services provided over it. It is also harder to regulate the relationship between the competitive and monopoly parts, particularly the terms of access to a vertically integrated incumbent, than to regulate consumer prices in a vertically integrated utility. There may be further economic and political costs if the potentially competitive parts are not adequately competitive (distortions, reduced incentives for efficiency, and an unattractive distribution of the benefits).

The electricity supply industry provides a concrete example of de-integration to introduce competition. Recent technical advances in combined cycle gas turbine technology have dramatically reduced the minimum economic scale of generation, so that new entrants into the British electricity market have typically less than 2 percent of total capacity. Most of the larger industrial economies and any with access to gas are therefore able to support a number of competing generating companies, each large enough to realize all the economies of scale in generation. The state of Victoria, Australia, created five generating companies around the five major power stations, whose combined maximum demand was only 7,000 MW. Argentina was restructured to give over 30 generating companies with about 18,000 MW capacity, in which the largest had less than 8 percent of total capacity.

The high-tension grid is a single natural monopoly within a particular area, as are the local distribution companies (though there can be several local distribution companies of optimum size served by a single grid). Transmission and distribution must therefore be regulated. The policy question is therefore whether it would be desirable to split off generation and leave it unregulated subject only to normal competition laws. The answer will depend on whether the generating companies would retain too much market power to be left unregulated, and whether the short and long-run problems of coordinating the operation and investment in transmission and generation can be overcome. It may be possible to secure these economies of scope with a well-chosen set of regulated prices for access and use of the grid, but it may be that these coordination benefits can be achieved at lower cost in an integrated utility. If the industry is kept as a vertically integrated monopoly, only the final electricity prices need to be regulated, and there is no need to design the complex set of access and use-of-system prices for the grid.

Whether the benefits of de-integrating the electricity supply industry exceed the costs is an empirical question, which may have a different answer for systems of different sizes, based on different fuels, with different institutional endowments. For the moment all we need to note is that if regulation were efficient there would never be any reason to split up a vertically integrated utility or liberalize access to the network, so the first step is to demonstrate that regulation is inherently inefficient.

4.1   Normative and Positive Theories of Regulation

There are two different approaches to the theory of regulation: The normative theory prescribes the way in which regulation ought to be designed to maximize social welfare, while the positive theory predicts the way regulation will work in practice. The normative theory has much in common with the theory of optimal taxation, while the positive theory is more akin to public choice theory. One standard objection to any normative approach is that the idea of social welfare is operationally meaningless. Arrow's (1951) impossibility theorem states that there is no nondictatorial method of aggregating arbitrary individual preferences to give social preferences, and hence no acceptable way of deciding what should be done. The reason is that individual preferences about the organization of society or the choice of policies are likely to conflict, especially when choosing taxes to transfer income from one group to another.

This objection may be fatal to the idea that we can resolve all issues uncontroversially by voting, but does not undermine the concept of social welfare as reflecting ethical judgments, not personal preferences. Many institutions operate on the principle that provided our personal interests are not involved, we will be able to reach agreement on what is just or ethical. Rawls (1971) suggested that ethical judgments could be made by imagining their effects on other members of society. Suppose that you had to make a judgment or choose a policy on the assumption that after the choice you would be randomly assigned to become any member of that society, with their preferences, property, and position. Your own preferences and position would now be irrelevant, and this thought experiment should reveal what is the right decision and therefore good for society. Harsanyi (1955) earlier argued that this would provide a way to construct a social welfare function, for if you were asked to choose policies with an equal chance of filling any individual's shoes, you would rationally choose policies to maximize expected utility, $\Sigma U^i/N$, where U^i is the utility of person i, and $1/N$ is the chance of being one of the N different individuals. This would be equivalent to maximizing the utilitarian (additive) social welfare function ΣU^i.

This thought experiment has been institutionalized in the British Monopolies and Mergers Commission, which also examines disputes between utilities and their regulator. The Commission has to advise the Secretary of State on "whether the utility operates or may be expected to operate against the public interest," and if so, what remedy might be available. No doubt other competition authorities are given similar instructions. For a well-trained welfare economist, "the public interest" seems operationally equivalent to the economic concept of social welfare, while the idea of recruiting Commission members from a range of occupations and ensuring that they have no financial stake in the outcome of the inquiry is designed to ensure an impartial judgment. The normative approach offers guidance in such cases.

The positive theory of regulation tries to explain the form of regulation as the outcome of bargaining between various interest groups. If agents agreed on objectives, the two approaches would coincide, but the essence of bargaining is that the interests of one group are opposed to those of the others and can only be advanced at some cost to the others. The problem with the normative approach is that the public interest is rarely the same as the interests of the various participants in the regulatory game, and the normative approach may therefore make poor predictions about the likely outcome of such bargaining.

Whether there is a substantive difference between the normative and positive theory of regulation depends on the case in question. In the simple model of regulation in which there are only two agents—a regulator who represents consumer interests, and a utility maximizing its profits—social welfare corresponds closely to consumers' (long-run) interests, and as voters they should support those who represent these interests. Provided that the regulator is not captured by the utility, and has to satisfy these voters, the positive theory predicts that the normative result will be chosen. If there are several interest groups, there is room for difference between the predicted outcome and the social optimum, since relative bargaining strengths are unlikely to coincide with relative weights in the ethical balance of social welfare. For our immediate purpose, though, both approaches agree that regulation will be inefficient, since both describe imperfectly informed attempts to redistribute income.

The normative theory of regulation of a natural monopoly largely consists in defining the prices that the monopolist can charge. Ideally these prices would be set at the efficient level subject to the obvious but important constraint that the utility is able to finance its investment and cover its operating costs. With constant or decreasing returns to scale, competition could produce the efficient prices, but the essence of a natural monopoly is that competition is inefficient and hence not a sensible option. In such a case the best regulation can do is to aspire to the competitive ideal, though in practice it is hard to detach the price set from the observed cost of the natural monopoly, given the obvious difficulty of discovering what the efficient cost should be. If price is based on observed costs, then there is little incentive for efficiency.

This problem can be addressed in two ways. If there are many comparable utilities (e.g., regional distribution companies for electricity and gas, regional water companies), then the price can be based on the costs of the *other* companies, just as firms in competitive industries face prices set by other (marginal) firms. Such yardstick regulation in which the target for one utility depends on the performance of other comparable utilities has the advantage of using relevant cost information while preserving incentives for cost reduction (Shleifer 1985). Where this is not feasible (e.g., where there is only one utility as with the electricity grid or telephone network), then it may be possible to construct a set of accounts for a model company—an approach that has been adopted in Chile formally for telecoms and electricity, and informally in Britain by using consultants to estimate the costs of efficient operation.

Regulation therefore involves balancing two conflicting aims. If consumers are to benefit from low prices, prices must be kept close to costs, but not so low as to discourage investment. If this can only be achieved by relating prices to costs, then efficiency is discouraged. If it is achieved by relating prices to benchmark costs, there must be a sufficient margin to allow the actual utility, which may be less successful or less fortunate than the benchmark ideal, to survive. The inefficiency of regulation thus derives either from the deadweight losses of excessively high prices, or the inefficiency of excessively high operating costs, or some mixture of the two.

The formal expression of this argument (Laffont 1994; Laffont and Tirole 1993) is cast in a principal-agent framework in which the regulator (as principal) knows less about the production possibilities and opportunities for cost reductions than does the utility, or agent (i.e., the principal suffers from asymmetric information). The regulator attaches a lower weight to profits than consumer welfare (to keep prices close to costs) and has to determine allowable revenue, R, say. The simplest rule for setting revenue is

$$R = b\overline{R} + (1-b)C,$$

where the target revenue $\overline{R}$ is independent of the utility's total cost C. The term b is the *power* of the regulatory incentive scheme, with $b = 0$ (the lowest power) corresponding to cost-of-service regulation and $b = 1$ to a high-powered scheme such as price regulation. The central insight of this Bayesian optimizing approach to designing the best incentive scheme given asymmetric information is that there is an inescapable trade-off between greater efficiency and greater rent transfer to the utility (as in the closely related field of optimal taxation) and that typically the optimum involves some intermediate level of incentives. Periodic price reviews, or regulatory lags in rate-of-return regulation, proxies this. Problems of regulatory credibility and commitment make this trade-off less advantageous, since high-powered incentives increase the risk of regulatory opportunism, as we saw in chapter 2.

4.1.1   Positive Theories of Regulation

One of the limitations of the normative theory of regulation is that it seems so static: There would seem little reason to change the system of regulation if that regulation were the best feasible. The other limitation was well expressed by Coase (1964, p. 195), who argued that it was fundamentally misguided to concentrate solely on finding the conditions for an optimum without asking how the policy would be put into practice: "It is no accident that in the literature . . . we find a category 'market failure' but no category 'government failure.' Until we realise we are choosing between social arrangements which are all more or less failures, we are not likely to make much headway."

Similar objections were made about the advice given to nationalized public utilities for setting prices and selecting investments. It was not too difficult for economists to work out how this should be done, and even to persuade the government to publish White Papers setting out the rules: Price at marginal cost and select investments by cost–benefit analysis. They assumed uncritically that the industries could be relied upon to do this honestly and impartially, without inquiring too closely why they should, or whether they might be pursuing other aims that might differ, and if so, what they might actually do if told that all projects meeting the specified criteria would be financed, no questions asked.

The positive theory of regulation addresses this critique by first observing that there is a demand for regulation both by utilities and their customers. Customers demand protection from the utility's potential exploitive power through the political process, while utilities seek to protect the future profitability of their large sunk investments from the demands of the mass of local voting consumers. The utilities need the cooperation of local or national political power to grant them rights of way and protection against expropriation and/or competition which threatens future profits, while politicians demand benefits for their electorate—reasonable prices, adequate supply, and no (visibly) unfair discrimination. The theory then asks how the demand for regulation is likely to be met, and what the supply side of the equation might look like. If demand and supply are in balance, the present regulatory system can be both explained and examined for its efficiency, and if not, then it may be possible to explain changes in regulation as adjustments of supply to demand.

The various political theories explaining the supply side of the market for regulation have been surveyed by Noll (1989). The optimistic *public interest theory of regulation* claims that competition between political entrepreneurs will result in the least-cost remedy, just as competition between agents in the market place leads to least-cost production.

Noll (1989, p. 1260) lists the predictions made by this theory. First, regulation becomes more likely as the severity of market failure increases, because the costs of taking remedial action are likely to remain fairly constant. Second, the transaction cost of renegotiating regulation limits the extent to which any group can be disadvantaged by regulation (and hence the overall levels of inefficiency). Changes in costs and benefits can therefore precipitate reform, and deregulation should take place when the costs of regulation outweigh the gains by enough to cover the transaction cost of repeal. Ellig (1989) gives the example of the gradual deregulation of gas in the United States. Regulation designed to hold down consumer prices eventually reduced supply, created shortages and disruptions, and produced larger inefficiency costs for consumers than their gains from lower prices. Deregulation followed. Finally, evolution should lead to the form of regulation that sustains the largest benefits net of the costs of inefficiency. It implies that ways will be found to minimize the transaction costs of regulation, by ensuring that regulation is transparent and that information is disseminated widely.

4.1.2   *Interest Group Theories of Regulation*

There are sufficiently many obvious counterexamples to the claim that regulation is the least-cost solution to market failures to reject this simple view, and replace it with a more general *economic* or *interest group theory of regulation*, which recognizes that competition among interest groups is imperfect or oligopolistic and can reallocate returns in socially undesirable ways. Regulators are seen as utility-maximizing arbiters between these various interest groups. Different interest groups have different bargaining power, depending on their costs of organizing and the benefits of manipulating outcomes, and they will intervene to redistribute benefits to their group at some additional inefficiency cost. Just as the central insight in public finance is that redistribution creates deadweight costs that must be balanced against the distributional gains of taxation, so interest group theory recognizes that policy interventions will be biased in favor of some groups at the expense of others, and at some cost in extra deadweight losses. The outcome may bear little relationship to the best feasible that a benevolent dictator might choose in the public interest, and they certainly need not minimize efficiency losses.

The groups that are likely to be favored are those with benefits that are large relative to organizational costs, particularly those organized around production (managers, workers, trade associations of producers and suppliers) rather than customers, though large consumers exposed to international competition are likely to form trade associations to lobby for preferential treatment, while political entrepreneurs will represent some consumer/voter groups. The gains to be distributed are the monopoly rents, which Peltzman (1976) argues will be distributed approximately in proportion to the net benefits (benefits less organization costs) of the interest groups. If there is one dominant interest group (usually the regulated industry), there will be "capture" (Stigler 1971). The theory predicts that regulation is likely to restrict entry as the incumbents have more bargaining power than potential entrants, and their rents will be threatened by competition. If entry makes negotiation more costly, increasing deadweight losses, then even consumers could be persuaded to oppose competitive entry by cross-subsidies (Posner 1971) or targeting benefits appropriately (Crandall 1983). Liberalization may well be successfully opposed.

The theory predicts important similarities and differences between public ownership and regulated private ownership. Under public ownership, interest groups will compete in the political market place for benefits, while under private ownership, the regulator will represent the interests of the nonowning groups. This can be clearly seen by comparing the electricity industries in Britain under public and subsequent private ownership with private integrated electricity companies in Germany and Spain. Regardless of ownership, all three countries evolved systems of protecting high-cost domestic coal producers and recovering these costs from electricity consumers, though in Britain subsidies fell dramatically when the market was liberalized.

The best way to create and protect rents for distribution to the incumbent interest groups is to maximize the horizontal and vertical extent of the utility's monopoly, and the best way to shift the balance of bargaining advantage toward consumers is to minimize both extensions of monopoly. The fact that these industries are so often vertically and horizontally integrated suggests that well-organized groups have succeeded in capturing the rents at the expense of consumers. But how should this be if one of the main reasons for public ownership or regulation is to defend the interests of voting consumers?

There are three related and supporting answers. First, vertical integration enhances the utility's ability to control information to defend its interests. Second, the utility can argue that economies of scale and scope make integration efficient. Third, unbundling the different stages increases risk as prices for intermediate services reallocate profits up or downstream, while competition increases risk directly. A franchise monopoly protected against entry lowers the cost of capital by reducing market risk, and enables politically desirable cross-subsidies to be financed by implicit rather than explicit taxation (most visible in the transfer from long-distance to local calls in telecoms). Cross-subsidies buy political support to protect the franchise. Utilities are therefore able to argue convincingly that there are genuine benefits of integration, while concealing information about the costs of inefficient bargaining that might be revealed if parts of the industry were exposed to the discovery mechanisms of competitive pressure or comparative performance.

The amount of rent dissipated in inefficiency is likely to depend on the extent of conflict between groups, the number of dimensions in which they can bargain (the fewer, the cruder, and more costly the outcome), the transactions costs involved in reaching agreement, and the difficulty of credibly enforcing agreements. As a general rule, most policy reforms that appear Pareto improving (e.g., reforming the grotesquely inefficient and inequitable Common Agricultural Policy of the European Union) are not credible because they are either not durable or because they make explicit the nature of the transfers that were previously concealed. Buying off farmers with lump-sum payments would make more sense than subsidizing their production, but if provided in one lump sum, it would be considered outrageous and deeply inequitable because larger farmers would get most. Avoiding this by annual lump-sum transfers initially agreed is not credible, since explicit subsidies would be subject to annual fiscal scrutiny and, once the new agricultural deal is in place and delivering consumer benefits, would be voted down. So inefficient but well-concealed transfers persist because they have proved durable. Given the risks that interest groups may lose their benefits, much effort will be invested in ensuring that the gains are concealed and entrenched, and such actions are likely to further increase inefficiencies.

Historical experience suggests that reforms leading to large redistributions are likely to be delayed long beyond the point of realizing considerable net benefits, which means that reforms to regulatory systems require profound economic or political changes. Joskow and Rose (1989) observe that much regulation in the United States dates from the turbulence of the Great Depression of the 1930s, and reforms, particularly the move to deregulate, occurred after the macroeconomic shocks of the 1970s. Another interpretation is that deregulation occurs when the regulatory compact is weakened by excess capacity—the benefits of competition outweigh the needs to reassure investors that their investment will be adequately rewarded, as argued in chapter 2. Finally technical progress and market growth may make it possible for smaller entrants to compete with incumbents, undermining the natural monopoly defense. This lowers the cost to society of breaking the regulatory compact and turning to alternative suppliers, again as illustrated in chapter 2.

Two examples illustrate the influence of interest groups and their effect on efficiency, as well as the dynamics of change. The English electricity supply industry was nationalized in 1948, restructured in 1989, and privatized in 1990. The Bell Telephone System remained a private regulated utility throughout, but liberalizing entry precipitated its breakup in 1984.

4.2   Interest Group Influence on the English Electricity Industry

The British electricity supply industry (ESI) was nationalized by the Labour government in 1947, and for most of the postwar period, the Central Electricity Generating Board (CEGB)[1] operated all generation and transmission in England and Wales as a vertically integrated statutory monopoly, with twelve area boards acting as regional distribution monopolies. The importance of the ESI in the national economy can be gauged from the fact that in the first fifteen years after nationalization it accounted for on average 8 percent of total British capital formation, rising to 12 percent with the nuclear program of the early 1960s. Figure 4.1 shows the remarkably high level of investment as a share of revenues until 1966–67, falling rapidly and then stabilizing at about one-fifth of its earlier share. Note that investment in the earlier period greatly exceeded cash flow, entailing heavy borrowing.

The main weakness of nationalization was that it had no clear objective to guide its policy once it had achieved the initial task of rationalising the industry, which happened fairly rapidly in the postwar reconstruction period. This failure to specify clear objectives is symptomatic of a deeper problem. Public ownership inevitably allowed the various interest groups a stage on which to influence outcomes and thus ruled out the pursuit of any simple single objective. These interest groups included the management and unions within the industry, the coal industry, the equipment suppliers, major energy users, the Treasury, both as financier and the body responsible for macroeconomic management, and of course the politicians, supporting these and other interests such as defense, security, and technological leadership.

Coal supplied 80 percent of the fuel for generation in 1960, and although this share fell slightly over time in 1990, over two-thirds of electricity was still generated from coal while power generation took 80 percent of the output of British Coal by that date. This is clear in

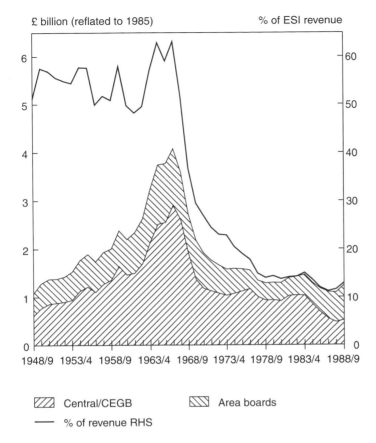

Figure 4.1
Capital investment in electricity: England and Wales, 1948 to 1989.
Source: Electricity Council (1990).

figure 4.2, which shows the evolution of fuel used in the U.K. electricity industry, of which the CEGB provided about 90 percent.[2] The nationalized industries dominated the Trades Unions Congress, which in turn had close links with the Labour party that had nationalized these industries. Domestic coal has thus been protected against imported coal and heavily subsidised, particularly in the period 1974 to 1992, when the subsidies averaged 19 percent of the sales revenue of the CEGB (Newbery and Green 1996, p. 57).

This heavy reliance on indigenous coal was obviously in the interests of the coal miners, still numbering three-quarters of a million workers in 1955. There was little conflict of interest while the world coal market was underdeveloped and British coal was cheap and

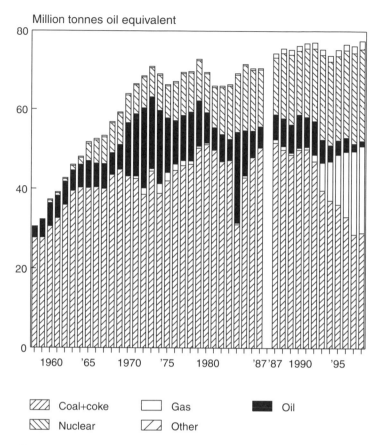

Figure 4.2
Fuel used in electricity generation: The United Kingdom, 1958 to 1998.
Source: DTI (1999).

in excess demand, as was the case in the early period of national ownership. Indeed, faced with a projected shortage of coal, the Central Electricity Authority (the immediate predecessor to the CEGB), a naturally conservative organization, wished to continue constructing coal-fired stations and import coal (presumably until adequate domestic supplies were again available). The Treasury argued that oil was cheaper, and that the industry was overdependent on one supplier, the National Coal Board. Fourteen stations were converted from coal to oil in 1954 and greatly benefited from lower fuel prices. By 1958 coal was in surplus, and the government, fearing redundancies among politically powerful miners, required the CEGB to stop building the lower cost oil-fired power stations. This reduced its planned oil burn but at considerable financial cost.

This was the first of a series of costly bargains with mining interests. In 1973 the dramatic rise in the price of oil greatly increased the bargaining power of the miners, who demanded higher wages. The subsequent miners' strike in early 1974 brought down the Conservative government, and Labour was returned to power. The strike ensured that the next Conservative government would prepare their future strategy toward the miners with considerable care to ensure a more successful outcome in any future confrontation. The subsequent 1984–85 year-long miners' strike was defeated by the Conservative government under Mrs. Thatcher, in part because of the presence of carefully prepared coal stocks and a considerable if costly switch from coal to oil—the oil burning increased from less than 3 mtoe (million tonnes oil equivalent) to nearly 24 mtoe as coal dropped from 46 to 24 mtoe (as revealed in figure 4.2).

Clearly the conflict over fuel rents was intense and costly. It must have strengthened the case for privatizing both the ESI and the coal industry. When the ESI was privatized in 1990, the generators were sold with three year take-or-pay coal contracts to ensure a smooth and uncontroversial transition to the private sector, and to delay any confrontation with coal miners until after the 1993 general election. As the coal contracts matured, hard bargaining between the generators and the still public British Coal Corporation revealed a large discrepancy between what the generators were willing to pay, rather than import coal or burn gas, and the cost of mining the coal. At the contract price of British coal, it was commercially attractive to invest in new gas-fired combined cycle gas turbines (CCGT), and in the liberalized market for power, new independent power producers could and did enter on the back of long-terms contracts for gas supply and electricity sales.

Within three years of privatization the new and incumbent generators had signed contracts for 8.7 GW of CCGT plant, which would displace about 25 million tonnes of coal, compared to the 1992 coal burn of 60 million tonnes. The impact this had on the negotiations for new coal supply contracts between British Coal and the generators was dramatic; it led British Coal in October 1992 to announce the closure of more than half the remaining deep mines. The number of mine workers had dropped from 160,000 at the time of the 1984 strike to about 50,000 in 1991, before the 1992 announcement of 30,000 redundancies. By the time coal was finally privatized in 1994, the number had fallen to about

10,000. The sharp fall in coal consumption can be seen clearly in figure 4.2, and is projected to continue. By 1998–99 coal accounted for less than one-third of electricity generated in England and Wales, while the gas share had risen from nothing to one-third, slightly more than coal.

One rather cynical view of electricity privatization is that it was part of a campaign against the overmighty public sector unions which was designed to undermine the power base of the opposition Labour party. An alternative view is that the costs and benefits of transferring rents to miners had changed. The concentrated worker power represented by the miners in earlier periods (three-quarters of a million workers in 1955, still half a million in 1965) would have successfully resisted privatization or even liberalization of generation, with its economic imperative to buy the cheapest fuel. The opportunity cost of not buying international fuel was low compared to the number of benefiting miners. By the latter part of the 1980s, with miners declining rapidly in numbers and falling international fuel prices, the costs of sustaining these transfers exceeded the political benefits of not confronting the miners, or destroying their market power by privatization, and this duly occurred.

Energy policy in Britain, as in most countries, is almost by definition politicized, for to leave the choice of fuel to an undistorted market is thought to characterize the lack of an energy policy. Even after the privatization of all the energy industries, the British government felt the need to defend its unprecedently noninterventionist stance after the collapse of the coal market in 1992 by arguing that "The aim of the Government's energy policy is to ensure secure, diverse and sustainable supplies of energy in the forms that people and businesses want, and at competitive prices." (DTI 1993, p. 12) "The Government's energy policy therefore centres on the creation of competitive markets." (DTI 1993, p. 3) Nevertheless, the government still retains power to enforce strategic fuel stock holding at power stations and controls access of Norwegian pipeline gas to the U.K. market. In 1998 the newly elected Labour government imposed a moratorium in new gas-fired generation.

In the postwar years, energy policy meant above all political interventions to influence the fuel burned by the CEGB, understandable in a world still far from the ideals of free trade and currency convertibility, with a thin international coal market, recovering from a war in which control over oil supplies had been a decisive strategic weapon by the major powers (and the *casus belli* of the Japanese). Into this arena

came the Atomic Energy Authority, heavily involved in weapons production and as such at the heart of British defense policy. This large
and rapidly growing body was clearly anxious to develop a civil
nuclear industry, initially to supply plutonium for the weapons
program but later perhaps more for reasons of technological imperial-
ism, and to diversify their sources of support. Their advocacy was
greatly enhanced by their ability to not inquire too closely into the true
cost of nuclear power, and the belief they fostered with politicians that
nuclear power not only provided energy diversity and independence;
it was also a field in which Britain lead the world. Building up the
nuclear construction industry was therefore a key part of the strategy
of industrial revival and exploiting technological advantage.

Their moment came when the 1956 Suez crisis revealed the insecu-
rity of oil supplies, and they were successful in convincing politicians
(who needed little persuasion) to dramatically increase the amount of
nuclear capacity ordered. This was achieved against strong resistance
from the CEGB, who knew that the costs of new coal-fired stations was
falling rapidly. The CEGB was sceptical of the reliability of the
unproved technology and the accuracy of the cost forecasts of the
Atomic Energy Authority (which failed to allow for known improvements in coal plant) (Hannah 1982, p. 177). Later the ill-fated Advanced
Gas-Cooled Reactor program provided further evidence of the success
of the nuclear lobby, while the Government's concern to ensure the survival of three nuclear construction companies resulted in the construction of five full-scale stations to at least three different designs based
on the experience of only a single 30 MW prototype (i.e., less than 5
percent of the design size). A more realistic assessment of the relative
costs of different designs would almost certainly have selected the
foreign water reactor design, (probably a boiling water reactor). In 1987
the pressurized water reactor (PWR) was finally selected after an
exhaustive inquiry (started in 1982) for a new generation of nuclear
power stations for the 1990s. Only one, Sizewell B, was built, and plans
for later stations were dropped after a government inquiry (DTI 1995)
concluded that nuclear power was uneconomic in Britain.[3]

In later years both British and European energy policy continued to
influence the choice of fuels. Coal has been protected in Britain by a
hydrocarbon duty on oil since 1961. This duty was extended to Orimul-
sion (a suspension of bitumen in water that can be burned in oil-fired
thermal stations) when that fuel, priced at international coal parity, and
in many ways resembling coal, looked likely to undermine the market

for British coal after electricity privatization. The only logic for the hydrocarbon duty is protective—carbon or sulphur taxes would also be applied to other fuels, whereas coal is exempted from all excises.

The European Community prohibited the burning of gas in electricity generation until the late 1980s, on various very doubtful grounds—that it was a premium fuel to be reserved for high value use, that it would increase dependency on Russian supplies, but most plausibly that it would threaten the indigenous coal industry in Europe. Finally environmental pressures, particularly over sulphur emissions from coal-fired electricity generation and concerns over global warming from carbon dioxide emissions, provided additional reasons for allowing gas to be used as a fuel for generation. In most European countries gas-fired generation is now cheaper than any alternative for new power station construction. Of course, Britain is not alone in politicizing energy policy, and energy security has been critical in past conflicts, as Yergin (1992) convincingly demonstrates. Indeed, the very difficulty of conceptualizing and measuring energy security offers scope for spurious political arguments designed to support particular fuel or industrial interest groups.

As in most countries, both domestic and major energy consumers are important interest groups, and they influence the level and structure of tariffs. The major energy users have some bargaining power through their ability (in some cases) to autogenerate.[4] Most are in traded goods sectors facing stiff competition from foreign rivals, who in turn are often given preferential tariffs for electricity. In Britain this was achieved by setting tariffs by reference to the imported price of coal, not the domestic price, thus exempting energy-intensive industry from the implicit cost of the coal subsidy. More controversially, they also appear to have paid short-run avoidable costs rather than long-run marginal costs, but since capacity was in excess supply in the later period, this could be defended as economically efficient.

Domestic consumers are voters, and their influence was decisive in discouraging the Labour government from raising prices in the late 1940s, despite a desperate shortage of electricity-generating capacity and fuel. As coal was rationed to domestic customers, they switched to electric space heating, which made the shortage of coal worse and resulted in extremely costly power cuts to industry. The Labour government had to contend with Conservative newspapers like the *Evening Standard* carrying the headline "You own the electricity industry . . . AND UP GO THE PRICES" (cited in Hannah 1982, p. 33). Public opposition prevented the major price rises that were required to discourage wasteful domestic electricity use. A serious lack of economic understanding about the principles of efficient pricing, in both government and the industry, did not help. Later economic analysis arguing for a rather simple version of marginal cost pricing did little to encourage a sensible level of prices in this highly capital-intensive industry, and the result was that over the entire period of nationalized ownership the rate of return on investment was only 2.7 percent in real terms (Newbery and Green 1996).

The other main interest group in any large nationalized industry is the workers. We have seen how the power of the miners influenced British fuel policy. German miners were similarly successful in defending their interests by forcing electricity consumers to pay high taxes to pay for the subsidies to coal mines (Newbery 1995a). Power workers had an even more direct strike threat over electricity supply. Centralized wage bargaining kept basic hourly wage rates relatively low in the 1950s, and large-scale overtime working was used to raise earnings, but lowered productivity. Despite various changes, manual workers' earnings were still below the average for manufacturing industry in 1970, and an overtime ban to support a pay claim caused the government to declare a state of emergency in December 1970. The ban was called off after a week, and the resulting Court of Inquiry recommended a large increase. Since that action, workers in the industry have tended to be near the top of the "earnings league," and there has been very little further industrial action in the industry leading to disruptions in supply.

A more dramatic illustration of the rents enjoyed by workers under public ownership comes from the considerable reductions in employment in the successor companies to the CEGB after privatization. In 1989, on the eve of privatization, the CEGB employed 47,000 workers, but by 1996 the four successor companies together employed just over 21,000 workers, or 44 percent of the earlier figure, producing about the same amount of electricity. The individual generators experienced an even greater decline in workers per kWh generated, achieving reductions between 58 and 62 percent in the six years from 1990 to 1996, while the absolute numbers of workers fell by 73 percent in National Power, by 64 percent in PowerGen (both of which closed plant as well), and by 39 percent in the still public Nuclear Electric.[5]

We saw in chapter 3 that one of the motives for privatization in developing countries has been the heavy burden state enterprises placed on public finances, and the apparent difficulty of financing needed investment by further state lending. This argument carries no weight when applied to the electricity industry; as figure 4.1 shows, the state was well able to finance the extraordinarily high rates of investment in the austere postwar period up to the mid 1960s. Since then the industry's investment needs have been very modest, with the Treasury requiring net transfers to the Exchequer. Indeed, chapter 6 will present the results of a social cost–benefit analysis of restructuring and privatizing the CEGB, which shows that the government probably made a financial loss from the sale, even though the restructuring was socially beneficial. Nor did most consumers benefit, suggesting that the restructuring and privatization was primarily driven by the quest for efficiency, of which the obverse side was a desire to take on the public sector unions that were seen as the main source of Britain's inefficiency and poor competitiveness.

It is difficult to judge how far changes in the balance of interest group bargaining power, or in the costs and benefits of regulation, were responsible for the restructuring and regulation proposals. Certainly introducing competition in generation was the swiftest way to reduce the power of the coal lobby, which was clearly a political aim. It also had the unintended and politically unattractive consequence of undermining the case for nuclear power, which had been championed by Mrs. Thatcher. A simpler explanation is that BT and British Gas had been privatized as de facto monopoly utilities, and there was considerable public opposition to the concept of transferring unrestructured public sector monopolies directly into private ownership. In the words of the 1993 Conservative Manifesto: "Merely to replace state monopolies by private ones would be to waste an historic opportunity. So we will take steps to ensure that these new firms do not exploit their powerful positions to the detriment of consumers or their competitors." Electricity privatization offered a realistic opportunity to address that criticism. The consequent collapse of the market for coal seems to have come as a surprise to most politicians (though it was completely predictable, and was predicted in confidential studies produced in preparation for privatizing the coal industry).

4.3 Dynamics of Regulatory Reform in the Bell Telephone System

Restructuring network utilities to introduce competition is far easier if they are initially in public ownership, for competition normally involves rebalancing tariffs to align prices closer to costs. The pattern of regulated tariffs and charges in a private vertically integrated network utility normally creates reasonably secure and predictable income streams as part of the regulatory compact. While the utility remains a vertically integrated statutory monopoly protected against entry, any cross-subsidies are purely internal transfers that cancel out. The utility is less concerned with the structure of tariffs for different services offered than their overall revenue producing ability.

If the industry is split up or liberalized, then the various parts of the industry become keenly aware of the revenues allowed to that part or service, and these revenue streams will be capitalized into the market value of that part of the business. If cross-subsidies cannot be sustained in the face of competition, then the income streams may have to change considerably and with them the asset values. The resulting wealth redistributions are likely to be fiercely resisted by those who lose. For example, if electricity consumers are allowed to contract freely with any generator, and if the regulator mandates open access to the trans-mission network, so that the utility is obliged to treat all customers and generators equally when scheduling capacity and transmission, then it will no longer be possible to charge the average total cost of expensive nuclear plant when independent power producers can enter and gen-erate with cheap CCGT technology. The nuclear power stations will be "marked to market" or revalued in the same ruthless way that futures contracts to buy or sell a commodity at some future date will be repriced each day in the market.[6] The future revenue stream selling electricity from the nuclear power station at a price that cannot rise above the cost of new generation will be discounted over its remain-ing life to give a modern equivalent asset replacement value, which may be a small fraction of its written down original construction cost. Owners of such power stations will resist reforms that prevent them from recouping their sunk investment, arguing that to do so breaks the original regulatory compact.

The history of the Bell System leading to the breakup of American Telephone and Telegraph Company, AT&T, provides an excellent example of an induced structural change in a private utility caused by regulatory pressure, which may be contrasted with the more planned restructuring of an industry facing privatization. The unfolding drama is told with a keen sense of lost opportunities by Temin (1987), and a more positive assessment of the economic costs and benefits of liber-alization by Crandall (1991). The telecoms industry, like the electricity industry, is both large and capital intensive. The value of gross capital stock of all telecoms (including noncommon carrier systems) in the United States was $525 billion or just under 3 percent of gross reproducible fixed assets in 1988. Employment was 639,000 in 1371 companies with 130 million access lines, though by 1993, employment had fallen to 536,000 while the number of lines had risen to 149 million, suggesting an increase in labor productivity of lines per employee of 37 percent in five years or 6.5 percent per year.[7] The gross capital stock of the common carriers was $438 billion with annual revenues over $100 billion (about 2 percent of GDP) in 1988 (Crandall 1993, pp. 7, 49).

AT&T was, until 1984, also remarkably integrated, not only in the long-distance and local telephony market but also into equipment manufacturing (Western Electric) and R&D (Bell Labs). This integration undoubtably helped to achieve equipment compatibility and the rapid and efficient diffusion of technical improvements throughout the system. Although under integrated ownership, AT&T was organized into local operating companies and a long-distance carrier (Long Lines). The local operating companies were distinct legal entities with separate accounts, regulated by the state Public Utility Commissions (PUCs), while Long Lines was regulated at the federal level by the Federal Communications Commission (FCC).[8]

The source of the tensions that set liberalization in train was the imbalance between long-distance and local tariffs. During the Second World War there was excess demand for long-distance traffic, which generated large accounting profits in Long Lines. Rather than reduce interstate tolls and exacerbate excess demand, it was decided to reallocate costs and revenues between the local and long-distance carriers. Long Lines allocated more of the cost of equipment to local operators, which justified them in receiving a larger share of the revenue. This was used to subsidize domestic and rural consumers, and thus to help realize the company's vision (and legislative goal) of universal service.

The interest groups are easy to identify: The domestic consumers' interests are defended by the state regulator, who has an incentive to reallocate the rents on interstate calls to his clients. This could be achieved and concealed by the complexity of cost allocation in an interconnected system such as Bell's, where much of the equipment serves both local and long-distance needs. A significant fraction of the cost of the network lies in the local loop from the subscriber to the local exchange, and thereafter calls can be sent by switches along a variety of possible routes. Such switches typically serve the network as a whole rather than local or long-distance calls exclusively. For example, when it came to allocate equipment between the separated companies in 1982 to 1984, there was considerable dispute over the class 4 switches (extremely sophisticated electronic switches costing $20 million each) which were primarily involved in long-distance routing but designed to handle some local switching functions (Temin 1987, p. 330).

Given the degree of arbitrariness in allocating joint and common costs, it was not difficult to argue for a more favorable allocation to the better-organized local interest groups. The same process can be seen in most telecoms companies, most noticeably for international calls, which typically generate large profits to subsidize domestic services. In 1947 AT&T decided to allocate costs between local and long-distance calls in proportion to relative use, known as "subscriber line use" or SLU, and this basis for cost allocation was supported by the FCC. Over time the costs of the local loop, which is labor intensive to install, kept pace with inflation, but switching and the capacity of long-distance lines experienced rapid technical progress. As long-distance costs fell relative to local costs, and interstate traffic grew rapidly, so local regulators pressed for more of the rents to be reallocated to the local operating companies. They succeeded by obtaining congressional support and overruling the wishes of the FCC, so that by 1980 four times as much interstate plant was allocated to (and charged out by) the local operating companies than under the SLU allocation (Temin 1987, p. 26).

Figure 4.3 shows the evolution of U.S. telephone prices deflated by the consumer price index on a logarithmic scale from 1970 to 1996. (Equal percentage reductions in the real price are therefore represented by equal vertical distances.) Until 1984, local, intrastate and interstate charges moved almost in line with each other, falling about 35 percent over the period or 3 percent per year (i.e., RPI − 3). Thereafter the series rapidly diverge as rates were rebalanced. While local charges rose somewhat, interstate calls fell at RPI − 5.5 for the next 12 years, indicating the degree of rebalancing that was possible (and which was still not exhausted by 1996).

The development of microwave radio technology put this overpricing of interstate calls at risk from entry, and the FCC, anxious to encourage competition in equipment (Motorola manufactured microwave radio systems) and also service, decided in 1959 to allow entry where this would be cheaper than the existing service—in part to allow users to choose a lower-price, lower-quality service.[9] This would have been

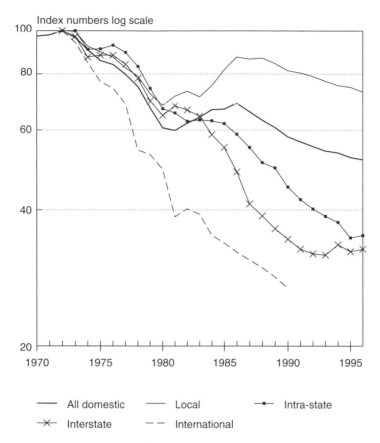

Figure 4.3
U.S. real telephone price indexes, 1972 = 100, deflated by CPI.

fine if the tariffs charged by AT&T reflected cost, in which case an entrant with lower costs than the tariff would indeed have been of lower cost, but otherwise it could lead to cream skimming with possibly inefficient entry.

AT&T wished to forestall this by competitive pricing on routes vulnerable to entry (high volume intercity routes); they introduced new tariffs that on some routes cut charges by seven-eighths (Temin 1987, p. 32). Bell argued that the existing averaged rates had encouraged universal service, and should be protected against inefficient entry, which should be subject to close scrutiny, and against which Bell should have the right to respond with tariff realignments—so that it would have the power to defend its monopoly by competitive pricing but competitors would have little encouragement to enter. This understandably provoked the Justice Department into charges of predatory pricing to forestall entry. "AT&T wanted to act like a competitive firm in defense of its monopoly over telephone services. The FCC . . . wanted the Bell System to act like a regulated monopoly in a market that the agency had just recently made competitive" (Temin 1987, p. 39).

The Justice Department, presumably less well informed about the complexities of cost allocation and tariff setting, and less subject to the tensions between the FCC and the state PUCs over the allocation of costs and rents between their constituencies, had long been suspicious of the market power of AT&T and its potential for abuse. When entrants into the long-distance carrier market like MCI complained about the terms of access to the local loop, they were sympathetic to the claims of foreclosure, rather than seeing the access issue as complicated by cross-subsidies. Access pricing is a complex problem which has only recently attracted the careful analytical study that it deserves, and in the early 1970s regulatory understanding of the allocative role of pricing was minimal.

If the FCC was not well informed on these issues, the Justice Department, whose role was to uphold the antitrust legislation on the statute books, took an even simpler view of the issue. Consequently the Justice Department filed a suit against AT&T for monopolizing interstate communications in 1974.[10] Once the matter was in the hands of the courts, legal interpretation was clearly going to be decisive over economic argument. The FCC allowed the court to have a free hand, arguing that it had no jurisdiction over restructuring AT&T, which should properly be handled as an antitrust matter.

In due course AT&T realized that the only resolution to the problem of cross-subsidy and interstate competition was to divest the local operating companies, and in 1982 AT&T proposed a Modification of Final Judgment (MFJ), that is, of the 1956 Final Judgement (Consent Decree) that it replaced, to separate the regional Bell Operating Companies (RBOCs) from AT&T, to restrict their actions to local exchange operations (and not to compete in interstate traffic), and to grant equal access to all interstate carriers. This divestiture, completed by January 1, 1984, thus removed the opportunity and incentive for anticompetitive cross-subsidization, and constituted a structural remedy to the perceived anticompetitive behavior of AT&T. Temin concludes (p. 336) that three factors contributed to the breakup: intercity competition was a destabilizing and cumulative process, the ideology of deregulation was important, and the rigidity of AT&T impeded adaptation to meet these challenges, since it was too well adjusted to life as a public utility monopoly. In that sense AT&T's own interests were less effectively pursued than those of its competitors, the agencies, and the courts.

The political pressures to cross-subsidize local consumers from interstate traffic remained, and the access charges to the RBOCs were still set by the local PUCs, though limited by the possibility of local bypass, that is, for large users to connect directly with long-distance carriers. The access cost of the local loop is a fixed cost, independent of usage, but the FCC regulates interstate carrier access by a subscriber line charge ($3.50 per month in 1993), and an access charge of 7 cents per minute regardless of time of day or duration of call. According to Hausman, Tardiff, and Belinfante (1993), these access charges comprised 40 to 50 percent of long-distance carriers costs and were five times the incremental cost of long-distance access. Thus the FCC continued to ensure that transfers are made to the RBOCs, who in turn could use the revenue to subsidize local use. This they did by subsidizing the fixed costs of the local loop. The average monthly fixed charge in 1990 was $17.79 (including taxes and the FCC-set subscriber line charge for long-distance access), while the incremental cost of providing access varied from $18 to $24 per month for residential customers. The authors argue that PUCs are motivated to keep fixed charges low and tax long-distance calls in order to meet universal service goals, but these equity goals would be better met by raising the fixed charge and lowering the long-distance tax, as well are reducing the substantial inefficiency in this form of cross-subsidy. Their argument is that demand for a telephone is determined by the total cost of access and use, and even poor customers make sufficient long-distance calls to benefit from an efficient rebalancing.

More recently, Wolak (1996) has used household expenditure data to estimate the welfare gains from a revenue-neutral rebalancing of reducing long-distance rates and increasing local charges. The results show that if the revenue-neutral change requires an equal percentage change in both, then more than half the phone-owning population is (very slightly) worse off, but if long-distance rates are cut by twice the percentage increase in the local charge, then just over half the population gains. Faulhaber in his comments on the paper argues that the second case is closer to a revenue-neutral switch, but even so, it would require a sophisticated consumer to work out by how much its use of long distance would increase before more than half believe the change would be desirable.

Crandall and Waverman (1999) have used a more informative sample of household bills, which describe the telephone rates faced by each household, to perform a similar exercise, and they also find that more than half the sample of all but the richest group of consumers would be worse off, as would more than 40 percent of the richest class. The unweighted total benefits are large, but they are concentrated on a minority of phone users (fairly evenly distributed by income). The losses from rebalancing for most customers were tiny (less than $6 per year), while the average gain was much larger.

Pressures to liberalize the Bell System reflected the changing balance of interest groups precipitated by technical change, but although the form of regulation had to change in response to the restructuring, the objectives of the local interest groups continued to be served despite the resulting inefficiencies. It is hard to believe that the result would have been chosen if the sole criterion had been the public interest, though it was an understandable outcome of bargaining over the rents.

Kaserman, Mayo, and Pacey (1993) test the interest group theory of regulation against the public interest theory on the regulation of intrastate long-distance calls after the liberalization of the long-distance market, which should have removed the need for regulation. Intrastate, as opposed to interstate, calls are subject to regulation by the PUCs rather than the FCC, and differences between states can therefore be used to identify the factors influencing the choice of regulation. The question addressed is which set of variables best predicts whether a given state will deregulate intrastate long distance. The answer is that the interest group theory variables (representing the strengths and stakes of the major interest groups) are statistically significant and have the right sign, while variables representing public interest (strength of competition, extent to which universal service is met) are not significant. The results also help to explain the lethargic pace of deregulation of this industry.

In a subsequent work Caudill, Im, and Kaserman (1993) test the interest group or economic theory of regulation against a range of alternatives, such as the public interest theory (interpreted as following the advice of the regulatory agency), the capture theory, and simple rules of thumb, in making a regulatory ruling. The ruling was the allowed rate of return for private electricity utilities, and the result was that the economic theory was statistically better than any other alternative, though some of these alternatives "came uncomfortably close to equalling the performance of the former." The evidence from these two papers strengthens the anecdotal case history evidence given earlier that regulation reflects interest group pressure, and will therefore be less socially efficient than the public interest or normative theory of regulation would suggest.

4.4   Assessment of the Dynamics of Regulatory Change

A pessimistic conclusion from the positive theory of regulation is that there is no room for economic analysis or policy advice, for what happens is the inexorable working out of the initial balance of power, and the evolution of technology and demand. Such a Newtonian or even Marxist theory of economics is anachronistic—we live in a period familiar with contingency, chaotic systems, and history-dependent evolution rather than the gravitational attraction of a unique equilibrium. What is strikingly evident from the historical record is that periodically an industry may reach a crux or turning point, when several alternative evolutions open up and one is chosen. At such moments information and analysis or vision can transcend sectional interests, usually because the future implications of action are sufficiently opaque that it is difficult to discern where interests lie.

To take a recent example, the structure of the British electricity supply industry chosen for privatization was dictated by the pressure of the Parliamentary timetable, coupled with a contrived ignorance in government about the costs of nuclear power. A well-briefed Department of Energy should have argued that the nuclear stations were always going to present commercial difficulties. The evidence showed that their sale should await a clarification of their costs, which would be greatly eased by creating a market for their product—in short, waiting until they had been marked to market before attempting their sale. Had that simple decision been taken early, more time could have been devoted to deciding the number and size of the conventional generators, with considerable benefits to competition, entry, and the fate of the coal industry. The decision was muffed because the Department of Energy failed to inform itself about the economics of nuclear decommissioning and the commercial realities of selling unspecified but potentially enormous liabilities to private investors.

In that, they were repeating earlier mistakes repeatedly made by politicians, advised by their ministries, about the commercial logic of nuclear power—in their choice of design, size of program, and the lack of willingness to stabilize the design before construction. The enthusiasm of scientist/engineers to try out full-scale models at public expense is not surprising. That the civil service failed to suspect their motives and collect sufficient information to give pause for thought by their political masters is a measure of their technological and economic naivety. It need not have been so, and in France it probably was not so. What emerges is that the power of some interest groups derives from the willful ignorance of decision makers, rather than their ability to inflict damage if not successful. From that, economists should take encouragement that informed analysis can have decisive effects at critical moments.

The Bell System case shows clearly that both the Justice Department, in bringing suit, and the FCC, in allowing competition but not tariff rebalancing, had considerable autonomy in taking actions which had enormous long-run repercussions on the structure of the industry. Brock (1994) gives an insider's view of the conflicts between the different public agencies, which he defends as the necessary price for the doctrine of checks and balances to prevent the potentially abusive concentration of power in a centralized government. He observes that unlike airline deregulation, there was never any consensus on what reforms were needed. The Department of Justice believed that the FCC had been captured by AT&T and hence sought a structural remedy rather than a regulatory remedy, which would have been left to the FCC to devise.

Justice was also anxious to keep the FCC out of subsequent regulation, which it believed would be achieved by divesting the Bell Operating Companies that operated within states, and were therefore subject to regulation by the PUCs. There was a subsequent and considerable dispute over the setting of access charges. Logically these largely nontraffic sensitive costs should be included in the local rental fee, and the PUCs argued plausibly that such fees should be set by the PUCs, not the FCC. As a result of the FCC's determination to retain control over these charges, they eventually reached an inefficient compromise in which part of the long-distance rent transfer to the local companies would be made by increased monthly charges and the balance through a fixed charge per minute.

It is difficult to judge how far the agenda of the Justice Department and the FCC was dictated by their (imperfect) understanding of economic issues (market power, foreclosure, access pricing, tariff setting), rather than the pressures of interest groups (though the agenda may have been set by these interest groups). Brock (1994) argues that the agencies were frequently operating on factually doubtful premises, about the size of the benefits from operating an integrated system (which ex post seemed smaller than claimed), about the amount of cross-subsidy (shown to be much larger than claimed), or about economies of scope in the provision of services by the RBOCs, which the FCC initially thought low but was subsequently persuaded that they were higher.

The power of economic analysis and economic facts in influencing change was thus potentially present, though economists were arguing on both sides of the liberalization debate and may have canceled out. AT&T certainly had access to very considerable economic talent to defend its policies, and the rapid development of utility pricing theory was partly prompted by the problems AT&T faced (e.g., see Sharkey 1982; Baumol, Panzar, and Willig 1982).[11] On the other side, economists were increasingly arguing that deregulation and liberalization would yield efficiency gains. We will consider further below whether the outcome was beneficial, even if the Bell System were broken up for the wrong reasons.

4.5 Competition versus Regulation

The claim made at the beginning of this chapter was that regulation is inevitably inefficient and would be better replaced by competition where this is possible. The sources of inefficiency are several: regulated prices may deviate from costs in order to transfer rents to favored groups, noneconomic objectives may be important and costly (universal service, energy security), while cost-of-service regulation reduces incentives to improve efficiency. Public ownership is rather like cost-of-service regulation, and costs may be inflated through excessive employment and excessively expensive capital. Price-cap regulation attempts to improve incentives by mimicking a competitive market in which the producer cannot influence the market price, and can therefore only increase profits by reducing costs. The problem with price-cap regulation is that to secure adequate investment, it must err on the side of allowing above-average profits, since the risks of an investment strike exceed the costs of higher prices and profits. It therefore runs the risk of becoming politically unsustainable unless the price-caps are periodically reset in line with costs. This will be fully appreciated by the utility, with the result that price-cap regulation acts more like a profit-sharing form of regulation in which the utility keeps profits created by cost reductions until the next price review, but thereafter transfers them to consumers in lower prices. Such profit-sharing schemes inevitably reduce the incentives for cost reduction.

The idea of using business models to benchmark utilities and hence reduce the information asymmetry about the feasible level of costs is attractive, and has been written into the Chilean legislation. It seems to offer the incentive advantages of price-cap regulation and the cost-based advantages of rate-of-return regulation, but in regulation, as elsewhere, there is no free lunch. The obvious problem is that the utility will argue that the model ignores important features of reality. The water regulator in Britain is specifically enjoined to use information from the other water companies to assess comparative performance. Horizontal mergers between water companies are automatically referred to the Monopolies and Mergers Commission, and one of the questions asked is whether the claimed reduction in costs is sufficient to offset the loss of information which would otherwise be provided by having a separate comparator company. This information is used by the regulator to set the price controls, and with fewer observations he has less information to lower prices to the expected level of efficient costs. The MMC has so far rejected several mergers because the value of the information that would be lost with the merger was thought to be higher than the efficiency gains from merging, indicating the potential value of such benchmark models.

Nevertheless, each water company argues that its own costs will be higher than the benchmark for local reasons—hillier country, drier climate, porous soil, more agricultural residues, more urban streets, lower population density—and it is almost impossible to take these into account in the benchmark model without using cost information from the local water company. The problem is more acute in water than in electricity, while telephone models may be less sensitive to local conditions. Nevertheless, as long as utility-specific information is needed to calibrate the model, there is some loss of incentive compared to a truly external competitive test.

There are several further problems with the use of industry models for benchmarking. In Chile the industry counterproposes its own model, which of course is designed to produce a more generous outcome and to justify the industry's choice of investment and consequential costs, restoring the link between cost and price. Adjudicating between models can be costly. If the regulator insists that only his model is valid, there are still problems. The regulator must choose whether the model assumes that the utility made the right choice of investment, or whether it starts afresh each time and asks what is the current best practice choice. If this differs from the existing capital stock because of technical progress or changes in fuel prices (e.g., of gas vs. coal), then earlier investment choices will have to be depreciated faster.

In a truly competitive market managers judge the period over which they have to recover their costs, and the price needed to achieve this, and then choose whether or not to invest. In a regulated market, the investment must be made, and the regulator decides what cost of use, including depreciation, to allow. Again, it is hard to divorce the estimated cost of depreciation from the actual investment decisions made. The regulator faces the unenviable choice of either validating all investment and ensuring that its full cost is recovered, or deciding what depreciation should be allowed, which may not be enough to cover unforseen technical progress. The longer these business models are maintained as the benchmark for determining prices, the closer they are likely to have to become to the actual industry, again weakening the incentive effect of using a truly independent benchmark.

The final step in the argument for replacing regulation by competition is to demonstrate that competition does indeed create the claimed incentives for cost reduction. This is not immediately obvious because at one level the principal-agent problem facing the regulator in inducing the utility to perform efficiently is rather similar to the problem facing the owners of the large corporation run by managers whose ownership stakes are relatively small. Even if incentives to pursue profits vigorously may be muted in both competitive and regulated firms, the incentives to avoid bankruptcy are quite different. Most regulated firms operate under laws that guarantee their ability to finance investment, and hence insure them against the risk of bankruptcy. Firms in a competitive market have no such guarantee, and for competition to replace regulation, it must be possible for new firms to replace old firms should they go bankrupt. If a generation company goes bankrupt, the plant will normally be sold to another company which can continue to operate it (and any creditors will surely insist that the plant continue to operate while a new owner is found, so there should not be any disruption to supply). The most obvious example where removing the threat of bankruptcy reduces efficiency can be found in the Soviet-type economies of Eastern Europe which operated under extreme forms of low-powered incentive schemes and guaranteed survival.

When the first network utilities were privatized as monopolies in Britain, it was claimed that competitive pressures would still compel efficiency, if not in the product market, then in the capital market, where takeover raiders would buy up shares of underperforming utilities, sack the incompetent managers, and reorganize them to increase efficiency. This argument lacked credibility for huge companies like BT and British Gas (with stock market values of £26 billion and £12 billion, respectively, in September 1995), but it was demonstrated to be highly relevant for the regional electricity companies. These local distribution franchise monopolies had been privatized in 1990 with golden shares that allowed the government to block any takeovers until 1995. When these shares lapsed, there was an unprecedented takeover wave, starting in December 1994 with Trafalgar House's bid for Northern Electric, which was beaten off by a counteroffer from the target REC, thereby revealing the size of the cash mountain on offer to raiders.

Table 4.1 shows that in the following few months eight of the twelve RECs were targeted, and six were successfully acquired, two by other

Table 4.1
Bids for RECs

Bidder	Target REC	Offer made	Flotation value	Bid amount	Outcome
Trafalgar House	Northern	Dec 1994	£295 m	£1.2 b	Fail
Southern Co.[a]	SWEB	July 1995	£295 m	£1.1 b	Success
Scottish Power	Manweb	July 1995	£285 m	£1.1 b	Success
Hanson	Eastern	July 1995	£648 m	£2.5 b	Success
Texas Energy[a]	Norweb	Sep 1995	£415 m		Fail
NW Water	Norweb	Sep 1995	£415 m	£1.8 b	Success
PowerGen	Midlands	Sep 1995	£503 m	£1.9 b	Blocked
National Power	Southern	Sep 1995	£648 m	£2.8 b	Blocked
Central & SW[a]	Seeboard	Nov 1995	£306 m	£1.6 b	Success
Welsh Water	Swalec	Nov 1995	£244 m	£872 b	Success
Avon Energy[a]	Midlands	May 1996	£503 m	£1.73 b	Success

a. U.S. utility.

U.K. regulated utilities, one by the vertically integrated Scottish electric utility, Scottish Power, and two by U.S. utilities. The two RECs targeted by the two major generating companies, PowerGen and National Power, were blocked by the government, but one was subsequently bought by another U.S. utility group.

Why were the RECs so attractive to the bidders, and to what extent were the takeovers evidence of effective competitive pressure on the RECs? First, the RECs were sold with little debt, generous price-caps, and relatively little need for new investment, so they could (and did) run down their debt from their large cash flow. The RECs were faced with a choice: Should they seek profitable investments for their surplus cash outside the regulated business, where they had little expertise, should they hand back large dividends to shareholders while choosing a higher and more appropriate gearing (as Northern successfully did in its defense against Trafalgar House), or should they carry on as before, enjoying large profits, handsome managerial rewards, with little pressure to cut costs? Those that chose the last route allowed bidding companies to borrow the funds to finance the buyout, effectively returning cash to the shareholders, reasonably confident that the future cash flow would cover the debt, and perhaps permit the surplus to be transferred to profitable investments available to the larger more experienced buyers. The effect of privatizing the RECs with inadequate debt has been to capitalize a strong cash flow into transfers to shareholders rather than reductions in the national debt.

There is no doubt that these takeovers put competitive pressure on the companies, as any obvious inefficiency would certainly have made the companies even more vulnerable. The problem is that even efficiency did not necessarily save them, since the raiders had other advantages; they could write off unexhausted tax credits against the high profits of their acquisitions. The more favorable depreciation rules under U.S. accounting standards allowed them to declare higher profits to their U.S. shareholders than the RECs were able to declare to the U.K. shareholders. The main reasons for the takeovers may have been tax arbitrage rather than efficiency enhancements. That said, the message sent to incumbent managers is that shareholder value is paramount, costs have to be reduced and profits increased, or managerial jobs will be at risk. However, once the utilities are acquired by diversified institutions, they are somewhat protected from these takeover threats and may again relapse. Product market competition is harder to escape.

4.5.1 Evidence from U.S. Airline Deregulation

Just how effective it is to subject a previously regulated industry to competitive pressure can be seen in the consequences of the *Airline Deregulation Act* of 1978 in the United States, itself one of the main arguments for regulatory reform in other industries. The consequences of airline deregulation have been extensively documented and are usefully summarized in Evans and Kessides (1993).

The consensus of these studies is that deregulation enabled airlines to reduce operating costs, increase load factors, and reduce the average ticket price in real terms (often by offering discount tickets to casual passengers), without adverse effect on safety or the availability of service. The operation of competitive pressures was positively Darwinian, for between 1979 and 1983, 49 new airlines were certified for domestic passenger service and by 1985 had captured 23 percent of revenue passenger miles. With this entry came rapid exit and consolidation so that of the 29 airlines operating in 1978, only 12 survived to 1992 and only 3 of the larger new entrants had survived. Competition at the level of the individual route increased from an average of 1.5 equivalent airlines in 1978 to 2.5 in 1988 (defined as the inverse of the Herfindhal index). Released from the constraints of regulation, the industry reorganized itself onto the hub-and-spoke system to gain economies of density, and possibly also to increase their market power at the level of the hubs.

Most studies have concentrated on the effects of deregulation on prices, which have fallen in real terms, as have fuel costs, while passenger demand has risen. The dramatic fall in real prices in the early 1980s was reversed in 1983, prices then fell to 1985 and rose to 1988, indicating that prices are procyclical. Evans and Kessides (1993) find that between 1978 and 1988 median real prices per mile fell by 16 percent, but the variance of prices increased very substantially so that the bottom quartile fell by 25 percent while the top quartile increased by 11 percent over this period. Although the new entrants had lower costs per seat mile and lower prices, they also experienced lower load factors, suggesting that the incumbents had significant advantages in marketing and seat reservations. Controlling for route characteristics, the impact of actual competition on prices appears quite small, with prices falling 3.3 percent when a route moves from monopoly to duopoly, while adding an additional carrier reduces prices by a further 1.5 percent, suggesting that monopolies do not have much market power and supporting the potential contestability of these routes. On the other hand, dominant firms at a hub obtain a price advantage of between 4.7 percent and 16 percent, with this price advantage correlated with the market share of the dominant regulator.

Morrison and Winston (1996) note that since deregulation the airline industry has been characterized by periodic fare wars that have greatly increased the volatility of profits, and lowered profits by some $8 billion, to the considerable benefit of customers (though this transfer represents only about 10 percent of the consumer benefits of deregulation). The worry is the increased volatility will lead to successful calls by the industry for re-regulation, though the authors argue convincingly that volatility and price wars are a sign of healthy competition which benefits consumers and puts downward pressure on costs.

Disentangling the effects of deregulation on costs in a dynamic industry experiencing rapid technical progress and increase in consumer demand with possible economies of scale is obviously very difficult. Baltagi, Griffin, and Rich (1995) have estimated a cost function for airline variable costs and used this to construct a comparison between a counterfactual regulated airline and the actual unregulated airline to identify the effects of deregulation. They distinguish between trunk airlines and nontrunk airlines, which have substantially higher costs than trunk airlines. They find that they can attribute real cost savings of 9.3 percent for trunk airlines and 19.9 percent for nontrunk airlines to deregulation over the period 1976 to 1986, observing that nontrunk airlines still finished this period with 11 percent higher average costs than trunk airlines. The lower survival rate of the nontrunk airlines may have been the incentive to cut costs faster. They certainly increased output more quickly through lower fares, thereby reducing average cost per revenue seat mile. Their higher initial costs may also allowed them to reduce costs more quickly. The cost savings came from improvement of load factors, which accounted for a 4 percent cost saving, a reduction in union wage rates, which lowered costs by 4 to 5 percent, and cost reductions owing to a shift to hub-and-spoke operation. Lower fares allowed faster growth and increased density reduced average costs relative to the counterfactual with continued regulation, particularly for nontrunk airlines.

Airline deregulation thus confronted airlines with the realistic threat of bankruptcy, and these threats caused a radical restructuring of traffic to the hub-and-spoke system which may have created sufficient market power to ensure survival of some carriers despite their higher operating costs compared to new entrants. Opening markets to competitive entry lowered real costs and prices, though not uniformly, and the incumbents retained considerable advantages. This suggests that replacing regulation by competition is potentially attractive, but market power issues may remain; regulation may need to take positive steps to encourage effective competition. The next chapter looks at the experiences of introducing competition into the network utilities, to see how far these predictions are realized in practice.

5   Introducing Competition into Network Utilities

Competition is more effective than regulation at cutting costs to improve productive efficiency, and aligning prices with costs to improve allocative efficiency. If prices have to be held down by a regulator or set by the public owner, then there is an inevitable tension between incentives to improve efficiency and the credibility of the commitment not to claw back those efficiency gains. The ideal solution is for competition to provide both the incentive for efficiency and the means to transfer the gains to consumers. That leaves no rents for renegotiation and hence no threat to the credibility of the arrangement. The most effective place to introduce competition is for the services provided over the network. The aim of liberalization and restructuring is to confine regulation to the core network and thereby minimize the extent of regulatory inefficiency.

The argument for liberalization is that competition provides stronger and less manipulable incentives to efficiency than regulation. Perfect competition would provide the strongest incentives for efficiency and would transfer all the gains to consumers and thus solve the problem of bargaining over rents. But competition is never perfect, and the practical question is how competitive markets have to be in order first, to yield higher efficiency than regulation, and second, to transfer efficiency gains to consumers. The following figures show that the two questions need not have the same answer.

Figure 5.1 shows the evolution of the relative productivity of the CEGB (i.e., electricity generation and transmission in England and Wales) and also that of BT.[1] BT was privatized with no restructuring in 1984, but there was little change in its relative rate of growth of productivity after privatization until the entry of a large number of new competitors after the duopoly review of 1991. In contrast, the CEGB's productivity growth, which had been about the same as U.K. industry

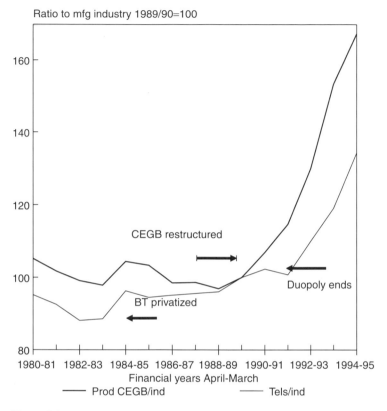

Figure 5.1
Productivity of CEGB and BT relative to the U.K. manufacturing industry.
Source: Newbery and Pollitt (1997).

until privatization in 1990, dramatically accelerated thereafter as a result of restructuring and competition.

Figure 5.2 compares the real prices (i.e., deflated by the RPI) of domestic telephone services and domestic electricity. Real telephone prices rose somewhat after privatization in 1984 as a result of rebalancing but then fell by a quarter, while real electricity prices rose slightly. Tight telecoms regulation transferred the efficiency gains to consumers, while competition in electricity cut costs but raised profits rather than lowering prices.

Competition in network services should lower their cost, but the core network remains a natural monopoly, and remains essential for the delivery of the service. The central structural question is how best to organize the relationship between the network and service providers.

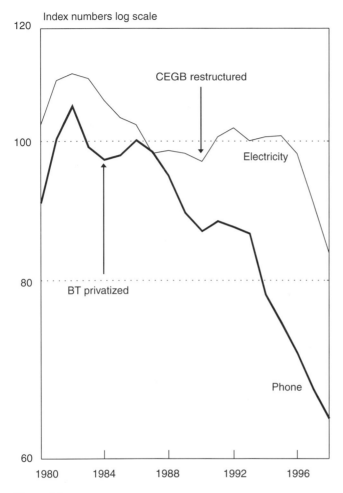

Figure 5.2
Real phone and electricity prices for U.K. domestic customers.
Source: ONS (1999).

They are interdependent: Efficient service delivery requires an efficient network, and investments in one may reduce the costs of the other. For example, if power stations are large, far from demand centers, and have diverse costs (nuclear, coal, hydro), then the electricity grid will need to have high carrying capacity to deliver power from the cheapest source to each demand centre. The least-cost way to expand such a system to meet new demands requires the careful coordination of investment in new generation and in strengthening the grid. It may be

cheaper to locate a power station in a higher-cost location to avoid the
need for new grid investment, or it may be better to build a more
distant or larger, lower-cost power station and strengthen the grid. If,
as in Britain before the creation of the Central Electricity Board, there
is no mechanism for taking such strategic choices, then power stations
are likely to be too small and too dispersed. The evidence from Britain
was that the CEB lowered costs substantially, demonstrating that the
economies of scope between generation and transmission are important and worth securing or protecting.

Coordinating network and service is simple within a vertically integrated utility with a franchise monopoly. Vertical integration allows
service and network to be coordinated, while the franchise makes
demand more predictable and provides the captive market to finance
the investment. If markets replace central planning for services, how
are services and the network provision to be coordinated, and at what
extra cost? Will the fall in costs from competition in services be larger
than the possible loss of efficiency in coordination? Will free entry into
the market for service provision lead to excess entry and excessive
investment, or will the increased uncertainty facing each service
provider about the size of its market raise investment costs and reduce
investment? Will new opportunities for service providers to devise new
services encourage technical progress, or will the loss of a secure franchise market undermine the finance of R&D, which is a public good
prone to market failure? Will market risks encourage a short-term view
of investment compared to the long-term vision of a centrally planned
vertically integrated utility, biasing choice away from high capital cost
but low operating cost investments (in nuclear power, large-scale
hydroelectric schemes), or will competitive pressures eliminate the
gold-plated overengineered state-of-the-art but untried technologies
favored by engineers and encouraged by rate-of-return regulation (the
Averch-Johnson effect)?

Structural reforms to introduce competition are likely to have far-
reaching effects on the distribution of rents, the distribution of risks,
the rate and direction of technical progress, the choice of investment,
and the forms of regulation required. The costs of restructuring are considerable; restructuring will only be worth undertaking if the gains are
larger. The argument of this chapter is that the design of structural
reforms has a considerable impact on both the costs and benefits of liberalization. The costs increase with the amount of restructuring, while
the benefits depend on the speed of introduction and effectiveness of

competition. As always, the range of feasible choices is circumscribed by the balance of interests affected—politics is the art of the possible. It is well to be aware of the redistributions that might occur, the strength of groups adversely affected, and whether there are alternative reforms which are almost as good and which will attract less resistance, or which will lead to the same ultimate destination by a less divisive and costly route.

This chapter compares the two major ways of introducing competition into network utilities: unbundling, or separating out the competitive activities from the core network, and liberalizing access to a vertically integrated utility. The CEGB and BT illustrate the two approaches: the CEGB was unbundled, but BT (and almost all telecoms companies that have been liberalized) was kept vertically integrated. This chapter will set the scene for the detailed industry studies of the next three chapters; it will suggest that there are strong regulatory pressures for unbundling gas and electricity, where the economies of scope or coordination seem modest, but not for telecoms, where these economies appear more important.

Institutional reforms may also have a profound effect on the path of future regulatory reform by encouraging or discouraging competition and innovation. Statutory monopolies at one extreme protect incumbents from the need to experiment to find the least-cost solution to consumers' needs, while offering opportunities for building technically attractive solutions to the company's desires. A large part of the case for allowing competition is to liberate the potential for both discovery and market testing, so that bright ideas that fail the market test can be weeded out without consumers having to bear the cost. If regulators have to approve investments (as under cost-of-service regulation), then they may both be too cautious in allowing new developments, and too slow to rule against uneconomic investments, in both cases because they share the responsibility for protecting both consumers and the utility. Hausman (1997) estimates that regulatory reluctance to let AT&T develop mobile telephony may have cost consumers lost consumer surplus of up to $50 billion per year and perhaps $100 billion in total. Similarly, lifting the regulatory restrictions on voice-messaging services in 1988 ten years after they were proposed, led to annual welfare gains of $1.3 billion, suggesting that the regulatory delay cost consumers billions of dollars. In electricity, the costs of uneconomic nuclear power investment have been borne by consumers, not by the shareholders who in a competitive market would shoulder the risk.

The reasons for regulatory caution and protection are understandable. Franchise monopolies have huge power to cross-subsidize new ventures from their existing captive market, so they may use the franchise to develop sources of unregulated income, leaving consumers to pay for any losses but allowing shareholders to capture any profits. Similarly regulators are willing to enter into a compact to allow the utility to recover the costs of investment provided that they are judged prudent, used and useful, at the time of the investment in order to both encourage investment and lower its cost by reducing risk. With the benefit of hindsight, some of these investments may turn out to be white elephants. If they were provided in a competitive market, consumers may pay higher prices for successful projects (which have to include a return to cover the risk of failure) but will avoid the costs of failed projects. More to the point, failures may be abandoned more quickly, reducing the total cost to society, while the prospect of high returns to success may create goods or services that regulators could not imagine.

If network utilities are already in the private sector, then liberalization may precipitate restructuring (as in the case of AT&T) or require it as a condition for participating in reforms (as with the U.S. electricity supply industry). Where the network utilities are publicly owned, there is a prior question of whether privatization is necessary for competition to achieve its full potential benefits, or whether part or even the whole of the existing utility can remain in public ownership.

5.1   State Ownership and Competition

The main goal of utility reform in Britain was to transfer ownership to the private sector rather than to introduce competition. In contrast, in New Zealand and Norway the main goal was to improve the efficiency of the network utilities by introducing competition, without necessarily privatizing them.[2] Other countries with a strong tradition of public ownership of public utilities are now required to liberalize access to their networks—in Europe under pressure from various directives of the European Union, and in Canada as a requirement to continue trading with the United States. The raises an obvious question: Is it possible for publicly owned utilities to be restructured and regulated to introduce competition in such a way that the benefits of competition are realized without the state losing its claim on the increased profits from increased efficiency? That is, is competition compatible with public ownership?

If we look around the world, it is clear that there are a number of possible models of competition involving state-owned utilities, each of which raises different issues. In Britain, the nuclear power stations proved unsalable when the electricity supply industry was restructured in preparation for privatization in 1989, and they were withdrawn from the sale. In England and Wales, the nuclear power stations were placed in a public limited corporation, Nuclear Electric plc, whose ownership remained with the government. Nuclear Electric competed with the privatized generating companies in selling electricity into the Electricity Pool (the spot market) each day, though initially it was restricted in the contracts it could sign. Its performance dramatically improved, and in the five years after restructuring in 1989, labor productivity increased 88 percent, output increased by nearly 50 percent in the troubled advanced gas-cooled reactors (AGRs), and the fuel cycle contracts were renegotiated. Operating costs for all Nuclear Electric's stations fell from 5.2 to 2.7 pence per kWh.

It had always been the government's intention to review the nuclear industry in 1994, and this was completed in May 1995 with a recommendation that the newer types of nuclear stations (AGR and PWR) should be privatized. This was successfully done in June 1996, with the older stations retained in public ownership and eventually merged with British Nuclear Fuels Ltd., the publicly owned nuclear fuel reprocessing company. The British experience is therefore one in which a state-owned enterprise competed in an industry that was always intended to be privately owned, and where public ownership was really only a default option with an effective sunset clause—when the older stations are closed down the state-owned company will exit, leaving the industry completely private.

Norway, in common with several other countries, has municipally owned generation and distribution companies competing in a pool, with high-tension transmission in public ownership as Statnett. Municipally owned utilities coexisting with privately owned utilities were common in the early days of public utilities, but typically they had local franchises and so hardly competed directly, either with each other or with private companies. The innovation in Norway was to restructure the industry to create direct competition, though it seems less likely that municipally owned utilities will invest outside their local jurisdiction, making it important that entry by private generators be allowed.

Municipal ownership differs from state ownership in several important respects. Most obviously different utilities in the same industry have different owners and are thus motivated to compete. Different companies with the same state owner might be encouraged not to compete, or only to compete in certain allowed dimensions. Municipalities have harder budget constraints than the state, and the city fathers are less likely to allow speculative or uncommercial borrowing. Instead, they often look to the utility to behave commercially and to be profitable to create resources for other civic activities. The main concern, which may be serious, is that the utility might provide the means for patronage through excess employment, to which the obvious remedy is competitive pressure. Municipal ownership without a local franchise monopoly has more in common with private ownership than liberalized but vertically integrated state ownership, which brings us to the next model.

5.2   Liberalizing Entry while Retaining State Ownership

Britain attempted to liberalize the electricity industry with the Energy Act 1983, which allowed private power producers to sell direct to final consumers using the national grid as a common carrier. The Act also required area boards to publish tariffs for transmission and to specify the prices at which they would be willing to buy power for their franchise customers. Whether because there was excess generation capacity or because the CEGB restructured its tariffs to make entry unattractive, the Act failed to encourage any entry, which may have contributed to making the later restructuring proposals more radical.

Liberalizing entry into a vertically integrated utility which remains both vertically integrated and state owned is the least disruptive reform, and is one of the models allowed by the European Commission in its Electricity Market Directive (EC 1997). That Directive allows member countries to choose between three models of liberalization: the single-buyer model, third-party access, and a pool. In the single-buyer model, the vertically integrated incumbent publishes transmission tariffs and must be prepared to buy from a buyer and sell to its contracted customer, charging only the published tariff. In addition the transmission business must be informationally separated (by "Chinese walls") from other parts of the business (generation and supply) and must keep separate accounts. These restrictions are intended to ensure equality of treatment between the incumbent's own competitive activities and those of entrants. Under third-party access (TPA), transmission is transferred to a separate company. Buyers and sellers negotiate contracts for power with each other and either pay the transmission company a regulated tariff or negotiate a transmission tariff.

Several European countries, notably France, seem determined to keep the existing electricity supply companies in state ownership, and they have accepted the Electricity Directive under pressure rather than with enthusiasm. One imagines they would not be very upset if negligible private entry took place, and they do not place much emphasis on the benefits of encouraging competition. The single-buyer model can be used to deter entry by keeping transmission tariffs high and cross-subsidizing generation to undercut potential entrants. If the incumbent were solely concerned with efficiency, then it should always be willing to offer its own generation at the relevant marginal cost (depending on the duration of the contract, this might be short-, medium-, or long-run marginal cost). This would ensure that entry only occurs if the entrant is able to provide power at lower total cost for the whole industry, in which case the incumbent would be able to meet consumer demand at no cost penalty to itself. Transmission tariffs could be raised to recover any shortfall (if needed) between marginal and average generation cost. In this case liberalization makes the market contestable and ensures that demand is met at least cost, while not encouraging inefficient entry.

However, it is unlikely that the incumbent is concerned solely with satisfying customers at least cost because it desires either to retain its monopoly profits if privately owned or to enjoy the same monopoly profits in the form of excessive costs or various forms of patronage if in the public sector. Competitive entrants reveal potentially embarrassing information to regulators or government audit committees about the true costs of the industry, and this can lead to a tougher and less attractive regulatory regime for the incumbent. The obvious temptation is for the incumbent to conceal the true avoidable cost of its contestable activities by transferring costs to the monopoly network and by keeping its accounts in an opaque or misleading form. Activity-based cost accounting might exaggerate the extent to which costs are fixed by concentrating on the very short run, while there is an obvious incentive to choose excessively capital-intensive methods of production that have lower avoidable costs (but higher average costs); nuclear power and hydroelectricity are leading examples. The result would be predatory pricing, that is, pricing below the relevant marginal cost. The evidence from a wider variety of examples suggests that it requires aggressive regulation to prevent abusive entry deterrence by vertically integrated incumbents.

If the country wants to retain public ownership and is not committed to competition, then the single-buyer model provides the best defense against entry and hence the best method of retaining complete state control. Separate financial accounting for transmission may make it harder to cross-subsidize the competitive parts of the company, but this can be continued by revaluing assets, writing down those in the competitive divisions and revaluing those in the core network.[3]

On the positive side, the existing SOE may be so inefficient that liberalization does lead to entry, which may have a variety of beneficial effects. Entry may restrict the cross-subsidy from industrial to domestic customers, should provide external performance standards which assist regulation, and in capacity-constrained countries may reduce supply interruptions. The worry is that entry may not happen.

5.3   Procompetitive Reforms of State-Owned Utilities

The most interesting case is where the country is committed to competition but wants to retain public ownership. There can be several reasons for this, including waiting to see whether privatization might be attractive later. Delay might give more time for the regulatory framework to demonstrate its effectiveness, and for the assets to be properly valued as efficient going concerns. The most serious political objections to privatization seem to arise where hydroelectricity is currently severely underpriced. Hydroelectric schemes rarely pay any water rent to the central government. Their operators prefer instead to distribute the rent to their consumers in the form of low prices. Liberalization opens up the prospect of raising prices to efficient levels, set either by marginal thermal plant within the country or in an export market where the price of electricity is substantially above the domestic level.

Thus the Pacific Northwest of the United States might experience a price rise of 58 percent (from 1.91 ¢ to 3.02 ¢/kWh) as a result of moving from the present regulated price to a market determined price as a result of liberalization, and a further 6 percent rise (from 3.02 ¢ to

3.19 ¢/kWh) as a result of opening up trade with California (Hadley and Hirst 1998). While the second increase is modest compared with that owing to moving from a regulated to a market determined price, consumers are likely to view the reason for liberalization as a drive for profitable export markets by the power companies and to resist both. Similar concerns influence attitudes in Norway, where domestic electricity prices were only 68 percent of those in Denmark in 1997,[4] a country to which Norway would like to increase exports. Quebec, with its vast hydro resources and low domestic prices, is also resisting privatization, though it will have to unbundle transmission if it wishes to continue exporting electricity to the high-price New England market south of the border.

While it would be theoretically possible to overcompensate domestic consumers in cheap hydro regions for moving to a market determined price of electricity, it is implausible that consumers would believe in the durability of such compensation. Privatization removes the political control that transfers the hydro rents to consumer/voters, and is likely to crystalize those rents as profits.

New Zealand offers an interesting case in which state-owned electricity supply industry was restructured and corporatized under the State-Owned Enterprise Act 1986 but had still not been privatized twelve years later. The Act had as one of its stated objectives that "The principal objective of every State enterprise shall be to operate as a successful business, and, to this end, to be (a) as profitable and efficient as comparable businesses that are not owned by the Crown; and (b) a good employer; and (c) an organization that exhibits a sense of social responsibility by having regard to the interests of the community in which it operates and by endeavouring to accommodate or encourage these when able to do so." The Act led to the creation of ECNZ, the Electricity Corporation of New Zealand, among others, and to the amendment of the monopoly provisions in the Electricity Act 1968 and the obligation to supply.

The electricity supply industry was gradually restructured from June 1992, when the government published its Energy Policy Framework which sought to improve efficiency by introducing competition (Barton 1998). The high-tension grid was separated from ECNZ and placed in the state-owned enterprise (SOE) Trans Power New Zealand Ltd. in 1994, while Contact Energy Ltd., a company with about one-quarter of the country's generating capacity, was split off as another SOE in 1995. ECNZ sold a combined cycle gas turbine and some smaller hydro generators to third parties, but the market dominance of ECNZ remained a problem. In late December 1997 the government announced its intention to split ECNZ further. Nevertheless, ECNZ remained state owned, and one of the reasons for delay was a lack of clarity as to who owned the large number of local electricity supply authorities and particularly the power boards. (Culy, Read, and Wright 1996). The public objected to selling shares in assets which they argued they had already paid for, while a free distribution of shares was criticized because it might lead consumers to sell out and create ownership concentration.

Compared to Britain, then, SOEs remain dominant in the electricity supply industry, and are supposed to create competition largely by competing with other SOEs, at least until more private generators enter, or existing SOEs are privatized. New Zealand is a test case in the viability of state-owned companies competing with each other, despite sharing a common owner.

There is no doubt that exposing SOEs to the rigors of the competitive market place can dramatically improve operating efficiency. Culy, Read, and Wright (1996) report that between 1987 and 1992 ECNZ nearly doubled its labor productivity (from 4.5 to 8.5 GWh per employee (though some of this was cosmetic as the amount of contracting out increased dramatically). ECNZ reduced unit operating costs (excluding fuel and capital) by 13 percent in real terms, increased average plant availability from 73 to 91 percent for thermal plant and from 87 to 95 percent for hydro, and increased profits from N.Z. $262 million to over $400 million while reducing wholesale prices by 8 percent in real terms.[5]

The more interesting question is whether competitive pressure can be sustained in the longer run against other SOEs with the same shareholder. Suppose that one company is more successful than the other SOEs at cutting costs. It could stay the same size and earn higher profits, but it is more likely that the incentives facing management would encourage output maximization through cutting prices.[6] The other companies would then probably make losses, and the state as owner might attempt to broker a more collusive and less competitive outcome to avoid these losses.

ECNZ offers several salutary lessons about the problems than can be encountered with continued state ownership. Despite having backward linkages to coal and gas corporations, it has not attempted to vertically integrate into fuel supply, nor to compete downstream with the distribution companies, perhaps because it would be seen as an abuse of its dominant position. More worrying, Culy, Read, and Wright (1996) note that ministers have the right to instruct the company on certain matters (which have to be publicly reported), and although that right had not been exercised, there has been evidence of political influence. After a government inquiry into a hydro crisis in 1992 (which found no fault with ECNZ), half the senior management left the company, and it is becoming difficult to recruit good senior managers when they are so exposed to public criticism.

It is interesting to contrast the U.K. utilities, particularly water, where public and government criticism is also severe but where managers accept that it goes with the territory. It may be that some of these concerns in New Zealand would be alleviated if there were more competing SOEs in each sector, as each might then feel less exposed. It may be, though, that the U.K. utility managers take comfort from knowing the difficulty the government would face in taking steps against any one of them or their companies, whereas a state owner could do just that. High salaries also provided considerable compensation.

Devolving investment decisions is even more difficult. If SOEs compete with private companies, there is a concern that since SOEs have an owner who cannot go bankrupt, they will always be able to borrow on more favorable terms and enjoy a lower cost of capital (higher gearing *and* lower debt interest). Public and private companies facing different costs of capital will not allocate investment funds efficiently between them, nor will the public firms be under such pressure to minimize investment (and other) costs. If SOEs are free to issue debt and compete with each other, they may overinvest, both because the cost of capital will be understated by the riskless interest rate at which they can borrow and because each SOE will have an incentive to expand at the expense of the other, with little penalty if they become loss making. If they are not free to issue debt, then the state will have to manage the investment budget, and the different SOEs will effectively be branches of a single ministry. After a while the state as owner may be increasingly convinced of the "inefficiency of wasteful competition" and recombine the companies back into a single company, or it may be persuaded that the only solution is the final step of privatization. It is interesting to observe that several state-owned utilities on the continent have been active buyers of foreign utilities when they were privatized. Some of these were European telecoms companies that may well be privatized, but there seem to be no such plans for Electricité de France (EdF), an active foreign investor who bid for the privatized

London Electricity REC in 1998—renationalization by another means? Perhaps foreign investment by SOEs can be handled as efficiently as by private shareholders, where the record of British utilities is not that impressive.

There is one interesting exception to the argument that public networks cannot sustain efficient competition with private networks, and that is provided by the BBC (British Broadcasting Corporation, which was the first public corporation and the model for the Central Electricity Board). The BBC is financed by compulsory license fees, and it competes for audiences with privately owned radio and television companies, which are financed by advertising. The BBC is debarred from commercial advertising in the United Kingdom, though it is free to sell its programs to foreign media companies. It is structurally divided into different channels (BBC1 and BB2, Radio 1–5). These are intended to appeal to distinct audiences, and they compete more directly with their functional equivalents in the private sector than with each other. This rather uneasy form of ownership and competition periodically comes under attack by those who argue for complete privatization of all public media, and it is equally strongly defended by those who argue a merit good case for public support. If this merit good case is accepted, then competition appears to have considerable advantages over the previous public monopoly, in terms of both efficiency and democratic accountability.

To summarize, it seems difficult to accept the logic of maintaining state ownership of enterprises that can operate effectively in a competitive market, except as a transitional state in which the regulatory institutions are established and developed, interest group opposition overcome, the best industrial structure evolved without the pain of stranded assets, and the assets properly priced in a market that has increasing confidence in the commitment of the government to the new structure and ownership patterns.

These strictures do not apply to municipally owned utilities, though other considerations may require a change of ownership. We have seen how in Britain municipal ownership prevented utilities reaching viable economic scale because of the difficulty of joint ownership and/or the unwillingness of the citizens of one jurisdiction to volunteer control to those of another jurisdiction. Where economies of scale dictate larger entities some other form of ownership—perhaps a joint stock company with shares held by the municipalities—may prove superior,[7] and may have to be imposed by the central government.

5.4   The Case for State Ownership of the Network

The argument that privatization is needed if competition is to be efficient and sustainable does not apply to the core network, where competition is not feasible. As the network must be regulated, there may be a case for public ownership, which provides a different form of regulation. Statnett, the electricity grid in Norway, is state owned, though admittedly there is a strong tradition of public ownership with widespread municipal ownership of the local electricity companies with their dams and local distribution networks. Local networks, such as the regional electricity distribution companies, typically provide rather simple services. They are simpler to regulate and value than the core network such as the high-tension grid or the high-pressure gas pipeline system. Local networks are therefore easier to privatize, but they may not be so inefficient under municipal ownership if they operate in competitive markets for the services supplied over the networks. Culy, Read, and Wright (1996) note that the electricity distribution utilities appear to operate well under local public ownership, where competition has increased their responsiveness to customers and reduced cross-subsidies.

The core networks, on the other hand, have a monopoly at the country or state level and usually require a more complex range of services to operate efficiently (frequency and voltage control, storage, etc.). They are therefore harder to value, since it may take longer for their revenue from access and other charges to stabilize and for the mix of regulated and competitive services to reach equilibrium. Selling them early runs the risk of selling them for less than fair market value, and that was certainly the experience for the British National Grid Company, which dramatically appreciated in value between privatization in 1990 and its sale by the Regional Electricity Companies in the flotation of 1995.

Are there any problems with keeping the core network in public ownership while privatizing the competitive services? After all, roads remain publicly owned, while the vehicles operating on them are private, and the same model has been proposed for various continental rail reforms. Of course, if the state continues to own upstream or downstream companies in competition with private companies, there is the normal fear of discriminatory treatment, as with a liberalized vertically integrated company. The test case therefore is where state ownership is confined to the network, and instructed to operate in the public interest. If there is already an independent industry regulatory agency, then logically it should be subject to the same oversight as the rest of the industry, but if the competitive activities have been both unbundled and horizontally divided to create adequate competition, it might not be thought necessary to have a specific industry regulator, but just the normal competition authorities. This is the case in New Zealand, which has adopted "light touch" regulation and reliance on fair trading laws.

The main argument for privatizing even the regulated core is that the capital market can still apply a competitive threat to inefficient management which encourages cost reductions and stimulates innovation. National Grid Company in Britain has divested its Pumped Storage Business and invested in a telecoms company, Energis, which uses the high-tension pylons to provide rights of way for long-distance telephony. It is active in managing and buying foreign transmission systems, which it would find difficult to do under the stifling Treasury rules as a public corporation. EdF, though, does not seem to suffer the latter handicap.

The other worry about state ownership of the network is that it is an essential facility to which access might be controlled to secure political goals (e.g., forcing generators to buy British coal) or which might be used to extract monopoly profits for the state, which is effectively another form of taxation. The U.S. regulatory system suggests that this can also happen with investor-owned networks.

5.5   Assessment of Competition and State Ownership

Restructuring publicly owned network utilities to introduce competition inevitably raises the question of privatization, and the evidence suggests that while there may be good reasons for delaying privatization, it is hard to imagine that effective and efficient competition is sustainable in the public sector. There are obvious advantages in restructuring some time before privatization, to ensure that the new companies are viable, to test the new markets and establish market prices for the services, to ensure that regulation is effective, and to create a set of accounts on which the businesses can be valued. There are also advantages in making it clear early on that the ultimate goal is privatization, as that is likely to provide stronger incentives to managers to improve performance.[8] The real question is whether the benefits of competition are sufficient to offset any loss of economies of scope from unbundling. If economies of integration are strong, the choice is to continue with public ownership of a franchise monopoly, or to privatize the integrated utility and liberalize entry. The combination of a liberalized, but vertically integrated, state-owned utility looks even less likely to encourage the kind of entry that puts competitive pressure on the incumbent than a privately owned utility, given its inherent advantage of access to cheap finance and political power over entrants.

In Britain, while there is widespread agreement that the economy benefited by privatizing telecoms, electricity and gas, there is less agreement that the water and rail privatizations were beneficial. In the case of water, the prospects for competition are extremely limited, and a cynical view is that privatization was a way of the government abandoning its long-standing resistance to what it (and many consumers) saw as expensive upgrading to meet new EU pollution standards of doubtful economic merit. Public ownership with its likely restrictions on the ability of the water companies to invest by keeping prices low might have been economically defensible, though politically difficult in the European context. In the case of rail, competition for franchises largely substituted for competition among train-operating companies, and the jury is still out on whether the high costs of restructuring and the loss of the benefits of integration will at some stage be offset by improved efficiency.

5.6   Vertical Separation or Liberalized Access?

For competition to be effective, new firms must be able to offer the utility's customers some service, and if their costs are lower than those of the incumbent utility, it must be possible for them to be able to undercut the incumbent and secure access to those customers. At a minimum this requires that they have a legal right to offer the service— that is, to end any statutory franchise—and that they are protected from unreasonable discrimination either by fair trading laws or regulatory oversight. The two main types of service are those offered to final customers over the network, and those offered to the network operator. Electricity can be generated but needs to be transmitted over the network of wires to reach the final customer. Gas storage or frequency stabilization are services that may be competitively offered to the gas and electricity network operators, respectively, to assist them in providing stable and reliable services. Meter reading, planning, and building new electricity transmission lines or new gas pipelines need not be provided by the incumbent utility, but they often are.

The importance of the distinction is that services offered to the network have only one buyer. So, although there may be competition between service providers, there is no guarantee that the market will work efficiently. The incumbent may favor more costly in-house provision whose cost (plus an attractive profit) can be recovered through the regulated business. Services that are offered to final consumers have the potential to be competitive if each side of the market has an adequate range of choice of suppliers or customers. The problem then is one of fair access to those customers through the network of the utility. There are in turn two main ways in which access may be granted, either by structural separation or liberalized access. The more drastic reform of structural separation or unbundling separates ownership of the network from that of the services offered over it. This should ensure that all service providers have equal access to the network, which has no reason to favor one over another.

Liberalization requires no restructuring of the incumbent utility but that entrants have the ability to access customers over the network in competition with the incumbent's own services. The worry is that the incumbent will discriminate in favor of its own service provider. Each has its advantages and drawbacks. Vertical integration facilitates coordination and may economize on transactions costs, but ensuring equal access may increase regulatory costs and create other inefficiencies. Separation may avoid the regulatory problem of ensuring equality of access but creates other regulatory problems in the design of access pricing to retain coordination benefits.

5.6.1 *Restructuring Options in Different Utilities*

Restructuring a previously vertically integrated network utility to separate off the potentially competitive parts requires defining boundaries between the core natural monopoly and the rest of the industry. In electricity this is reasonably simple—the wires businesses (both the high-tension grid and the lower-tension local distribution systems) are the obvious natural monopolies, while generation and supply (i.e., contracting with, metering, and billing the customer) are potentially competitive. Various ancillary services to maintain stability and security of supply may need to be centrally managed but can be competitively supplied (through tendering, through contracting, or through the market). A fully competitive solution also requires open access to transmission and distribution, and a electricity market into which any (licensed) generator is free to sell and all customers above a certain size are free to buy.

There are variants on this theme, which simplify regulation in some respects but may require greater vigilance against other kinds of abuse. If customers are denied access to the electricity market, then some of the problems of pricing transmission are avoided. The utility owning transmission then acts as a monopsony buyer in the market, and generators would need long-term contracts to avoid exploitation. There could be competition to build, and possibly to own and operate new generation, though there may be conflicts of interest if the utility also owns or can build new plant. Another configuration is one in which the grid also owns significant generation but is a common carrier serving an electricity market open to large customers as well as other generators. The major competition issues have to do with policing competition between companies that combine monopoly and competitive activities, and these are most easily avoided if generators are denied ownership stakes in the grid.

In the case of gas, the natural monopoly elements are the high-pressure transmission system and the lower-pressure distribution systems, though there is some ambiguity about what kinds of storage are so critical that they should be managed by the pipeline operator.[9] Production is obviously tied to the gas field in a way that thermal electricity generation is not tied geographically to its fuel source, though hydro power is. Gas production may need a dedicated pipeline connection to the high-pressure system, and whether competition is feasible will depend on the number of gas sources supplying the system. In Britain there are many competing fields, and the situation is similar to electricity. In the state of Victoria, Australia, though, there is a single company controlling the pipeline and gas field, making competition problematic (though long-term contracts for gas and transport could be allocated among various competing companies provided that those contract terms were cost related). Most continental countries are interconnected and go to considerable lengths to ensure diversity of suppliers, so again "gas on gas" competition is feasible, even where vertical integration limits explicit competition. In the United States competition has been actively promoted by the regulatory authority. Given competition in production and the existence of a reasonable number of gas traders (including producers), competition in supply becomes feasible, as with electricity.

In telecoms separation is more problematic, as modern packet-switched systems can route calls along any path, not necessarily the shortest route nor one lying within a defined geographic area. We have already seen how difficult it was for AT&T to agree the appropriate allocation of its valuable Class 4 switches between the local and long-distance companies, and one could argue that there is no natural boundary for the natural monopoly, which must be drawn pragmatically at the place where the efficiency gains of increased competition outweigh the benefits of integration. The answer will vary with the size, sophistication, range of services (broadband vs. voice), and rate of expansion of the system, as well as on regulatory constraints on the range of services that may be provided, the degree of cross-subsidization required, and so on.

As the costs of switches comes down (and, as they are essentially computers, they are subject to Moore's Law, according to which the cost of microelectronic devices halves every 18 to 24 months) and the demand for data transmission capacity increases, the amount of capacity required to connect each major population center will increase and will support an increasing number of parallel circuits. In most countries everything beyond the local loop ("the last mile") will cease to be a natural monopoly. One version of unbundling would then be to allow competition between different network owners by ensuring that they all have access to the local loop. The main problem is that one of the networks will normally own this local loop, which acts as a bottleneck to the customer and allows the exercise of market power unless carefully regulated. One theoretically attractive solution to this problem which virtually avoids the problem of natural monopoly is for subscribers to pay for and own the local loop to the nearest switch, leaving them free to decide whether to replace, upgrade, or duplicate the connection (Schecter 1996).[10]

The other approach to unbundling telecoms (and other apparently natural monopolies) is to allow competitors to share the natural monopoly facilities upon payment of an appropriate usage charge to the owner. Again, bottleneck facilities give the owner monopoly power to exploit rivals, which can be avoided by requiring that owners grant access at charges set by the regulator at the correct level. This is easier said than done and could well create a regulatory nightmare. Either the incumbent is able to deter entry by offering unfavorable access terms, or there is little incentive to build infrastructure because other competitors are free to use it without risk and at low cost.

Even where the potentially competitive part can be readily defined, as in gas and electricity, whether it would actually behave competitively if separated will depend on the number of viable competing companies that can be sustained. In the case of gas, this depends on the number of sources connected to the transmission system, while in the case of electricity it will depend on the size of total demand relative to plant size, which in turn will depend on fuel type and age (older plants were usually smaller). For both fuels competition will be affected by the extent of transmission constraints and the contestability of the market, which will depend on the market structure and regulatory constraints. Again, the balance between regulatory inefficiencies ("government failures") and market power inefficiencies ("market failures") determines where or whether the boundary should be drawn.

Finally there are important physical differences in the networks that influence policy. In both electricity and gas, consumers are indifferent as to who supplies the power—there is no need to define property rights in electrons or gas molecules, so there is no need to physically match up individual producers and consumers. Pooling, in which agents are paid for delivering supplies or charged for taking supplies, regardless of destination or source, makes sense. In telecoms, end-to-end integrity of the link is essential, so each transaction is personal. In electricity, supply must be continuously adjusted to demand, and the laws of physics determine electricity flows, with important externalities (loop flows). In gas, short-term storage (line pack) can buffer fluctuations in demand and supply, but while electricity fails to safety, gas fails to danger, making adequate storage and supply continuity paramount. In telecoms, switches route calls but may be congested with call loss, calls are multidimensioned (in demands for bandwidth, peak/mean bit rate, urgency, integrity, error rate), and sophisticated charging may soon become a real-time option (though facilities are normally bundled and sold under simpler contract prices, e.g., per minute, or through line lease). The network is potentially intelligent and perhaps decentralizable and therefore contestable.

5.6.2   Restructuring Choices and the Dynamics of Unbundling

An economist might argue that there is a most efficient industrial structure for each network utility, which will depend on the type of utility, the size of the market (which will depend on population, density, and wealth), the state of technology, and access to resources (gas, hydro, etc.). Any restructuring that fails to achieve this efficient structure will create tensions that can only be resolved by further reforms. A political scientist would probably add that the equilibrium structure will depend on the institutional maturity of the country, and this may impede progress to apparently more efficient—typically more pro-competitive—structures. The rest of this chapter illustrates some of the structural choices of recent reforms, before assessing the options for introducing competition into each industry in more detail in the next three chapters.

Both main types of reform—liberalizing access while leaving the vertically integrated incumbent essentially unchanged and restructuring to separate off competitive parts of the industry—can be observed in Britain. The early privatizations (BT, British Gas) maintained vertically integrated utilities but liberalized access, and it was not until electricity privatization in 1990 that the alternative of structural separation was attempted. The British Telecommunications Act 1981 separated British Telecommunications (later to become BT) from the Post Office and ended its statutory monopoly over the network. The small company Mercury was licensed in 1982, but BT was privatized in 1984 without restructuring, as the sole owner of the network, under the regulation of Oftel. Mercury was licensed as the sole competitor until 1990, and built its own fiber-optic network originally linking large population centers. Mercury had to negotiate terms of interconnection with BT, so that its customers could dial up those subscribing to BT, and vice versa. Clearly, if BT had complete power to set interconnection terms, it would effectively be able to prevent any competitive entry by setting a high enough charge. Not surprisingly, Mercury and BT failed to reach agreement on these interconnection charges. They were referred to the regulator to adjudicate, and access charges were set at a pro-competitive level.

The duopoly was finally terminated in 1991 with any application for a license thereafter to be considered "on its merits." By 1995 there were over 150 operators licensed to compete with BT, including 125 cable TV companies who could offer telephony with cable (of which 80 were actually providing service; Bell 1995). Each operator had a possibly small network connecting his subscribers to a switch which gives access to all other networks, enabling connection to anyone with a registered phone. By January 1997 some 8.4 million out of 22 million U.K.

households were passed by a cable company with a telecoms franchise, and this rose to 12 million households by October 1998 (Oftel 1999). Take-up was 3.4 million by October 1998, and BT's (revenue) share of the domestic market had fallen to 64 percent in 1997–98, and to under 40 percent of international business calls. Although BT remains dominant in the domestic market, the fact that customers can now switch carrier without changing their number (and phone directory entry) makes the market considerably more contestable than it was before.

In contrast, AT&T was restructured by the Modified Final Judgement of 1984, which separated the local Bell Operating Companies (thought to be natural monopolies) from the potentially competitive long-distance carrier. Between then and 1997, any long-distance call has to pass between at least two and usually three different companies. On the other hand, local calls remain within a vertically integrated franchise monopoly. Finally, after lengthy public discussions, the Communications Act 1934 was revised by the Telecommunications Act 1996, which was intended to protect and expand universal service, encourage competition by allowing local carriers, long-distance and cable companies to enter each others' markets, and to facilitate the creation of a "national information infrastructure." Whether these worthy aims are compatible with effective competition and how likely the Act is to achieve these various goals will be discussed in chapter 7.

As with BT, so it was with British Gas. The Oil and Gas Enterprise Act 1982 removed the statutory monopoly British Gas had on the pipeline system but left British Gas free to negotiate the terms for access. No entry occurred, and British Gas was free to foreclose any downstream competition by specifying uneconomic access charges. The Gas Act 1986 set privatization of British Gas in train and specified the regulatory structure of the privatized industry, but British Gas was kept intact with all the original assets, and granted a licensed monopoly except for large customers (above 25,000 therms per year, lowered to 2,500 therms per year in 1992).[11] Access conditions were left for entrants to negotiate, though they could appeal to the regulator, Ofgas. Between 1982 and 1990 there were ten attempts to secure access, but none was successful. Ofgas felt constrained by the Act to allow transport tariffs at the average cost of transport, which were above the marginal cost. This was in sharp contrast to Oftel's pro-competitive access charging adjudications.

It was not until the Office of Fair Trading forced British Gas to contract for no more than 90 percent of new gas supply in 1989 that entry finally occurred in 1990. Before that, though, a series of investigations by the Monopolies and Mergers Commission and the Office of Fair Trading found that British Gas used its market power to deter entry and competition, and culminated in the recommendation that the trading activity of British Gas should be divested, leaving British Gas with just transportation and storage, as the only way to ensure equal access to these services. The Department of Trade and Industry rejected this recommendation in favor of full accounting separation, mainly because of the government's desire to introduce competition into the domestic market as soon as possible, which complex restructuring would impede (Stern 1994; Spring 1995).

Progress in retail liberalization (i.e., allowing gas traders to offer domestic customers gas supplies) has been rapid, starting with the southwest in April 1996 and extending to all parts of the country by May 1998. The new entrants had the advantage that current supplies of gas are available at considerably lower cost than the earlier long-term contracts signed by British Gas. About 30 percent of customers have switched as each region was opened to competition, in response to a price reduction of about £50 per year or 15 percent of the annual gas bill.

British Gas remained vertically integrated until 1997. Its offshore gas fields (in competition with other gas producers) delivered gas to the beachhead, where it was taken by the National Transmission System to the local distribution zones and to the final destination, along pipes all owned by British Gas. Other suppliers could purchase gas at the beach and pay the charges for using the pipes to deliver to final customers in competition with the incumbent British Gas. In 1997 British Gas decided on commercial grounds to undertake a restructuring similar to that recommended by the MMC. Most of the assets were transferred to BG plc, which owns TransCo, the onshore pipeline system and storage system, and Exploration and Production, which is one of the six largest holders of U.K. hydrocarbon reserves. The other holding company, Centrica, owns British Gas Trading, which in 1996 (before retail competition) supplied gas to 19 million domestic customers, and Hydrocarbon Resources, that owned the two Morecombe gas fields supplying over 11 percent of total U.K. gas requirements in 1996. Thus, although both successor companies are still involved in gas production, supplying customers is now quite separate from the onshore gas transportation business—a condition that seems inevitable if British Gas was to avoid continual regulatory conflict over the introduction of retail competition.

The process of unbundling has continued, for the regulator, Ofgas, has required storage to be competitively auctioned. British Gas (Storage), a subsidiary of TransCo, is already accounted for separately but, despite industrial consultation and regulatory pressure, remained within the same revenue cap as TransCo in the 1998–99 gas year. By 1998, then, the gas industry had been restructured to allow competition into almost every contestable part of the industry, with the remaining parts due to be opened up within a short period.

If BT was liberalized, but remained vertically integrated, while British Gas was compelled by regulatory pressure to unbundle in response to liberalization, the electricity supply industry was the first example where the industry was restructured before privatization. The Central Electricity Generating Board of England and Wales was restructured in 1989 to create three generating companies and a separate transmission company, National Grid Company, whose shares at privatization were owned by the 12 Regional Electricity Companies or RECs, but later floated as a separate quoted company. Competition in supply (i.e., contracting with and billing customers) was originally intended for large customers, but at relatively late in 1989 it was proposed to extend it to all consumers by 1998. Initially only some 5,000 large sites with a demand above 1 MW could buy directly from the pool, and they accounted for about 30 percent of total supply. In 1994, 50,000 customers with demand above 100 kW could buy direct, bringing the competitive share up to about a half. The remaining 20 million consumers were able to choose their supplier from late 1998, again opening up almost all the competitive parts to free and symmetric entry.

The Scottish electricity industry in contrast was organized into three parts: a nuclear generating company (state-owned until 1996), and two vertically integrated generation, transmission, and distribution companies, each of which had long-term contracts with Scottish Nuclear Limited. Second-tier suppliers (i.e., licensed suppliers other than the local distribution company) are free to enter and offer to supply eligible customers and can purchase bulk electricity from the incumbent companies (at the bulk selling price in the English Pool) and pay the (regulated) transmission and distribution charges to the company owning the wires connecting the generator to the customer. As in many similar instances of liberalization without unbundling, entry has been effectively deterred. The regulator has a program of work reviewing the Public Electricity Suppliers over the period 1998 to 2000 and has been clearly concerned to make the Scottish market more contestable. Offer (1998a) gives a list of examples where potential entrants have been discriminated against and deterred from entry.[12] One solution proposed was to separate out the transmission businesses of the Scottish companies, and to create an independent system operator to ensure competitive trading arrangments there. Once again, regulatory pressure may lead to the unbundling of a liberalized but vertically integrated utility.

The new Labour government elected in June 1997 ordered a review of utility regulation and published the Green (i.e., consultation) Paper *A Fair Deal for Consumers* in March 1998, suggesting, among other regulatory reforms, that the supply business should be separated out from distribution, and therefore that the RECs would no longer have a mix of competitive and natural monopoly activities within the same company. Among other advantages, this would allow generators to vertically integrate into supply without owning the wires that give access to consumers. Generation and supply have a natural affinity as a risk-sharing corporate structure. If suppliers contract with customers to sell electricity at a predetermined price (as effectively they must to domestic customers), then higher spot prices in the pool mean higher profits for generators at the expense of the suppliers, while lower spot prices mean higher profits for suppliers at the expense of generators. Volatile spot prices randomly shift profits up- and downstream, imposing risks on both parties that would cancel out if they combined.

Contracts between generators and suppliers can reduce this risk, but the natural contract is for a fixed quantity of electricity (which may vary by time of day and at weekends) at a specified strike price. If demands or supplies differ from the specified amounts, then the differences are normally priced at the (unpredictable) spot price, leaving some residual risk that would be avoided by vertical integration.[13] The main objection to this proposal was the possibly high cost of implementing it. The industry will spend some £800 million setting up the system for retail competition and operating it for the first five years, and has argued that it could easily spend as much again separating out supply from the distribution business. It may be that complete unbundling is not worthwhile, though as we will see below, the initial restructuring in England and Wales was economically justified.

British Rail has been restructured under The Railways Act 1993 in the most drastic reorganization of any network utility. Railtrack owns the infrastructure, signaling, and stations, and its shares were sold to the public in 1996. Three rolling stock leasing companies lease rolling stock to train-operating companies which bid for franchises to operate services on specific network routes. Railtrack procures services from infrastructure service companies and leases most stations to train operating companies, operating under the Office of the Rail Regulator. In 1995–96, the regulator approved 523 station access agreements, as well as 18 passenger track access agreements and 129 freight access agreements. Despite this high degree of unbundling, most of the train-operating companies are protected against competitive entry into their markets for the first four years, have limited protection for the next three years (i.e., until the end of the typical seven year franchise), and only thereafter face full competition (Winsor 1996). We await to see whether this highly complex and costly restructuring is economically justified.

Liberalization, if successful, puts competitive pressure on the incumbent utility and, if unsuccessful, creates pressure for regulatory reform. If the utility remains both integrated and dominant, then it will continue to require regulation, and even if entrants demonstrate that the market is contestable, access terms will still need regulation. Separation may allow regulation to be confined to the natural monopoly elements, but if competition in the separated part is inadequate, the benefits of competition may not be transferred to consumers and may not even be realized if competitive pressure is no tougher than regulatory oversight. The next three chapters consider how successful the various attempts to introduce competition into the network utilities have been in practice, and what lessons can be drawn from these experiments in regulatory reform.

6   Reforming the Electricity Supply Industry

Until recently almost all electricity supply industries (ESIs) were vertically integrated statutory monopolies, operating either under state ownership or as regulated utilities. In 1989–90 the British government restructured the state-owned Central Electricity Generating Board, separating generation from transmission, allocating generation capacity between different companies, and creating a spot market for wholesale electricity to make generation competitive. In the following seven years liberalization spread round the world. Pollitt (1997) found that the ESI had been liberalized to some extent in 51 out of the 62 countries he studied, with privatization in 30 countries, and vertical separation either in place or planned in 27 countries. (See also IEA 1997.)

The industry has probably attracted more discussion over the best way to introduce competition than any other utility, partly because it raises such a variety of complex issues but mostly because a very large number of countries are or have recently reformed this sector. Rail reform may be even more complex. Few countries have embarked on serious reform to date, while electricity reform is on the agenda almost everywhere, impelled by external pressure (e.g., the European Commission Electricity Directive, or the U.S. Federal Energy Regulatory Commission, which also affects exporting provinces of Canada), the need to raise revenue by privatization (Eastern Europe), or the need to attract in private finance in developing countries.

The English model of vertical separation is rapidly becoming the reference model for reform in developed economies where the ESI is mature provided that the system is large enough to support a number of competing generation companies (or has gas, which greatly reduces the minimum viable size of generation companies). It is not, however, the only model, and it may not be the most suitable model in some countries. This chapter discusses the British experience in some detail, as one of the best and longest running examples of a major restructuring to introduce competition, but also surveys some other examples. The first question to address is whether it is possible to introduce competition into the ESI in a way that improves efficiency, transfers the benefits to consumers, and minimizes regulatory problems. If so, then what is the best way of doing so, and what lessons can be learned from recent reforms?

It is too soon to say whether competitive ESIs are sustainable in the longer run, but there are obvious pressures that can already be identified. There are political and regulatory concerns that adequate investment in both base-load and peaking plant will not be forthcoming if the industry is sufficiently competitive to keep prices close to costs. There are commercial pressures to re-integrate the industry and to avoid "excessive competition" by horizontal and vertical mergers. There are concerns about the degree of market power of incumbents, and about the neglect of fuel diversity and longer-run security issues, as well as the social problems of "fuel poverty," and the high prices faced by noncreditworthy customers. One view, which we will need to examine seriously, is that introducing competition into electricity is a transient phenomenon that addresses some currently salient problems but is not consistent with a long-run sustainable equilibrium. If it does not prove possible to create or sustain adequately intense competition to keep prices low, so that generation has to be regulated, then the arguments for vertical unbundling are weakened. If commercial pressures then argue for re-integration in exchange for re-introducing regulation, perhaps privatization will be the only enduring reform in the ESI. These are pessimistic possibilities, but the pressures that might bring them about need to be understood, if only to see how to ensure the sustainability of the most efficient industrial and regulatory structure.

Some of these pressures could be seen at work in Britain when the Conservative government, the proponent and architect of utility privatization, was defeated decisively at the polls. In May 1997 a Labour government was elected with a landslide majority, after 18 years of successive Conservative governments. In opposition, the Labour party had opposed each privatization and strongly criticized the high level of profits earned (and high executive salaries paid) by the regulated network utilities. One of their first actions after the election was to implement one of their Manifesto pledges to impose a windfall tax on all privatized utilities, arguing that they had been sold too cheaply and had made unreasonable profits. They also commissioned (on June 30, 1997) a review of utilities and their regulation, whose terms of reference were "to consider whether changes are required to the system of regulation of the utility industries in order to ensure open and predictable regulation, fair to all consumers and to shareholders, and which promotes the Government's objectives for the environment and sustainable development, while providing sufficient incentives to managers to innovate, raise standards, and improve efficiency." (DTI 1998, Annex A)

The utilities review was prompted by general concerns about the ability of utility regulation to transfer efficiency gains to consumers, but there were particular and long-standing criticisms of the way the competitive market had operated in the ESI. In response the minister for science, energy, and technology asked the electricity regulator to review electricity trading arrangements in October 1997.[1] The English example is instructive, therefore, not only for its early achievements (which were considerable) but for the difficulties revealed when creating competition in electricity.

6.1   Vertical Separation in Electricity: The English Example

The electricity supply industry consists of four distinct activities; generation, high-tension transmission, lower voltage local distribution, and supply (i.e., contracting for and billing final consumers). In Britain, generation accounts for around two-thirds of the industry's costs, transmission for 10 percent, distribution for 20 percent, and supply for the remaining 5 percent. Transmission and distribution (the "wires" businesses) are natural monopolies that require regulation, but generation and supply are potentially competitive. A liberalized and competitive electricity supply industry must have a market (or markets) into which generators sell and from which customers and traders can buy, a transmission and distribution system that acts as a common carrier, with freedom of entry in generation, and freedom for final consumers to choose from whom to contract for supply.

A completely unbundled industry would be one in which the four activities were under different owners, in which no company in any one segment owned assets in any other. This is an extreme and not very common practice. The critical element of vertical separation is to ensure that the link between generation and transmission is severed so that generators do not own transmission and the transmission company does not own generation (except perhaps for a limited amount of fast response generation, e.g., peaking gas turbines, storage hydro, or pumped storage for system stability).[2] Regulation is simplified if generation and distribution are also separate, for then the boundary between the natural monopoly and potentially competitive parts is clearly defined.

If we look at the United Kingdom, almost every ownership combination can be observed. In England and Wales (with a population just over 50 million and a peak demand of just over 49,000 MW)[3] the industry was under public ownership from 1948 to 1990, and for most of this period, the Central Electricity Generating Board (CEGB) operated all generation and transmission as a vertically integrated statutory monopoly, with twelve area boards acting as regional distribution monopolies. The CEGB had interconnectors to Scotland and France, with whom it traded electricity. Scotland (with a population of 5.1 million and peak demand of 5,600 MW, including exports of 800 MW to England) has always retained a degree of autonomy (in law and government) within Britain, while England and Wales are normally treated as a single country.[4] The same is true in the electricity supply industry. In Scotland there were two vertically integrated geographically distinct utilities, combining generation, transmission, and distribution, one serving the north and the other serving the south. Northern Ireland (with a population of 1.7 million and peak demand of 1,500 MW) is physically separate from the mainland, and the grid connection with Eire in the south had been severed by terrorist activity so that it was a small isolated system. It included all four functions within a single vertically integrated state-owned company, Northern Ireland Electricity (NIE).

The Electricity Act 1989 divided the CEGB of England and Wales, with its 74 power stations and the national grid, into 4 companies. About 60 percent of conventional generating capacity, namely 40 power stations with 29,486 MW capacity, were placed in National Power, and the remaining 40 percent or 23 stations of 19,802 MW were placed in PowerGen. The 12 nuclear stations with 7,973 MW capacity were placed in Nuclear Electric, and the high-tension grid, together with 2,000 MW of pumped-storage generation,[5] were transferred to the National Grid Company (NGC). These four companies were vested (i.e., created) as public limited companies on March 31, 1990, at the same time as the 12 distribution companies, now known as the Regional Electricity Companies (RECs). NGC was transferred to the joint ownership of the RECs, and the RECs were sold to the public in December 1990. Sixty percent of National Power and PowerGen were subsequently sold to the public in March 1991, with the balance sold in March 1995.

The original plan was to place the 12 nuclear stations in National Power, which had been given the bulk of the fossil generation in the hope that the combination would be financially viable, but at a late stage it became clear the nuclear stations were not salable at a reasonable price. They were transferred to Nuclear Electric and kept in public ownership, until a further restructuring when the 5 newer advanced gas-cooled reactors (AGRs) with 4,750 MW were transferred to British Energy and privatized in 1996. The 7 remaining old Magnox reactors with 3,223 MW (which had negative net worth) were transferred to the publicly owned British Nuclear Fuels plc, the fuel (re)processing company. The pumped-storage generation of NGC was separated and sold to Mission Energy at the end of 1995, and the RECs sold their shares in NGC when it was floated on the Stock Market, also at the end of 1995.

After privatization, almost all of the RECs became joint investors with Independent Power Producers (IPPs) in building gas-fired combined cycle gas turbine (CCGT) generating stations, whose high efficiency, low capital costs, modest economic scale, and use of cheap fuel made them attractive competitors to the predominantly coal-fired generation of National Power and PowerGen. The next major structural change occurred in 1996, when under regulatory pressure, National Power and PowerGen leased 6,000 MW of coal-fired generation to Eastern Group, one of the largest RECs, which thereby became a major generator with significant distribution assets. Further divestiture of 8,000 MW took place in 1999, again under regulatory pressure.

The Electricity Act 1989 set out a timetable for introducing competition into supply. At privatization the 5,000 consumers with more than 1 MW demand were free to contract with any supplier (or directly from the Electricity Pool), but all other consumers had to buy from their local REC, which had a franchise monopoly. In 1994 the franchise limit was lowered to 100 kW, and another 45,000 customers were free to choose their supplier. From late 1998 the remaining 22 million customers have that right and the REC franchises came to an end.

The Scottish system, with about 10,000 MW capacity, was restructured on March 31, 1990, when the North of Scotland Hydro-Electric Board became Scottish Hydro-Electric, and the nonnuclear assets of the

South of Scotland Electricity Board were transferred to Scottish Power. Both were privatized as vertically integrated regulated utilities in June 1991, free to sell into the English market and use the English Pool price as the reference price for Scottish trading. The two nuclear stations (both newer AGRs) were transferred to Scottish Nuclear and remained in public ownership until they were transferred to British Energy and sold in 1996. Supply competition parallels that in England and Wales.

Northern Ireland was different again. The four power stations (with rather less than 2,000 MW, and a peak demand of 1,500 MW) were sold in a trade sale to three different companies in 1992. NIE, which now just contained transmission and distribution, was sold to the public in 1993. There is no supply competition as all electricity is sold to the Power Procurement Business of NIE under long-term contracts.

Thus England and Wales have gradually moved to an almost completely unbundled structure, as NGC was spun off and divested generation, except that the RECs have subsequently integrated into generation. Scotland contains two vertically integrated regulated utilities who can compete for customers (and sell in England and Wales). Northern Ireland has separated generation from the wires businesses, but transmission, distribution, and supply are combined in a regulated franchise monopoly. NIE's electricity prices were about 23 percent higher than on the mainland in 1996, and the gap widened to 42 percent by 1998 because of the lack of competition in generation and the protected long-term contracts with the generators. Scotland is the farthest from the ideal of separating generation from transmission, and perhaps as a result, supply competition is relatively weak. Consequently there are pressures for further restructuring in both Scotland and Northern Ireland.

6.2 Creating Markets for Electricity

Until recently electricity within an area was invariably centrally dispatched, and the idea of a spot market was almost inconceivable, which raises the obvious question, What is special about electricity that seemed to require centralized control rather than decentralized markets? Why is electricity not like other commodities? In some ways electricity is very like those primary commodities that are traded sight unseen on futures and spot markets. It is remarkably homogeneous (all electrons are identical), and, like other commodities, must be distinguished by time and place—a MWh at 5:30 pm on a winter weekday is very different from (and is often 20 times as valuable as) a MWh at 3 am the following morning. Likewise electricity in the northeast may not be substitutable with electricity in the southwest during periods when transmission between the two is constrained.

The key difference between electricity and other primary commodities is that producers and consumers must be physically linked, with changes in supply and demand propagated through the entire network at the speed of light. Since electricity cannot be stored, supply and demand must be kept in balance second by second. Gas is similar in that producers and consumers must be linked by pipelines, but its physical flow is relatively slow (50 kph or less), it can be stored within the pipe (line-pack) or at storage sites, and its flow through each link separately controlled. Electricity, in contrast, chooses a path through the network satisfying Kirchoff's laws, whereby any change in demand or supply at any node immediately affects the pattern of flows through all the links in the network. The power losses on any link depend on (and increase as the square of) the current flowing along the link, and these transmission losses therefore depend on the geographical pattern of demands and supplies. Changes in supply by any producer or demand by any consumer thus create external effects on all others connected to the network, and these externalities threaten the efficiency of decentralized markets.

Each link in the network has a maximum rated capacity for carrying current, so the flows into each node have to be controlled and may have to be constrained to prevent these transmission limits being exceeded. In addition the quality of electricity (frequency, voltage, phase angle) must all be maintained within tight limits. This makes refined power (meeting these quality standards) different from raw power (MWh), and requiring a host of ancillary services to transform raw into refined power. For example, the immediate impact of an increase in demand (or a fall in supply) is that voltage will drop somewhat, reducing the load, while frequency will fall slightly as turbines slow down as they are called on to work harder. This voltage reduction sometimes shows up as a dimming of lights if a large extra load is switched on, since the power and brightness of incandescent lights is extremely sensitive to changes in voltage. It is therefore important to match supply to demand as closely as possible at the standard voltage and frequency to avoid power fluctuations in consumers' appliances. Finally, in the event of a loss of load or outage, special procedures are required to restore power safely—at least some generating stations must have the capability of starting without an existing power supply, known as black-start capability.

The idea of central dispatch stems from the obvious need to meet all these requirements efficiently, at a speed measured in milliseconds, and to handle all the interactions that give rise to externalities. The systems operator or dispatcher starts with a forecast of demand at each offtake node at each moment, based on past experience, temperature, time of year (which affects lighting demands), working or nonworking days, and allowing for special events.[6] Generating plant is distinguished by how much it costs to start up, maintain idling under no load, and produce power at different levels of utilization, as well as how quickly its power can be increased (how many MW per minute), and whether, as with nuclear stations, they are slow to restart if shut down or not. Given a forecast pattern of demand and set of transmission constraints, the dispatcher can compute the least-cost solution to meeting that demand. The result will be a dispatch order, telling each station when it needs to be available to generate, when to turn on, and what level of output to produce.

If everything were perfectly predictable, that would be the end of the story. But plant may fail, as may transmission lines and transformers, while demand may differ from that predicted. Given the reliability of the various components and the uncertainty of the forecast, a certain amount of reserve capacity will be needed to make sure that any shortfall in supply is rapidly met. Some events, like equipment failure or demand surges, require almost instant responses, which can come from a number of sources. Storage hydro (and pumped storage) can be switched on and run up to full load almost instantly, while some load may be interruptible and can be shed to reduce demand; some thermal stations can be run at part-load, with the ability to rapidly increase output. Other events can be anticipated some time before (bad weather increasing demand), giving time for stations that are available but were not originally scheduled to run to be called upon to generate. Each deviation from the original schedule must be checked to see that it does not overload transmission links (nor increase the risk that the links would be overloaded in the event of a further unforseen failure), which may require running plant that is far "out of merit order"—significantly more costly to run than the set of plant originally chosen. A reliable and stable supply of electricity requires the system operator to ensure an adequate margin of reserve capacity (of generation and transmission) that can be called on over different time scales to meet imbalances in any part of the system but that will normally not be required.

In addition to the short-run problem of operating the existing system efficiently, the system will need to be expanded to meet growing demand. This will require decisions on the timing, size, type, and location of new generation and transmission capacity, again with the object of securing least-cost expansion and delivery to final customers. The problem is difficult to solve since time lags are long (4–8 years for traditional thermal or nuclear plant, though 2–3 years for modern CCGT plant), demand forecasts and future fuel prices uncertain, as are future technologies, environmental and safety constraints.

In most systems a computer-optimizing package is used to produce the dispatch schedule and indicate which plant should be held available, and in the CEGB the program was called GOAL (generation ordering and loading program). The longer-run problem of choosing the type and location of power stations and transmission reinforcements should also have been a technical problem of finding the least-cost expansion path given probability distributions of demand and relative fuel prices. In practice, investment decisions were heavily influenced by political concerns over security of supply, ensuring a market for British coal, and developing a nuclear capacity to diversify risks and support an industry in which Britain had established, but then lost, an early world lead. Improving these investment decisions offered the best chance of lowering the cost of electricity.

6.3   Restructuring the CEGB and the Creation of the Electricity Pool

The decision to introduce competition in electricity was political and strongly supported by the secretary of state for energy, the prime minister, and the chancellor, all of whom were aware of the earlier unpopularity of privatizing British Telecom and British Gas as monopolies. The Department of Energy was charged to propose a method of creating competition, and they hired Merz and McLellan as consulting engineers to advise.[7] They also appointed management consultants, merchant bankers, and legal experts to advise on restructuring and market design issues. Stephen Littlechild, who subsequently became the director general of electricity supply (DGES), that is, the regulator, was invited to advise on regulation. The key questions they faced were whether a market-based system would deliver the "merit order"(i.e., the least-cost system of dispatch) and whether the grid could be controlled to ensure stability and security in a decentralized system (critically, whether the lights would stay on).

Breaking up the CEGB was bitterly opposed by its chairman, who argued that the obligation to supply meant that someone (the CEGB) had to ensure that adequate capacity was built in time. This would best be done using the single-buyer model, as the 1998 European Union *Directive on Electricity* would eventually name it, in which the CEGB contracted with independent power producers for adequate capacity, and would be regulated in the charges it could levy so that it would recover its costs and avoid stranding assets. This did not meet the requirements of a competitive market, and the technical consultants were asked whether it was possible to separate transmission from generation and organize a spot market. When they agreed that it could, the die was cast and the decision to unbundle the CEGB was taken and set out in the Government White Paper of February 1988 (Department of Energy 1988).

The practical problem was that the merit order was defined by the short-run avoidable cost of generation, which is largely the fuel cost and only about half the total cost. A market that only paid the short-run avoidable cost would bankrupt the generators, whereas one that paid the average cost might fail to dispatch plants according to their avoidable costs. Early proposals considered a variant of the single-buyer model, in which buyers (the RECs) would hold long-term contracts with individual stations and pay a capacity charge to cover the fixed costs, and an energy charge that covered the avoidable cost of generation (including any start-up and shutdown costs)—effectively a two-part tariff. The complexities of creating a market in these individual contracts with their two prices were too great. The idea was abandoned and replaced by a single market, the Electricity Pool. The final design to emerge owed much to preserving what were felt to be the desirable features of the old CEGB system of dispatching stations, including the GOAL scheduling program, except that this would now receive information submitted by the companies acting commercially rather than using the technical details of station performance.

The Pool operates as a daily, day-ahead, sealed bid auction. Every morning before 10 am, generators must declare which of their generating sets will be available the next day[8] and announce five prices for each generating set that will hold for the following day. The five prices are the start-up cost in £, the no-load cost (£/h), and three-generation costs (£/MWh) for three ranges of output to allow for the systematic way in which thermal efficiency varies with utilization. In addition generators can also vary the large number of technical parameters specifying the rate at which the station can be run up or down, and any limits on its range of output, for example, in each day's bid. At the same time all suppliers submit estimates of the demand at each of the grid supply points from which they take power, for each half-hour of the following day. NGC then runs GOAL exactly as in the CEGB days, except that this now uses bids rather than costs and hence tries to minimize the financial operating costs over the next day. The output of this program is known as the unconstrained schedule, since it ignores all transmission constraints.

In order to encourage truthful revelation of avoidable costs, the market is run as a last-price auction in which the system marginal price (SMP) is set equal to the bid price cost of the most expensive generating set called on in that half hour.[9] This would work if there were a sufficient number of independent bidders, so the chance of any one influencing the price is small. If the price is set by another company, then the best response for a generator is to bid avoidable cost and earn profits equal to the SMP less these avoidable costs. If he bids higher than avoidable cost and above the SMP, he forgoes this profit, while bidding below avoidable cost runs the risk of being asked to generate at a loss.

Unfortunately, there were initially only two companies with plant whose output could be varied and who could therefore set the price. Each one could, by raising the prices of marginal plant, increase the revenue earned by all of its inframarginal plant and hence had an incentive to distort its bids to the Pool. On the other hand, setting a single price payable to all generators dispatched mimics a competitive market and allows generators with low avoidable but high fixed costs to recover at least some of their fixed costs in the market. The problem of ensuring adequate reward for making plant available (and building plant to ensure adequacy of supply) was met by paying a capacity charge for each unit of capacity declared available to generate, whether or not it was called upon. The capacity element is given by LOLP × [VOLL − max (SMP, the set's bid price)], where LOLP is the loss of load probability, the risk that demand will exceed capacity, and VOLL is the value of lost load, which was set administratively to reflect the cost of demand exceeding supply at £2/kWh in 1990–91 indexed to the retail price index. For sets in operation, SMP exceeds their bid price, and the sum of SMP and the capacity element gives the pool purchase price, PPP. All companies buying electricity from the pool pay a pool selling price, PSP, whose difference from the PPP is the uplift, which covers a variety of other payments made to generators.

Some of these payments are for essential ancillary services, such as the provision of reactive power to keep the transmission system stable. Others reflect the fact that the unconstrained schedule, on which the payments are based, is not the actual operating schedule. Transmission constraints, and unexpected changes in demand and plant availability, mean that some sets will be run when they were not due to run in the unconstrained schedule. They are paid their bid prices, which exceed SMP (since they would have been operating under the unconstrained schedule if their bids were lower). Sets that are unable to operate because of transmission or other constraints are paid their forgone profit, equal to the SMP less their bid price, as compensation for the inability of the grid to accommodate their bid. (In effect, they have a firm contract for the right to be dispatched, and are compensated if this cannot be exercised.) Finally the capacity payments to generators who are not called upon, and payments for providing reserve, must be financed.

The uplift is set so as to recover all of these costs on a daily basis, and was initially smeared over all consumers, rather than borne by the grid (for failing to provide transmission capacity and to provide it with appropriate incentives for reducing their cost), and/or to those consumers responsible for constraining on more expensive plants. As a result of an enquiry, a share of these costs was subsequently allocated to NGC. Generators also pay an annual fee proportional to declared net capacity to remain connected to the grid (and hence available for dispatch). This fee varies across the country, and can be negative for zones in which there is a shortage of capacity relative to demand.

Eligible consumers can buy directly from the Pool, or under contract from a supplier (who might be a generator, or a REC, or a trader who in turn contracts with generators and buys in the Pool). Large customers need a meter that records consumption every half-hour and suppliers have to pay transmission use of system charges to NGC, and distribution use of system charges to the local REC, while domestic customers pay a modest fixed charge and a price per kWh to cover generation, transmission and distribution charges. Transmission and distribution are regulated by the Office of Electricity Regulation, Offer.

The Electricity Act 1989 allows the regulator acting in consort with the Office of Fair Trading to refer noncompetitive behavior to the Monopolies and Mergers Commission (which the secretary of state for trade and industry has power to block; see appendix B at the end of chapter 2). The idea here is that the potentially competitive parts should be subject to normal competition law.

6.3.1 Dealing with Risk and Transition: The Role of the Contract Market

Pool prices vary significantly over the course of the day, the week, and from month to month. For example, in 1995, the minimum pool purchase price (PPP) per MWh was zero, the maximum was £1,108 (U.S.$1,835) and the (time-weighted) average was £24 (U.S.$39.7), while the coefficient of variation (CV, which is the standard deviation/average) was 1.9. In 1997 the CV had fallen to 0.6, while the CV of pool prices in three other countries (Victoria, Australia, the North Island of New Zealand, and Norway) varied from 0.3 for the hydro system in Norway to 4.4 for the coal-based system in Victoria in 1997, though the last was around a price less than one-third that in the English pool (Offer 1998b, app. 1).[10] On a typical day the maximum price may be three to five times the minimum, but it can be far larger. Figure 6.1 shows the variation in the monthly average prices over the year (which suppresses the considerable variability over each day and week), as well as showing the evolution of both the level and volatility of the pool prices since privatization in real terms.

As with other volatile commodity markets, such price risks need to be (and mostly are) hedged through financial instruments or contracts. The normal contract is a contract for differences (CfD) under which a generator receives, in addition to the normal pool price for any sales, a sum equal to the specified strike price *less* the pool price, multiplied by the specified number of units contracted. In addition to contracts for differences there is a market for electricity forward agreements (EFAs) which allow the main components of electricity price uncertainty (e.g., the spot price between certain weekday hours, or the capacity charge) to be hedged on a short-term basis. This differs from a classic futures market primarily in its lower liquidity and the resulting difficulty in pricing and liquidating specific EFAs, which may have been responsible for the disappointing performance of the market to date.

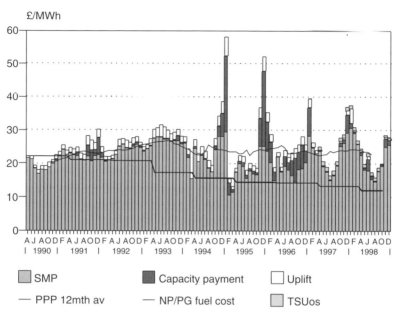

Figure 6.1
Prices in the electricity pool.

Contracts were also critical in managing the transition from a vertically integrated company able to pass all its costs through to its captive customers to a competitive industry in which customers were free to buy from the cheapest supplier. The two major transitional problems facing the designers were that British coal was considerably more expensive than imported coal (and was soon to be revealed uncompetitive against gas) and that the average costs of nuclear generation, once all the decommissioning and fuel cycle costs were included, were considerably above the likely equilibrium pool price. The second problem was dealt with by imposing a nonfossil fuel obligation (NFFO) on the RECs (to buy electricity generated from nonfossil fuels, overwhelmingly nuclear power) and imposing a fossil fuel levy (FFL) on all fossil generation (initially at the rate of 10.8 percent of the final sales price). This levy was paid to Nuclear Electric to build up a fund to meet its decommissioning liabilities (of about £9.1 billion or U.S.$15 billion, which can be compared with the privatization proceeds from selling off the CEGB of just under £10 billion).

The first problem was handled by a series of take-or-pay contracts between the generators and the still state-owned British Coal for the first three years at above world market prices. The generators in turn held contracts to supply the RECs for almost all their output, for up to three years, that allowed the costs of the coal contracts to be recovered from the revenue from these contract sales. There was the additional and very important benefit that the profit and loss accounts of the generators and RECs could be confidently projected for the first three years, and these provided the necessary financial assurance for the privatization to proceed.

The electricity market can thus be thought of as a number of interacting and interdependent markets—a physical market for spot energy (the pool) and markets for risk sharing (the contract and EFA markets which trade financial instruments). The contract market also gives a market for medium-run trades (from 1–3 years), while the mechanisms of capacity payments defined by VOLL and LOLP gives market signals for investment (or retirement) decisions, and thus deals with the long run.

The generators have to make three strategic choices—how to bid in their available plant each day, what level of contract cover to arrange, and how much plant to make available (normally each year when connection charges are incurred, but plant must also be withdrawn for maintenance). Together these choices determine the daily range of the PPP and the long-run average around which they fluctuate. The spot and contract market are closely interrelated, and the contract price must be close to the expected spot price, otherwise buyers or sellers will prefer one to the other. Both are influenced by the amount of capacity, which will depend on the decisions of incumbents and entrants.

Anticipating the argument below, there are two routes to effective competition in generation. The first and obvious route is to ensure that capacity is divided between sufficiently many competing generators that no one generator has much influence over the price—an option available but not taken at privatization. The second, indirect route is to induce generators to sell a sufficiently large fraction of their output under contract and expose them to a credible threat of entry if the contract price (and average pool price) rises above the competitive level. Contracts and entry threats are complimentary—entry threats encourage generators to sign contracts and contracts facilitate entry. The advantage of the first approach is that it does not need to rely on the continued contestability of entry, and it works well even when the competitive price is well below the entry price in periods of excess capacity.

In either case, one would expect generators to seek ways of reducing the intensity of competition in order to enhance their profits. Firms selling homogeneous products in fiercely competitive markets will be attracted to merge to create market power, while firms facing the threat of entry will endeavour to create barriers to entry. Vertical integration may be attractive in either case as a way of securing markets and reducing the intensity of competition. A proper study of competition in newly restructured industries like electricity needs to be aware of the dynamic forces shaping the evolution of the industry and to avoid the temptation of comparing alternative initial structures, some of which may not represent long-run equilibrium configurations.

The proper test of the success of the initial restructuring is whether it enables the industry to adapt to changing circumstances (new technology like CCGT, changes in fuel prices) without excessive cost, prices, or profits. The industry was privatized with only two price-setting generators, and the obvious concern is that they would have the ability and motive to manipulate their bids into the pool, though somewhat restrained by the threat of entry. In order to test this suspicion, we need a model of bidding in the pool and of the effects of entry threats and contracts. The key market to examine is the pool, which differs from normal auction markets in that it determines 48 half-hourly prices from one set of bids (submitted the day ahead by each generator). Instead of a single price, each bidder submits a whole schedule of prices and quantities, which can usefully be thought of as a supply function (giving the price required to elicit the next unit of generation as a function of total supply offered up to this price). Indeed, National Power has explicitly referred to its bidding strategy as one of submitting a supply function.

Suppose initially that there are no contracts. A generator with a significant share of capacity in some active (i.e., price-setting) part of the aggregate supply function sets price for some fraction of the time and can, by raising his price over this range, increase the SMP and his revenue from all despatched plant. If the bid price of the set is too high, then another generator would undercut, set the SMP, and the plant would not be despatched. The spot market is in equilibrium when each generator is content with its own supply function, given the chosen supply function of all other competitors.

Competition without Contracts

Green and Newbery (1992) showed how to find equilibrium supply functions using the theoretical model of Klemperer and Meyer (1989) calibrated to the cost and demand conditions of the English electricity industry of 1990. (See the appendix at the end of this chapter for details.) They showed that in the absence of contracts, and with no threat of entry or collusion, there was a wide range of possible equilibrium supply functions, lying between a high-price function that would maximize collective short-run profit and a low-price function. Any one of the possible equilibrium supply functions would be self-enforcing in that any generator deviating while the others continue to supply as before would reduce his profits. The range of possible equilibria (and the highest equilibrium price) would, however, be dramatically reduced by increasing the number of competing generators from two to five.

Figure 6.2 illustrates this finding. The line labeled "marginal cost" represents a smoothed approximation to the marginal avoidable generation costs of the two main generators in 1990 in £/MWh at each level of total output. Since 1 MWh is 1,000 kWh, £20/MWh is equal to

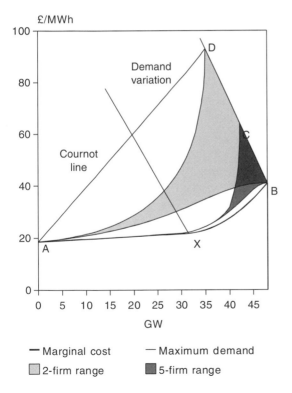

Figure 6.2
Feasible supply functions—duopoly and quintopoly.

2 p/kWh in units familiar to domestic consumers. Output is measured in GW (1,000 MW) and demand is shown varying over a winter day. The curved line *AD* represents the highest-price feasible equilibrium aggregate supply function of a symmetric duopoly (each firm would submit half of the total amount shown at each price). It meets maximum demand vertically at *D* and is equal to marginal cost at zero output at *A*. The lowest feasible equilibrium duopoly supply function, *AB*, meets the marginal cost schedule at *B* horizontally, and defines a range of feasible uncontracted duopoly supply functions shown as the lightly shaded area *ABD*.

If the available capacity were to be divided equally among five companies (and, conveniently, such an allocation of the conventional power stations was feasible since there were ten large and comparable stations), then the highest feasible equilibrium supply function would be *AC*, and the lowest one *AB*, defining the darkly shaded area *ABC* of feasible equilibria. (Again, each company would bid a supply function one-fifth of the total). *AC* also meets maximum demand vertically, and *AB* hits marginal cost horizontally. These two features define the bounding equilibrium supply functions. Any outside this range would be infeasible, either turning back or down, neither of which would be accepted by the scheduling program.

Note that the range of equilibria is dramatically reduced by increasing the number of competitors from two to five, and that for much of the range of output the two ranges do not overlap. Green and Newbery (1992) calculated that if the duopolists coordinated on the high-price equilibrium, average prices would be well above costs, causing large deadweight losses.[11] Had the generating plant been divided among five equal-sized companies, then each generator's market power would dramatically decrease. The five-firm supply function converges rapidly toward marginal cost at lower levels of demand, and losses would have been reduced to only 6 percent of their duopoly value.[12]

Competition with Contracts

Contracts and the threat of entry dramatically alter this picture. Consider the effect that contracts have on the incentives generators have to bid high. If a generator has sold CfDs exactly equal to the amount despatched in some period, then its income is entirely determined by the strike price of the CfD. It would have no incentive to manipulate the Pool price to either raise or lower the SMP, as this would not affect its revenue. Indeed, if it bid a set above its avoidable cost, it would run the risk that it would not be despatched and would lose the difference between the SMP and the avoidable cost, while if it bid below avoidable cost it might have to run the set at a loss. It would therefore do best by behaving as a competitive price-taker and bidding at short-run avoidable cost. More generally, the incentive to raise pool prices depends on the amount of uncontracted pool sales, since only this benefits from the higher prices. The larger the contract cover, the smaller the incentive to manipulate pool prices, and the more competitive the resulting pool prices will be. On vesting, the three generators were provided with CfDs for virtually their entire forecast output, for periods of between one and three years, and matched with comparable (take-or-pay) contracts to purchase British coal. As noted, this solved the problem of high priced coal and made their income and expenditure streams highly predictable for the prospectuses on which they were to be sold. It also reduced their incentive to exercise spot market power to negligible levels, though not their ability to take advantage of transmission constraints and to game capacity availability. Figure 6.1 shows that for the first year pool prices were indeed low, and below the average fuel cost of the price-setting generators.[13]

When the time came to renew contracts, the generators were faced with a difficult choice. If they reduced contract cover, they would have the incentive and ability to increase their bids in the pool, and raise the average level of prices, revenue, and profits. Meanwhile IPPs, usually with equity participation by RECs, had demonstrated a technique for making the electricity market contestable. They could sign fifteen-year contracts with their REC for the sale of electricity, provided the REC could demonstrate to the DGES that these contracts met the economic purchasing condition of their license (Offer 1992c). Given then prevailing pool prices, forecast coal and gas prices, the risk of carbon taxes and other environmental restrictions likely to raise the price of coal-fired generation, and the desirability of encouraging entry and competition, the DGES was prepared to accept that the contracts met that test. The electricity contracts in turn provided security for signing fifteen-year contracts for the purchase of gas, issuing debt to finance the purchase of the plant, creating a highly geared financial structure with low risk, and hence relatively low cost.

Such a package made the generation market contestable, since the potential entrant could lock in future prices and hence avoid the risk of retaliatory pricing behavior by the incumbents. So attractive was this package that within a few months contracts had been signed for some

5,000 MW of CCGT plant, which, in addition to the incumbents' planned 5,000 MW of similar plant, would displace about 25 million tons of coal, or nearly half the 1992 generation coal burn of 60 million tons. The new CCGT capacity amounted to about one-sixth of existing capacity, which was in any case more than adequate to meet peak demand.

Every MW of additional capacity created by entry would displace a MW of existing capacity and hence result in the loss of the difference between average pool price and cost for the owner of that MW of capacity. Faced with this credible entry threat, incumbents had an incentive to commit themselves to bidding in such a way that the time-averaged PPP was just below the price at which contract-backed entry of IPPs was attractive. This they could do by signing contracts, which both were directly comparable to those offered by IPPs and which would induce the incumbents to bid more competitively into the pool, ensuring that contract and pool prices converged. Newbery (1995a, 1998b) showed that the best strategy for the incumbents was to use contracts to lower the time-averaged price, while increasing the spread between peak and off-peak prices, raising the demand-weighted price and increasing price volatility in the pool.

Contracts are thus doubly critical for competition. The contract cover reduces the incentive to exercise market power in the pool, while contracts make entry contestable. This gives the incumbents an incentive to keep pool prices down, which they can do by selling contracts. Figure 6.3 illustrates the effect of contracts, enlarging the right-hand part of figure 6.2. The entry price is shown at £28/MWh—the estimated average contract price that would cover the total operating and capital costs of a new CCGT generating station at the gas prices in 1990. The lowest duopoly supply function without contracts, AB of figure 6.2, is shown at the continuous line in figure 6.3, and the point Ep is the expected or average price as demand varies, considerably above the entry price. With five firms and no contracts, the lowest supply function (shown dashed) has an average price just below the entry price and would deter entry. But, if the duopolists were to sign base-load contracts for 30 GW, their residual equilibrium supply function (i.e., the uncontracted excess supplied at pool prices) can be brought down as shown (the S-shaped dot-dashed line), and the average price could be held down to the entry price (if desired) by increasing the level of contract cover.

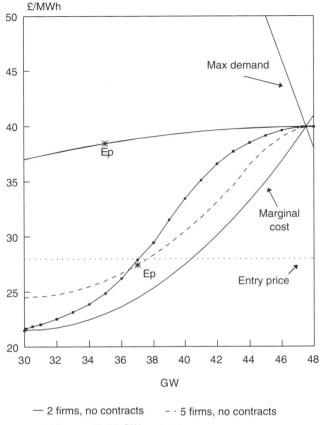

Figure 6.3
Entry-deterring supply functions: Effect of contracts.

Indeed, the best strategy for entry-deterring duopolists to coordinate on is to choose a level of contracts and a residual supply function that maintains the average price just below the entry price, while making the residual supply as steep as possible. This will maximize the spread in prices between peak and off-peak, and give the highest revenue to the duopolists, who increase their output at times of peak demand, compared to the entrants who run on base load. Over time the volatility of pool prices (i.e., the range from peak to trough) has increased as the incumbent generators have adjusted to this contracting and bidding strategy; this can be seen in figure 6.1. The reason why this strategy is attractive is that the incumbents have almost all the mid-merit and peaking plant, which they can use to increase their output in periods of high price. The main constraint limiting mid-merit and peak prices is the risk that IPPs may find it attractive to build plant specifically to meet these parts of the load duration curve if the peak price rises sufficiently high.

Choice of Capacity

The generators can further influence both the average price and its volatility by removing capacity from the system. Capacity payments are extremely nonlinear in the margin between capacity declared available and peak demand. If this margin falls from 20 percent of capacity to 10 percent, then the capacity payments increase from negligible levels (a few pence per MWh) to more than £20/MWh. In deciding whether to pay the connection costs and the workforce needed to keep the least efficient power station available (as compared to disconnecting and keeping it on a care and maintenance basis), the company can estimate the annual capacity payments and the pool revenue from the small number of hours it will run, to see if it covers these costs. If not, it is withdrawn until system capacity falls enough to increase capacity payments. One of the curious features of the industry since privatization is that in the first five years, despite substantial new capacity coming on stream, the total declared capacity actually fell as the incumbents adjusted capacity to produce satisfactory returns to marginal or peaking plant, further adding to pool volatility.

Figure 6.1 shows that the monthly capacity payments rose sharply at the end of 1994, when their annual moving average rose to just under £30/kW and gradually increased to over £50/kW in 1996 before falling back to £30/kW in 1997 and £8/kW in 1998. The level of annual capacity payments needed to keep a generator on the system or to induce entry will depend on the excess of average value of the SMP over avoidable (fuel) costs, which will depend on the age and fuel use of capacity in use and on the annual connection charges, which in 1997 varied from £8/kW to −£10/kW (i.e., a payment to the generator of £10/kW of peak output produced). If reserve is provided by an open cycle gas turbine costing perhaps £150/kW and located in a capacity constrained zone with negative connection charges, then the target of £35/kW set at vesting could surely be lowered to nearer £15/kW, and possibly less for existing plant. Critics argue that both VOLL and LOLP have been exaggerated and that as a result capacity payments are too high, as the figures for 1995 to 1998 suggest.

However, if the incumbents have enough market power to choose their contract level and price and their bidding strategies to set both the SMP and the capacity payments, and hence the PPP, they still have to worry about entry threats, which are affected by the PPP, and not its component parts. If capacity payments fall, as they did in 1997–98, then SMP can be increased, as figure 6.1 shows they were, comparing the winters of 1996–97 and 1997–98. The regulator strongly criticized the generators for this behavior in Offer (1998d). He found that SMP was over 26 percent higher in real terms in winter 1997–98 than in winter 1996–97, despite an increase in the capacity margin and a fall in fuel prices (see figure 6.1). Capacity payments fell by more than half, so the PPP increased by a more modest (but still excessive) 15 percent. In defense, the generators argued that higher SMP was to be expected when capacity payments were low, since customers were concerned with the pool selling price, not SMP, though the generators' motives clearly had more to do with setting the PPP, guided by the threat of entry. Reducing capacity payments in an uncompetitive market may therefore not have much impact on the final selling price, though in a competitive market capacity payments play a critical role in determining the size of the reserve margin and hence the risk of power cuts.

6.3.2 Progress in Introducing Competition

The failed attempt to privatize nuclear power led to a flawed structure in generation (which could not be remedied in the time available in the electoral cycle), but the flotation was skilfully managed to ensure a smooth transition to private ownership. The two fossil generators were sold almost fully contracted, both for the sale of electricity and the purchase of coal. This gave predictability to revenue streams and dividend forecasts and delayed the impending politically divisive collapse of British Coal. It also provided incentives to the companies to cut costs and equip themselves with the commercial expertise needed to trade in the pool and contract markets. Full contract cover created incentives for competitive bidding in the pool, and pool prices were considerably below contract prices, though naturally they increased to the entry price over the next few years as contracts came up for renewal, as shown in figure 6.1.

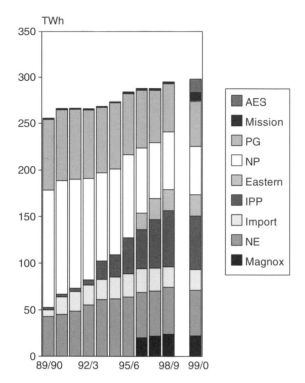

Figure 6.4
Generation in England and Wales.

The effect of restructuring and competition on generation has been dramatic. Figure 6.4 shows the generators' output since 1989–90, together with a forecast for 1999–2000. The increase in Nuclear Electric's (NE) output is due largely to the improved operating performance of the company's stations, encouraged by the competitive environment that the company faces. Imports from France and Scotland also rose when the trading rules were changed with the restructuring: The importers now sell at the market price in England and Wales, rather than at the (lower) average of the two system's costs, as before.[14] There has been a dramatic increase in independent generation (IPP), while PowerGen's and (particularly) National Power's output has fallen.

There has also been a dramatic switch from coal-fired to gas-fired generation, shown in figure 6.5 (for the United Kingdom as a whole, though almost all gas generation is in England and Wales). There was no gas-fired capacity in 1990, but 17.1 GW had been connected by 1997–98. Just over half of this was built by independents. By 1998–99,

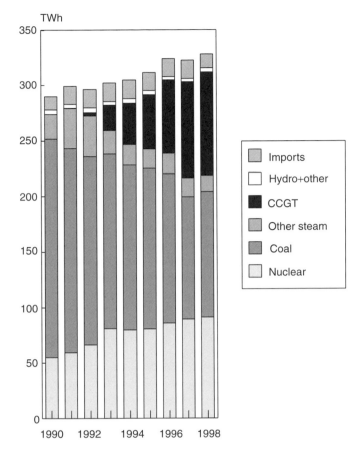

Figure 6.5
U.K. electricity supply by fuel.
Source: DTI (1999).

gas was the fuel for 34 percent of the electricity sold in the pool (Pool *Statistical Digest*, April 1999). The main source of these changes was the rapid development of combined cycle gas turbine (CCGT) technology in the late 1980s, which offered potential entrants a technology that could be introduced at modest scale (300–600 MW), short construction times (24–36 months), and with low capital and operating costs. At the same time the European Community rescinded its prohibition on gas-fired electricity generation and tightened emission limits for sulphur dioxide. To meet the limits, National Power and PowerGen would have to retrofit some of their coal stations with expensive flue gas desulphurization equipment or to replace some of their coal burn with gas, which emits no sulphur dioxide. Given the relative prices of gas and coal, National Power and PowerGen decided to replace small old coal plant with CCGT technology rather than retrofit.

Eleven of the twelve RECs also invested in CCGT stations, generally in partnership with independent power producers (IPPs). The stations sold long-term contracts (typically fifteen years) for their expected output to the RECs, on terms which allowed them to be largely debt financed. The RECs were able to argue to the regulator that these contracts were competitive with the prices then being indicated by the major generators, although there were worries at the lack of serious negotiations about those prices, and the fact that the RECs were equity participants in the stations and were expected to pass their contract costs through to the franchise market until 1998. Before privatization, it had been proposed that the RECs should be subject to yardstick regulation for their power purchase costs, so they would only have been able to pass on the average of all REC power purchase costs to the franchise market. It was then recognized that this would discourage the RECs from contracting with new entrants, and at a late stage they were allowed to pass through all contract costs (Hunt 1991). The RECs duly obliged by facilitating considerable entry.

The RECs also argued that the IPPs were desirable on wider grounds than price alone. Not only would the new stations provide more competition, but gas generation reduced the risks associated with coal's environmental impact. In the early 1990s the EC was discussing a carbon-energy tax that would have fallen more heavily on coalfired than gas-fired generation, while the United Nation's Second Sulphur Protocol (not finally agreed until June 1994) similarly threatened to increase costs for coal-fired generation (House of Commons 1993).

What did these REC-IPP contracts cost the franchise consumers? In 1996–97 the RECs purchased 71.7 TWh of electricity under the coal contracts (discussed below) at 3.92 p/kWh and 28.9 TWh from IPPs at 3.84 p/kWh, when the time-weighted pool selling price (PSP) was 2.572 p/kWh and the demand-weighted price was 2.793 p/kWh (Offer 1997). If the IPP contracts were essentially base-load contracts for which the time-weighted PSP is the relevant comparison, then they cost nearly 50 percent more than buying in the pool. Offer (1997) suggests that the IPP contracts are more like contracts bought for the nonfranchise market (which will be less peaky than overall demand, but more peaky than a base-load contract), which were 2.93 p/kWh, making the IPP contracts 31 percent more expensive than these contracts.

The ending of the franchise, subsequent improvements in CCGT efficiency and continued falls in gas prices, have reduced the break-even prices of new CCGTs, perhaps to as low as 2p/kWh.[15] They resulted in asset write-downs on the RECs balance sheets, so in retrospect the investments may have turned out less well than anticipated, though selling at these contract prices would have been highly profitable while it lasted. The RECs may retain sufficient market power over domestic consumers to continue to pass on some of these purchase costs after the end of the franchise, though the prices they can charge customers who remain with their old REC supplier will be capped until 2000.

The "dash for gas" associated with the entry of IPPs caused a collapse of the British coal market and the closure of more than half the remaining deep pits when the coal contracts came up for renewal in 1993. This prompted a parliamentary inquiry, which asked whether the new investment was justified on economic grounds. The eventual conclusion was that the ever-tightening sulphur limits would indeed require a shift of this magnitude to gas generation by the end of the century, but that about half of the new capacity could usefully have been delayed several years, since the relevant economic comparison was between the total cost of new CCGT generation against the avoidable cost of coal-fired generation valuing the coal at import parity prices (Newbery 1994b). The option existed for the incumbent generators to import coal, and although the vesting contracts for coal specified a substantially higher than import-parity price, these contracts were take-or-pay, which if anything depressed the opportunity cost below import parity. The incumbent generators undoubtably increased their bargaining power with British Coal by reducing their domestic coal dependence (they also invested in coal import capacity to the same end), making their choice of gas commercially sensible, if not socially least cost.

During the parliamentary inquiry the industry was put under considerable pressure to sign five-year coal contracts, again at above world prices. The RECs signed five-year coal-backed contracts with the generators and were allowed to pass through the extra costs to the captive domestic customers (at well above pool prices, as discussed above). The new coal contracts made it possible for the government to privatize the coal industry for an acceptable price. The contracts were timed to expire with the planned end of the domestic franchise in March 1998, precipitating a further crisis, discussed below.

The initial vesting contracts, followed by rapid entry, and the recognition that contracts could be used to manage pool prices and deter excessive entry, meant that the outcome was more competitive than a simple analysis of duopoly bidding would suggest. Nevertheless, in the first three years the two fossil generators set the pool price 90 percent of the time, and as contracts expired, they raised pool prices even though fuel costs were falling (figure 6.1).[16] The regulator had already criticized these two generators on a number of occasions, and two parliamentary select committees had recommended that he consider referring them to the Monopolies and Mergers Commission (MMC) to investigate their abuse of market power. The final straw came with the sharp increase in pool prices in April 1993, as the final vesting contracts ended on March 31 (Offer 1994a). Faced with the alternative of a reference to the MMC, the generators agreed to a price-cap on pool prices for the two financial years 1994–95 and 1995–96. They also agreed to divest 6,000 MW of plant (4,000 MW from National Power compared to its capacity of 26,000 MW; 2,000 MW from Power-Gen compared to its capacity of 20,000 MW) which they duly did, selling (strictly, leasing) it all to Eastern Group, the largest REC. The duopolists' share of generation fell from 54 percent in 1995–96 to 39 percent in 1998–99 as a result (figure 6.4).

The price-cap was presumably intended to restrain the exercise of market power until the divested plant was in the hands of competitors who would increase competition in the price-setting part of the market. The price-cap specified both a time-weighted level of 2.4 p/kWh and a demand-weighted price of 2.55 p/kWh (both in October 1993 prices, which in 1996–97 prices would equate to 2.6 and 2.77 p/kWh). As a measure of the ability of the two generators to control pool prices, demand-weighted prices were within 1 percent of their capped level each year. The price-cap was not renewed, in the hope that the industry would no longer be vulnerable to the exercise of market power. This hope was not realized, perhaps because the divestitures included an "earn out" clause, under which Eastern has to pay the sellers £6/MWh generated. This encouraged the stations to bid above marginal cost, which is somewhat anticompetitive but is intended to keep their present place in the merit order.[17]

The regulator criticized the high SMP ruling in winter 1997–98 compared to the year before despite increased spare capacity (Offer 1998d). The average prices bid by coal-fired power stations owned by National

Power increased by 4 percent to £24.4/MWh, those (essentially identical stations) owned by PowerGen increased their bids by 26 percent to £20.8/MWh, while Eastern raised its bids by 63 percent to £46.7/MWh (compared to the peak-lopping pumped storage generation of First Hydro which bid £43.5/MWh). The average SMP set by each generator (i.e., the prices of the sets that determined the SMP) increased considerably more, by 18 percent for National Power, by 43 percent for PowerGen, and by 22 percent for Eastern. As a result of their bidding strategy, National Power reduced its output 2 percent, PowerGen by 6 percent, while Eastern's output increased by 33 percent and First Hydro increased by 24 percent. This suggests that the two majors were bidding high and accepting a fall in market share, confident that the high prices would be supported by Eastern and First Hydro, who, acting more as price takers, were able to win market share.

The regulator observed that increased competition from entrants and lower fuel prices should have led to "significant decreases in generation prices at this time. In this context, the ability of the two major generators to prevent such falls in generation prices as costs fall and new entry increases, and indeed to increase SMP, demonstrates an unacceptable extent of market power, which is being exercised at the expense of customers, and also at the expense of coal as a fuel for electricity generation. . . . The most effective route for increasing competition in the short term would seem to be to transfer more of National Power's and Powergen's coal-fired plant into the hands of competitors, who may be expected to use it more actively to compete" (Offer 1998d).

The high pool prices and the low gas prices (caused in part by increased gas competition and the rapid maturation of a gas spot market) encouraged continued entry of gas-fired CCGTs, and exactly as in 1993 the high-priced coal contracts have matured and were not being replaced. This time the Labour party was in power, a traditional supporter of coal miners. Their immediate response was to prohibit any further gas-fired generation until the issue of coal was resolved in the now traditional inquiry. In due course the Trade and Industry Committee independently produced *The Coal Report* (House of Commons 1998a). The inquiry opposed the moratorium on gas but urged the regulator to find ways of making redundant coal-fired power stations available to competitive generators, and it criticized the Environmental Agency for accelerating the imposition of tough emissions limits that made coal uncompetitive.

6.3.3 Competition in Supply

In the first year that the 1 MW market was opened to competition, the RECs lost two-fifths of their sales volumes, and their market shares have continued to decline, so by 1996–97 Offer estimated that the RECs supplied less than 30 percent of this demand in their local market, with generators and other RECs competing to supply these customers. The size of the competitive market increased in April 1994, when the 50,000 sites with demands of between 100 kW and 1 MW were allowed to change their supplier. One-quarter of them did so in the first year, and half had done so by the following year. Prices fell, mostly because the nonfranchise market was able to escape the coal contracts whose costs now fall on the remaining captive franchise customers.

One of the main benefits of supply competition is that it makes it harder to sustain uncompetitive but politically attractive interventions to support favored fuels like domestic coal. Of course, a determined government can still impose uncompetitive fuels on the industry. The nonfossil fuel obligation and the fossil fuel levy used to subsidize nuclear power provide an immediate example, but at least they were passed in legislation after democratic debate and were imposed using taxes and transfers. The FFL and NFFO survive as mechanisms to sub-sidize renewable energy, where the revenue collected makes up the shortfall between the contract price of the renewables bid in a periodic auction and the pool price. The distortions caused by this system of support are minor, for they do not affect bidding in the pool and are confined to the demand side of the market, raising prices by rather less than 2 percent.

The plan was to allow the remaining 20 million consumers (with half the total demand) to choose their supplier starting in September 1998, making it difficult for RECs to pass on any uncompetitive contracts (with coal producers, or with equity-participating "independent" power producers). It has, however, proved very difficult to design a cheap and simple form of domestic retail competition, and the costs of setting up the new system and operating it for the first five years are estimated at £726 million (U.S.$1,200 million; House of Commons 1998b). There are no new meters, and the costs arise from the very complex system of estimating and re-estimating the billing costs to charge to each supplier and the new IT systems needed to keep track of a changing portfolio of customers. The potential efficiency gains are small as the supply business's own costs are only about £600 million

($1,000 million) per year. Of course, the potential benefit of removing the ability to tax consumers for inefficient regulatory choices is much larger, but this could surely have been achieved at lower cost.

In late 1998 it was too soon to say how domestic competition would work in electricity. We can look at evidence from the domestic gas market, which was gradually opened up from April 1996. Until then British gas was vertically integrated and signed long-term contracts for beach deliveries of gas, which it transported and sold to its 18 million customers. The gas industry has been gradually unbundled, a spot market has emerged, and the spot price of gas is about half the old contract price. New gas is therefore cheaper, and new suppliers can offer considerable discounts on the British Gas price, effectively stranding the old contracts. About 30 percent of customers switched in response to a price reduction which was about £50 (U.S.$80) per year or 15 percent of the annual gas bill. British Gas has responded to competition as it lost market share, partly by promising a better deal for the combined supply of electricity and gas.

In electricity, the regulator will cap prices sold by RECs to their incumbent domestic customers and this regulated ceiling will fall by about 9 percent, reflecting the end of the overpriced franchise contracts discussed above. These caps are set rather high, and RECs are offering reductions of up to 10 percent outside their area.[18] Industry analysts were expecting a rapid concentration in the supply business as companies merge or exit. By 2000 the regulator will need to decide whether to deregulate supply completely. If about one-half to two-thirds of customers are reluctant to switch, then incumbent RECs and Centrica (British Gas) may be left with a comfortable quasi-monopoly position, much as the High Street banks have in Britain.

6.3.4   Competition in the Capital Market

If private companies have market power, the product market may not be able to provide adequate incentives for cost-cutting and the search for increased efficiency, as the survival of the firm will not be imperilled if it fails to make such improvements. The worry is that managers will seek to enjoy a quiet life rather than relentlessly minimising costs. But publicly quoted companies can be bought on the stock exchange by those who believe that costs can be cut and profits increased, and the threat of takeover, and particularly the threat that lazy managers will be fired, is argued to be an important spur for efficiency. The RECs had been privatized with the government holding a golden share in each, which could be used to block any takeover, but these shares lapsed in 1995 soon after the regulator had reviewed distribution prices, cutting the companies' revenues by £2.5 billion over the next five years. The subsequent takeover wave culminated in the attempted restructuring of the electricity supply industry by vertical integration between generation and distribution.

The first bid, Trafalgar House's attempt to buy Northern, was made in December 1994 but was beaten off by a counteroffer from the target. This was a pyrrhic victory, since it revealed the size of the cash mountain on offer to raiders and persuaded the regulator to reopen the distribution price control review. In July 1995 he announced that he would cut the RECs' prices by a further £1.25 billion over the next four years. In the following few months eight of the twelve RECs were targeted, and six were successfully acquired (see table 4.1). Two were bought by their local water and sewerage companies (also regulated utilities), one by the vertically integrated Scottish Power, one by the conglomerate Hanson plc, and two by U.S. utilities. The remaining bids, by National Power and PowerGen, were referred to the MMC and are discussed below. One of the target RECs, Midlands, was bought by another U.S. utility group soon afterward. Three more U.S. utilities made successful bids in late 1996, and one in early 1997, so that by July 1997, only Southern Electric remained independent.

The reasons why the RECs were so attractive to the bidders have been discussed in 4.5. They were sold with little debt, and generous price caps, while their investment has generally been covered by their (current cost) depreciation charges. Could this have been avoided in the distribution price control? Although the initial controls were widely agreed to be too lax, the regulator resisted attempts to bring forward his scheduled review, or to claw back past profits, because this would reduce the companies' future incentives to cut costs and would have threatened regulatory credibility. The review cut prices by £2.5 billion over the next five years, but even this reduction was based on a relatively generous treatment of the RECs' asset base. The assets inherited at flotation were included not at their initial market valuation but at a 50 percent premium to it (Offer 1994b). The second review reduced this premium (to 15 percent) which, with some other adjustments, produced a further £1.25 billion for customers (Offer 1995). But a tighter price control might have been justified, and it would have reduced the RECs' cash flow, transferring rents to consumers rather than shareholders. Although much of the damage was done by the initial controls, part of the problem lay in the lack of information available to the regulator, and more especially to outside observers. The United Kingdom clearly required more complete disclosure of all information on the accounts and operations of regulated monopolies like the RECs, following the U.S. model, and this may be introduced after the 1998 utilities review (DTI 1998).

6.3.5   Vertical Re-integration and the MMC Generator References

PowerGen announced a bid for Midlands in September 1995, and National Power responded with a proposed merger with Southern shortly after. These bids were referred to the MMC, which reported to the secretary of state for trade and industry, on March 29, 1996. The MMC found that the bids could be expected to act against the public interest but recommended that they be allowed to proceed under certain conditions, though one member wrote a dissenting report. On April 24, the Minister announced that he was rejecting the bids by National Power and PowerGen and therefore not accepting the recommendations of the MMC. Most commentators noted that the government's rejection of the advice left the electricity industry unsure of the government's intentions for its desired evolution and its policy more generally on competition. In response to speculation about a bid for National Power, on May 2, the government announced that it would block any bid for National Power or PowerGen, at least until "there is adequate competition in the generation and supply markets" (DTI 1996).

Horizontal mergers between water companies have been strongly resisted, and similar mergers between RECs would certainly be referred to the MMC, if only because they reduce the number of comparators and hence the quality of information needed to set the distribution price controls, but there have been no such attempts to date. Mergers between RECs and companies in other sectors or countries have been accepted subject to safeguards on the ability of the REC to finance its investment even if the parent company runs into financial difficulties. The previous Conservative government took a very relaxed view on foreign (U.S.) ownership of English RECs, confident in the ability of the regulators to protect English customers, but the incoming Labour government thought otherwise. The first bid by a U.S. company (Pacificorp) for Energy Group, of which the REC, Eastern is a subsidiary, was referred to the MMC in 1997 after it had been cleared by both Offer and the Office of Fair Trading. The secretary of state stated that she considered that the merger raised important regulatory issues that needed thorough investigation—the first time a utility had been referred for reasons other than competition.

The Conservative government had already privatized the Scottish electricity industry as two vertically integrated companies in 1991. Regulated vertically integrated utilities might be preferable to an unbundled structure for small and isolated systems, and that was presumably the reason for the Scottish structure, though this was signaled as in need of reconsideration in 1998. The English RECs had been allowed limited vertical integration into generation,[19] and most (except Manweb) had taken advantage of this possibility. Eastern was later allowed by the regulator to buy all of the 6,000 MW of divested plant from National Power and PowerGen, thereby creating a significant vertically integrated utility entirely in the English market. The limit on own generation had to be lifted to allow the purchase to go ahead. Why, then, were the two vertical mergers involving the two main generators deemed to be undesirable?

The normal argument is that if vertical integration does not affect market power either upstream or downstream, it will only be privately profitable if it lowers costs, and this will be socially beneficial. There may be additional social gains if the intermediate market (the pool in this case) is uncompetitive, for then vertical integration eliminates the double marginalization (buying above marginal cost, and then marking up on this price rather than on the underlying marginal cost). This benefit can also be obtained by allowing generators to sell directly on contract to final customers, and this already happens on a significant scale, so vertical integration offers no extra benefits over the existing opportunities of direct sales, and such benefits cannot be allocated to vertical integration. If integration reduces competition either upstream or downstream, then there must be sufficient cost savings to offset any reduction in competition. The RECs' ventures into generation probably increased total generation costs in the short run but were allowed partly because they increased competition in generation. Most competition policy decisions involve balancing damage against gain, and this one is no exception.

The MMC reports recognize that market power is primarily exercised by setting prices in the pool and deterring entry (MMC 1996a, b), but thought that with safeguards, competition could be made adequate to remedy the damage. A dissenting report raised the dynamic issue of whether approving the mergers would create pressure for further mergers and vertical integration, possibly ending with an industry of four or five integrated companies. The author of the dissenting report believed that the electricity market would not become sufficiently contestable for the mergers to have no adverse effect on competition.

The key questions are how much power over price-setting these generators would have, whether they could use this power to deter entry, and whether vertical integration would affect the extent of this power. At the time of the reports it was too soon to predict the bidding strategies of the players in the future, particularly as Eastern had only just acquired the 6,000 MW of divested plant, but it was assumed that the two generators would maintain a dominant position in non-base-load generation, which sets the price most of the time. The MMC estimated that the two generators' share of the non-base-load market would fall from 85 percent in 1995–96 to between 58 and 65 percent in 2001, confirming their dominant position in terms of combined share (see figure 6.4).

The mergers would have no effect on generator market shares, and it is argued that they therefore do not affect the degree of competition in the market, which is described as "a broadly satisfactory competitive environment in generation from 1997 onward in the absence of the merger" (MMC 1996a, 1.6; but not the subsequent view of the regulator, who drew attention to the high prices in 1997–98 discussed above and in Offer 1998d). The main argument that the duopolists would not be able to exercise market power in the price-setting part of the market is that competition to supply base load would be intense, as 38 GW of nuclear, CCGT and large coal-fired plant could be competing for 21 GW of base load by the turn of the century (MMC 1996a, 5.93). Any attempt by one company to raise pool prices by bidding high runs that risk some of this potential base-load plant (particularly CCGT, the divested plant, and electricity supplied through the interconnectors) would underbid and be preferentially dispatched, thereby setting the price at a lower level.

The second main plank of the MMC's argument on competition is that entry would continue to be relatively easy, as they argued that the market for the contracts needed to assist entry would remain both broad and liquid. But past entry was predicated upon two important features that no longer continue after 1998. First, IPPs signed contracts for fifteen years for base-load power with the RECs because the RECs had a franchise market on which to write such contracts. Second, older coal-fired base-load stations were vulnerable to entry by cheaper CCGTs. In 1998 the franchise market ends, and RECs are likely to be more cautious in signing long-term contracts with IPPs. By 1997–98 nuclear and gas generation together accounted for 55 percent of generation, considerably more than the summer minimum load of 21 GW. Entry will now be in direct competition with existing similar-fueled generation which is both young and has low avoidable cost. The fact that the one-year CfD (contract for differences) market may be liquid is little consolation in the absence of longer-term contracts, since an acceptable entry-supporting base-load CfD for one year offers no guarantee of likely future prices.

In the winter periods of 1996–97 and 1997–98 National Power was bidding in its gas-fired stations at an average price higher than its coal stations, as was PowerGen in 1996–97. Pool prices had risen, and they continued to attract entry from CCGTs until the moratorium on further gas entry was imposed in 1998. This excess entry was induced by the signaled behavior of the major generators that they would rather maintain high prices and lose market share than lower prices to deter entry, probably because they anticipated that the coal-fired generation would shortly need to be withdrawn by the ever tighter emissions limits.

The dissenting report argued that the proposed remedies to counter the adverse effects of the mergers did not address the problem of market power, and that it was too soon to tell whether the ending of the franchise market would encourage competition or discourage entry. In addition vertical integration would greatly increase the difficulty of regulating against discriminatory contracts. The argument against these vertical mergers is therefore that the two generators would be able to keep pool prices high while keeping contract prices (and direct sales prices from their downstream businesses) low enough to deter suppliers arbitraging the pool price, and targeting the customers of entrants with rather more favorable deals, undermining those customers' willingness to sign long-term contracts with entrants. The option of waiting to see how competition develops after the ending of the franchise was surely valuable, and would be foreclosed by premature restructuring.

If the two majors were to divest more plant so that there were four to five comparable sized price-setting generators (i.e., with flexible mid-merit plant), and if RECs were required to separate off their supply businesses as was being contemplated in the utilities review of 1998, then vertical mergers between the competitive generation and supply businesses might be less objectionable. It would still require a contestable bulk electricity market into which entrants could rely on selling, for otherwise the daily repeated game played out in the spot market might facilitate collusion and high prices. Vertical integration would eliminate much of the purpose of the spot market, which would only need to survive as a balancing market, making entry difficult. Even vertical integration with an apparently competitive structure might still lead to uncompetitive prices.

Private companies best protect their profits by reducing the intensity of the competition they face, by merging and deterring entry. When there are apparent cost synergies from merging, then a narrowly focused competition policy view, perhaps encouraged by politicians reflecting other constituencies, might from time to time accept proposed mergers. It may be that the only equilibrium to this process is a moderately concentrated vertically integrated industry, with muted competition and limited entry threats. If so, then unbundling the ESI without legislatively entrenched ownership restrictions on vertical mergers may yield only transient competitive gains. Are the gains from competition worth the costs of restructuring, and are the benefits of competition sufficiently large that they should be more aggressively pursued at privatization and defended against the pressures to reintegrate the industry? The next section addresses these questions.

6.4   Was the Restructuring of the CEGB Worth It?

Since privatization, costs have fallen dramatically in generation, but the margin between fuel costs and prices has increased, and the efficiency gains elsewhere in transmission and distribution were only passed on to consumers in the period after the first price review in 1995. Competition in supply has eliminated cross-subsidies from the competitive part of the market. Supply only accounts for a small proportion of the industry's costs, so the main savings, if any, must come from changes in generation, and increased efficiency in the regulated wires businesses.

Newbery and Pollitt (1997) have looked at the changes in generation and transmission in England and Wales, reconstructing the accounts of the four successor companies to the CEGB and comparing the outturn with various counterfactuals about what might have happened without such restructuring. The effect of privatization on labor

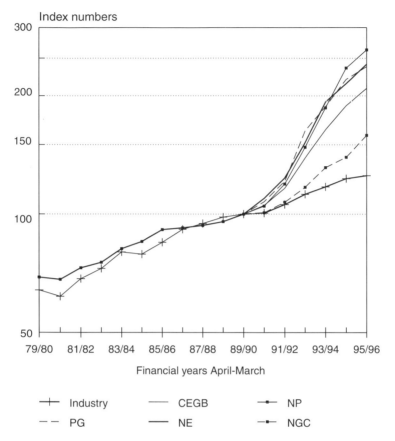

Figure 6.6
Productivity of CEGB and U.K. industry index numbers compared, 1989/90 = 100.
Source: Newbery and Pollitt (1997).

productivity has been impressive. Figure 6.6 gives electricity sales (in TWh) per employee of the whole CEGB or its successor companies (including NGC) over the period before and after privatization, as well as the individual generators post vesting. These are graphed on a logarithmic scale and can be compared with productivity in manufacturing industry—lines of constant slope exhibit constant rates of growth of productivity. Note that while matching manufacturing productivity growth before privatization, it has increased relatively by 60 percent since privatization. The absolute productivity growth of the three generators from 1990 to 1995 was 119 percent for National Power, 98 percent of Powergen, and 117 percent for the still public Nuclear Electric, largely achieved by increased output rather than reduced employment as for the other two. National Grid also improved its productivity, but less dramatically than the generating companies. There was clearly a discontinuity in the rate of productivity growth for all companies compared with the period before privatization.

Delivered coal prices fell by 20 percent in real terms and purchases of British coal fell from 74 million tonnes to 30 million tonnes a year. Fossil fuel costs per kWh fell by 45 percent in real terms. The switch from coal and the "dash for gas" has reduced the number of British coal miners from nearly one-quarter of a million at the time of the 1984–85 coal miners' strike to about 10,000 in the now privatized coal industry, and it has contributed to the substantial drop in acid rain and CO_2 emissions. The parliamentary inquiry into the collapse of the British coal market resulted in a clear statement of the Conservative government's commitment to market forces as their energy policy. The events of the first five years therefore transformed British energy policy as well as the electricity and coal industries.

The fall in unit costs was not translated into corresponding falls in prices but into increased profits. In the five years after privatization, electricity share prices outperformed the stock market by over 100 percent. Although real consumer prices fell, fuel costs fell faster, and the margin for the electricity industry's own costs and profits rose by almost 0.5 p/kWh, or by nearly 25 percent of the difference between the average industrial price and the fuel cost, as figure 6.7 shows. In current cost accounting terms the successor companies tripled their return on assets from 3 to 11 percent, 1.5 percent higher than non–North Sea British companies.

Table 6.1 summarizes the results of Newbery and Pollitt's (1997) analysis. They considered two counterfactuals. One, labeled "pro-privatization" in table 6.1, is their best estimate of what might have happened under the CEGB had it continued to behave as in its very well documented past. The other, labeled "pro-CEGB," is a less plausible counterfactual that assumes that coal production costs and gas prices would have been reduced as aggressively without the energy market liberalization as they were in fact, and that the CEGB would abandon its nuclear power program after the next planned station, rather than continuing on its stated path. It also assumes that the efficiency gains in nuclear power were not dependent on the competitive pressure of selling into the pool each day.

Table 6.1 shows the results of discounting the future costs and benefits at the government's social discount rate of 6 percent real, and at

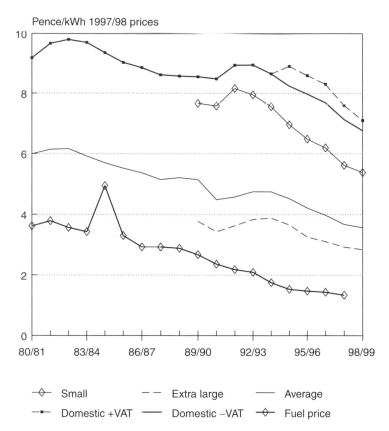

Figure 6.7
Real electricity prices: CEGB industry and domestic.
Source: DTI (1999).

the higher rate of 10 percent (to assess sensitivity to discounting). The first column thus presents the preferred estimates, and it shows that the £3.3 billion saved by abandoning the nuclear construction program was largely transferred to Electricité de France by allowing them to sell their nuclear power into the English pool at the specially favorable nuclear price. The net cost saving of switching from coal to gas was £3 billion. Overall the impact of the fuel switches caused by market liberalization was £3.6 billion.

The major benefit from restructuring and privatization (R&P) was the efficiency gain from cutting nonfuel costs, estimated to be worth £8.8 billion in present value terms. An overgenerous estimate of the restructuring costs is £2.8 billion (overgenerous because all workers left voluntarily and were therefore probably overcompensated). The

Table 6.1
Net benefits of privatizing the CEGB (billion £ at 1994–95 prices)

Discount rate percent[a]	Social weight	Pro-privatization		Pro-CEGB	
		6%	10%	6%	10%
Sources of cost savings					
U.K. nuclear		3.3	3.3	2.8	2.9
French imports		−2.6	−2.7	−1.5	−1.6
Coal		16.4	15.3	11.1	10.3
Gas		13.0	−12.1	−12.7	−11.7
Other fuels		−0.5	−0.4	−0.5	−0.4
Total fuel switching		3.6	3.4	−0.7	−0.5
Restructuring costs		−2.8	−3.2	−2.8	−3.2
Efficiency gains[b]		8.8	5.1	7.6	4.4
Total net benefits of R&P		**9.6**	**5.2**	**4.1**	**0.7**
Equivalent levelized cost reduction, % 1995–96 PPP		6.5%	4.9%	2.0%	0.5%
Who gains?					
Government sales proceeds	0.5	9.7	9.7	9.7	9.7
Prices converge		*From 2000*		*From 2010*	
Consumers	0.975	−1.3	−2.2	−9.5	−9.4
Government excluding sales proceeds[c]	1	−8.5	−4.1	−12.9	−6.6
Net government position		1.2	5.6	−3.2	3.1
After-tax profits[c]	0.5	19.4	11.5	21.2	13.3
Social welfare		**4.8**	**4.3**	**−6.7**	**−4.2**
Externality benefits					
SO_2 at £125/tonne		1.0	0.9	0.7	0.6
CO_2 at £12/tonne C		1.4	1.2	1.2	1.1
Total externality benefits		2.3	2.1	1.9	1.7

a. Discounted to April 1995.
b. Assumed cost savings: Pro-privatization: CEGB costs fall by 1 percent p.a. Pro-CEGB: costs fall by NE expansion.
c. Tax on profit: 25 percent for pro-privatization case, 14.5 percent (average 1991–96) for pro-CEGB case.

resulting total net benefits (excluding environmental gains) amounted
to £9.6 billion, which can be compared with the privatization proceeds
of £9.7 billion, and it represents a 99 percent return on the sales price.
A better measure of the asset value (as the assets were shown to have
been sold for less than subsequent value by the subsequent stock
market appreciation) is the current cost accounting book value of about
£25 billion, on which the net benefits amounted to 38 percent. Alternatively, the net cost reductions were equivalent to a permanent cost
reduction of 0.16 p/kWh, or 6.5 percent of the 1995–96 time-weighted
pool purchase price.

The bottom three lines of the table estimate the environmental benefits, valuing the reductions in sulphur emissions at £250/tonne and
CO_2 at £12 per tonne carbon.[20] The environmental benefits are worth
£2.3 billion, almost as much as the fuel benefits alone. If the environmental benefits are added, the present value rises to £11.9 billion, or 48
percent of the (CCA) capital value of the CEGB of £25 billion. Discounting at 10 percent, the levelized cost saving (ignoring environmental gains) falls slightly to 4.9 percent of generation costs. These
effects are large enough to be robust to moderate changes in the
assumed counterfactual, although the study did not ask whether privatization with a more competitive structure might have yielded still
greater benefits.

Newbery and Pollitt (1997) also attempted to find out how these efficiency gains were distributed among consumers, shareholders, and the
government, on various assumptions about how future electricity
prices will evolve and would have otherwise evolved under public
ownership. Prices increased relative to plausible views of what might
have happened under continuing public ownership, but costs are
falling and at some stage competition should transfer some of these
cost reductions to consumers. If prices converge to the public ownership counterfactual by 2000, and the tax on profit is 25 percent (compared to recent historical average of 14.5 percent), then at a 6 percent
discount rate, consumers lose £1.3 billion in present value terms as
shown in table 6.1. The government loses £8.5 billion in revenue
streams but sells the industry for £9.7 billion, and thus gains £1.2 billion
including sales receipts. Shareholders receive after-tax profits with a
present value (at 6 percent) of £19.4 billion for their outlay of £9.7
billion, or a net gain of £9.7 billion. Table 6.1 suggests (and the source
defends) social weights that might be used to aggregate across these

different groups, to give a net social welfare gain (excluding environmental benefits) of £4.8 billion.

If, however, prices are not expected to converge until 2010, and if the current rate of profits tax persists at 14.5 percent, then on the pro-CEGB counterfactual, consumers lose £9.5 billion, the government loses £3.2 billion (including sales proceeds), while shareholders gain £21.2 billion gross. Social welfare becomes negative at −£6.7 billion. The distributional impacts are thus very sensitive to future price movements, which are unknown, to the effective marginal rate of taxes on profits, and to whatever assumptions are made about efficiency gains. They are not, however, very sensitive to the discount rate. These calculations also exclude the windfall profits tax of £2 billion on the post-CEGB companies announced in the 1997 July budget.

6.4.1 Cost–Benefit Studies of the Rest of the U.K. ESI

Michael Pollitt (1997, 1999) has applied the same cost–benefit methodology to measuring the benefits of restructuring and privatizing the ESI in Scotland and Northern Ireland. The results throw an interesting light on the relationship between the structure chosen at privatization and the extent of gains and consumer benefits. Scotland was privatized with little restructuring as two vertically integrated private regulated utilities, and a state-owned nuclear company that was sold as part of British Energy in 1996. The two electricity companies, Scottish Power and Scottish Hydroelectric, are viewed as national champions and protected against takeover by permanent golden shares, though this has not stopped them buying up other utilities in England and Wales. They are viewed with pride as very successful companies, but the detailed cost–benefit evidence provides a less flattering assessment.

Pollitt argues that restructuring and privatization (R&P) had beneficial effects on the nuclear industry, by advancing the closure of the loss-making old Hunterston A station and extending the life of the profitable Hunterston B. The interconnector to the south was strengthened with beneficial effects, and altogether the investment effects were comparable to those in England and Wales (shown in table 6.1 as total fuel switching benefits), at about one-third turnover.[21] The environmental effects were small but negative, deriving from the early closure of Hunterston A and the increased interconnector capacity displacing CCGT output. The present value of the efficiency gains under the pro-privatization counterfactual were small (10 percent of turnover in Scotland compared to over 50 percent in England and Wales) but canceled by the restructuring costs, which were also small (since little restructuring actually occurred). Under the pro-public ownership case the efficiency gains are negative and quite large (one year's turnover). The total efficiency gain was about zero, though a pro-public sector view would have given a discounted loss of 74 percent of turnover.

The distributional effect of R&P were somewhat worse than for the CEGB. Consumers lost £1.5 billion (80 percent of turnover, compared to 8 percent in England and Wales), the government sold the assets for £3.6 billion but suffered a fall in discounted receipts of £5.2 billion (excluding the subsequent windfall tax), while the owners received a profit stream worth £6.7 billion for their payment of £3.6 billion.

Northern Ireland is smaller but has adopted a structure that appears to offer greater incentives for efficiency, though apparently less ability to transfer the benefits to consumers. The generating stations were placed in three companies and sold in a trade sale with long-term power purchase agreements with the franchise transmission and distribution company, NIE, as explained above. The generating stations have considerably improved performance and cut costs, but the power purchase agreements initially prevented these gains from being transferred to consumers. The investment (fuel switching) effects of R&P appear modest (10 percent of turnover, compared to 34 percent in Scotland), and again a pro-public counterfactual would make them negative (a loss of 20 percent of turnover). The environmental effects were negligible (though would have been 19 percent of turnover under a pro-public counterfactual in which more fuel switching occurs), while the restructuring costs were high (£118 million, 24 percent of turnover) and were criticized by the Public Accounts Committee. The efficiency savings were, however, very large at £974 million, 195 percent of turnover (compared to 55 percent for the CEGB).

The net efficiency gains (excluding the negligible environmental benefits) discounting at 6 percent were £533 million on a sales value of £909 million, a return of 60 percent compared to the equivalent return of 99 percent for just the CEGB alone (which is flattering, since it ignores the value of the RECs). These efficiency gains were, as in the other cases, very unequally distributed. Consumers gained £1007 million (200 percent of turnover after a price review had considerably lowered prices), the government realized a sales value of £909 million while forgoing future revenue streams worth £64 million, and owners lost £410 million (again as a result of the price review) at 6 percent for their outlay of £909 million.

6.4.2 An Assessment of the Three ESI Privatizations

The main conclusion is that competitive pressures created significant operating efficiency gains in generation. In England and Wales, daily bidding of each station into the pool concentrated the minds of power station managers wonderfully, many of whom received bonus payments linked to station performance. In Northern Ireland, the Power Purchase Agreements provided strong incentives for plant availability (which provided half the generators' income in 1995). Plant availability improved remarkably, overall from 74 percent to 88 percent, and for the two smaller stations to over 95 percent (Pollitt 1997). In the short run the effect was to increase electricity prices, and since there is excess capacity, the advantage of deferring new investment is small. In Scotland, in contrast, vertical integration appears to have muted incentives for improving efficiency, except for the nuclear power stations. The Scottish companies would argue that efficiency was already good but that just emphasises the point that it is liberalization rather than privatization that is the key to improved performance.

The second finding common to all three cases is that the price-cost margin widened, to the advantage of the producers but harming (or failing to adequately benefit) consumers. In Britain (England, Scotland, and Wales) the fossil generators were split between just two companies. In Northern Ireland, although they were split into three companies, they sold all their output under long-term contracts. Prices only fell in Northern Ireland as a result of regulation, and only after 1998. Duopolies do not bid competitively into electricity pools; they are only constrained by the threat of entry, which limits the extent to which prices will fall when there is excess capacity (as there was in all systems).

The third finding, which at first sight seems rather surprising, is that the dynamic efficiency gains of improved investment were smaller than might have been expected, and smaller than the X-efficiency gains in station operation. The CEGB had been cogently criticized for its inefficient investment performance, where the consensus was that its power stations cost between 50 to 100 percent more than in other developed countries, took as much as twice as long to commission, and rarely achieved the economies of replication that a large buyer might reasonably have expected. Instead the CEGB was pressured by an industrial policy that aimed to keep alive an unreasonable number of internationally uncompetitive British firms.[22] The effects of this strategy can be seen in their least favorable light in the disaster of the Advanced Gas-Cooled Reactor nuclear power program, and they are detailed in depressing detail in Layfield (1987). Jeffrey (1988) cites the cost for the AGRs as £2,446/kW actual capacity (at 1988 prices), compared to 1997 CCGT costs of £350 to £500/kW capacity.

The explanation for the apparently modest investment effects are linked to the lack of price competition in the pool, for the high prices induced excess investment, reducing the considerable gains in the efficiency of individual investment projects. In Britain, abandoning the nuclear power program and closing inefficient pits saved large sums of money, but much was dissipated in transfers to the French nuclear power industry, or in excess entry by CCGT stations. But why did the incumbents allow excess entry, if they believed that the maximum sustainable price was going to be set by the cost of entry, and that excess entry would permanently deprive them of a market which was profitable at the entry price for existing plant? Initially, the answer may have been that they underestimated the ease with which contract-backed CCGT entry could occur. The may have thought that offering entry-deterring contracts to the RECs would have been viewed as predatory by a regulator who was committed to encouraging competition but had inherited a very uncompetitive initial structure. That might explain the first "dash for gas" of 1991 to 1993 but not the second in 1996 to 1997 which caused the Labour government to impose a moratorium on new gas plant.

Offer (1998d) observed that "the evidence on changes in output and capacity suggests that the strategy of these two generators has been one of profitable withdrawal from the coal-fired sector of the generation market of England and Wales. . . . Both companies have declared strategies of increasing activities overseas." A critic might argue that the companies expected the end of the domestic franchise in 1998 to eliminate the willingness of RECs to sign long-term contracts with IPPs, making entry more difficult, and perhaps also believed that coal would be protected against entry from gas (as proved to be the case). In both cases, entry barriers would rise, allowing higher prices in the pool. They were also faced with increasingly stringent emissions limits, which would force closures of many remaining coal-fired stations, and might therefore have taken the view that the cost of forgoing the market for these coal-fired stations was smaller than the profit from keeping pool prices above the entry level. Finally, the gas market has dramatically changed since 1996, with the unbundling of British Gas, the emergence of a liquid gas spot market, and hence a growing reluctance of customers to sign long-term gas contracts. One of the few ways in which a gas producer can hedge its risks is to diversify its portfolio, and a CCGT provides a way of transforming spot gas into spot electricity, which can be attractive even without a long-term electricity sales contract. Again, the incumbents may have underestimated this threat.

High electricity prices in Northern Ireland and Scotland are also attracting the attention of entrants. A gas pipeline has been built from the mainland to Northern Ireland, which allows one of the existing stations to switch from oil to gas, and several large industrial users are considering generating their own power. An electricity link is also planned, though neither of these interconnections is justified at the avoidable cost of Northern Ireland electricity. PowerGen was attempting, so far unsuccessfully, to obtain permission to site a CCGT in Scotland, even though there is substantial excess capacity in Scotland and a constraint on exports. The vertically integrated companies have been rather successful in creating entry barriers. Here is the dilemma. If the incumbents were efficient, then entry might be wasteful. However, without the credible threat of entry, there is little pressure on the incumbents to become efficient. The same criticism can be leveled at the permanent Scottish golden shares that prevent takeover threats.

The message for England and Wales is that vertical integration appears to reduce competitive pressure, which is presumably one of its attractions to the major generators, and a reason to resist further re-integration, at least until the majors have been further fragmented. Although the Environment Agency may be having a benevolent effect on the environment, its impact on competition in electricity has been adverse. The EA is removing the advantage that comes from the inherited portfolio of plant of varying marginal costs and degrees of flexibility.

The fourth finding is that the government has not been very successful in obtaining value when privatizing the ESI, normally because it failed to appreciate how profitable the companies would become through improvements in efficiency or increases in prices relative to fuel costs, or both. The government appears to have sold the industry at a price that assumed it would be competitive but with a structure that encouraged oligopolistic behavior.

Finally, creating an adequately competitive and contestable bulk market for electricity appears to be a necessary step for improving efficiency and transferring the gains to consumers. Power purchase agreements mimic a competitive market in that the price paid to the generators is not affected by their actions, but it has difficulty in reducing the price as costs fall, as would happen in a competitive market.

6.5 Creating Electricity Markets in Other Countries

Competition requires a market, so creating an electricity market or pool is a critical element in liberalizing the ESI. It is also one of the most difficult institutions to design, given the many tasks that it has to fulfill, discussed in section 6.2. In Britain, growing dissatisfaction with the electricity pool led the Labour government, elected in May 1997, to call for a review of electricity trading arrangements in October 1997. The electricity pool set up the Pool Review Steering Group to agree a set of objectives for these trading arrangements. The overall objective was "that trading arrangements should deliver the lowest possible sustainable prices to all customers, for a supply that is reliable in both the short and long run" (Electricity Pool 1998). In section 6.6 below we shall examine the specific criticisms leveled at the English pool, and discuss the proposed remedies, but it is helpful first to look at the experience of creating electricity markets in other countries.

6.5.1 Scandinavia

Norway first set up an electricity spot market in 1971 to coordinate the use of the large number of different hydroelectric generators (of which there were about 80). The resulting energy "pool" (*Samkjøringen*) was run as a generators' cooperative and designed to allow trading between the generators to meet their demands at least cost. Most trading was for bilateral physical contracts with the pool acting as a voluntary balancing market for about one-fifth of the electricity traded. Generators who were short of water could buy electricity rather than run down their reservoirs or sell surplus power to other generators, so the pool acted rather like a spot market in stored water.

In 1991 Norway unbundled its ESI with the Energy Act, splitting the vertically integrated company Statkraft into a generation company (also called Statkraft) and a high-tension transmission company Statnett. The old power pool became Statnett Marked, a competitive pool open for buying and selling spot power, though it acts for marginal exchanges, with most electricity sold under firm contracts (Moen 1995). Norway is overwhelmingly hydro with substantial storage, and many utilities are integrated with both generation and distribution. At some pool prices they utilities are willing to sell, and at lower prices to buy depending on the state of their reservoirs. The pool thus has both a demand and supply schedule actively determining the price. As in Britain, generators and distributors are licensed, the natural monopoly parts are regulated (by NVE), and the competitive parts are supervised by the Norwegian Competition Authority and NVE. Unlike Britain, the restructuring took place with no change in ownership, and Statnett remains state owned. The private company, Norsk Hydro, accounts for about 20 percent of generation, with most of the rest being supplied by about 30 municipal utilities.

The effect has been to integrate the market for electricity. Norway has a large number of small producers and small distributors, with about one half of the market serviced by twenty-five vertically integrated utilities, though most of the remainder have long-term relationships with wholesale power companies. Before the reforms the Norwegian Electricity Board had responsibility to coordinate expansion but local interests, and environmental lobbies have effectively obstructed least-cost coordinated expansion. The fragmented nature of the industry and the locally negotiated long-term contract prices for many major energy users leads to high price dispersion and potentially large allocative losses (estimated at $900 million per year by Bye 1991). Creating a transparent market should considerably reduce this loss, and Moen (1995) noted that price dispersion had fallen.

All Norwegian customers, including households, are free to choose their supplier since the 1990 Energy Act. Although competition for larger customers has been fierce, this has been less true for households. The range of household prices in 1994 was from 12.7 Nøre/kWh to 19.6 Nøre/kWh, but in 1997 the range was from 10.5 Nøre/kWh to 45.9 Nøre/kWh. Since then NVE has eliminated the switching fee for changing suppliers, and has removed the need for an hourly meter. Small customers can now pay on an assumed load profile, and as a result the number of households choosing an external supplier increased from less than 5,000 in early 1997 to over 90,000 by the start of 1999.

Sweden similarly unbundled transmission from the state-owned company Vattenfall, and introduced competition from January 1, 1996, the same date that Sweden and Norway integrated their markets into

Nord Pool, 50 percent owned by each grid company. Whereas Norway was 99 percent hydro, Nord Pool is only 64 percent hydro, with 28 percent nuclear and the balance thermal. Initially all customers with an hourly meter were free to choose their supplier, and as a result very few households switched, despite large price dispersions between different retail suppliers. As a result metering requirements were replaced in 1999 by a system in which small users will be charged on the basis of standardized load profiles. In response, major suppliers offered household tariffs in the range 15 to 17 öre/kWh, compared to 19 to 33.8 öre/kWh before the change was announced.

Finland reformed its ESI with the 1995 Electricity Market Act, and has combined its two grids into a single company, Fingrid, which also owns the interconnectors with Sweden and Russia. Consumers with demand above 500 kW can enter the competitive market, both Nord Pool and the local El-Ex market, and all consumers with hourly meters were free to buy competitively from 1997, though the metering costs made this uneconomic for domestic customers. By 1999, El-Ex had merged with Nord Pool to give a combined market of just over one-half hydro, with the rest roughly equally divided between thermal and nuclear power. On June 30, 1999, west Denmark joined the Nordic Power Exchange so that the spot price (Elspot) could be arbitraged over a wide area.

The Scandinavian system is interesting as it involves both restructuring (unbundling and liberalizing) as well as cross-country market integration, and is therefore a possible model for the development of the Continental electricity system. Unifying markets is likely to both raise prices where they were cheap (Norway) and lower them where they were based on expensive thermal power, at least in years of abundant water supply. The resulting unified market should reduce both generation and investment costs.

For outside observer, the most interesting aspect of the reforms is how the markets have been structured, and how well they operate, particularly as they have to trade electricity over long distances where transmission constraints are important. Each grid company provides systems operation, and Nord Pool remains a voluntary pool, with most trading continuing as bilateral physical contracts. Nord Pool operates a day-ahead spot market (as in England and Wales) as well as a forward and futures market. The day-ahead market differs from the English Pool in that participants submit both supply and demand schedules for each hour of the following day. Nord Pool takes account of existing physical contracts and computes the intersection of the hourly supply and demand curves to give the hourly prices. If all trades can be conducted with no transmission constraints, the price will hold for the whole market, but if transmission constraints fragment the market, then Nord Pool computes and, by 2 pm, announces the market-clearing price in each constrained region. Therefore the prices in southern Norway, northern Norway, and Sweden may all differ.[23] Participants then have 30 minutes to confirm their bids, after which they become binding physical commitments, and all participants must inform the systems operator of all their intended generation or offtakes at each grid point by 7 pm. The final balancing of demand and supply is managed by the system operators. In Norway, Stattnett accepts bids from participants who are willing to increase supply or reduce demand at 15 minutes notice. In Sweden, Svenska Kraftnät also runs a balancing market which accepts bids up to 2 hours before dispatch. The prices in these balancing markets are then used to settle any imbalances in the day-ahead commitments.

The key difference with the English pool is that there is no central dispatch, and generators schedule and dispatch themselves guided by their commitments and the price in the balancing market, leaving the system operators to maintain system stability by adjusting trades in the balancing market. It clearly helps that the system has such a large amount of storage hydro which is available at a moment's notice to make adjustments and ensure stability of frequency and voltage. The other important difference is that there is no mechanism for capacity payments, again reflecting the fact that Scandinavia is so well endowed with storage hydro, which is energy rather than capacity constrained. Prices then tend to be fairly stable over periods of a day or a week but vary markedly from season to season depending on rainfall. Hydro generators are continually trying to predict how high prices will need to go to balance consumption over the season with the level of water in the dams. At present there is normally excess capacity, but eventually prices will presumably increase until on average they are high enough to justify further investment.

Nord Pool also operates a futures market in contracts for differences, which with the pool are gradually replacing physical contracts. In 1997 43.6 TWh were traded through the spot market and 53.6 TWh through the futures market, when total consumption was 260 TWh. Nord Pool cleared 147.3 TWh of bilateral contracts, thereby reducing transaction costs and providing counterparty security.[24] The futures price typically has two prices—one for winter and one for summer—while the weekly average spot market price in 1997 moved in a rough U-shape from 250 NOK/MWh (U.S.$34/MWh) in week 1 to about 100 NOK/MWh (U.S.$13.67/MWh) in mid year before returning to its long-run average winter level of about 175 NOK/MWh (U.S.$24/MWh).[25] The weekly range (from lowest to highest spot price) is normally only 50 NOK/MWh, though it can be higher in the summer when water is spilled at some times.

6.5.2 Latin America

Chile's reforms have already been described in section 3.4.3. The two state-owned integrated companies, ENDESA and Chilectra, were divided into separate generation and local distribution companies in 1982. ENDESA was divided into five separate generating companies and eight distribution companies. ENDESA survived as the largest generating company in the central interconnected system with over 50 percent of capacity, also owning the interconnected transmission system, thus retaining vertical integration, while opening the market for generation. There are two economic load despatch centers or CDECs (one for each grid) which are also required to ensure orderly and economic trading between the two systems. The CDECs compute short-run marginal costs (SRMC) and long-run marginal costs (LRMC) according to formulas. The spot price is a combination of SRMC and a firm power component, equal to the nonenergy costs of a reference gas-turbine plant ($/kW capacity per month), varied hourly and used to price bulk transfers between generators. End-users with a demand above 2 MW can freely negotiate prices with generators.

Transmission charges for distribution companies are determined by the regulatory agency, CNE, based on their distance from a balancing point. CNE computes the maximum prices for electricity at each node from the transmission charges and a dynamic programming model that forecasts the average marginal cost (i.e., the forward-looking long-run marginal cost) over the following three years as a function of fuel prices and reservoir levels (and Chile generates about 80 percent of its electricity from hydro power). These nodal prices are set for periods of six months, though they are adjusted if fuel prices or dam levels indicate that a change of more than 10 percent is required, and they are capped to be no higher than 10 percent above the competitive wholesale price (Spiller 1996). The distribution charges are based on a model system adjusted to the size of the distribution company's area, so all the components of the final price cap are determined by formulas rather than actual costs. The formula price cap provides strong incentives to reduce costs but also allow predictable cost changes to be passed through to consumers (in contrast to the situation in Northern Ireland). The market for electricity in Chile is thus largely simulated, though its cap is linked to the free wholesale price so that it retains some contact with a conventional market-determined price.

The benefits of restructuring and price regulation are that prices now reflect regionally differentiated economic costs, which are related to SRMC as efficiency requires. In addition, although prices are close to marginal costs, the companies have made reasonable profits and have been willing to invest in new hydro capacity as well as in transmission and distribution (Spiller 1996). The worries lie largely on the degree of competition in the system, which will affect the costs used to set the prices. ENDESA has been strongly criticized for its monopoly over transmission, which allowed it to limit access by other generators.[26] These generators also disputed the pricing of transmission. ENDESA also has dominance over current generation capacity (over 50 percent in the central system) and over access to water rights for future hydro power (over 40 percent of economically viable water). New generation plant has been small scale, built when needed rather than reaping economies of larger scale, suggesting that ENDESA may not be subject to much competitive pressure.

In Argentina radical reforms starting in 1992 transformed the structure, ownership, and regulation of the ESI (Perez-Arriaga 1994). Argentina had a population of 34 million, generation capacity of 16,000 MW, and consumption of 51 TWh (1994), though capacity availability was initially very low (at 45 percent). The generation mix was fairly balanced, with 44 percent hydro, 45 percent thermal, and 11 percent nuclear (rather like Sweden). As in England, restructuring de-integrated the industry into generation, transmission, and distribution. Distribution is regulated as a natural monopoly, and the generating companies were so divided that no generator had more than 10 percent of capacity initially. By the end of 1993 there were 70 firms trading in the bulk supply market. By 1997 there were 40 generating companies, most of which were by then private, and over 20 distribution companies, many of them provincial. The national grid and the three federal distribution companies were privatized, as were about half the provincial distribution companies.

Large customers (above 100 kW in 1997, and above 30 kW by the end of 1998) can buy directly on bilateral contracts, or from the wholesale electricity market (WEM). The operations of the WEM (scheduling, dispatch, price setting, setting reserve levels, and settlement) are carried out by the private company CAMMESA, though in contrast to Norway, bilateral contracts do not take precedence in drawing up the dispatch schedule, which is in strict merit order, originally based on audited costs. The spot market computes hourly energy spot prices which are now based on the fuel prices declared by the generator (subject to a cap, and may only be varied every six months), and the technical characteristics of the generators, while hydro generators can only change the value of water every six months. The spot price is the price of the last generator dispatched; it defines the system marginal price, computed not from the unconstrained schedule (as in most pools) but ex post from the actual despatch.[27] In addition to the SMP, the generators receive a fixed payment for capacity of U.S.\$10/MW (which has remained at the level set on May 1, 1994) available for dispatch for each of 18 nonvalley weekday hours, and a variable capacity charge that reflects the tightness of demand relative to supply (as with the VOLL–LOLP system in England and Wales, where in this case the value of lost load, VOLL, is set at U.S.\$1,500/MWh or about one-third the English level). As in Chile there is considerable emphasis on using computer models to compute prices, and distribution uses differentiated nodal prices to reflect regional transmission cost differences.

CAMMESA's board has representatives from the associations of generators, transmission owners, the distribution companies, and large users, and the Secretary of State for Energy, each with 20 percent of the votes. They can propose changes to the Secretary of State for Energy who decides whether to approve and implement it. The wholesale market rules are issued by the Secretary of State and can be imposed without the approval of the other participants. The regulatory agency, ENRE, awards licenses, determines tariffs, and resolves disputes, subject to supervision from the Secretary of State for Energy but with considerable autonomy. ENRE also authorizes tenders to build additional transmission in response to a request from potential beneficiaries of the line.

The obligation to supply is placed on distribution companies, who have to ensure adequate contracts to meet their obligations. They specify their maximum demand for each six month period and are penalised for exceeding this. The price-cap on distribution is set on the basis of the seasonal market price and the original vesting contracts (which amount to less than 50 percent of their sales); it does not reflect the costs of any other contracts the companies choose to sign. This may reduce the incentive on the distribution companies to enter into the contracts that might support additional investment. The penalty for failure to meet supply obligations is set at the VOLL, namely U.S.$1,500/MWh. The penalties are large compared to the profits of these companies (about U.S.$7–9/MWh), and it is not clear that they are credible. The companies' slowness to sign contracts may reflect current excess capacity in the system, and this may be quite rational.

The reforms have had a very positive effect on plant availability (which increased from 45 to 72 percent) and power outages, while the pool prices are giving market signals not only for investment in generation but also in transmission. For example, gas-fired thermal generation at the gas well in Comahue has an estimated marginal cost of U.S.$3.75/MWh, compared to U.S.$21/MWh in Buenos Aires (Kleinwort Benson 1995). As a result generators located in Comahue are encouraged to contemplate financing an additional transmission line to Buenos Aires. The average cost of thermal generation installed since 1992 has been $11.27/MWh (Mateos 1998), varying from $6.82/MWh to $13.27/MWh (the latter in Gran Buenos Aires). The Yacyretá hydro scheme, which is jointly owned with Paraguay, has a power purchase agreement with the government of Argentina at U.S.$32.40/MWh, though the government can sell at any price into the WEM or abroad (e.g., to Brazil where prices are higher). The government keeps any profits from selling at above this price, and makes up any shortfall as part of its financial arrangements with the World Bank. Yacyretá started to generate in 1994 with about 1,400 MW, with a planned final capacity of 3,100 MW capable of producing 17 to 20 TWh/yr. In the year to June 1999, it produced 12 TWh or 18 percent of Argentine consumption of 67 TWh/yr.

The monthly average price in the WEM has fallen from about $45/MWh (with peaks over $70/MWh) steadily down to about $16/MWh in 1998. Despite the fall in prices, 4,927 MW net additional capacity has been added to the system, while available capacity has increased from 5,930 MW in 1992 to 13,530 MW in December 1997. More than half of the new capacity was hydroelectric (all commissioned before the reforms), though the trend demand for gas has almost doubled over the period. The availability of abundant cheap gas, as in Britain, greatly assisted the transformation of the electricity sector. The wholesale electricity market appears to be operating extremely competitively, though there are criticisms that regulatory constraints, methods of calculating prices, and price caps interfere with efficient functioning of the markets. Specifically, the capacity payments which are set at $10/MW do not reflect opportunity costs, and the system of smoothing prices for distribution companies discourages them from contracting. The regulated prices fail to reflect costs, and it would be preferable to allow prices to track costs moment by moment, even though the underlying prices would be more volatile, and to encourage distribution companies to buy on contract to hedge these risks, rather than discouraging them by not allowing them to pass through any contract costs to final customers.

The system of financing new transmission investment has also been criticized. Apparently there were concerns that the transmission company would be overencouraged to build excess transmission (as have many transmission companies in other countries), but the system now makes it harder to finance cost-justified expansions. The law requires CAMMESA to allocate the financial cost of any new transmission investment in proportion to the benefits received, both now and in the future. Computing who benefits and by how much in an integrated network is complex, and in practice, the charges are levied in proportion to changes in quantities flowing in the zone of the expansion. Agents can and do make side-payments to build coalitions to support investments, and the generators in Comahue have built such a coalition to support the "fourth line" project, after examining the cost allocations proposed by CAMMESA. The worry is that such coalition building will raise transaction costs and may delay or even prevent worthwhile projects, lowering the quality of supply. Indeed, a more general criticism leveled at the regulatory framework is that it pays inadequate attention to quality and fails to penalize those who degrade quality or adequately reward those whose actions improve quality. Nevertheless, the new system has motivated generators to improve availability with dramatic results, with a consequent improvement in system reliability compared to the earlier regime.

It has also been argued that because gas pipelines operate under a more sensible contractual regime, the decision between building pipelines to transport gas to demand centers for generation compared to generating electricity at the gas field and transporting electricity has been distorted. It is more likely that the balance between gas-fired generation and hydroelectricity is distorted. It is normally cheaper to transport gas than electricity, and since the discouragements hinder the building of electricity transmission lines to distant areas, they tend to exaggerate the advantage of moving gas. However, distant hydro schemes are discriminated against under the present system of electricity transmission finance.

6.5.3 Australia

Australia has a federal structure with individual states responsible for restructuring and regulating the electricity supply industry (ESI) within a framework set by the ACCC, the federal competition authority. The state of Victoria was the first to restructure its industry when it unbundled the vertically integrated state utility in 1993 into six generating companies, four of which with low-cost brown coal generation have been privatized, the transmission company, Powernet, and five distribution companies. The Victorian Power Exchange is responsible for system control, the mandatory real time spot market Vic Pool, and planning grid extensions. Supply competition has lowered the threshold from an initial 5 MW down to 750 MWh per year and then to 160 MWh from July 1998. Full competition is planned to start in 2001. Capacity is 8,400 MW (of which 1,000 MW is Victoria's entitlement to the Snowy Mountain hydro scheme), peak demand is 7,100 MW, and generation is about 70 percent from brown coal, 20 percent hydro, and 10 percent gas.

South Australia, which is interconnected with Victoria, also unbundled the Electricity Trust of South Australia in 1995–96, and initially trades in Vic Pool. New South Wales legislated the unbundling of its ESI in 1995 to create the transmission company Transgrid, three generation companies, of 4,640 MW, 4,240 MW, and 2,640 MW capacity, and six distribution businesses, though privatization has been resisted and delayed. Including NSW's entitlement of 2,170 MW of the Snowy Mountain scheme, generation is supplied 79 percent from black coal, 19 percent hydro, and 2 percent gas. Transgrid is also the system operator, and it operates the spot market for New South Wales and the Australian Capital Territory (ACT, which lies within the state). The NSW wholesale market started in May 1996 and the first stage of a national electricity market (NEM1) started in May 1997, involving Victoria, NSW, and ACT, with South Australia participating via its membership of Vic Pool. Queensland started a spot market in 1998, and the full national economic market NEM with a single set of rules for all participants under the management of NEMMCO started on December 13, 1998, ending Vic Pool. Prices in NSW and Victoria are kept close by the considerable interconnection capacity, but prices in both South Australia and Queensland have been on average considerably higher, reflecting transmission constraints. Thus in the first three months of 1999, prices in NSW averaged \$A21/MWh, in Victoria \$A24/MWh, in South Australia \$A56/MWh, and in Queensland \$A83/MWh.[28]

Victoria's electricity market, Vic Pool, initially ran as an ex post market setting SMP retrospectively for each half-hour. Since 1997 Vic Pool, followed by NEM1 (and in due course NEM), has operated as a five-minute ex ante market, effectively setting the SMP in real time. Generators indicate their half-hourly maximum availability for up to seven days ahead under competition rules that penalize gaming. By 11 am each generator bids each unit for a 24 hour period starting at 4 am the following day. Generators are allowed to determine when to synchronize with the system, and such self-commitment is mandatory for generators who cannot respond to dispatch orders within 30 minutes. The self-commitment minimum generation level is included in the daily bidding, with up to ten incremental prices for increments of output above this level. Generators can also specify two negative bids as payments they would require to reduce output. These bids determine the order in which plant is off-loaded and output is reduced. Plant that can be made available in less than 30 minutes is centrally dispatched and thus provides flexibility.

The bid prices cannot be adjusted during the 24 hours, but the step width can, effectively allowing the supply schedule to be adjusted up to one hour before despatch. Every half hour the Victoria Power Exchange and Transgrid forecast demand and a pre-dispatch schedule for up to 41 hours ahead. They inform generators of their current operational schedule and the forecast SMP. The plant is then dispatched in five-minute intervals with any deviations after that dealt with by ancillary services. There is no capacity payment, but if there is inadequate generation capacity, the price becomes VOLL, initially set at the U.K. level of A\$5,000/MWh (U.S.\$3,700/MWh). The Osborne power station has set the price at this level on April 14, 1999, and prices have exceeded \$A3,000/MWh on several occasions. The average price for the half-hour determines the settlement price paid to all generators.

Apart from setting prices in real time, the distinctive feature of the Australian market is that there are no separate payments for startup, and the generators must choose a schedule of prices that covers any fixed costs involved. The technical constraints on the rate at which plant can be varied in output is still communicated to the dispatcher and taken into account in the five-minute final dispatch schedule.

With four large comparably sized low-cost but relative inflexible brown-coal-fired generating stations, the Victorian market is intensely competitive, and in the early period competition was increased by the desire by the state-owned companies in NSW wishing to retain market share and accepting prices below avoidable costs. (Black coal used for generation in NSW has an export value that is higher than the value of brown coal used to generate electricity in Victoria.)

Australia provides an interesting comparison for Britain, as it is a primarily coal-fired thermal system, initially with excess capacity, and has had to deal with interconnected systems (like England and Scotland). It avoided the mistake of overconcentrated generation and succeeded in creating a competitive and rather simple market. Figure 6.8 gives the weekly average settlement price in Vic Pool (which is also the SMP and PPP), the 4-week and 52-week moving averages, all at 1997 prices. The annual average price has fallen in current price terms from A\$42/MWh (U.S.\$31/MWh) in 1995 to A\$19/MWh (U.S.\$12/MWh) in 1998, when Vic Pool ceased to exist. Since then prices in Victoria have increased somewhat, to A\$24/MWh in the first quarter of 1999 (compared to A\$10/MWh in the first quarter of 1998) and to A\$29/MWh in the

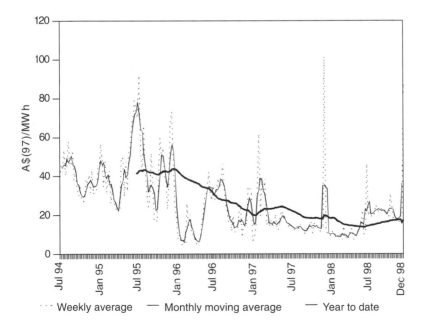

Figure 6.8
VicPool system marginal price, 1994 to 1998 at 1997 prices.

second quarter of 1999 (compared to A\$13/MWh in the second quarter of 1998). The price duration curve (i.e., the number of hours the price was greater than some specified amount) reflects this greater competition and is nearer to the reverse L-shape that a perfectly competitive market with constant marginal costs would attain.

6.5.4 New Zealand

New Zealand (population 3.3 million) has an ESI somewhat smaller than Victoria, with capacity of 7,100 MW, peak demand of 6,200 MW, and generation 71 percent hydro, 17 percent gas, 6 percent geothermal, and the balance of thermal being mainly coal. The transmission company, Trans Power, was separated from the state-owned company ECNZ in 1993 when the 50 local distributors lost their monopoly franchises (see also section 5.1.2). In 1996, 22 percent of ECNZ's generation assets were transferred to the state-owned company Contact Energy, and wholesale market started operation in October 1996. Plans to privatize and possibly further restructure generation have run into political opposition and have been delayed.

The spot market is voluntary, though over 93 percent of total power flows through this spot market as transaction costs are lower than in the bilateral market. Buyers and sellers specify their demand and supply schedules at each grid point and as in Australia Trans Power produces a forecast of prices. Bids can then be revised up to two hours ahead of each half-hourly trading period. The dispatcher includes bilateral deals and then computes the dispatch schedule and the nodal prices using a DC power flow model to optimize consumer benefit. The model calculates the prices at each node and settlement is based on these ex post prices. As in Australia there is no separate system for paying for capacity, but unlike Australia there is no upper limit on market prices, although there is currently excess capacity. Nevertheless, in dry years prices can increase dramatically, and at such times the demand responses bid into the pool are important at limiting the market price.

6.5.5 United States

In the United States, most utilities were vertically integrated geographical monopolies, with three-quarters of capacity in regulated investor-owned utilities and the balance under public (or cooperative) ownership. Under the old regulatory compact utilities ensured adequate, possibly excessive, capacity as part of their public service obligation to ensure security of supply to all, in return for a fair return on all that capacity. This compact has been eroded by the high cost of that excess capacity, the irrationality of the rate structure that evolved under political pressure to sustain it, and its vulnerability to "cherry picking" by bypass. The same forces that brought to the Bell telephone system the breakup in 1984 have been operating in the electricity industry. The mismatch between regulated prices and the cost of new generation in some states and the development of efficient small-scale generation units has combined to suggest that competition promises benefits to consumers and the prospect of increased efficiency for the industry.

Evidence for the mismatch between prices based on the costs of older plant and the costs of newer plant is plain to see. Diabolo Canyon nuclear power plant in California was receiving 11.5 cents/kWh, while new gas-fired plant is competitive at rates one-quarter as high. The divergence of rates from marginal costs have been estimated to cause losses 7 percent of costs (Gilbert and Henly 1991). The inefficiencies of the old cost-based regulation took various forms. Employment may have been 20 percent too high (Kahn and Gilbert 1996a), and investment costs may have been 10 to 15 percent too high (Kahn 1991). We have already noted in section 3.5.1 that the lack of a transparent power pool combined with open access to the grid is potentially very costly in failing to secure the gains from trade between neighboring utilities. White (1995) estimated the potential gains from introducing pooling to California, to replace bilateral deals between the four major electric utilities might be about 4 percent of total costs or $240 million per year. If competition reduces these inefficiencies, provided that the costs of creating and operating the new system are not too high, the gains will well be worth having.[29]

The Federal Energy Regulatory Commission (FERC) encouraged modest steps to deregulation in the Public Utilities Regulatory Policies Act 1978 by opening the wholesale market to independent generators with qualifying facilities, and forcing utilities to offer them "must take" contracts at avoidable cost. In some states this was to store up future problems with stranded contracts, since avoidable cost was interpreted to mean long-run marginal cost, often with pessimistic views of future oil prices under which investments like Diabolo Canyon could be justified. The Energy Act 1992 created exempt wholesale generators, and the Act greatly reduced barriers to entry, encouraging utilities to

purchase from distant generators, and to wheel the power over neighboring grids. To assist this option, the Act allowed FERC to mandate
transmission access. The object of these initial steps was to make the
building of new generation contestable, and to encourage the utilities
to contract for least-cost new capacity, though it was difficult to ensure
that utilities would not favor their own plant through their control of
contracting and despatch. Between 1991 and 1994 nonutility generators
built over half all new capacity (Berg 1995).

The efficiency case for liberalization was that investment and operation costs could be reduced, but the pressures compelling reform were
distributional, as White (1997) and Joskow (1997) document. The
average price of electricity in the United States in 1995 was 6.9¢/kWh,
but in California it was 9.9¢/kWh, 10.3¢/kWh in Massachusetts, and
10.5¢/kWh in Connecticut (Joskow 1997). Residential prices in those
three states were 11.6¢, 11.4¢ and 12¢, exceeded only by New York at
14¢/kWh, compared to the U.S. average of 8.4¢/kWh. These variations
in price mostly reflected variations in the sunk costs of generation and
power purchase contracts, and the issue that this evident variation in
prices raised was who should bear the costs of these apparent past
mistakes.

Not surprisingly, given the high consumer prices, California was one
of the first states to press for reform. In early 1993 the president of the
California Public Utilities Commission (CPUC), Dan Fessler, proposed
what was then thought to be a radical solution of "retail wheeling," or
allowing customers to contract directly with generators. Consumers
would then gain the benefits of the low price of new plant, though the
incumbent utilities strongly resisted the implied write-down in or
stranding of the value of their old, high-cost assets and contracts. Since
then much effort has been devoted to devising methods to recover
these stranded assets without completely sacrificing the potential gains
from liberalization. In 1994 the CPUC issued the "Blue Book" with proposals to alter the regulatory system (e.g., see Blumstein and Bushnell
1994). The four (interconnected) grids then vertically integrated with
their local utilities would form a regional transmission grid under a
systems operator, and would make regulated payments to the utilities
for the use of their assets, thus gaining the benefits of state-wide efficient despatch. Larger customers would be allowed to buy from any
supplier, and the CPUC invited comments on whether this should be
achieved through an English-type compulsory pool or through bilateral contracting, with a voluntary balancing pool.

The latter system seems to work well in the dominantly hydro Scandinavian system, and California has 25 percent hydro (together with 38 percent gas, 17 percent nuclear, 11 percent renewables, and 9 percent coal), as well as links to the hydro systems in the north. One argument for a balancing pool, which would operate on the day, is that it might eliminate forecasting errors and reduce uplift, but the objection to both pool bypass and a separate physical market is that both run the risk of out-of-merit running for no obvious gain. Stoft (1997) has cast doubts on the motives of those arguing for it in California, and he suggests that it may lead to considerable efficiency losses.

FERC has jurisdiction over interstate trade in electricity, and in an integrated system coving the United States, actions of any generator anywhere will inevitably have implications for interstate flows of electricity. This, and the Energy Act 1992, gives FERC the power to make rules for trading electricity. In 1994 FERC published a Notice of Inquiry on alternative power pooling institutions, followed in 1995 by its Notices of Proposed Rulemaking (NOPR) on access to transmission services and the recovery of stranded costs, the so-called Mega-NOPR (FERC 1995). The Mega-NOPR provoked widespread criticism for its rather simplistic approach to defining transmission services, but it marked a decisive step forward in recognizing that control of transmission gave the incumbent utility huge market power over consumers requiring access to alternative generators. If participants in wholesale markets were to have nondiscriminatory open access then FERC argued that the public utility would need to "functionally" unbundle transmission; that is, the operation of the transmission would have to be provided by an independent system operator (ISO), though the utility would not necessary have to sell the assets. FERC also proposed that liberalizing the wholesale market would "require the applicant and its affiliates to demonstrate that they lack or have mitigated market power in generation and transmission."

CPUC adapted its proposals to satisfy the Mega-NOPR, and proposed a compromise solution to the debate over pools or bilateral trading in which the pool (known as the California Power Exchange or PX) would be optional, and would compete with other exchanges and with trading bilaterally outside the PX. The PX and the ISO were separately incorporated as independent pro bono nonprofit corporations, with no financial interests in generation. The PX sets ex ante prices for the day ahead derived from an auction process in which generators and buyers submit offers and bids for each hour in a sequence of five iterations. After each iteration, provisional prices and schedules are published and can be revised only according to specified activity rules that have been designed to discourage gaming. The final iteration determines the ex ante clearing price and quantities, which are firm, and the day-ahead schedule is submitted to the ISO.

Those players choosing not to trade through the PX submit their bids and offers to scheduling coordinators who in turn submit balanced schedules to the ISO. The ISO operates a real-time balancing market and purchases ancillary services to ensure system stability and also manages transmission congestion. The ISO determines an ex post price at which any divergences between notified bilateral contracts are settled, and charges for the other services it supplies. The motivation behind having a number of different power markets is to provide competition between the activity of market making to determine the least-cost method of trading. Although large generators are required to trade through the PX until 2001, thereafter the most successful market maker will presumably capture most if not all the trade.

The market was scheduled to open at the beginning of 1998 but was delayed by computer problems until March 30. In its early stages almost all transactions were either subject to price caps or under transitional contracts, both of which greatly reduced the role of supply competition. Until July, prices in the day-ahead PX market remained below $40/MWh but gradually drifted upward in response to growing peak demand during July, and exceeded $160/MWh in a heat wave in early August. Prices exceeded $40/MWh about 25 percent of the time in July and August but then fell back to between $20 and $30/MWh for the rest of the year. The time pattern of prices is strongly correlated with demand both within the day and over time, suggesting that the market is working well (and contrasts with the poor correlation between price and demand in the English pool).[30] The PX price appears to track the bilateral contracts prices and the hour-ahead market (for which there was little experience) closely. In the first year of operation to March 31, 1999, 80 percent of the time prices were below $30/MWh, and the average hourly price was $24.44/MWh.

The graph of the PX market-clearing price against the market-clearing quantity (which is an averaged supply function) is fairly elastic up to about 30,000 MW and $40, but it rapidly becomes very inelastic and essentially vertical at 35,000 MW. Approximately 20,000 MW of plant is must-run plant that bids zero, and the PX price has fallen to zero for 43 hours in May and 87 hours in June. The result is that the price-setting part of the market is relatively thin, and of the 30 sellers in the market, only four were important price setters once prices exceed $75/MWh, with fewer playing a price-setting role as the prices rose further (Bohn, Klevorick, and Stalon 1998). Not surprisingly, the Market Monitoring Committee expressed its concern about market concentration.

In contrast to the systematic relation between prices and quantities in the PX market and other evidence of a functioning market, the ancillaries service market operated by the ISO performed very poorly, at least in the first few transitional months, in the view of the surveillance committee (Wolak, Nordhaus, and Shapiro 1998). From March 30 until June 30, the market was subject to cost-based caps for most services, during which there was a chronic shortage of capacity. From July 1, several generators that had been divested from their parent utility received FERC authorization to receive market-based rates rather than cost-based rates, and prices moved from their cap of $10/MW or less to highs of $5,000/MW and $9,999/MW, with huge volatility—the price in the hour following the last $9,999/MW bid on July 13 was $0.01/MW. The PX market for energy and the closely related ISO market for related services of balancing and reserve did not appear to have been efficiently arbitraged.

The surveillance committee identified nine major structural faults with the ancillaries services market, one of which is that more reserves seem to be needed in a fragmented market than in the previously vertically integrated one, possibly in part because the ISO does not bear the cost of ensuring system stability but would attract the odium of failing to provide it. In addition the ISO follows rigid and highly predictable rules that allow suppliers to predict when their own supply is critical and hence can be highly priced. This appears to be exacerbated by breaking the region into zones in each of which the ISO must purchase these services. The surveillance committee has made recommendations for improving market performance, and suggested that these early problems were probably unavoidable given the complexity of the task and the short time in which it had to be completed. They also point out that some of the problems derive from the mismatch between allowing some participants freedom to trade on markets while others are subject to restrictive rules.

It is therefore too soon to tell whether the gains from liberalization will offset the considerable costs of setting up and operating the new trading system, not to mention the possible inefficiencies that perverse pricing and incentives may cause. One of the hoped-for benefits was that creating a wide-area market should provide additional gains from trade, allowing cheaper power from one area to replace more expensive generation in another. Kahn, Bailey, and Pando (1997) have attempted to quantify these gains and suggest that they may be remarkably small. Their model of the Western System Coordinating Council region (which runs from British Columbia in the north, to Baja California, Mexico in the south, and as far east as Utah) estimates the benefits of pooling as $31 million/year or one-third of 1 percent of avoidable costs. This estimate is only about one-tenth the benefits estimated by White (1995), perhaps because White ignored the extra transmission losses, which could be important as pooling can have a large impact on the volume of trade. The model predicts that California will increase its imports from 62 to 84 TWh, or to nearly one-third of total consumption. If marginal losses are as high as 6 percent, the extra transmission costs would be about 0.5 of 1 percent. White also examined a single month which may have been atypical, whereas Kahn, Bailey, and Pando looked at the entire year. White's figures should therefore be treated with some caution.

Other states, particularly those with high retail prices where consumers saw advantages in liberalizing access, were also actively discussing reform, and some have been operating power pools (confined to utilities) for many years. The United States presents a fascinating test bed for institutional reform, since each state is largely free to determine its own restructuring, subject to approval by FERC, and most are under some pressure to liberalize if customers within the state can see lower spot prices in neighboring areas. Over the next few years, different models will be tried and some will be found better than others.

6.5.6   Transmission Pricing and Investment

The main objection to separating generation from transmission is that some of the coordination benefits of vertical integration might be lost. For example, it may be cheaper to choose a more expensive location for generation in order to economize on investments in transmission. Any country or state deciding to unbundle generation from transmission has to decide how to price transmission services, and how to decentralize decisions on generation location and investment in new transmission. In Britain, with a mature and dense transmission grid, and excess generation capacity, the problems of ensuring efficient pricing of the grid did not seem serious at the time, and were left for later review. Countries with sparse grids, or distant hydro resources, or those with rapid electricity demand growth, need to think more carefully how to preserve these coordination benefits, while the evidence in Britain and the United States suggests that even mature countries can make mistakes, some of which may be very expensive.

Electricity is transmitted between different locations by a network according the laws of physics, not the contracts between generators and buyers. The efficient solution to generating and delivering electricity over a constrained network with losses has associated with it the normal set of dual prices, one for each node. Are these shadow nodal prices just notional, or can they be made manifest in markets and used for decentralized decision making? This may sound like an abstract question, but it is at the heart of debates on how best to restructure the U.S. electricity system, where different parts of the interconnected network are under different ownership and control. Nodal pricing has already been chosen in Scandinavia and Latin America. It is interesting to compare the two different approaches to decentralizing the transmission system.

The English solution is to ignore differences in nodal prices, and adopt the single integrated market as the benchmark, with a contractual right to transmission. Where transmission constraints prevent the despatch of stations in merit (i.e., having a bid below the system marginal price, or SMP), they are compensated with their lost profit (SMP *less* the station's bid). Stations that bid above SMP but are required to run are paid their bid price. The extra cost is then recovered from all consumers, not just those whose demands caused the extra cost. In the longer run, connection and use-of-system charges are regionally differentiated so that consumers and generators take transmission costs and constraints into account when choosing where to locate.

This concept of a single countrywide price with station-specific adjustments may be contrasted with nodal pricing, where all suppliers and consumers within a zone (defined as having no internal transmission constraints) face the same price, which may differ between zones. The choice between these two concepts of the market is fundamental and problematic. The English system is simple to operate, but it faces the objection that generators have an incentive to exploit any capacity constraints by manipulating their bids. The same is also true with nodal pricing, but with an important difference. Generators in an importing zone can exploit the transmission constraints to raise zonal prices, but those in an exporting zone will only be paid the SMP (the bid price of the most expensive generator) within that zone, which will be less than the systemwide SMP. Zonal pricing thus penalizes exporters rather than compensating them as in the English system. Given that there will typically be a range of equilibrium bidding strategies and resulting prices, the real question is whether the threat of entry somewhere into the system better restrains bidding behavior when prices are set zonally, or when there is a systemwide price directly affected by entry anywhere.

The attraction of nodal prices is that they define the value of the transmission link connecting adjacent nodes and provide an appealing solution to two difficult problems: how to signal where consumers and generators should locate, and how to decide when and where to build additional transmission capacity. The main criticism of vertical de-integration is that generation and transmission investment must be coordinated to minimize total system costs: It may be cheaper to pay more to locate generation near demand to avoid the cost of building extra transmission. The English solution of signaling where to locate by a centralized calculation of regional connection charges failed its first test because the locational prices were insufficiently differentiated. In the "dash for gas" new entrants located in areas of excess supply. Perhaps markets could do better. The problem is that any power flows between two nodes changes the pattern of flows over the whole network, creating the kinds of externalities that normally cause market failure. It is now well known that it may be profitable to build a network link (paid for by the flow times nodal price difference) that actually increases total systems congestion and cost (Braess's paradox—e.g., see Kelly 1991; Bushnell and Stoft 1995).

The counterargument is that market power and externalities can be handled by contracts. These will be necessary in any case, as market-determined nodal prices would be even more volatile than pool prices. The natural counterpart to systemwide English CfDs are nodal CfDs, or, equivalently, a single CfD plus a set of transmission congestion contracts (TCCs) that allow the holder to receive the difference in nodal prices at each end of the transmission line for each MW contracted. As before, the incentives for noncompetitive behavior are eliminated if agents are fully contracted (Green 1999; Newbery 1995a). Bushnell and Stoft (1995) claim that if all agents are fully contracted (defined as a set of TCCs and CfDs corresponding to a feasible despatch), then no party has an incentive to make disadvantageous grid investments; the investor would effectively have to compensate all other agents for externalities. This approach of "completing the market" for externalities (Newbery 1989), coupled with full contracting to eliminate market power, has considerable theoretical appeal but doubtful practicality. Such an approach might work in a completely predictable world, but competitive nodal prices change on a time scale of hours, while grid investments may last for decades. Nor is it clear why agents would choose to be fully contracted and forgo their market power.

At the heart of the debate between nodal pricing and a single pool is the question how well markets might work in practice. We have a growing experience with unified pools, but less with market determined nodal pricing, though there are some revealing insights from laboratory experiments. Vernon Smith (1996) suggests that generators are adept at exploiting their market power at the expense of transmission owners when uncontracted, but we wait evidence on whether contracts will emerge that are adequate to handle nodal price differences. Scandinavia and California operate zonal pricing systems where congestion constraints can cause prices to diverge in neighboring zones, but they both have sufficiently strong transmission systems that price variations have been modest to date. New Zealand has significant transmission constraints but the generators are few in number and remain publicly owned, so the present nodal pricing pattern may not accurately reflect that of a genuinely competitive market. For more evidence on the performance differences between the two systems of transmission pricing we need to look to the Eastern United States.

Hogan (1998) describes the problem that the Pennsylvania–New Jersey–Maryland (PJM) interconnection market encountered in its original design of a zonal pricing system. FERC approved an interim transmission access and pricing system in March 1997 with a real-time spot market that computes a single price for the entire PJM system, thereby ignoring transmission constraints. Generators, however, did not have rights to firm dispatch and were paid zero if they were constrained off, in contrast to England and Wales where generators affected by constraints are compensated. In addition, participants could schedule bilateral contracts and pay their share of the total congestion cost. As Hogan points out, constrained-off generators faced with a zero payment from the pool could (and did) make a bilateral contract and force the ISO to constrain off some other generator or schedule alternative generation. The whole system threatened to unravel and the ISO had to intervene to avoid the market collapsing by banning bilateral trades in June 1997.

This flawed system was replaced by a nodal pricing system from April 1998 with some 2,000 nodes between which prices can differ. The difference between the lowest and highest nodal price in any hour in April was $282/MWh, and the median price range was $33/MWh. Hogan argues that it would take a very large number of zones, perhaps up to one hundred, to ensure that nodal price variations within each zone are small, though a more interesting question is how the dispatch efficiency (the total cost of generation and transmission) compares in this system and one with a smaller number of zones and constraint payments made to generators (and perhaps compulsory dispatch). Tabors and Galindo (1999) take issue with this claim. They argue that a limited number of zonal prices for the whole of the Northeast of the United States would capture 98 percent of the price variation. They suggest a "hub and spoke" simpler compromise solution.

The English experience with a single zone has had its difficulties as well, though it is far from clear that they would have been resolved by nodal pricing, given the underlying problems of market power even in the unified Pool. At privatization the initial transmission charges were drawn up rather hastily, to be reviewed after two years. Unfortunately, very substantial entry occurred before appropriate price signals were put in place. For example, several new entrants required connection in the north where there was a shortage of transmission capacity to the main centers of consumption in the south. Under the existing rules the substantial cost of strengthening transmission fell in the first instance on NGC.[31] Had the generator been connected further south, the small extra generation cost would have been greatly outweighed by the saving in transmission investment. The system of constraint payments provides somewhat perverse location incentives, for a constrained-off plant is compensated for its notional lost profit. This can encourage generators to locate in an export-constrained area and bid zero for periods they can expect to be constrained off. NGC should perhaps not offer the same right of secure transmission to generators who choose to locate in regions that may be export constrained and where their capacity is less valuable. In due course the locational charges were revised, using a methodology that averages the extra costs incurred by entry (or exit) over the relevant zone, rather than charging entrants the "deep connection" charge, or the increase in total cost incurred as a result of entry.

The original annual use-of-system zonal charges for generators ranged from £3.13/kW in the northeast, down to zero in London; but by 1997–98 the range was from £7.98 in the north down to −£10.11 in Peninsular (i.e., the far southwest), where generators are paid to be connected to the system.[32] Losses have increased from 1.6 percent in 1990 to a high of 2.4 percent in 1999, mostly because of high peak power flows from north to south, in part because generators are locating too far from load centers. NGC (1997, tab. 6.7) shows that a new power station in the north generating 100 MW only meets 93 MW of national demand averaged across the system at the predicted 2003/2004 winter peak, while 100 MW located in Peninsular meets 110 MW of demand by alleviating power losses—or 18 percent more than the northern station. Since all the capital cost should ideally be collected at system peak, this differential implies that lifetime generating costs might be 12 percent too high for an incorrectly located station (on the assumption that half the cost is capital, and operating losses add another 4 percent).[33] Clearly, the costs of inefficient location can be large compared to the benefits of competition, which Newbery and Pollitt (1997) put at 6.5 percent of the wholesale electricity price annually (see section 6.4 above). It remains to be seen whether the more highly zonally differentiated charges correctly reflect the costs of location.[34] The pool also proposed a system of charging generators for zonal losses, but this was appealed against by the adversely affected northern generators. The regulator has decided to revisit issues of transmission pricing at the next transmission price review (Offer 1998c).

6.6   Electricity Markets: Lessons from the Case Studies

The Argentine electricity reforms suggest that the lessons of radical restructuring in England can be applied to state-owned systems in developing countries providing sufficient care is taken to design the structure, the markets and their operation, and the system of regulation. In many ways the Argentine solution is more sophisticated than the English solution, in the management of the bulk electricity market, the contestability of transmission, and the attempt to base prices on costs rather than bids, thus potentially reducing the market power of generators. As in England, the regulatory system is buttressed by licenses that can be protected through the courts, and the impact of its reforms have been similarly dramatic in increasing the efficiency of generation. It remains to be seen whether the rather complex system of regulation and price setting can achieve the potential benefits that their designers anticipated, and it is too soon to judge the robustness of the regulatory system against political intervention or economic crisis. That in turn will determine whether the industry remains capable of financing investment.

The major economic differences between the different cases lie in the organization of the electricity market and the treatment of transmission, though there are also important differences in the governance structures for these markets, discussed in Barker et al. (1997). The main problems facing the designers of an electricity market are how to dispatch plant (taking account of transmission constraints) to minimize generation and transmission costs, and how to secure adequate (but not excessive) payment to cover fixed costs and ensure a willingness to invest to expand capacity when required. The first requirement normally requires plant to submit their short-run avoidable costs, but these are typically only half the average total cost. Paying just the marginal energy price will therefore fail to meet the second requirement, while accepting bids based on average costs risks running plant out of merit order.

The three solutions that have emerged for the electricity market are as follows:

1. Variants on the Argentine system. This is the closest to the older system of merit order dispatch based on energy cost data with additional computed availability and/or capacity payments.

2. The English system of a compulsory pool with commercially determined bids and an additional calculated system of capacity payments.

3. Models based on commodity markets, with voluntary trading, no capacity payments, and a balancing pool.

There are differences in whether physical trades are allowed (and take precedence over the balancing pool). Most, if not all, pools at the moment determine a system marginal price paid for all transactions in that pool, though most trade is covered by bilateral contracts at mutually agreed prices, so only the difference between contracted and actual trade is ever priced at the SMP.

Which model delivers the best performance? That was the question posed by the incoming British Labour government in 1997 to the director general of electricity supply (DGES, the regulator), reflecting the growing dissatisfaction with the performance of the English Electricity Pool. The overall objective of the pool review was "that trading arrangements should deliver the lowest possible sustainable prices to all customers, for a supply that is reliable in both the short and long run" (Electricity Pool 1998). The pool review steering group also listed a number of subsidiary objectives—that the trading arrangements should facilitate efficiency in generation, transmission, distribution, trading, and consumption; they should minimize entry and exit barriers, should support systems security, minimize transactions costs, and minimize unnecessary and unmanageable commercial and regulatory risk.[35]

Ideally one would compare the costs and benefits of each trading model, and attempt to relate these to the technical and institutional features of the different electricity systems. Perhaps the most important of the technical features are the extent of market power of the incumbent generators, the size of any barriers to entry, the extent of storage hydro (which greatly reduces short- and medium-run price volatility), the amount of excess capacity, and probably the extent to which the country has access to cheap gas and can benefit from quickly built and competitive CCGT generation. Institutional differences are even wider. The extent and nature of ownership and regulation, the system of market governance, environmental constraints, and the maturity of the legal and administrative system of the country are all important and differ widely. Given the large number of possible factors that might explain differences in performance of different trading arrangements, and the short time period over which most have been tested and adjusted, the empirical evidence is far from decisive as to which design suits which set of circumstances. The debate has therefore been largely driven by a priori arguments, analogies, or the expectations (often overoptimistic) of different special interest groups who can see opportunities for gain from changes to the existing system (Stoft 1997).

The main criticisms of the English pool are about market manipulation, market design (including criticisms about capacity payments, constraint payments, and transmission charges), and the governance structure. Because pool members must sign the Pooling and Settlement Agreement, which is an indefinite contract, changes at present require the agreement of the parties affected. Since almost all changes redistribute costs or revenues, they are usually blocked. Consequently, reforming (or replacing) the present governance structure is critical to making any other changes.

The most serious criticism of the performance of the electricity market is that the restructuring in 1990 created an effective duopoly, in which National Power and PowerGen set the price over 90 percent of the time. These two firms have maintained their price setting ability, despite the subsequent massive entry of gas-fired combined cycle gas turbine plant. Even after National Power and PowerGen were induced to divest 6,000 MW of coal-fired plant to Eastern, they did so with earn-out payments that encouraged Eastern to bid the plant exactly as before, and if anything National Power and PowerGen raised their prices in winter of 1997–98, sacrificing market share to Eastern and other generators in a successful attempt to keep pool prices up while fuel costs continued to fall. The DGES criticized this behavior and recommended that these two generators be required to divest more coal-fired plant (Offer 1998d).

This bidding behavior of coal-fired plant came at a sensitive moment, when the five-year coal contracts forced on the industry in 1993 after the first collapse of the coal market were set to expire. Faced with a second "dash for gas" further eroding the market for coal, the government imposed a moratorium on building gas-fired plant until it had reviewed its energy policy. If the avoidable cost of existing coal-fired plant is below the total cost of new CCGT (which may well be the case), but is bid in at a price above this cost, then inefficient entry will occur and coal will be displaced. The sensible remedy is to cure the market power that leads to distorted bidding, rather than to prevent entry of the one source of competition that might put a cap on the average pool price.[36]

The *Review of Electricity Trading Arrangements* (Offer 1998c) concentrated its attention on market design issues, where the main criticisms are that it is only half a market with inadequate representation of the demand side, that is opaque, unpredictable, and therefore hard to hedge using standard contracts, and that is compulsory, which prevents trading outside the pool and hence discourages contracting. Paying all generators the same marginal price (except to those constrained) further discourages contracting and aggressive bidding, and the SMP is typically between twice and four times the marginal energy price that the scheduling program relies on to select the merit order. In addition capacity payments are claimed to be volatile, unpredictable, and excessive.

The review process argued that the complexities of price formation in the pool allowed the generators to exercise more market power than would have been possible had the market been structured like a classic commodity market. The pool review recommended that the Pooling and Settlement Agreement be replaced by a Balancing and Settlement Code. The pool as such would end and be replaced by four voluntary, overlapping, and interdependent markets operating over different time scales: bilateral contracts markets for the medium and long run, forward and futures markets operating up to several years ahead, a short-term bilateral market, operating from at least 24 hours to about 4 hours before a trading period, and finally, a balancing market from about 4 hours before real time. The system operator would trade in this market to keep the system stable, and use the resulting prices for clearing imbalances between traders' contracted and actual positions. This structure mirrors that emerging in the British gas market, and it has similarities with electricity markets in Scandinavia, Australia, and California. The main questions about these proposals are whether they would deal with market power without restructuring generation, whether they would be improve efficiency if generator market power were dealt with by restructuring, and whether they are likely to prejudice a move toward a competitive market, all of which are disputed by the author (Newbery 1998a). Finally, will the gains outweigh the costs?

The pool review attempted a rough calculation of the costs of restructuring (Offer 1998c, §8.72) and put them at £100 million to £110 million per year for the first five years, representing about 1.25 percent of the average pool price. No estimates of the benefits are provided, though it was observed that a 1 percent fall in retail electricity prices (2 percent fall in wholesale electricity prices) "would more than cover a conservative estimate of the costs" (§8.74). A fall in prices is not the same as a fall in costs (and the net benefits of restructuring at privatization described above (in §6.4) were associated with an *increase* in consumer prices relative to the counterfactual). Unless costs also fall, it is doubtful that prices can be sustainably reduced without a change in the market structure to create more competition. If, as hoped, the market is restructured to make it more competitive, then prices will be set closer to costs, and any further lowering of prices would need a lowering of costs.

Will the proposals lower costs (or even prices)? Will the trading reforms create markets with the efficiency of commodity futures markets or markets for financial instruments? Is electricity more like cocoa or life insurance? Cocoa, cotton, and the like, are traded in highly liquid markets for remarkably small trading costs, allowing ownership of claims on the underlying commodity to change hands perhaps 10 to 20 times with transaction costs measured in tenths of a percentage point or less. Financial products are also traded on very liquid markets, but they need to be bundled and rebundled by portfolio managers at considerable cost. Consider a typical unit trust with annual management fees of 1 percent of revenue, as well as entry and exit charges that can amount to 5 percent of capital value. If, over long periods of time, real returns are 6 percent, and if holding times are five years, then the management and entry/exit fees absorb one-third of the total profit. High Street banks extract an even larger fraction of the return on the assets they manage for their services.

The key question is whether all these new markets and incentives or requirements to hedge will more closely emulate the low-transaction costs of commodity futures markets or the high-transaction costs of more individualized financial markets. Given the highly non-homogeneous nature of electricity, with 48 half-hourly prices for 365 days per year (not to mention the problematic ancillary services that have given the California ISO so much grief), it is difficult to see the commodity futures market for highly standardized products being a good analogy.

When it comes to arguing that the proposed trading arrangements will lower prices, the claim is that delinking the balancing market from the contract and forward market will make the influence of the price-setting generators on the price level less direct, compared to the present system in which the balancing market is the pool which determines the price for all generation and serves as the guide price for setting contracts. The argument here is that because any generator can sell into the pool without any contractual cover and receive the PPP, while any consumer can buy at the PPP (plus uplift) instead of on contract, in the long run the contract prices can only differ from the relevant average Pool price by a (modest) risk premium. If, on the other hand, the balancing market is thinly traded, dominated by the small number of generators with flexible plant, and viewed as an unpredictable and possibly penal alternative to bilateral contracting, then the prices revealed there will not be relevant for contracting, while the incentive to contract will be greatly increased and will be driven by the normal balance of commercial considerations which guide price formation in other markets. The central part of the claim is that because participants can no longer rely on buying in the pool they will have to contract. Since some 90 percent of electricity is already traded under contracts, that is hardly new.

It is also argued that the pool is too transparent to the price-setting generators, who can craft their bids to maximize their profits, and possibly even tacitly collude, in a way that a less transparent contract market might make harder, offering as it does opportunities for price shading, underbidding, and other competitive rather than cooperative strategies. It is hard to reconcile the claim that, on the one hand, price discovery will be encouraged once the pool price ceases to be a good guide to trading terms, while on the other hand, the lack of a clear reference pool price will encourage harder bargaining over the terms of these contracts, and they will be driven closer to cost. If plant owners know the likely contract price, why should they accept less? Why should this be any different from the present situation in which plant owners cannot predict the future pool price with any confidence (as convincingly demonstrated in the reports to the review) and so must choose on what terms to contract?

Perhaps the argument is that removing the option of being guaranteed sale at pool prices alters the outside option in the bargaining game between the generator and supplier, forcing down the bargained price. This may be true in the short run, but what effect will it have on the conditions of entry? At various points it is recognized that the pool reduces the entry risks for new entrants (especially merchant plant) by providing them with this outside option. If the returns for entrants are made riskier and less attractive, the obvious conclusion is that there will be less entry, and that the threat of entry will have less downward pressure on prices. If there is no change in the ownership of capacity, what will be the response of the incumbents? Surely they will raise prices, if not immediately, then as soon as the market tightens because of a reluctance to enter?

The criticisms in the pool review about capacity payments are telling, and have been made elsewhere (Newbery 1995a, 1998c) and in section 6.2.1 above. The method of computing the loss of load probability greatly overstates the actual probability of a loss of load, and hence provides overgenerous capacity payments. While there is much wrong with the present system of capacity payments, their effects can be exaggerated. At present there is evidence that average pool prices are set by the conditions of entry, and it is therefore no surprise that if capacity payments go down, SMP rises correspondingly to preserve the PPP. (The evidence for this inverse relationship can be found in Offer 1998d.) The more interesting question is what might happen in the pool if the capacity payments were reduced, logically by a more accurate estimate of LOLP.

On the assumption that entry remains contestable, the PPP is fixed by the costs of entry, in which case if the incumbents have the power to raise the SMP by the amount that the capacity element is reduced, they will do so. The amount of spare capacity will be reduced (for it must cover its fixed costs from the expected capacity payment, which has fallen), and the variability of prices might at first sight be expected to fall somewhat, since capacity payments are concentrated on a small number of hours where the peak payments may now be lower. On the other hand, the profit-maximizing strategy of the incumbents is still to maximize the volatility of prices, subject to not inducing entry of peak capacity, which has been made less likely by the lower capacity payments. Incumbents may therefore increase base load contractual cover to induce lower base load prices and raise peak prices in compensation, essentially restoring the original volatility. The pool selling price (PSP) should fall as the level of unscheduled availability payments, which was about £260 million in 1997; this will fall in line with the fall in the reserve margin. If the payments were to fall by one-third, the PSP might fall by 0.04 p/kWh or by a little over 1 percent.

The average *cost* of electricity for the incumbents will also fall, as capacity utilization of the incumbents will have risen (but this will not affect any base-load IPPs), so incumbent profits should rise, as will the risk of power cuts. The end result looks like a potential public relations disaster: The generators make more profits for less reliable power at only a marginally lower price.

What would happen if there were more equally placed generators bidding into the spot market and hence making it more competitive, as in Victoria? Then entry threats would not be necessary to keep prices low, though at some stage as demand expands relative to capacity, new plant will be required, and entry will only be justified once the average price rises to the average cost of new plant. This is essentially the same condition as in a contestable market. If there were no capacity payments, the situation would be rather like commodity markets with durable investment. Aluminium is a good example, where heavy investment in smelters makes the avoidable cost low compared to the total cost, just as in electricity. The aluminium market is characterized by long periods of rather low prices close to marginal avoidable costs, punctuated by periods of very high prices, during which the producers recover all their fixed costs. Prices have to stay high enough long enough to convince investors that entry is desirable, given the high sunk costs and the risks of low prices after they have expanded capacity. Capacity payments should mitigate this extreme and probably politically unsustainable volatility.

Several conclusions follow from this analysis. Provided that entry remains contestable, and that some new capacity would be economic as a result of a growth in demand and the need to replace older stations, the incumbents will be forced to keep the prices at competitive levels on average, and will be encouraged to mimic the extreme daily and seasonal volatility of a competitive market. Second, the level of the PPP, which includes the capacity payments, may not be very sensitive to the exact form of capacity payments where the incumbents retain available price-setting power. Third, the degree of system security may be quite sensitive to the exact form of these capacity payments, as will the cost of providing the security. Fourth, the main deviation of market behavior in the pool from competitive behavior is likely to occur in periods when entry is not a threat, typically when there is excess capacity and no economic case for investment, or if barriers to entry appear, or if the willingness of counterparties to sign long-term electricity contracts weakens. Finally the relatively benign experience of the English pool (where prices have not risen as much as was feared would follow from the unfettered exercise of market power by two price-setting generators) depends critically on the ease of entry at modest scale with CCGT plant. This in turn depends on the availability of cheap gas in the presence of aging coal plant. This experience will not necessarily translate to other countries with different plant and fuel prices, and was put at risk by the 1998 moratorium on gas entry into the English market.

Changing the form of capacity payments to meet objections will not be easy. The advantages of a decentralized market mechanism are considerable but uncomfortable. It encourages generators to make plant available when it is most needed, but to retire plant that cannot cover its annual costs. It forces those overseeing the industry to question closely the value of lost load, and, if this is not rather high, to accept the higher implied risk of system losses of load (in addition to the existing frequency of local outages). It encourages consumers to consider the value of reducing demand at the peak, and it may prompt a variety of lower cost solutions to the peak than centrally despatched plant with the attendant need for adequate transmission capacity. It moves electricity pricing closer to the efficient ideal where overhead costs are loaded onto the peak or expected peak, even where the spot market may not be very competitive—at least provided that the market remains contestable.

The alternative in which generators bid a simple price high enough to cover all costs will either dampen these signals if generation is not sufficiently competitive or, if it is, may lead to periodic crises in which the market fails to provide an acceptable level of reserve capacity. This may require the system operator to contract for reserve capacity. If he overcontracts, then pool prices will remain low and no investment will take place, effectively forcing the system operator to take on the functions of the former franchized utility, but if he undercontracts, the problem will remain. Unfortunately, given the extent of excess capacity in most liberalizing electricity industries (which is no coincidence), it may take many years to discover the best form of rewarding reserve capacity.

Vic Pool is a good example of a very competitive market where prices have drifted down as the market has been widened to include more generation (see figure 6.8), but it has had problems with adequately rewarding capacity. California's PX also has simple bids, though the ISO pays for reserves through ancillary services, and that market worked very poorly, at least in its early period. The PX market behavior exhibits a very steep supply function, which is consistent with the competitive model just described, but clearly the market will continue to evolve given the close regulatory scrutiny it has attracted.

One of the problems with the U.K. pool review is that it lacked a vision of how the industry might evolve, either without reform or with some restructuring to increase competition, or under the proposed changes to the pool. The argument of this book is that competition is preferable to regulation, but that for competition to deliver benefits to consumers, market power must be abated, and that seems most likely in electricity with a structure of competitive generation with no cross-ownership with other parts of the industry. If so, it seems that the only way to sustain a competitive structure once it has been created is to preserve a single-price open-access pool and prevent horizontal and vertical mergers. On this view the pool review's proposals went in exactly the wrong direction, for they seemed likely to precipitate vertical mergers that would be justified as reducing the transaction costs imposed by the new market structure. The almost certain outcome would be toward a more vertically integrated industry with a small number of players who would benefit relative to their rivals from their ability to internalize risks after the removal of existing markets and instruments that allow other independent generators to manage their risks.

There is already some evidence for this with the agreed merger between Powergen and the U.S.-owned English REC East Midlands in August 1998. The government has clearly been tempted to accept vertical integration in return for some divestment of further coal-fired generation, as a mechanism to help protect coal. PowerGen agreed to divest 4,000 MW (two stations), while National Power sold Drax, at 4,000 MW the largest coal-fired power station in Europe, and equipped with flue gas desulphurization. Together with changes in the trading arrangements, vertical integration might discourage entry by independent gas-fired generators, while at the same time forcing down the prices paid to existing nuclear and independent CCGT base-load plant, giving higher revenues to the owners of the coal-fired stations through their control over flexible plant, and an overall but rather short run price fall. It must be doubtful that lower prices would persist as demand rises, since it will be less easy to enter such a vertically structured market with no pool, and hence the incumbents can gradually tighten the market to support more profitable prices.

6.7 Conclusions

An open, transparent single-price pool is the critical element in introducing competition into generation. It allows entry at the choice of the entrant, which puts downward pressure on prices, contract terms, and undermines collusion between incumbent generators. It follows that the main criterion in designing a market for bulk electricity is to ensure the efficient contestability of the market place. Efficiency requires that the correct signals on location, fuel-type, reliability, and degree of excess capacity are transmitted to generators, and this places a heavy burden on the design of access and use-of-system pricing of the transmission system. The alternative is one in which entry is at the discretion either of an independent grid company or central purchasing agency, possibly publicly owned, or at the whim of an incumbent, vertically integrated utility. Some publicly owned transmission systems may operate in the public interest, others will be subverted by the political process. Privately owned natural monopolies like transmission systems can be efficiently regulated but may be captured. Separating transmission from generation potentially increases the transparency of charges, provided that these are not obscured by confidential, long-term contracts, and reduces the risk of subversion. Transparency is unattractive to established incumbents who will attempt to suppress open market prices and will argue strongly for confidential bilateral contracting that takes precedence in dispatch.

Contestability is facilitated by long-term contracts from buyers, which in practice means the distribution companies. In the past their incentive was increased by equity participation in the IPP projects, legal in Britain but probably not in the United States. Such participation requires regulatory oversight to prevent profits being transferred from the captive-regulated domestic market to the IPP shareholders and hence requires an independent and trustworthy regulatory system. RECs would have an incentive to sign long-term contracts if they could capture some of the profits on these contracts compared to the possibly more expensive alternative of a sequence of pool-related short-term contracts from incumbents. Yardstick regulation in the domestic market would encourage this at some increase in risk and hence cost. Now that more than half the market is unregulated, this should provide incentives for RECs to contract for competitive electricity supply.

The practical question is who bears the risk of investment in capacity. In the past these risks were passed through to the final customer, whose price reflected the costs, possibly mistaken, of investment decisions. The same is true with rate-of-return regulation and vertical integration. If generation is split from distribution, then it critically depends whether all customers are free to choose their supplier, as was the case in Britain after 1998. Before that date, there was a franchise market, and the RECs could contract for electricity to meet demand in that market, confident that if they can satisfy the regulator that they had met the economic purchase condition, they would be able to pass on these contract costs. Once customers are free to switch to whoever offers the best current price, the RECs face the prospect that long-term contracts may be stranded if the pool price falls or new cheaper generation occurs, though if pool prices rise, they can make a profit on their contract selling at higher current prices.

This increase in income uncertainty and risk will make them less willing to sign long-term contracts or will require a discount for the extra risk borne, which will make entry less attractive. Risk sharing among the generator, REC, and customers would reduce the cost of the aggregated and partly offsetting set of risks. The financial challenge will be to devise a low-cost method of disaggregating and rebundling such risks. This problem will become more important as new entrants will soon cease to run on base-load, and their position in the merit order and hence the amount of time they run will depend on uncertain movements in the prices of gas and coal, as well as on uncertain demand. Later entrants will therefore face increasing price and volume risk, in addition to the loss of the secure franchise market. In contrast to bidding for oil fields, the "winner's curse" of entry is visited upon all existing generators in lower prices.

If generators bear the risk by selling at pool prices (or on pool-price-related contracts), they may be able to pass these risks back to the gas (or coal) supplier (by linking the gas price to the pool price), or by integrating with a gas producer. They may also share risk with a diversified parent company such as a foreign electricity utility, and these risk-sharing devices may lower the cost of risk sufficiently to preserve contestability. One obvious response to future pool price risk is vertical integration between generation and distribution, and this trend is already visible in England. Long-term contracts by RECs are a market version of the same risk-sharing mechanism. As already observed, they need regulatory oversight if the REC has a captive market, and even if all customers are free to choose their supplier, most small domestic customers are likely to stay with their local REC. It may be that some market power is worth trading for reduced risk.

Contestable base-load entry affects pool prices through setting a limit on the time-weighted price that can be maintained over the medium run. A small number of price-setting generators can keep prices at the entry-deterring level, which in periods of excess capacity may be substantially above the efficient level. A large number of actively competing price-setting generators will give greater volatility to average pool prices from year to year, around the same medium-run entry-determined time-weighed price but with a lower demand-weighted price. Oligopoly provides price stability which is inefficient in terms of short-run allocative decisions, but which may reduce imprudent investment choices. Volatility provides incentives for innovation in supply security, in metering, in demand-side management, and in decentralized small-scale generation.

Compared to vertically integrated regulated or state-owned ESIs (which have close similarities) de-integrated private electricity supply may lead to higher profit margins and lower costs, with ambiguous consequences for consumer prices. Given the attractive trade-off between lower costs and excess profits shown in figure 3.7, creating a market in electricity generation is attractive providing it can be made adequately competitive, and that in turn will depend on the size of the market, the nature of scale economies (which will depend on fuel type) and the institutional design and oversight of that market. The U.K. experience suggest that the potential benefits are real and worthwhile, and the dangers ought to be avoidable with more careful institutional design and careful thought about the number of initial generating companies to create.

Appendix: Modeling the Electricity Pool[37]

There are two contending models, the first based on Klemperer and Meyer's (1989) (KM) supply function equilibrium model and the second based on an explicit discrete bid auction model. The claim here is that any equilibrium of the first is also an equilibrium of the second, but not necessarily vice versa. KM explore the Nash equilibrium in supply functions that must be committed to before the realization of uncertain demand. Green and Newbery (1992) noted that the uncertainty of demand was mathematically equivalent to the daily predictable time-varying demand, and they numerically solved a model calibrated to the 1990 English market.

The other approach is exemplified by von der Fehr and Harbord's (1992) model in which each generating company submits a single price for each generating set. This gives a stepwise supply function rather than a continuous schedule. They showed that for some patterns of demand and allocation of capacity among generators there would be no equilibrium in pure strategies. Prices would be inherently unstable as in Edgeworth duopoly, and they claimed that observed pool price behavior revealed such instability. They suggested that the correct way to think of the problem of setting up an electricity market was one of auction design, which is useful in identifying the relevant theoretical literature (e.g., McAfee and McMillan 1987). Unfortunately, it is very hard to solve repeated auctions that lack pure strategy equilibria, leading to an apparent impasse. There is a tractable modeling approach that assumes continuity of the supply schedules, which is subject to the criticism that the indivisibility of the generating sets rules out continuity and drastically affects the nature of the equilibrium, or an alternative that avoids that criticism but is intractable.

This conflict may be more apparent than real.[38] Newbery (1992b) argued that the continuous supply function approach can be adapted to deal with discontinuities caused by the discreteness of each generating set. He noted first that the number of generating sets bid was large (over 200) and each set could submit bids for up to three specified tranches of the set's capacity (e.g., for the first 100 MW, the next 150 MW, and the final 80 MW). If the bids for each tranche are chosen appropriately, and the sizes of the tranches randomly chosen from an appropriate probability distribution, any monotonic supply function can be constructed that is continuous in expectation. Any equilibrium continuous supply function can thus be replicated by introducing a very small amount of randomization. It remains an open question whether there are other plausible mixed strategy equilibria that cannot be found by the supply function approach, but discreteness of the individual sets is not an argument for rejecting the supply function approach.

Newbery (1998b) shows how to solve for the simultaneous equilibrium in spot and contract markets in the case of an analytically tractable model—a task that remains incomplete because of the complexity of interactions between the spot and contract markets (e.g., Green 1999; Powell 1993). The natural approach to modeling electricity markets as supply function equilibria has the drawback that equilibrium is typically not unique. Newbery (1998b) proposed a unique equilibrium in the case where entry may be backed by contracts, and determined the level of contract sales that incumbent generators will sell to sustain this equilibrium. This appendix sets out the basic model and indicates how it can be used to explore equilibrium in an electricity pool.

Equilibrium in Supply Functions

Firm i is assumed to submit a smooth supply function, $q_i = S^i(p)$, relating amount supplied, q_i, to the system marginal price, p. We look for an equilibrium in which each generator has a single chance to bid and does not wish to change its bid given the actual outcome. More collusive outcomes might be sustainable in a repeated game where the players bid against each other every day, so this equilibrium concept tends to underestimate market power, though entry threats neutralize this criticism. The simplest case is that of a symmetric n-firm oligopoly, which can be extended (with some computational difficulty), to the practically important case of an asymmetric duopoly. The notation and argument follows Klemperer and Meyer (1989) closely, who provide proofs of the claims advanced here. The main difference is that we consider variations over time rather than states of the world.

Suppose that the load-duration curve net of nuclear supply at any moment during the day is predictable with certainty and given by $D(p, t)$, where t is the number of hours of demand higher than D. The net demand facing firm i at moment t when the other firm(s) j together have a supply schedule $S^j(p)$ is $D(p, t) - S^j(p)$. Let the generating costs of supplying q be $C(q)$ with marginal cost $C'(q)$. Each firm submits its supply function to the grid despatcher a day ahead, and the despatcher then determines the spot price and hence the order in which to call each firm's generation sets by solving for the price-output pair which equates supply to demand at each moment. That is, at each moment t the despatcher announces the lowest price $p(t)$ such that $D(p(t), t) = S^i(p(t)) + S^j(p(t))$. Valid supply functions are increasing in price, so there is a one-to-one relationship between price and quantity for each supply function, and so the profit-maximizing solution can be found by maximizing profit, $\pi_i = pq_i - C(q_i)$ with respect to p (instead of the less convenient q_i). Profit for firm i is

$$\pi_i(p) = p[D(p, t) - S^j(p)] - C(D(p, t) - S^j(p)), \tag{6A.1}$$

so the first-order condition setting $d\pi_i/dp = 0$ can be written (after rearranging) as

$$\frac{dS^j}{dp} = \frac{q_i}{p - C'(q_i)} + D_p, \tag{6A.2}$$

where $D_p = dD/dp < 0$ is the slope of the demand schedule. Solving for the symmetric n-firm solution in which $q_i = q$ and $S^j = (n-1)q$ gives

$$(n-1)\frac{dq}{dp} = \frac{q}{p - C'(q)} + D_p. \tag{6A.3}$$

This differential equation defines a family of supply functions with positive slope, all passing through the origin (i.e., the point of $q = 0$, $p = C'(0)$) and bounded by (q, p) pairs that satisfy

$$C'(q) < p < C'(q) - \frac{q}{D_p}. \tag{6A.4}$$

With a single exception, for sufficiently large q or p the solutions to the differential equation (i.e., the trajectories) intersect one or other of the boundaries defined by (6A.4) and thereafter cease to be economically valid supply functions. Consider first the boundary defined by the equation $p = C'(q)$. This is the supply schedule of a perfectly competitive firm, and along this curve $dq/dp = \infty$ from (6A.3), so $dp/dq = 0$. Any trajectory that intersects the lower stationary reaches it with horizontal slope, and once it has crossed the stationary, it will slope down and eventually reach the q-axis.

Figure 6.2 above illustrates this for the Green and Newbery (1992) model calibrated to the English market during the winter of 1990. The lowest line is the marginal cost of each level of output, and the figure illustrates the range of equilibria for a duopoly, or a quintopoly (of five firms). The two bounding curves though A and B are solutions to the two and five-firm case (as discussed later) which reach marginal cost at B horizontally.

If the trajectory reaches the upper stationary AD (labeled in figure 6.2 as the "Cournot line") given by $p = C' + q/(-D_p)$ at point D (on the maximum demand schedule, DB), its slope will there be $dq/dp = 0$, or $dp/dq = \infty$. It will cross the stationary vertically and then bend back, eventually reaching the p-axis. The upper stationary also has a simple interpretation as the Cournot supply schedule, for if firm j has unresponsive output k_j, then firm i chooses supply independent of firm j, with $q_i = D(p, t) - k_j$. The profit-maximizing choice of p satisfies $q_i + [p - C'(q_i)]D_p = 0$, or $p = C'(q) - q/D_p$, the equation of the upper stationary of (6A.4). The Cournot supply schedule is the locus of points that are profit maximizing for firm i when the aggregate supply functions of its rivals are locally constant, as demand varies and the market clears. The Cournot *supply schedule* should thus be distinguished from normal concepts of Cournot output, in which a firm chooses a fixed level of output in a Nash equilibrium. Figure 6.2 actually shows *aggregate* supply functions, the *aggregate* Cournot schedule, and total demand. The figure for an individual company would have all quantities reduced by a factor 2 or 5 for the same value of price.

Candidates for equilibrium supply schedules must not cross either stationary over the range of possible price, output pairs; otherwise, they would no longer be monotonically increasing schedules. KM prove that there will be a connected set of equilibria bounded by an upper and lower supply schedule. In general, the supply schedule could therefore lie anywhere between the competitive and Cournot schedules, that is, within the shaded areas ABD (for the duopoly) and ABC (for the quintopoly) in figure 6.2. All that we can say is that if firm i is known to have chosen $q_i(p)$, and if there are no capacity constraints, then the solution $q_j(p)$ to (6A.2) is the profit-maximizing response of firm j.

KM show that increased uncertainty about the residual demand facing the firm narrows down the range of equilibria. Figure 6.2 suggests (and Newbery 1998b proves) that increasing the number of competitors also narrows the range of equilibria. Entry threats, contracts, and capacity limits can narrow this range to give a unique equilibrium.

Effect of Contracts

Suppose that an incumbent (duopolist) firm i offers a (long-term) contract to sell a fixed amount of electricity, x_i, at price f per unit. Its profits are then

$$\pi_i(p, t) = p[D(p, t) - q_i(p)] - C(D(p, t) - q_j(p)) + (f - p)x_i, \qquad i \neq j. \qquad (6A.5)$$

The actual mechanics of contracting are well described by this formula, for the firm continues to supply all its output to the pool in exchange for the pool price p, and it signs "contracts for differences" with the buyer, under which it receives the difference (possibly negative) between the contract price f and the pool price p for the agreed amount x_i, very like a futures contract. The first-order condition for the supply function is found by differentiating (6A.5) as before and gives

$$\frac{dq_j}{dp} = \frac{q_i - x_i}{p - C'(q_j)} + D_p. \qquad (6A.6)$$

Compared to (6A.2), the effect of contract cover x_i is to shift the supply function so that instead of passing through the origin it passes through the point x_i, as in figure 6.9. (Note that figure 6.9 graphs quantity against price, rather than the converse in more conventional graphs of inverse supply and demand functions.) What this means is that if the generator sells more than contracted, or $q_i > x_i$, then the supply function slopes up and the generator wishes to raise the pool price above the marginal cost. If he is overcontracted, or $q_i < x_i$, then he would wish to drive the price below marginal cost, since he would be a net buyer in the pool. The aggregate Cournot schedule is similarly displaced, and figure 6.9 shows a duopoly with a linear demand, $D(p, t) = a(t) - bp$, so $D_p = -b$, and the aggregate Cournot schedule becomes $Q^C = \Sigma q_i^C = \Sigma(x_i + bp) = X + 2bp$, $X \equiv \Sigma x_i$.

Entry

High pool prices will attract entry, and this can be modeled by supposing the new entrants bid at marginal cost (both because they are too small to benefit from bidding higher and because they are likely to be fully contracted), and that entry will continue until profits are competed away. Contract coverage of the kind witnessed in the market makes this a riskless strategy. If the level of entry is z units of base-load

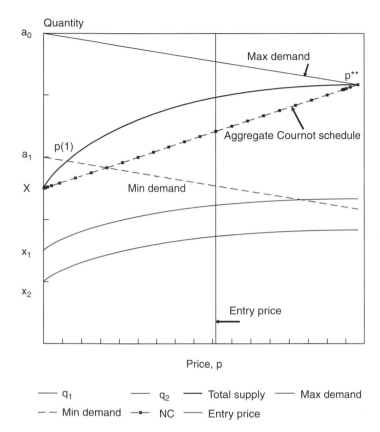

Figure 6.9
Supply function equilibrium with contracts and entry.

capacity with variable unit costs c, and daily (sunk) fixed costs r, then
the net demand facing the bidding generators will be $D(p, t) - z$, and
the equilibrium level of entry will produce an average price $\bar{p}$ that
satisfies

$$\bar{p} = \int_0^1 p(t)dt = r + c, \tag{6A.7}$$

where $p(t)$ ensures that supply equals demand at each t, $D(p(t), t) =$
$z + nq(p(t))$ and where $r + c$ is the average cost of the entrant that
must be recovered from pool prices averaged over the day (taken to be
one unit of time long) and n is the number of symmetric price-setting
generators.

The effect of increasing the number of competing generators and adjusting the level of contract cover to give the profit-maximizing entry-deterring equilibrium is shown in figure 6.10. The larger the number of generators, the more convex is the supply function, and hence the lower is the range of prices. To achieve the same average price, the upper price will therefore be lower and the lower price higher, the larger the number of competitors. This can be seen comparing 2, 3, and 5 generators in figure 6.10. With eight competing generators, entry is deterred without contracts for the parameters chosen, and any positive contract cover would reduce prices even further. If the generators are able to coordinate on a positive level of contracts and a maximum price to just deter entry, then the aggregate supply

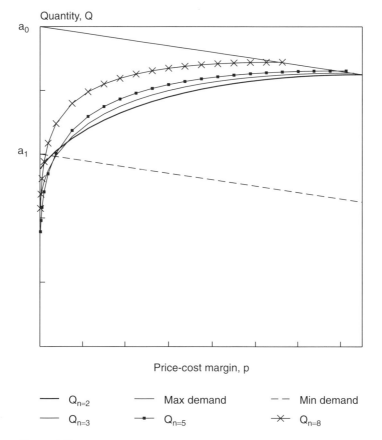

Figure 6.10
Supply function equilibrium varying the number of generators.

function is relatively insensitive to the number of competitors. As the number of competitors increases, it becomes increasingly likely that entry will be blockaded rather than deterred. In that sense a more competitive market is likely to have a lower average price than a less competitive market, provided that there is sufficient capacity to make further investment unnecessary.

If potential entrants can sign base-load contracts, then the generation market becomes contestable, since entrants can lock in the postentry price without risk. If the industry has enough total capacity (given the number of firms), the incumbents can sell enough contracts to drive the price down to the entry-deterring level, and they will find it most profitable to coordinate on the highest-price, highest-contracted supply schedule that sustains this price. The resulting equilibrium is one in which the level of contract cover and bidding strategies are both uniquely specified. The threat of entry will, in most cases, cause the incumbents to increase their contract cover, which will make their behavior in the spot market more competitive and reduce the average pool price. They will also maximize the variability of spot prices, and Newbery (1995a) provides evidence that the two price-setting incumbents in the English electricity market, once they grasped the reality of entry threats (or after they had allowed in sufficient competitors to satisfy the regulator's desire for more competition), rapidly coordinated their bidding strategy in a way consistent with the story presented here.

Increasing the number of competitors would reduce the maximum price reached in the pool, and this might also reduce the average price, depending on whether the equilibrium bidding behavior ignoring the threat of entry were sufficiently competitive to keep prices below the entry level. If not, then the average price would again be set by entrants, but the variability of prices would be lower the larger the number of incumbent competitors, to the benefit of consumers.[39]

The original model in Green and Newbery (1992) was calibrated to reproduce demand and supply conditions in 1988–89 (the latest year available at the time of the study). On the assumption that the incumbents faced no entry threats and would choose to sign no contracts (which, if they faced no entry threats would be an attractive strategy), the noncollusive maximum profit equilibrium involved a price rise of 50 percent and deadweight losses of some £340 million per year, or 6 percent of industry output, compared to a configuration in which the plant were divided up among five equal-sized competitors.

The model was then recalibrated for 1994 to allow for known capacity expansion plans, including expected nuclear performance improvements, and solved for the equilibrium level of entry on different assumptions about demand and bidding behavior, but again assuming that the incumbents were not able to commit to bid competitively through their contract positions. The central estimate was that the incumbents' bidding behavior would induce some 4 GW of entry and dissipate some £200 million per year in deadweight losses compared to the five-firm equilibrium.

In the event about 3 GW of IPP CCGT entered by 1993–94, rising to over 5 GW in 1995, so the predicted levels of entry were quite close. The assumption of no contract cover was not correct, and the arguments set out in this appendix suggest that contract cover can deter entry, providing the incumbents have sufficient capacity (and choose to follow this strategy). There are several possible explanations for why the incumbents nevertheless failed to deter entry: that some entry was seen as a necessary protection against more aggressive antimonopoly investigation, that there was in fact inadequate low-cost plant to compete against new CCGT, or that it was thought profitable to exploit dynamic entry barriers. That is, it would take time for entrants to build capacity and compete, during which the incumbents could reap monopoly profits. The simplest explanation is that the RECs could pass through the costs of IPP contracts and receive profits regardless of the pool price.

The models briefly sketched here and set out in more detail in Newbery (1998b) can be used to explore such issues. They have been influential in encouraging those planning the unbundling of generation to press for adequate numbers of competing generators, as in Victoria. The main lesson to add to Green and Newbery (1992) is that contracts and entry conditions vitally affect the equilibrium in the market, and they also need to be modeled.

Liberalizing the Telecommunications Industry

One of the subthemes of this book is the contrast between the energy network utilities of electricity and gas, and the more technically advanced telecommunications industry. The differences manifest themselves in various ways. Thus in Eastern Europe the case for privatizing telecoms is more compelling than privatizing energy because the gains from relaxing the constraint on investment are so much larger, and there is less concern on the part of buyers that the regulatory compact will fail. Demand growth is high, capacity needs to be expanded, and consumers are willing to pay high prices (relative to costs) to secure good service. The benefits of maintaining an adequate return to the investor and encouraging continued investment are high compared to the risk of alienating foreign investors. Typically social cost–benefit studies of privatization suggest large gains, which often benefit the government and consumers as well as the investors (with Mexico an interesting exception, for reasons discussed in chapter 3).

Electricity, in contrast, has often been privatized where there is excess capacity and modest demand growth, less need for new investment, and hence more concern that the regulatory compact will fail. The steps needed to convince private buyers of the security of their investments are more demanding, and they seem less likely to realize benefits for consumers and also profitable returns to the government. The potential efficiency gains in mature electricity systems seem modest, and it seems hard to design a set of markets and regulation that can divide these modest gains so that all benefit.

Countries where the existing electricity system is grossly inefficient (and there are many such in the developing world) face related problems. Often the inefficiencies stem from underpricing, which in turn reflects politically strong interest groups—farmers in India, energy-intensive industries in Eastern Europe, and urban consumers almost everywhere. Underpricing provokes excess demand and inadequate investment, and these are dangerous conditions under which to create liberalized markets, for the distributional changes are likely to be viewed as an unacceptable price to pay for improved allocative efficiency and ability to finance investment. Charting a route from the present unsatisfactory equilibrium through this phase of high scarcity prices to the eventual goal of demand satisfied at prices close to cost (including the right return on asset value) is difficult, especially if private owners are to be confident in the regulatory stability of the process. Telecoms industries, in contrast, are popular choices for privatization in almost every country—developed, developing, and transitional. Regulatory design does not seem so critical for profitably privatizing telecoms, while poor regulatory design can effectively prevent gas and electricity being sold for an acceptable price.

In industrial economies, pressure for regulatory reform in the energy utilities came after the core network was mature, when the benefits of increased efficiency from competition outweighed the earlier priority of financing the core infrastructure. This was greatly assisted by a fall in the ratio of the minimum economic scale of generation to the market, and amplified by inefficient cross-subsidies or overpriced assets. The same was true in the breakup of AT&T in 1984, but since then the pressure for reform in telecoms comes more from the extraordinarily rapid technical progress in equipment (digital switches, cellular phones, satellites, fiber-optic cables), software (for programming switches, compressing and routing data, encryption, billing, etc.) and the services that these technologies make possible. There is a growing conviction that cumbersome state-owned telecoms monopolies are unable to adapt to these rapid changes effectively, and that the competitive position of any advanced country will be seriously prejudiced if market forces are not allowed to shape the evolution of the industry. This is not the case in the energy utilities, where much of the pressure to liberalize comes from outside the countries—in Europe driven by the EU Directives on Electricity and Gas and in North America driven by FERC's requirements for trading with already liberalized markets.

7.1   Pricing and Regulatory Inefficiencies

In all network utilities the costs of inadequate supply are large, and these are of overwhelming importance in developing countries, and where investment has been held back in telecoms—in Britain during the post–oil-shock austerity period, and in socialist countries for most of their history. Once supply becomes adequate, the inefficiencies of poor regulation and inefficient pricing appear modest in the energy industries, but this is the final important contrast: They are huge in telecoms. The implication is that the problem of designing regulation for telecoms is significantly different from that for the energy utilities. Although, as just noted, it is easier to devise a regulatory regime to allow profitable telecoms privatization than it is for electricity and gas, this can hide the importance of ensuring that regulation is efficient. The fact that it is relatively simple to devise regulation that delivers benefits conceals the importance of designing regulation to maximize these benefits. The cost of falling short of this potential can be very high.

The reason is simple. Moore's Law states that the cost of microelectronics halves every 18 to 24 months, and since telecoms networks are increasingly controlled by sophisticated computer switching, this has had a dramatic impact on the cost of routing calls. At the same time the development of fiber-optic cables, more sophisticated data compression, and more efficient uses of the radio spectrum have increased the carrying capacity of the network and dramatically lowered the cost of carrying large volumes of voice and data. Falling costs have caused prices to fall, but since the cost structure of telecoms is opaque, the dramatic decline in costs has not been translated into such a dramatic fall in prices except where they have been forced down by regulation or by unusually intense competitive pressure, usually from new entry and bypass.

The resulting increase in the price–cost margin, which is masked by falling prices, can create huge profits for telecoms companies, which are partially reflected in the large bids companies are willing to make for the right to enjoy these profits.[1] The challenge facing telecoms regulators and governments in countries where telecoms are still under public ownership is to manage the transition to high-capacity, low-priced telecoms networks without unduly delaying network rollout and the introduction of new services, and without transferring too much of the rent to telecoms operators.

The stakes are high, both for profits (which governments may attempt to capture at the moment of privatization) and consumer surplus. Conflicts between these two are considerable, as the following example, taken from Robin Mason's (1998) study of internet telephony, illustrates. In 1995 the United Kingdom made 1.025 billion minutes of international calls to the United States at an average price of 55 U.S.

cents per minute and an average cost of 8.57 cents per minute (the details of the cost calculation are given in the appendix to this chapter). The price was therefore nearly seven times cost, largely as a result of the international settlement system. Figure 7.1 illustrates the situation. The profit on this single route (price minus cost times quantity, shown in black) generated by this distorted price was U.S.$476 million per year, but the potential consumer surplus (i.e., the extra area under the demand curve and above the cost schedule) of lowering price to cost would have been $885 million dollars at a price elasticity of demand of unity, implying a deadweight loss of $409 million per year (defined as this surplus, less the original profits, and shown shaded as DWL = 1 in figure 7.1).[2] At the efficient price, instead of 20 minutes per person

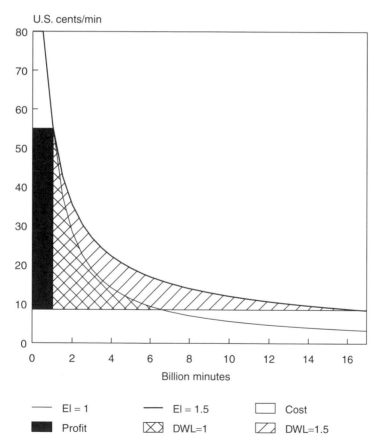

Figure 7.1
Rent and surplus from U.K. and U.S. phone 1995.

calling from the United Kingdom to the United States, we might have expected 138 minutes per person per year.

If the price elasticity of demand had been 1.5 (with the demand curve shown in figure 7.1 with a bold line as El = 1.5), demand might have increased to nearly 5 hours per person per year, and the potential consumer surplus available from lowering the price from 55 cents to 8.57 cents would have been $1.73 billion per year, implying a deadweight loss of $1,253 million per year (shown as DWL = 1.5).[3]

These numbers are large, and they can be compared with the global telecoms revenue for the United Kingdom (domestic and *all* international calls, not just those to the United States) of $27.6 billion (WTO 1998 and table 7.1). Deadweight losses, which as the name suggests are lost by consumers but not gained either by the government nor by the companies, on one route alone amounted to between 1.5 and 4.5 percent of global U.K. telecoms revenue, even though the revenue on that route was only 2 percent of U.K. global revenue. The deadweight loss on that route might have been between 85 and 260 percent of the total revenue received on that route. International calling prices between the United Kingdom and the United States have typically been lower than between most pairs of countries, so the estimated inefficiencies of mispricing are higher, and possibly much higher, elsewhere.[4]

Since 1997 the ending of the international duopoly in the United Kingdom has dramatically lowered these international call rates, to the point that domestic customers in the United Kingdom (and also in the United States) can subscribe to services offering calls between the two countries for between 5 and 16 cents per minute, considerably closer to cost (though, as Moore's law reminds us, that is a moving target and costs will have fallen further since 1995).[5] These services were still more complicated to use than the standard direct dialing service, since they require setting up a credit account and dialing four or more extra digits, but they indicate what competition might be able to achieve in lower prices. More complete liberalization would then have a dramatic impact on the profits and inefficiencies of operating the international telephone system between the United States and the United Kingdom, and where it is allowed to operate elsewhere, liberalization can be expected to have similarly dramatic effects.

Table 7.1 gives basic revenue data from WTO (1998) on the significance of telecoms revenues in 1995 for those member countries who have annexed schedules to the fourth protocol of the GATS by February 15, 1997, and penetration rate data for 1997 for the same countries

Table 7.1
Data on telecoms markets

Country	Telecoms revenues million $ R*	Population millions N	GNP/head U.S.$/head y	1995 GNP million $ Y = Ny	Lines '97 thousands L**	Lines/100 inhabitants L/N	Telecoms revenues As % of GNP R/Y	Per head $ R/N	Per line $ r = R/L	Line revenue divided by GNP/head r/y
Sweden	5,756	8.8	23,750	209,000	6,010	68.3	2.75	654	958	4.03
Switzerland	8,889	7.0	40,630	284,410	4,547	65.0	3.13	1,270	1,955	4.81
United States	178,758	263.1	26,980	7,098,438	170,568	64.8	2.52	679	1,048	3.88
Denmark	3,728	5.2	29,890	155,428	3,339	64.2	2.40	717	1,117	3.74
Canada	10,689	29.6	19,380	573,648	18,051	61.0	1.86	361	592	3.06
Hong Kong	5,113	6.2	22,990	142,538	3,647	58.8	3.59	825	1,402	6.10
France	27,162	58.1	24,990	1,451,919	33,700	58.0	1.87	468	806	3.23
Netherlands	8,488	15.5	24,000	372,000	8,860	57.2	2.28	548	958	3.99
Finland	2,534	5.1	20,580	104,958	2,866	56.2	2.41	497	884	4.30
Singapore	2,540	3.0	26,730	80,190	1,685	56.2	3.17	847	1,507	5.64
Germany	48,036	81.9	27,510	2,253,069	45,200	55.2	2.13	587	1,063	3.86
Norway	3,234	4.4	31,250	137,500	2,325	52.8	2.35	735	1,391	4.45
Australia	11,403	18.1	18,720	338,832	9,549	52.8	3.37	630	1,194	6.38
United Kingdom	27,647	58.5	18,700	1,093,950	30,678	52.4	2.53	473	901	4.82
New Zealand	2,019	3.6	14,340	51,624	1,840	51.1	3.91	561	1,097	7.65
Greece	2,798	10.5	8,210	86,205	5,329	50.8	3.25	266	525	6.40
Japan	93,855	125.2	39,640	4,962,928	61,526	49.1	1.89	750	1,525	3.85
Israel	2,249	5.5	15,920	87,560	2,656	48.3	2.57	409	847	5.32
Belgium	4,339	10.1	24,710	249,571	4,769	47.2	1.74	430	910	3.68
Austria	4,014	8.1	26,890	217,809	3,779	46.7	1.84	496	1,062	3.95
Taiwan-China		21.7	12,240	265,363	10,011	46.2				

Korea	8,728	44.9	9,700	435,530	20,423	45.5	2.00	194	427	4.41
Italy	20,004	57.2	19,020	1,087,944	25,259	44.2	1.84	350	792	4.16
Spain	11,008	39.2	13,580	532,336	15,854	40.4	2.07	281	694	5.11
Ireland	1,580	3.6	14,710	52,956	1,390	38.6	2.98	439	1,137	7.73
Portugal	2,775	9.9	9,740	96,426	3,819	38.6	2.88	280	727	7.46
Bulgaria	233	8.4	1,330	11,172	2,681	31.9	2.08	28	87	6.52
Czech Republic	890	10.3	3,870	39,861	2,817	27.3	2.23	86	316	8.16
Hungary	770	10.2	4,120	42,024	2,662	26.1	1.83	75	289	7.02
Slovak Republic	321	5.4	2,950	15,930	1,392	25.8	2.01	59	230	7.80
Turkey	1,674	61.1	2,780	169,858	15,744	25.8	0.99	27	106	3.82
Malaysia	2,098	20.1	2,890	58,089	4,236	21.1	3.61	104	495	17.13
Mauritius	104	1.1	3,380	3,718	223	20.3	2.81	95	468	13.84
Poland	2,162	38.6	2,790	107,694	7,510	19.5	2.01	56	288	10.32
Trinidad and Tobago	163	1.3	3,770	4,901	243	18.7	3.32	125	669	17.75
Argentina	6,009	34.7	8,030	278,641	6,120	17.6	2.16	173	982	12.23
Chile	1,321	14.2	4,160	59,072	2,248	15.8	2.24	93	588	14.13
Jamaica	314	2.5	1,510	3,775	353	14.1	8.31	125	888	58.83
Romania	423	22.7	1,480	33,596	3,161	13.9	1.26	19	134	9.04
Venezuela	1,594	21.7	3,020	65,534	2,804	12.9	2.43	73	568	18.82
Colombia	1,213	36.8	1,910	70,288	4,646	12.6	1.73	33	261	13.67
South Africa	3,675	41.5	3,160	131,140	4,646	11.2	2.80	89	791	25.03
Mexico	6,509	91.8	3,320	304,776	9,264	10.1	2.14	71	703	21.16
Brazil	8,622	159.2	3,640	579,488	15,106	9.5	1.49	54	571	15.68
Thailand	2,040	58.2	2,740	159,468	4,815	8.3	1.28	35	424	15.46
Ecuador	332	11.5	1,390	15,985	899	7.8	2.08	29	370	26.60
Tunisia	263	9.0	1,820	16,380	654	7.3	1.61	29	402	22.11

Table 7.1
(continued)

Country	Telecoms revenues million $ R*	Population millions N	GNP/head U.S.$/head y	1995 GNP million $ Y = Ny	Lines '97 thousands L**	Lines/100 inhabitants L/N	Telecoms revenues As % of GNP R/Y	Per head $ R/N	Per line $ r = R/L	Line revenue divided by GNP/head r/y
Bolivia (1993)	105	7.4	800	5,920	535	7.2	1.77	14	196	24.44
Peru	1,140	23.8	2,310	54,978	1,646	6.9	2.07	48	692	29.97
El Salvador	153	5.6	1,610	9,016	325	5.8	1.70	27	472	29.30
Morocco	659	26.6	1,110	29,526	1,378	5.2	2.23	25	479	43.11
Guatemala	197	10.6	1,340	14,204	430	4.1	1.39	19	459	34.22
Philippines	982	68.6	1,050	72,030	2,078	3.0	1.36	14	473	45.01
Indonesia	2,735	193.3	980	189,434	4,982	2.6	1.44	14	549	56.02
India	3,818	929.4	340	315,996	17,802	1.9	1.21	4	214	63.08
Pakistan	1,045	129.9	460	59,754	2,377	1.8	1.75	8	440	95.57
Sri Lanka	219	18.1	700	12,670	315	1.7	1.73	12	694	99.14
Senegal	108	8.5	600	5,100	116	1.4	2.11	13	927	154.45
Papua New Guinea	141	4.3	1,160	4,988	47	1.1	2.83	33	3,009	259.35
Cote d'ivoire	138	14.0	660	9,240	130	0.9	1.50	10	1,063	161.07
Ghana	65	17.1	390	6,669	78	0.5	0.97	4	833	213.68
Bangladesh	195	119.8	240	28,752	316	0.3	0.68	2	617	256.99
Total	548,885	3,131	8,104	25,371,938	619,642	19.8	2.16	175	886	10.93

Source: ITU World Telecommunications Development Report (www.wto.org/press/data3.htm).
Note: *Value of telecoms revenues 1995; **penetration data 1997.

from ITU (1998). The countries are ranked in order of telecoms penetration (measured by lines per 100 inhabitants), and not surprisingly, this correlates well with per capita income. Figure 7.2 shows revenue per line against income per capita (shown on a log scale). The line of best fit is plotted on the figure, but revenue per line correlates poorly with log income per capita ($R^2 = 0.2$), and is a surprisingly high $888 average per line per year.[6] This revenue can be compared with the cost of creating a network of perhaps $1,000 to 1,500 per line, and telecoms employment of 100 to 200 lines/employee, or possibly $100 to 300 per year.

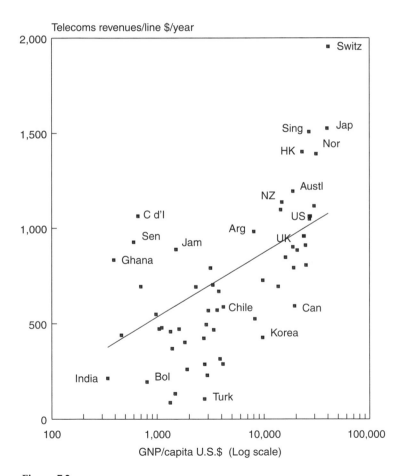

Figure 7.2
Telecoms revenues per line against per capita GNP.

One interesting consequence of this moderately constant revenue per line across countries is that the effective demand for phone lines (i.e., the penetration rate), is strongly negatively correlated with the effective cost (defined the annual revenue per line divided by the annual per capita income). Figure 7.3 plots data points for each country as a cross and shows the line of best fit, which might be thought of as a pseudodemand schedule for lines. A straight line on this double logarithmic graph exhibits a constant "price" elasticity of demand, which in this case is just over unity in absolute terms.[7] This picture tends to confirm that telecoms demand is price elastic, confirming that excessive prices are highly inefficient.

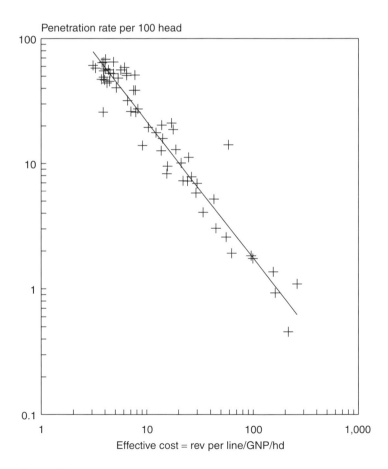

Figure 7.3
Pseudodemand for telecom lines logarithmic scales.
Source: WTO (1998); ITu (1998).

Why then do governments encourage such high prices for international and long-distance calls (and from business users)? The obvious reason is that they wish to keep the cost of line rentals and local calls low to domestic (voting) customers. This in turn can be defended to some extent as a subsidy to the network externalities at low levels of penetration, where the benefits to all users of increasing the number of those accessible are not captured by any single user. In rich countries, universal service is seen as essential to full citizenship, and cross-subsidies have been justified on income redistributional grounds, though neither the redistributional nor the externality argument seems sufficient to justify the very large markups over cost observed. A simpler explanation is that regulators or governments have been captured by interest groups (local voters and the company) and have used the largely invisible fall in costs to create profits and transfers, though at high opportunity cost in efficiency terms to the economy.

7.1.1   Pressures for Competition in International Telecoms Markets

International telephone rates are so out of line with costs that one is forced to ask why they are so high and how they can be sustained in the face of increasing competition. The answer is instructive, and illustrates the importance of bottlenecks in creating market power and supporting non-cost-reflective tariffs. The key to understanding the international market structure is that it derived from the days of a single monopoly provider in each country that controlled the delivery of calls and could charge whatever it liked to provide that service. Bilateral negotiations between countries established a largely secret set of *accounting rates* from country *A* to country *B* (not necessarily or even usually equal to those from *B* to *A*). The agreement then divided (usually 50–50) this rate between the two countries for originating and delivering the call. The amount paid to the delivering country is the *settlement rate*, normally half the accounting rate. The telephone operator in country *A* then charged its callers the *collection rate* for the international call, out of which it paid the settlement rate to the country called.

Table 7.2 gives information for international call charges (collection rates) and accounting rates from the United Kingdom to various OECD countries for selected recent years in U.S.$/min. The first three columns give the cheapest discount collection charges, the next three give the cheapest accounting rates,[8] and the last two columns give the margin

Table 7.2
Accounting and collection rates from the United Kingdom to other countries

Country	Cheapest discount collection charges (U.S.$/min)			Cheapest accounting rates (U.S.$/min)			Percent change 1991–99	Discounted collection rate less 1/2 account rate (U.S.$/min)	
	1988	1991	1995	1991	1995	1999		1991	1995
Australia	0.95	1.23	0.77	0.96	0.53	0.19	–80	0.75	0.51
New Zealand	0.95	1.23	0.77		0.82	0.17			0.36
Austria	0.64	0.69	0.51	0.56	0.47	0.13	–77	0.41	0.28
Finland	0.62	0.69	0.51	0.59	0.52	0.09	–85	0.39	0.25
Norway	0.64	0.69	0.51	0.54	0.38	0.06	–89	0.42	0.32
Sweden	0.64	0.69	0.51	0.55	0.31	0.06	–89	0.42	0.35
Belgium	0.49	0.52	0.38	0.45	0.41	0.07	–84	0.30	0.18
Denmark	0.49	0.52	0.38	0.48	0.50	0.06	–87	0.28	0.13
France	0.49	0.52	0.38	0.45	0.34	0.07	–84	0.29	0.21
Germany	0.49	0.52	0.38	0.57	0.44	0.06	–90	0.23	0.16
Greece	0.49	0.52	0.38	0.65	0.58	0.18	–72	0.19	0.09

Italy	0.49	0.52	0.38	0.56	0.53	0.07	−87	0.24	0.11
Netherlands	0.49	0.52	0.38	0.46	0.40	0.06	−87	0.29	0.18
Spain	0.49	0.52	0.38	0.57	0.58	0.14	−75	0.24	0.09
Switzerland	0.49	0.52	0.38	0.49	0.28	0.06	−88	0.28	0.24
United States	0.7	0.91	0.61	0.73	0.34	0.11	−35	0.55	0.44
Japan	1.42	2.06	1.27	1.92	1.37	0.43	−78	1.10	0.59
Average	0.65	0.76	0.52	0.62	0.52	0.12	−84	0.40	0.26
Standard deviation	0.24	0.40	0.23	0.37	0.25	0.09	5	0.23	0.14
Coefficient of variation (%)	38	53	43	60	48	76	−6	57	54
Groups									
Australia/New Zealand	0.95	1.23	0.77	0.48	0.67	0.18	−80	0.75	0.43
Japan	1.42	2.06	1.27	1.92	1.37	0.43	−78	1.10	0.59
Scandinavia	0.63	0.69	0.51	0.56	0.41	0.07	−88	0.41	0.31
EU + Switzerland	0.49	0.52	0.38	0.52	0.45	0.09	−84	0.26	0.15
United States	0.70	0.91	0.61	0.73	0.34	0.11	−85	0.55	0.44

Sources: OECD (1997); Oftel (1999).

received by the U.K. telephone company (the discount collection charge less the settlement rate taken as half the collection rate), which is to cover the cost of originating the call and half the cost of the international link. The countries fall into the five groups listed in the lower part of the table, within which collection rates are fairly uniform. The table shows that accounting rates have been falling sharply (by 84 percent from 1991 to January 1, 1999), and although the standard deviation of the accounting rates has fallen, the coefficient of variation has increased, indicating uneven progress in cutting rates. Collection rates fell an average of 29 percent between 1991 and 1995, while accounting rates fell by 22 percent over that period; however, collection charges seem far more uniform within groups of countries. The margin of collection charge over the settlement rate fell by 35 percent over 1991 to 1995.

Several points emerge from table 7.2. The margins vary considerably by country, and they are large compared to the costs of originating and carrying calls, suggesting that the UK operators were not behaving competitively on these routes. The margins are surprisingly high on the U.S. route where the settlement rate is low, and where the two countries are normally thought of as fairly competitive. Second, collection charges, which are published, are more uniform than accounting rates, which are secret (or were, until Oftel started publishing them). Third, if the accounting rate is just the cost of half the international link plus the delivery charge, figures of $4¢/min$ or less might seem closer to the 1997 costs (see the appendix to this chapter). By January 1, 1999, after rapid falls continuing unabated in 1998, the average is only three times as high, with some EU countries less than twice this amount. Finally, and coming back to the point of the previous section, the margins, which are the return to the originating telephone operator for originating and half the international link, and which might have been as high as $8¢/min$ in 1995, were three times this level.[9] Monopoly pricing seemed to be alive and well in both negotiating the accounting rate and setting the collection charge, though international prices are coming under increasing competitive pressure.

Both of these charges would be subject to competition if any telecoms operator in country A could install or lease a line between A and B, and pay the same local access charges at each end as the local phone company. A large part of the game of sustaining high international charges is therefore to prevent this happening, allowing the local phone company to retain a monopoly over access or call termination from abroad. Even though the telephone companies negotiate over the accounting rates, each has a monopoly on delivery and can therefore insist on a monopoly price for its part of the call. Worse, each company will treat the other's monopoly markup over cost as a cost and will mark that up in a double marginalization that will lead to a price above even the monopoly level.

The high margins to be made have nevertheless encouraged entry by callback operators, by those who lease international lines and resell their services, normally connecting them to a toll-free or local number, and by internet telephony, which uses the internet and avoids the accounting rate system altogether. Britain waited until January 1, 1997, to abolish the statutory duopoly on international calls, even though the domestic duopoly had been reviewed in 1991 and ended in 1992. Since 1997 discounted international call services have multiplied (there were 60 licensed at June 1998) and their prices have tumbled, putting pressure on the incumbent BT to match discounts to cheap destination countries such as the United States. The reason why competition has been delayed in both the United Kingdom and the United States is that a liberalized country is disadvantaged in dealing with a foreign monopoly operator. Allowing a foreign monopoly access to lower-priced delivery services increases their calls and hence their profits, and stimulates return calls on which they collect their high settlement rate. The problem is that the domestic regulator country has no jurisdiction over the foreign monopoly telecoms operator; it wishes to protect its own country from exploitation, in which domestic competitors compete away all the domestic profit, in the process transferring some part abroad.

Regulators have therefore frequently insisted that domestic carriers agree to set the same settlement rate with foreign carriers until the foreign market is deemed adequately competitive. This encourages the domestic carriers to behave as a cartel, and to negotiate an excessively high accounting rate. OECD (1997, tab. 3) notes that of all the countries listed in table 7.2, in 1995 only the United Kingdom had different accounting rates for the same country and only for the United States, though by 1998 all these countries were defined by Oftel as liberalized (and on these routes Oftel only publishes BT's accounting rate, not those of its competitors).

On August 7, 1997, the FCC adopted a Report and Order, setting lower-benchmark settlement rates of 15 ¢/min for upper-income countries from January 1, 1999, 19 ¢/min for upper-middle-income countries from January 1, 2000, and 23¢/min for lower-income countries from January 1, 2001, while admitting that these rates still exceeded costs. In addition the FCC will only permit a carrier to provide switched services over private international lines if more than half the traffic on that route is settled at rates no higher than the benchmark settlement rate, and U.S. carriers' foreign affiliates must settle at or below the benchmark rate.

On the international scene the World Trade Organization set a February 1997 deadline for signing up to more open telecoms markets and received offers from 69 countries, 56 of which committed themselves to "competitive" international supply (defined as permitting more than one supplier), most from January 1, 1998. Once countries allow operators access to the local telephone system (directly or through toll-free numbers) and to lease space on international lines (where there appears to be substantial excess capacity and even a spot market in that capacity), rates elsewhere will presumably fall as rapidly and as far as they have between the United Kingdom and the United States.[10]

7.1.2 Regulatory Inefficiencies

The inefficiency of regulation does not end with the overpricing of international and long-distance services. Hausman (1997) argues that one of the most costly consequences of traditional regulation as practised in the United States is the delay hindering the introduction of new services, caused by concern that these new services might be cross-subsidized from the captive customer base, as noted in chapter 5. Hausman gives two examples: voice messaging and cellar phones. AT&T originally wished to offer voice messaging in the late 1970s, which the FCC delayed until 1986 and which was finally allowed in 1988, when it was immediately introduced. The estimated consumer surplus it generated is estimated at U.S.$1.27 billion per year by 1994 (the estimated price elasticity of demand for messaging was −1.6), so the ten-year regulatory delay cost billions of dollars.

Cellular phones were apparently sufficiently advanced to have been introduced in the early 1970s, but regulation delayed introduction until 1983. Here the estimated demand elasticity was −0.4 to −0.5 (depending on estimation technique), giving an estimated consumer surplus from introducing cellular phones of $25 billion to 50 billion per year, and the total cost of delay possibly $100 billion. This is large compared with the 1995 U.S. global telecoms revenues of $180 billion in table 7.1.

Regulatory delays are one source of regulatory inefficiency, but not the only one. U.S. regulation probably involves more compromises in balancing the aims of different interest groups than some other countries, because of the division of responsibility between federal and state regulators, as discussed in chapter 4. Crandall and Waverman (1995) estimate the social cost of inefficient pricing as $8 billion per year in the United States, compared to RBOC revenue of $45 billion or total telephone revenues of $128 billion/year.

The lesson to draw from these examples is clear. Inefficient regulation and/or inadequate competition can be seriously damaging to consumer welfare and national prosperity. The two sources of inefficiency are interconnected. Regulation is typically required when markets cannot be made adequately competitive, but if the markets can be made adequately competitive, the case for regulation is diminished or eliminated.

7.1.3 Cross-country Comparisons of Telecoms

If costs have been falling rapidly, what has been happening to prices in different countries? How successful have competition and regulation been in reducing inefficiencies? Studying the evolution of telecoms prices over time is complicated by the huge variety of services and tariffs offered, even for the basic public switched telephone network (PSTN).[11] Thus tariffs may vary by time of day, destination or distance, total volume of calls, and the length of each call, as may the balance between fixed, variable, and installation charges, even before specially negotiated tariffs are considered. Making cross-country comparisons is further complicated by differences in purchasing power between countries, as well as country area, population, and density, each of which affects the costs of supplying telecom services. Most benchmarking comparisons consider a number of baskets of calls of varying types, times, and lengths. One of the most comprehensive cross-country studies (OECD 1995) uses published data of the dominant operator which ignores possible discounts to large users (especially important in the United States).

It is therefore difficult to reach unambiguous conclusions on the effect of liberalization and ownership on prices. Nevertheless, OECD

(1995) notes that across countries the usage charges are converging and decreasing, while the fixed charges are becoming more diverse and increasing, as tariffs are rebalanced and aligned in response to competition. For business users, the usage charges (in nominal $ at purchasing power parity) of competitive countries decreased 15 percent from 1990 to 1994, while for noncompetitive countries the decrease was only 7 percent. Competitive fixed charges rose less than noncompetitive fixed charges, so the cost of the total competitive basket fell by 9 percent compared to 3 percent for the noncompetitive basket. Rebalancing occurs either in response to competition, or in anticipation of future competition, as all EU countries face liberalization in 1998, and other countries are increasingly vulnerable to by-pass for the larger customers.

The OECD comparisons suggest that Sweden and Finland were cheaper for both business and residential users than the United Kingdom and the United States, with France and Germany cheaper for residential users than the United States and the United Kingdom, but more expensive for business users. Australia, with its lower population densities, was higher cost for both services, except for the sharp fall in residential costs in 1994.

More careful and detailed comparisons are harder to find, but Mason (1996) was commissioned by Oftel to make benchmarking comparisons of price and quality for business users between BT in Britain, and a number of other countries: Sweden, the United States, Australia, and France. Sweden's state-owned monopoly developed a modern service in the 1980s charging low prices as part of its social policy. The state-owned company, Telia, had no protection against entry other than its low prices, and these were low enough to deter entry until 1992. Sweden was the first country to introduce a mobile telephone network in 1981, and competition between the two providers led to low prices, high penetration, and presumably provided competitive pressure on the monopoly PSTN service. Mason's comparisons confirm that Sweden was the cheapest country for PSTN (which accounts for 75 percent of total business telecoms costs) for all sizes of business. The cheapest discounted U.S. PSTN services were almost as cheap as Sweden's and slightly cheaper than BT's, but the undiscounted U.S. service was considerably more expensive than BT's undiscounted service, and about the same level (for all sizes of business) as the most expensive countries in the sample, Australia and France. Australia was deregulated in 1992, but suffers from a high-cost low-density service, while France, with a recently created modern system, charged high prices with no discounts. It is noteworthy that the United States had the highest cost analogue and digital mobile services which is attributed to lower competition than in the other countries.

Several conclusions emerge from these studies. The modernity of the telephone system has a direct effect on cost and efficiency, regardless of ownership, as more recent switching technology, based on essentially the same computer chips as PCs, has fallen dramatically in cost, while fiber optics have displaced copper cables. State-owned telephone companies in countries like Sweden appear to have embraced best practice technology as well as or better than elsewhere. Second, prices can be held low by public policy as well as by competitive pressure, and since it is hard to observe costs (even if they correctly accounted for capital costs in the presence of rapid obsolescence), it is difficult to disentangle the effects of ownership on performance. Third, competition leads to price discrimination, which may avoid regulatory prohibitions by careful tariff design. Fourth, regulatory price controls may be more effective at cutting prices than the rather weak competition facing a well-entrenched dominant supplier. The difficulty is that tight regulation makes competitive entry harder, unless the entrants are favored (by concessional access charges and lighter regulation), and delays the move to an unregulated competitive market.

Whether regulation is required or competition can be relied upon to cause prices to follow costs downward depends on the ease with which effective competition can be introduced, and that depends on technology, which is still evolving rapidly, as the next section demonstrates.

7.2 Distinctive Features of the Telecoms Industry

Telecommunication differs from electricity and gas in that customers need two-way communication with specified partners, not the one-way receipt of anonymous electrons or molecules. Telecoms also experiences network externalities, where the value of the service provided to each subscriber increases with the number of others connected to the network. Regulation and competition must ensure this connectivity, cope with network externalities, and be able to adapt to rapid technical progress. So rapid and various have been these innovations that it is often hard to see where the industry is heading, what its equilibrium structure might look like, and how regulation should be designed or may evolve to rebalance the interests of consumers and providers.

We start by describing the distinctive features of telecoms that affect its industrial structure, the behavior of various players and the key regulatory issues, and then draw lessons from recent history. The traditional public switched telephone network (PSTN) provided approved apparatus (usually a telephone or telephone switchboard) for the consumer's premises (often rented rather than owned by the consumer), which was connected (normally by a twisted copper pair) from the premises to the nearest switch or concentrator (the "local loop"), and from there to the local exchange. The local exchange was connected to the remaining local subscribers, and to the rest of the network through a hierarchy of switches to other local exchanges and then to other customers and other networks. The main reason why the PSTN might need to interconnect with other networks was to make international calls, though in both the United States and the United Kingdom there were other telephone companies serving particular geographical areas that interconnected with the dominant incumbent. Telegraph companies delivered telegrams, telex machines provided a primitive form of electronic mail, and radio and television companies broadcast over the air waves (using portions of the electromagnetic spectrum).

Now almost every detail of this description has changed. Consumers are free to choose from a wide range of equipment to connect to the network—phones, faxes, computers, and video equipment—and are not forced to rent from the incumbent phone company. They may have a choice of network to which to attach, and often a choice of quality of connection (described by the bandwidth of the signal that can be carried). The local loop may now be a twisted copper pair, a coaxial cable with higher bandwidth, a fiber-optic connection (with very high bandwidth), or even a fixed radio link to a local aerial connected to a fixed network. The subscriber may also have a mobile phone which accesses a fixed network through the nearest aerial (normally on a building or tower) or possibly direct to a satellite. Portable pagers bleep when a message is to be collected, or receive short text messages, and may be able to send similarly short text messages. Computers can be linked by high-capacity networks and share resources, and computers can connect to external networks, including the phone network. Airline reservation systems, credit card companies, banks, and stock markets rely on being able to send and receive large quantities of data quickly, accurately, and securely over networks, and electronic commerce now reaches out beyond companies to individual consumers. In the United Kingdom in 1996 half the value of the total estimated telecoms market of $26 billion was data traffic, and while the fixed link PSTN was growing at 4 percent p.a., data traffic was growing at 25 percent or more, faster even than mobile telephony ($2 billion growing at 15 percent or more p.a.; Cleevely 1997).

The link between switches may be by traditional cable, but it is now more often by fiber-optic cable, with its vastly increased capacity, or by microwave. Different networks are interconnected at various points or switches, and they may be public (open to all as common carriers) or private (with restricted access). Cable companies that previously offered television programs are now often able to offer telecom services over the same cable, and telephone companies may be allowed to offer video services. Mobile phones use a variety of different technologies, which may or may not work in other areas and countries. They may be able to send and receive data, faxes, and connect to the internet. Personal computers can connect to the PSTN or cable networks and access the internet, send electronic mail (email) and even engage in voice and video telephony. Telegraph and telex have been replaced almost entirely by fax and email, while radio and TV can be delivered over cable to households just as phones can access the airwaves.

The range of services on offer shows even greater diversity, and there is a tendency for each type of network to be able to offer services previously only available from different types of networks—creating "convergence" between the different media, and presenting new regulatory challenges. The various media differ in whether they offer one-way simultaneous delivery to many receivers (broadcast), one-way simultaneous transmission to a single recipient (fax), two-way simultaneous communication, like voice telephony, or one-way delayed delivery (telegrams, email), and also whether the sender and/or recipient have to be fixed or can be mobile. Broadcast networks such as cable-TV typically use a tree-and-branch network with a single "pipe" serving a local distribution centre which delivers the message to the premises, traditionally without an upstream channel. Two-way networks like the PSTN have a star network with lines radiating from the local switch, which accesses a multiply connected core network, allowing many possible routes for messages from the local exchange. Older cable-TV networks were therefore not well designed for voice telephony, though newer cable networks often combine the coaxial cable for broadcasts with a traditional copper pair to a local switch, effectively using the same hole in the ground for jointly providing both services at little extra cost. It is also possible to add an upstream channel of limited bandwidth to an existing network, and this can work well for internet use, where the ratio of incoming to outgoing traffic is typically high. This might even allow older cable networks to provide access for internet telephony, which seemed set for rapid expansion in late 1998.

The PSTN was designed for simultaneous transmissions (with near zero delay). This was secured by *circuit switching* in which a circuit is set up between dialer and recipient. If all lines are busy, the call fails, but if not, a continuous path through the network is reserved with a specified bandwidth for the duration of the call, normally ensuring the quality of service of the call (no loss of connection or degradation of quality through loss of bandwidth). Clever software finds an alternative route if links on the first choice are congested, so a call may take a very indirect route (and use the resources of possibly many switches). Originally the voice frequencies sent out along the local loop were superimposed on a electronic signal at the switch and the resulting fluctuating frequencies carried over the wire as an analogue signal throughout the network, though by placing each message on a different carrier wave, many simultaneous messages can be carried over the same line. Now, most switches and hence the bulk of modern phone networks are digital. The voice is still carried as an analogue signal to the first switch, where the frequencies are sampled and converted into binary code (zeros and ones)—the language of microchips and computers (which is what modern switches are). Digital switches are cheaper, have more capacity, and can be programed and reprogramed to improve their efficiency.

Digitized signals can be compressed and manipulated to fit more signals onto a given link and to enable them to be stored easily for short or long periods.[12] It is also possible to digitize the signal before it leaves the premises, which means that more information can be carried over the local loop, giving access to a wider range of services. Fax modems give some idea of the improvements possible.

Delay tolerant messages do not require a continuous path to be established, and *packet switching* was developed to make efficient use of the bandwidth of the network (both links and switches). Each message is broken down into a number of packets with a fixed number of bits per package (e.g., 64 bits). Each packet has a header giving details of the destination, the order of the packet in the sequence (so that the message can be reassembled in the correct order), and requirements (specified in protocols) for service quality requested of the switches. The disadvantage of circuit-switched networks is that once the circuit is reserved, that bandwidth cannot be used for other messages even if the circuit is quiet or barely used. In contrast, a packet-switched network can fully use the resources available, and only makes resource demands in proportion to the message content, apparently using these resources more intensively. On the other hand, each packet carries the overhead cost of routing information that is only required to set up the original circuit for the circuit-switched network. Whereas switches in a switched circuit have a well-defined bit rate, and when fully loaded, tell requests for circuits to look for another route, a switch on a packet-switched network will share out resources (bandwidth) and slow down the rate at which the bits are delivered. This is painfully obvious when attempting to download pictures or documents on the internet but makes little difference for emails, which may just take a little longer before they arrive and sit around in the file server waiting to be read. Packets can be sent over the PSTN, so whether or not the network is packet switched is a function of the switching rather than the links.

Until recently all voice traffic was sent over circuit-switched networks, but the rapid growth in data traffic and of the internet, using packet-switched networks, has stimulated interest in IP telephony or internet protocol telephony, where the message header attempts to reserve sufficiently high-quality transit rights to ensure acceptable delay, especially on adequately sized or rationed networks. The advantages of IP telephony are several: as a cheap cost competitor to overpriced long-distance or international calls, as a method of using alternative networks to the incumbent's PSTN, possibly including older cable-TV networks, and for the additional functionality of combining voice and data, including possibly visual data, for distance working.

Networks therefore offer several types of service, measured by bandwidth, delay, whether digital or analogue, whether interactive (two-way) or not, and whether fixed or mobile. If we consider bandwidth for the moment, the variation is potentially huge. The PSTN receives voice analogue signals over the normal twisted copper pair and converts them to digital signals which require 64 kbs (kilobits, or thousand bits per second, i.e., 64,000 bits/s) to be carried at high quality. The signal can be compressed fourfold to 16 kbs so that more messages can be carried simultaneously (which is acceptable), or even to 8 kbs (which has noticeably lower quality). Asynchronous transfer mode (ATM) allows 1.5 Mbs (million bits per second) to be carried (for modest distances) on a twisted copper pair. A TV picture may require 1 Mbs without compression, and normally requires coaxial or fiber optic cable, though it could be carried by ATM on a twisted copper pair for perhaps 5 km. The early modems allowed communications at 300 bs, which is the speed of the old teleprinters (and of a normal computer keyboard).[13] The standard speed in 1997 was 28 kbs, with newer modems offering 56 kbs, a nearly 200-fold increase over the early modems, while ATM might allow a further 25-fold increase in capacity. Early internet links operated at 56 kbs, but the largest backbones now operate at 155 Mbs and MCI upgraded its backbone to 622 Mbs in 1998, an increase in speed of over 10,000 times.

A PC color display of 1,024 by 768 pixels at 30 frames per second would require 566 Mbs. If the picture area (or resolution) is reduced by a factor of 10 and the frame rate is reduced to once every 5 seconds (i.e., by a factor of 150), and data compression can achieve a 20-fold compression then the video signal would fit into 20 kbs, and could be carried on a normal phone line via a 28 kbs modem (Cawley 1996).

Data compression and other clever features (like ATM) enable more information to be carried over the existing network, while different networks can be configured to offer a greater variety of services. BT has been experimenting with sending video on demand over twisted copper pairs, while the packet-switched internet is rapidly developing real-time voice telephony and video conferencing. Cable TV companies can provide telephony and internet services, with some reconfiguration of their network topology, while new cable companies are designing networks that are already well configured to provide a wider range of services. Cable digital television offers the prospect of video conferencing and interactive programs. Faxes were once sent solely over the PSTN, but as they do not require simultaneity they can economize on bandwidth by being sent over a packet-switched network and are often sent to and from computers via a modem or other link.

A network can thus be thought of as the equipment in the customer's premises that generates a message, the medium that transmits the message (wire, cable, radio waves, etc.), and the switches that route it to its destination. The message will be encoded (perhaps several times) in a form suited to the means of transmission, then transmitted, and possibly stored, or buffered, at one or more nodes before final delivery. Once signals have been digitized, they can be handled similarly regardless of their original form, though their requirements for bandwidth and its variability, or burstiness, may depend on the source. Digitization, combined with the huge processing power now available from microchips and the comparably large bandwidth available on optical-fiber and high-frequency microwave transmission, allows different networks to offer a variety of overlapping services and enables convergence. One direct implication of this digital revolution is that if voice requires such little bandwidth compared with most other services, and can be carried by all of the competing networks, then the main source of revenue of the PSTN is under threat.

The demand for convergence—that is, not only the technical ability to offer these services but the regulatory right to interconnect and make them available—is driven by the desire of each network to offer a greater variety of services, and hence increase its market and benefit from economies of scale and scope. Entry into any market with large economies of scale and scope is difficult starting from no base if new facilities have to be built, but much easier starting from an existing network and customer base or if facilities can be leased or paid for on demand. Entry into particular markets is greatly encouraged by the extent to which prices in that market exceed marginal costs, which is a typical feature of inherited tariff structures.

7.3   Possibility of Competition

Before the digital revolution, the local network was a classic natural monopoly. Economies of scope—particularly of standardization in switches so that they all worked efficiently together—argued (less persuasively) for a single network provider. After the digital revolution, and the ensuing rapid growth in traffic, the advantages of a single provider rapidly decreased, starting with long-distance carriage and moving steadily closer to the subscriber's premises. Customer premise equipment was the first obvious liberalization, and it is doubtful if there was ever much reason to exclude other supplier's equipment.[14] If large increases in transmission capacity and switching are needed anyway, new entrants do not need to duplicate these facilities in order to enter, provided that they can interconnect with the existing network. The practical question is what fraction of the existing network needs to be upgraded (in terms of bandwidth and services provided) or extended, and what is the cost penalty, if any, in allowing new entrants to provide this upgrading or expansion rather than incumbents?

The regulatory issues are primarily those of ensuring that where competition is efficient or desirable, that it can happen, and where not, the natural monopoly facilities are properly regulated. The objective of the players (incumbents and entrants in facilities and services) is to make and defend profits by whatever legal means are available. Incumbents will wish to hang on to market power and deter entry, while entrants will wish to enter where they can in turn create a defended niche of market power. Market power can best be created and maintained by securing control over bottlenecks or essential facilities, though the more traditional means of deterring entry and discouraging customers from switching to rivals are also important. Telecommunications networks, more than most other networks, offer rich possibilities of creating or exploiting bottlenecks, entry barriers, and switching costs (i.e., the cost perceived by customers wishing to switch supplier). The proper study of telecoms competition requires a study of these bottlenecks and barriers.

The central question of telecoms liberalization is how best to achieve the potential welfare gains from competitive pricing and technical innovation, while the central question for regulation is how to foster that competition and restrain the exercise of market power created by control of essential facilities. The examples of regulatory reform in the United States and privatization and liberalization in Britain provide insights and lessons both for competition and regulation.

7.3.1   Liberalization in the United States

The forces that led up to the breakup of the Bell System in the United States on January 1, 1984, were described in chapter 4. Temin (1987) rather pessimistically concludes that "divestiture may well have sacrificed long-run gains in the quest for short-run goals." It is hard to test this counterfactual claim directly, and most observers are content to investigate the effect of the breakup on the trend growth in prices, costs, and productivity. The impact on prices is complicated by the fact that long-distance call charges are made up of the price of the long-distance service, and the access charge, which includes a cross-subsidy to the local operating company. Divestiture lead to a rebalancing between local and long-distance charges, so the access component of the long-distance price changed. One should therefore distinguish between changes in prices caused by rebalancing and those attributable to the competitive effects of restructuring.

The Modified Final Judgment (MFJ) of 1982 required AT&T to divest seven Regional Bell Operating Companies (RBOCs), each with about 12 percent of the total population of local subscribers. At the same time the country was divided into 161 local access and transport areas

(LATAs), within each of which the RBOC could offer local and short-distance calls but between which RBOCs were prevented from offering "long-distance" calls (which might geographically be rather short). The FCC in due course required the RBOCs to offer their customers equal access to all long-distance operators to create a genuinely competitive long-distance market.

One of the curious features of the breakup was that it was intended as a structural remedy to market abuse, to which the solution was competition, rather than regulation, but AT&T continued to be regulated on its long-distance service. At divestiture, AT&T still had 95 percent of the interexchange market, and its dominant incumbent position appeared to justify continued regulation by the Federal Communications Commission, but this rapidly changed. Taylor and Taylor (1993) observe that there has been massive entry and capacity expansion in the market—500 providers, four (instead of one) backbone long-distance networks, and a threefold increase in capacity. Demand doubled and real prices halved, suggesting that competition was not only potential but actual.

They go on to argue that all is not quite as it seems, and that the main reason that interstate prices fell so much was the rebalancing of the access charge (described in chapter 4). If these access charges are netted out, the real interstate tariff fell only half as fast after the breakup of AT&T as before, while demand grew no faster than would be predicted from tariffs, incomes, and population changes. They calculate that between 1984 and 1992, AT&T had benefited from paying reduced access charges by about $10.9 billion per year, while the effect of its price reductions was a cut in revenue of $8.22 billion per year. Thus over the period nominal net prices rose by 1.5 percent per year, and fell in real terms by 2.2 percent per year, compared to a real decline of 6.28 percent per year between 1972 and 1984. Although some routes that were subject to more intense competitive pressure experienced faster declines, and large businesses were also able to secure larger reductions, overall "these data are more consistent with the presence of a regulated price umbrella than with a competitive market" (Taylor and Taylor 1993, p. 189). If so, then presumably price-cap regulation was successful in preventing the exercise of market power in the less competitive (nonbusiness) parts of this market, though it could have been set more tightly, as in Britain.

Crandall and Waverman (1995) criticize the Taylor and Taylor (1993) study as relying on weak data, which they show has the implausible property that despite an acceleration in the rate of decline in the real cost of long-distance charges (which fell at 3.8 percent p.a. for inter-state calls between 1980 and 1986, but at 7.4 percent p.a. from 1986 to 1993) there was an apparent *fall* in the rate of growth of demand (from 11.8 percent p.a. from 1980 to 1986, to 5.7 percent p.a. from 1986 to 1993). They argue that the price data are inaccurate in excluding discounts and the quantity data even more inaccurate, for a variety of reasons. They attempt to correct the data and redo the analysis, finding in the process that "ordinary tariffed MTS (message telephone service) rates during peak hours reflect substantial competition in the longer mileage bands" (Crandall and Waverman 1995, p. 165). Presumably these longer-distance markets were markets where the price–cost margin was most excessive and which were therefore likely to attract competition sooner than in the shorter distance markets, where competition does indeed appear to have been more muted.

The overall effects of the breakup are set out extensively in Crandall (1991) and summarized in Noam (1993): Real telephone service prices have been falling since 1953, fell fastest between 1973 and 1978, but leveled off after 1983, while local services rose in real terms (as was to be expected by the rebalancing caused by long-distance competition). The price changes were mildly regressive. The lowest income quintile lost $16 per year, and the highest gained $15. Total factor productivity growth[15] of the whole system was 3 percent p.a. from 1961 to 1980, rose to 3.8 percent p.a. from 1971 to 1985 as competitive pressures increased, and to 3.9 percent p.a. from 1984 to 1988 after the MFJ (Crandall 1991, pp. 115, 68). According to Noam there was a slight fall in the rate of growth of total factor productivity for the Bell System from 1984 to 1988 which may subsequently have been reversed, but an apparent increase for the remainder of the sector. Noam concludes in favor of the case for liberalization, notes that there was no upheaval, the adverse distributional effects were small, and the industry has become more dynamic and innovative than before.

One of the more interesting developments has been the switch from rate-of-return regulation to price-cap regulation of the long-distance market noted in section 4.5. This was originally intended as a bridge between the old style cost of service form of regulation to a deregulated system, but one that allowed the relative prices to be adjusted more gradually by introducing a number of baskets. Under cost-of-service regulation, the access charges to the local exchanges were part of regulated costs, so there was no incentive for AT&T to avoid their payment by encouraging by-pass, or direct connection to large customers. One of the consequences of this regulatory change is that AT&T now has a positive incentive to minimize access charges, particularly where these include a large element of taxation to finance local subsidies, and so is a positive force for introducing competition into local markets. By 1992, competitive access providers had captured 40 percent of the 45 megabit service (used for large data transfers, especially by financial institutions) in New York and the Bell Atlantic area (Brock 1994).

This raises the question of how contestable the local areas are. Shin and Ying (1992) estimate cost functions for local telephony over the period 1976 to 1983 (i.e., before divestiture) and find that the conditions for natural monopoly (i.e., global subadditivity) in which one firm can produce more cheaply than two fail in two-thirds of the 21,170 hypothetical cases considered. The range of cost changes in moving to two firms ranged from savings of 17.5 percent to higher costs of 5 percent. They conclude that the benefits of introducing competition into existing local exchange markets, either by breaking up existing companies or allowing additional entry, would outweigh the potential efficiency losses. It follows that the long-distance market, which is less of a natural monopoly, would also benefit from competition. As ever, the practical question is how long adequate entry would take before competition could be relied upon to bring prices down, and whether this amount of entry would require excessive investment. The main problem with liberalization as a mechanism for introducing competition is that without breaking up the incumbent monopoly entry is the only way for this to happen. The attraction of restructuring a publicly owned utility is that competition can be introduced immediately. It is therefore disappointing when this does not happen.

The difficulty of creating adequately competitive markets can be seen in mobile telephony in the United States. Parker and Röller (1997) have studied the price-setting behavior of the regional duopolies that the FCC created in 1983. The FCC granted two licenses in each of 305 nonoverlapping geographic markets, one of which would only be given to the local telecoms operator (usually an RBOC) while the other was unrestricted. They find that the demand elasticity was high (−2.5), that the rate of growth of demand was very high (8.5 percent per month), and that pricing was more collusive than Cournot duopoly (which is the least competitive form of noncollusive pricing), with an implied price–cost margin of 35 percent. What is more interesting is that competition between an RBOC and an independent was somewhat stronger than between two independent operators (which occurred in about one-fifth of the markets studied), where the data were not able to reject the hypothesis of collusive pricing. Moreover, where these operators competed with each other elsewhere, they tended to collude more, supporting the theory that repeated contacts between rivals in different markets encourages collusion (by providing more opportunities to punish noncollusive behavior). They also find that regulation might if anything lead to higher rather than lower prices.

If competition was perhaps slow in delivering its promised lowering of prices toward cost, it was nevertheless firmly entrenched, and required some legislative response, as the 1934 Communications Act was clearly out of date. After much horse trading, the Telecommunications Act of 1996 was finally passed, allowing the RBOCs to offer long-distance service, though only after they had met onerous conditions for making their local markets competitive. (Other local operators like GTE were not so constrained by the MFJ and were already free to offer combined local and long-distance services.)

The Telecommunications Act also allowed cable television (CATV) companies to escape from rate regulation if the local phone company offered video over cable in competition, though as Harris and Kraft (1997) note, the Act is not symmetrical in removing rate regulation of the local phone company if the CATV company offers voice telephony. The conditions that the RBOCs have to meet to be deemed competitive are that they unbundle as far as possible all components of the network, each of which is then available for use by competitors for a cost-based charge, and to provide nondiscriminatory interconnection (for a negotiated access charge subject to PUC approval). Thereafter competition could take one of three forms along a spectrum ranging from entrants providing their own facilities ("facilities-based" competition) to entrants using the existing facilities together with some of their own facilities (e.g., switches), to resale, in which the incumbent buys the bundle of local services (at a cost equal to the retail cost less the amount saved by selling wholesale) and resells them to its subscribers.

The cost-based charges were to be set using the forward-looking TELRIC (total element long-run incremental cost) methodology, explained in the appendix to this chapter. Harris and Kraft (1997) argue that the 1996 Telecommunications Act was a compromise between powerful interests, each of which could have blocked its passage. Since its passing, most of the orders issued by the FCC under the Act have been contested in the courts, where the same powerful interests (incumbents, entrants, state PUCs, and the FCC) continue to pursue their conflicting objectives.

One of the more curious features of the Act is its stress on complete unbundling and cost-based pricing of all the elements of the local network, not just on the bottlenecks of the local loop (which is arguably unnecessarily expensive to duplicate) and call completion. If this is combined with incorrectly low estimates of the TELRIC-based charges (see the appendix), then it will inefficiently discourage facilities-based competition and leave local incumbents largely intact. One possible interpretation is that it puts pressure on local PUCs to rebalance tariffs toward costs; otherwise, entrants will buy for resale those parts that are underpriced and enter to compete with those parts that are overpriced. Given the durable nature of the politicoeconomic equilibrium that has sustained (economically) inefficient cross-subsidies, perhaps this was seen as the only way to disrupt that equilibrium. It could, of course, just be the outcome of a compromise in which neither the incumbent RBOCs nor the long-distance entrants really wanted to increase the intensity of competition, and decided to raise the stakes against any RBOC wishing to enter the long-distance market.

In the event the 8th Circuit Court of St. Louis overturned the FCC's pricing rules for unbundled components, arguing that incumbents are not required to provide combinations of network elements and are allowed to first disconnect those elements required by entrants and then charge for reconnecting them, thereby raising rivals' costs and reducing the competitive threat of entry into local markets (Riordan 1998).[16]

The other major tension created by the Telecommunications Act is that between the desire for competition and for universal service, which is interpreted as meaning cheap basic services for all domestic customers. The Act says that charges should be "reasonable," which, in the old view of the Supreme Court interpreting the Sherman Act on price fixing, means competitive, not necessarily cheap, and not below cost. The Act also requires that subsidies paid to achieve universal service must be paid by telecoms companies, who will therefore recover them by what is in effect a tax on other consumers. Logically this should be a lump-sum tax to minimize the efficiency costs, and should therefore fall on the line rental, but the FCC has imposed "mandatory contributions," which will collect $1.7 billion as a percentage of interstate telecoms revenues (presumably because it does not have jurisdiction over the local rates). These revenues also include internet revenues, and as Riordan (1998) points out, "the FCC is taxing a growing technology to subsidize an established one." The inefficiencies of this tax are large. Hausman (1998) calculated the efficiency cost of imposing taxes on interstate access charges for long-distance calls to finance school and library access to the internet as $2.36 billion/year, which is equivalent to a deadweight loss of just over $1 per $ of revenue raised—perhaps three times as high as using other taxes to finance what is thought to be a socially desirable program.

The U.S. experience is thus still very colored by its regulatory past, and competition has had to struggle against the well-entrenched interest groups with their inefficient systems of rent distribution. The goal of encouraging competition at the local level without breaking up the local monopolies has run into difficulties. Entrants are finding it costly to secure access to existing facilities, and the FCC is once again in conflict with the courts over jurisdiction.

7.3.2 Reforms in Britain

Britain provides an interesting contrast, since it lacks the regulatory history of the United States and avoids jurisdictional disputes by its unitary state structure. It has aggressively pursued facilities-based competition to deal with what was a very uncompetitive industry structure created at privatization, rather than making unbundled facilities available at cost-based charges. The British Telecommunications Act 1981 separated British Telecommunications (later to become BT) from the Post Office and ended its statutory monopoly over the network. The small company Mercury was licensed in 1982, but BT was privatized in 1984 without restructuring, as the sole owner of the network, under the regulation of Oftel. Mercury was relicensed as the sole competitor until at least 1990. It is interesting to observe that the United States achieved a greater degree of restructuring, despite the private ownership of the Bell System, than the British government was willing to contemplate, despite the greater ease given its initial public ownership and the prospect that any subsequent restructuring once privatized would be much harder.

Britain did, however, follow the U.S. model by licensing only two mobile phone companies, Cellnet (majority owner BT) and Vodaphone in 1985, though they were required to sell their services wholesale to competitive service providers who then repackaged them for retail sale. This arrangement ended in 1991 when two further mobile operators were licensed, with a guarantee of no further entry before 2005. From virtually zero in 1985, the number of mobile subscribers rose from a million in 1990 to over 13 million at the end of 1998, with all four operators covering more than 90 percent of the population (Oftel 1998b).

The failure to create a more competitive structure at privatization and the delay in allowing competition led Armstrong, Cowan, and Vickers (1994) to the judgment that "the duopoly policy has been detrimental to development of competition, and its main beneficiary has been BT itself" (p. 240). This does not mean that privatization was undesirable, only that opportunities were lost. Galal et al. (1994) provide a cost–benefit analysis of the privatization of BT based on data to 1990 (see section 3.5.5). They concluded that privatization benefited shareholders, government, and consumers as a whole, though business consumers did substantially better than residential consumers, many of whom may have suffered a net loss. The main sources of these benefits were changes in prices, improvements in the rate of investment once the constraints imposed by state ownership were removed, and after 1991, an assumption that BT's plans to cut the labor force by 30,000 by 1994 would be carried out without any adverse effects on output.

This assumption was justified, for the critical development, signalled in the original prospectus at privatization, was that the statutory duopoly would be reviewed in 1990. The review occurred and the domestic duopoly was terminated in 1991 with any application for a license thereafter to be considered "on its merits." (The duopoly on international calls did not end until December 31, 1997.) By 1995 there were over 150 operators licensed to compete with BT, including 125 cable TV companies who can offer telephony with cable (of which 80 were actually providing service; Bell 1995). The first six years of private ownership did not appear to change productivity compared to the experience of comparable companies elsewhere, though there is a sharp improvement in 1992. Figure 7.4 shows the ratio of BT's productivity to that of U.K. industry compared with the experience of the CEGB and its successor companies (which were shown in more detail in figure 6.6).[17] The figure strongly suggests that it is competition that leads to an acceleration of productivity growth, not privatization, for the CEGB was broken up to create competition from the outset.

Cleevely (1997) notes that BT's employment fell from 250,000 in 1989 to under 150,000 in 1995, while employment in other telecoms companies (including mobile) rose from 25,000 to 80,000. BT accounted for only half of total telecoms investment in 1997 compared to 82 percent

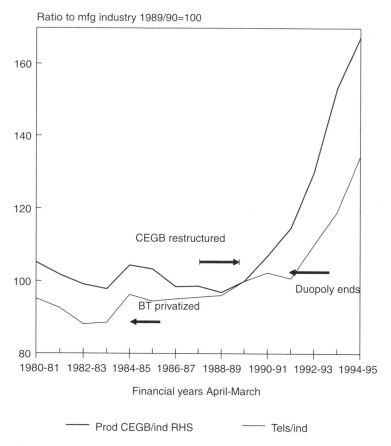

Ratio to mfg industry 1989/90=100

Figure 7.4
Productivity of CEGB and BT relative to the U.K. manufacturing industry.
Source: Newbery and Pollitt (1997).

in 1990. However, the dramatic improvement in BT's productivity can also be seen as a belated catching up with continental operators—BT had about 70 percent of the lines per employee that France Telecom had between 1985 and 1991, but is now equally productive. Indeed, what is striking in the evolution of productivity across Europe is that almost all telecoms companies experienced the same rate of productivity growth over the whole decade from 1985, except for BT after 1991.[18]

Figure 7.5 compares the real prices (i.e., deflated by the RPI) of domestic telephone services and domestic electricity. Real telephone prices rose somewhat after privatization in 1984 as a result of rebalancing, but then fell by over one-third in the next ten years. Real elec-

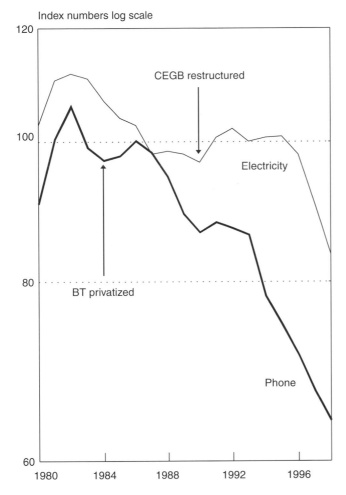

Index numbers log scale

Figure 7.5
Real phone and electricity prices for U.K. domestic customers.
Source: ONS (1999).

tricity prices rose slightly in the period after privatization until 1996, when regulation lowered the cost of distribution. Tight telecoms regulation transferred the efficiency gains to consumers, while competition in electricity cut costs but raised profits rather than lowering prices. The reason why the price-cost margin widened in electricity was discussed in the previous chapter, where, as with mobile telephones, two firms are too few to pass on the benefits of cost reduction to consumers under unregulated competition. Cleevely (1997) compares the evolution of business telecoms costs in real 1996 ecus per year in Finland,

France, Germany, and the U.K. from 1985 to 1997,[19] and shows that UK costs fell by 65 percent. From being the most expensive (60 percent more than Finland), it became the second cheapest (15 percent more than Finland). Germany's costs fell 33 percent, France's by 29 percent, and Finland's fell by over 50 percent.

Opening telecoms to competition requires defining the terms of access to the network, and this is complicated by any remaining desire to cross-subsidize some classes of consumer (usually domestic and/or rural consumers of local calls). Unrestrained competition forces prices into line with costs and eliminates cross-subsidies. In most countries that have embarked on liberalization, the government wishes both to keep domestic local calls cheap and to encourage entry. The obvious danger is that if the incumbent company is not allowed to rebalance charges, then inefficient entry may occur, and the revenue base of the incumbent may be unreasonably eroded.

In Britain these concerns were addressed by restricting (but not preventing) the rate of adjustment of the rental element, while capping the overall weighted price, initially limiting the number of entrants (to one, Mercury), and (after the 1991 Duopoly Review) determining the access charge to include an access deficit charge. This was designed to transfer the lost surplus on that part of the call not involving the local loop, and which would therefore continue to be available to BT to cover the deficit in providing access to the local loop. This access deficit charge was waived until an entrant had a market share of 10 percent or BT's market share fell below 85 percent, and ended in 1996 when BT was allowed to rebalance its line rental and usage rates (even though BT still had 87 percent of the residential fixed lines in 1997–98). Regulation therefore encouraged facilities-based competition by not compelling charges to be cost based. As a further incentive to facilities-based competition, Oftel did not permit BT to install broadband networks, to encourage investment by competing cable companies, and to create greater bargaining parity in negotiations over future interconnection terms.

Determining interconnection charges is complicated by the huge asymmetry between BT (97 percent of connections in 1991, and still 87 percent in 1998 after extensive entry) and other operators. The regulator has had to balance the need for BT to cover its universal service obligation and the subsidy to small users with its desire to encourage facilities-based entry. In an attempt to improve the transparency of costs and facilitate both negotiations and regulated access charges,

Oftel proposed accounting separation for BT into network, retail, and access businesses in 1994. This was agreed by BT and came into effect from 1995. This appears to have eased the problem of allocating common and joint costs, which may amount to 80 percent of the total, and BT and Oftel appear to be in agreement on cost models that can be used to determine access charges (Oftel 1997a).

The difficulty of determining the correct interconnection charges is compounded by rapid technical progress, which may be devaluing the sunk assets that generate the common and joint costs (see the appendix to this chapter). If cable companies can provide radio links for the final few hundred meters to each customer at modest cost (perhaps one-third that of the old copper cable), then the local loop becomes contestable, possibly reducing the asset value of the incumbent telephone company, or stranding its assets. New technologies involving wireless local loops (where a local radio transmitter can deliver calls to small receivers on houses within a small area) now appear to be competitive against the traditional twisted copper pair and, as they benefit from advances in data compression and technical progress in microelectronics, can be expected to become cheaper in the future.[20] By October 1998, CATV companies could provide telecoms connections to nearly 12 million houses, up 50 percent in two years (Oftel 1999), and by the end of the century 70 percent of residential customers are expected to have a choice between at least two local access suppliers (Barnes 1998). (Cambridge had a choice of three different technologies from 1997, though one, Ionica, declared bankruptcy in 1998.) Facilities-based competition seems at last to be on the verge of eroding BT's dominance in the residential market.

By 1998 the U.K. telecoms market was moving rapidly through a transitional phase from dominance by a regulated incumbent to a competitive and increasingly unregulated market, where regulation is confined to bottleneck facilities, and general competition policy largely replaces detailed regulation. The incoming Labour government picked up the reform of competition law left uncompleted by its predecessor. The Competition Act was passed in late 1998, bringing Britain into line with Articles 81 and 82 (ex 85 and 86) of the Treaty of Rome, including fines for the abuse of market power. The Telecommunications Act of 1994 already confers many of the other powers of these Articles on the regulator.

The system of regulation reflects this transition in other ways. The new price controls that run from October 1997 to 2001 have changed the basis of setting the interconnection charge controls from fully allocated costs to TELRIC (with a markup of 10 percent to cover common costs). BT is given freedom to set charges for competitive services. Those services that are prospectively competitive are subject to a price cap of RPI + 0 percent as a backstop until competition drives prices down in real terms, while interconnection services are divided into three baskets each of which is subject to a price cap (of RPI −8 percent). Dividing up services into separate baskets reduces the ability of the incumbent to cross-subsidize the more competitive elements from the less competitive elements, though at the cost of somewhat restricting the freedom to rebalance as costs change at differential rates. In addition BT's charges are subject to floors and ceilings, where the floors are set at TELRIC and are designed to prevent predation, and the ceilings are the stand-alone costs and are intended to stop exploitation. Both floors and ceilings are derived from the agreed cost models. BT therefore has considerable, but not unlimited, freedom to vary its charges in response to competition and changes in costs.

BT responded to the consultation over the new price controls by claiming that its access charges were the lowest in the world (Oftel disagreed but accepted that they were "amongst the lowest")[21] and that the shift to TELRIC would lead to stranded assets—a claim that Oftel examined and denied.

For competition to be effective, barriers to entry need to be low, and these have been considerably reduced by introducing number portability, which allows a subscriber to keep his telephone number when shifting to a new provider, at a charge based on cost and paid by the new provider. Meanwhile the EU proposed an Interconnection Directive (97/33/EC) which will require BT to offer carrier preselection (CPS) to its customers (though other competitive operators are not required to offer this service). This will allow subscribers to preselect a carrier who will carry the call without the need to dial extra digits (though the subscriber will still be able to choose other carriers by dialling in extra digits). The EU Directive requires CPS to be offered from January 1, 2000, though Oftel will apply to delay the more ambitious choices until January 1, 2001, since apparently U.K. switches require programming, while the switches of continental carriers already have this capability (Oftel 1998c).[22]

Some fifteen years after privatization, under the pressure of continued regulatory scrutiny and a form of regulation that encouraged facilities-based competition, Britain has become one of the more competitive telecoms markets, and is gradually becoming one of the cheaper telecoms markets, though local call charges still discourage internet use, and mobile phone charges are still well above cost.

7.4 Lessons to Be Drawn

The key questions that have to be addressed in restructuring and privatizing telecommunications can be listed as follows:

· Should the industry be unbundled, separating long distance from local, for example?

· Should any restrictions be placed on the dominant incumbent (asymmetric regulation), such as denying the right to offer cable TV or a mobile service?

· Should there be any restrictions on competition with the incumbent?

· What form of regulation is required, if any?

· What are the main regulatory issues to resolve?

There are other important questions (on universal service obligations, spectrum allocation, etc.), but they would take us too far afield. All the evidence suggests that modern dynamic economies can support competitive telecommunications markets, even for voice over wire, and greatly benefit from such competition. The main questions are therefore how best to create effective competition.

7.4.1 Restructuring at Privatization

If it is so desirable to create effective competition, and the industry is to be privatized, then it follows that the industry should be restructured to maximize competition, and prices should also be rebalanced and lowered toward cost. The argument here is that there seems to be strong persistence in pricing behavior without very effective entry threats, judging from the U.S. experience, and that therefore initial prices matter. It also avoids the unseemly re-opening and tightening of price caps once the regulator realizes how unbalanced and excessive prices are, as in Britain. The obvious objection to this strategy is that it will reduce the sales revenue from privatization. Since this may be a sticking point, it is worth making a number of arguments in favor of privatizing the most competitive structure even at the cost of a lower sales price, forgoing some of the discounted monopoly profits.

First, buyers are increasingly unlikely, given the WTO negotiations and U.S. FCC pressures, to believe that monopoly can be sustained for long, so they are likely to discount future offered monopoly profits heavily, though after the sale they will resist actual steps to liberalize markets if they were sold a monopoly. The worst of outcomes would be to sell the telecoms company for the price of a company in a competitive industry but to allow it to remain a monopoly. Second, allowing monopoly pricing (even if the resulting profits can be captured successfully in the privatization sale price) for a price elastic service with beneficial externalities is the least efficient form of tax for a government; it would be better replaced by a small increase in VAT rates on all goods if the object is to raise revenue. The evidence from figure 7.1 and Hausman's calculations showed that the deadweight losses of high telecoms prices are very significant and should be avoided where possible. Spectrum auctions are an even better way of raising revenue than taxes, since they also efficiently allocate a scarce resource.

If creating competition is so desirable, why did this not happen in Britain in 1984? Part of the explanation was that Britain suffered from a lack of parliamentary consensus on the desirability of privatizing utilities, which in turn meant that the Conservative government was always under considerable pressure to privatize each utility within the limited life of each Parliament. Given the substantial work required to prepare legislation and create the regulatory framework, this normally meant that inadequate time and attention were available to consider different structural options, and the early privatizations normally sold the whole of the previously nationalized industry intact. The obvious advantage of restructuring a dominant incumbent is that it should be possible to create several viable and potentially competitive companies immediately, rather than after a gradual process of entry with the slow transfer of cost reductions to consumers and the risk of some inefficient duplication of facilities.

The standard political objection to breaking up the incumbent is that a single national carrier may prove a viable international competitor, while a set of smaller national companies may be acquired by foreign telecoms companies, much as the regional electricity companies in Britain have almost all been bought out by U.S. electricity companies. In some countries this loss of national pride may rule out the competitive solution, but in smaller countries who are almost certain to form alliances with foreign Telcos, there are advantages in having several competing foreign companies, rather than being dominated by just one. In addition to the competitive advantages, there should be informational advantages to the regulator in benchmarking costs and prices of each company against the others.

7.4.2   Creating a More Competitive Structure

While it is easy to introduce competition into long distance via entry from new fiber-optic backbones (which are likely to be needed for internet and data traffic anyway), the harder part is to create competitive choice at the local level. The problem is that while local companies can be spun off the long-distance company, it is easier for local companies to enter long-distance than conversely (as the FCC has discovered), so creating an adequately competitive market may be difficult. The local company would be able to offer a bundled local and long distance service, whereas the long-distance company would find it hard to offer local services, unless it were able to secure access to all the local facilities on fair terms.

The various options that may assist the creation of more competition are to encourage facilities competition, in which entrants are given more favorable access terms if they build infrastructure, including local loops, or to enforce access to the existing infrastructure on "fair and reasonable" terms. The first runs the risk of inducing excessive duplication of facilities, while the second may create a regulatory nightmare. Either the incumbent is able to deter entry by offering unfavorable access terms, or there is little incentive to build infrastructure because other competitors are free to use it without risk and at low cost. The British solution has been to encourage facilities competition (which may not be too costly given the rapid growth in demand for bandwidth and need for new investment), while also encouraging reasonable access to the existing network. This is being achieved by firm regulation of access charges and conditions, number portability (on a reciprocal basis), and delaying BT's entry into some rival services until market shares are better rebalanced. The United States, in contrast, is attempting to enforce the sharing of existing infrastructure and to avoid "wasteful" duplication, but at the expense of much regulatory delay and hence lost consumer surplus. It also makes it less likely that new facilities will be created, in which case competitive choice at the local level will remain dependent on regulated access to the unbundled services.

How best to encourage competition remains contentious. The British solution of encouraging facilities-based local competition by itself is slow and runs the risk of encouraging inappropriate technologies.

Cable TV had relatively low penetration in the United Kingdom before BT was privatized, and risks being overstimulated by regulatory protection for joint telephone and TV services, only to be superseded by the next generation of satellite digital broadcasting. Farrell (1997) contrasts two views of the desirable form of competition. Sharing access to the bottleneck facilities and charging efficient fees for that access should encourage bypass only when the new facility is an improvement on the existing facility—in either cost or functionality—and thus lets the market decide while avoiding inefficient duplication. The other view is that only bypass with competing facilities will allow full deregulation. This is a goal worth pursuing as regulation, especially in the United States, has proved so costly. Farrell concludes that the best strategy is to allow entrants to choose between using regulated sharing of essential facilities or unregulated bypass, and to observe how the market evolves, and whether entry is inefficient or inadequate. That appears to be the pragmatic British view.

Another option might be to divide up the country into regions with a local phone company, possibly integrated into a nondominant long-distance carrier, and then allow rival phone companies to enter each other's local area (while allowing new companies to enter as well), rather than adopting the U.S. solution of only allowing local companies into long distance when they have created adequately competitive local conditions. The U.S. solution reflects an attempt to restructure an existing private regulated system where asset revaluations are opposed. Privatization offers the prospect of cutting through that objection and choosing the best final structure right at the start.

7.4.3   Restrictions on Competition and Asymmetric Regulation

The reasons why Britain adopted asymmetric regulation and placed restrictions on BT offering cable TV (though cable TV companies are free to offer voice telephony) is that BT is so dominant. If the market is to be made more competitive, BT needs to be actively restrained from foreclosure of new opportunities, while new entrants need to be protected against the fear of predatory actions by the incumbent. If the market can be made adequately competitive, then such restrictions are not necessary.

Restricting competition with an incumbent, as was done in Britain by giving Mercury a statutory duopoly position for a period, or preventing competition for voice telephony, is now widely regarded as an inefficient policy (Spiller and Cardilli 1997). The defense that it is needed to allow a competitor to reach critical size has been falsified by events—massive entry took place after the duopoly ended, with a considerable jump in efficiency gains (figure 7.4). These days large telecoms companies can build critical masses within previously closed markets within short periods by using rights of way held by electric transmission grids, waterways, and railway companies, creating internet or cable networks, or wireless local loops, so there seems no justification for protection in terms of supporting competition. Where entry is discouraged or prevented to prescrve cross-subsidies, there are better ways of meeting these social goals, either by general taxes to fund deserving services or by auctioning the right to receive a (minimum) subsidy to provide the service.

7.4.4 Design of Regulation

On the regulatory front, price-caps seem not only to be the most efficient method of regulating any residual natural (and unnatural) monopoly parts but the only viable form of regulation able to deal with the transition to a competitive and eventually unregulated market. Liberalization makes rate-of-return regulation obsolete or inappropriate. The breakup of AT&T provides a good example. Under the old system, proposals for tariff changes were subject to lengthy judicial hearings and were poorly adapted to the rapid changes of tariffs by competitors in the contestable long-distance market. Since 1989, the FCC has switched to setting price-caps for interstate services and allowing AT&T freedom to introduce new tariffs within those caps. The change made the whole system simpler and more flexible (Mitchell and Vogelsang 1991), and it reduced the extent to which competitors or incumbents could prevent moves to more competition by lengthy and legalistic rate hearings.

Price regulation has considerable attractions at the point of privatization. It appears to sidestep the question as to what the "fair" rate of return is, leaving it to "the market" (actually, the merchant banks pricing the shares) to determine, and it allows "the market" to take a view about the likely rate of efficiency improvement or cost reduction. This has attractions in Eastern Europe where the companies buying the utilities to be privatized prefer not to reveal what rate of return they require, lest this be thought excessive. There is little need to agonize either about the exact level for initial prices (for the basket of services)

P_0, provided that they are driven down reasonably close to TELRIC, or the rate of assumed productivity fall, X (in the price formula RPI − X) which governs the rate at which prices must fall. Lower values of P_0 (or, as a less satisfactory compromise toward pushing prices down toward costs, higher values of X) reduce the flotation value but benefit consumers directly in lower bills, and through large reductions in deadweight losses which outweigh any fiscal benefit from higher privatization receipts.

The main differences between rate-of-return and price regulation is that the former is based on actual costs, while in principle, the latter is based on projected efficient costs, that is, costs that the utility should be able to achieve (possibly after some reorganization) if it were efficient. Where there are many comparable utilities, as with the 10 major water companies and the 12 regional electricity companies in Britain, the regulator can estimate the efficient frontier cost function using information about costs from all companies; it can then determine how far from the frontier any individual utility is, and how rapidly it might be expected to reach the frontier. This kind of yardstick regulation in which the target for one utility depends of the performance of other comparable utilities has the advantage of using relevant cost information while preserving incentives for cost reduction (Shleifer 1985). It provides another argument for unbundling the incumbent to create a number of comparable companies, though international benchmarking is becoming easier with increased standardization and cost transparency.

A second difference is that although in principle, rate-of-return regulation could be indexed for inflation and based on a basket of services, in practice in the United States, it has typically not been indexed. The entire structure of rates has been set at the review, reflecting the interests of the various pressure groups, or at least preventing rapid changes in the rate structure that might disadvantage some groups. Thus telephone rates were highly averaged across groups with very different costs of service (remote rural vs. densely populated urban areas), with large cross-subsidies (from long-distance to local service, reflecting the power of state interests of the PUC compared to out-of-state interests), or from business to domestic customers, who had greater voting power. Any changes in cross-subsidies must be renegotiated and is likely to be resisted by those who lose. The British system aims at efficiency by ruling out most cross-subsidies in the Acts and encouraging competition, which forces utilities to align prices with costs. Utilities are therefore normally left free to rebalance tariffs between different classes of customers provided that they do not increase the price index for the basket of services, leaving distributional issues to be addressed through the tax system.

7.4.5 Access Pricing

Access pricing has emerged as the key issue requiring active regulatory oversight. The early argument that access pricing could be left to negotiation between the companies, as they should be skilled at negotiating efficient solutions, completely overlooks the problem that bottlenecks create market power which is not attenuated by competition between networks (at least, not unless the bottlenecks can be so readily bypassed that they cease to be bottlenecks). In Britain, Mercury was initially free to negotiate access charges with BT, with the right of appeal to the regulator in the event of a dispute. Mercury immediately appealed and was granted favorable interconnection terms. The interesting question is whether interconnection agreements can ever be left to the unregulated market, perhaps when competitors are more numerous and symmetric.

Armstrong (1996, 1998) and Laffont, Rey, and Tirole (1998a, b) have demonstrated that this is a subtle and complex issue. Not surprisingly, if a small entrant faces competition from a dominant incumbent, then it can pay the incumbent to charge a high access price to disadvantage the entrant. The more interesting question is what happens when competing networks are of comparable size so that market dominance is no longer an obvious issue. The answer depends very much on the nature of price competition, whether the networks are free to price discriminate and whether they are free to use nonlinear tariffs.

In the simplest case networks are differentiated but symmetric (i.e., if they charge the same price they will share the market equally) and are not allowed to discriminate, which can have two interpretations. Armstrong (1998) takes nondiscrimination to mean that operators must charge subscribers the same charge for calls delivered on or off net; that is, BT charges the same to connect to a BT customer as to a comparable Mercury customer. Armstrong shows that negotiations over the interconnect charge may facilitate joint profit maximization in the final market provided that the two networks are not too close substitutes. If the networks set interconnect charges noncooperatively, they would be set above the joint profit-maximizing level, and the double marginalization harms them as well as customers. If the networks are sufficiently close substitutes, then low interconnect charges emerge, making regulation unnecessary.

Laffont, Rey, and Tirole (1998a) take nondiscrimination to mean that the operators must agree the fee for completing a call from the rival network. With linear pricing, the access charge again provides an instrument for tacit collusion, under which each network raises the prices charged to final customers. The situation is similar to allowing users of a bottleneck facility to set a transfer price for trading capacity to raise prices in the downstream market. As before, if operators set access charges noncooperatively, there will again be double marginalization and a final price above the monopoly price.

If network operators can charge two-part tariffs, they may extract rent through the fixed charge, and let usage charges, including interconnect charges, move toward marginal costs. However, the incentive toward efficient pricing is constrained by the heterogeneity of consumers, and the tentative conclusion is that unregulated reciprocal or noncooperative access pricing may still be excessive. The question is probably academic, for with several competing networks, two-part tariffs are probably not sustainable.

Finally Laffont, Rey, and Tirole (1998b) show that the nature of competition changes considerably if networks can price discriminate between charges for calls terminating within or outside the network. As with other cases of price discrimination, the welfare effects are ambiguous. Price discrimination allows more intense competition at the margin, but because it is not related to final demand or prices, it introduces an additional pricing distortion. Not surprisingly, detailed modeling of pricing strategies and empirical evidence about both the industries' cost characteristics and the consumers' perceived costs of switching between rival operators will be needed to assess the benefits of unregulated competition. The evidence from the United States suggests that flexible rather than detailed regulation is preferable (Kaestner and Kahn 1990). States that offer greater flexibility to companies in setting tariffs have about 7 percent lower charges than those that do not (Mathios and Rogers 1989). The implication is that while it may be theoretically possible to improve on TELRIC, it has the great merit of mimicking the competitive outcome. Sophisticated mechanisms to improve social welfare are best left to the tax system, not to the regulators.

Access regulation also needs to consider issues of equality of access. If customers are to be given equal access to different carriers, to minimize the switching costs that allows or supports collusive pricing, then ideally any customer should be free to keep his or her number when switching carriers (number portability), and each should be free to designate a preferred long-distance carrier with a short access code, called carrier preselection.[23] The first has been introduced in the United Kingdom, and the second is mandated for EU countries by 2000; it was an integral part of the MFJ in the United States.

If regulating access pricing emerges as one of the key regulatory issues, then it is likely that a specialist regulator will be required, rather than the "light-handed" regulation espoused by New Zealand, which relied on existing antitrust legislation and institutions. These proved slow to deal with abuse, and unable to apply economic rather than legal reasoning. On the other hand, as competition increases, the style of regulation has to shift from primarily one of setting prices and terms of access to more general competition oversight. In Britain, this was recognized in giving Oftel powers which are more comparable to those available under Articles 81 and 82 (ex 85 and 86) of the Treaty of Rome than under the original 1984 Telecommunications Act. These have been extended by the 1998 Competition Act, which allows the regulator to penalize abuses of market power.

7.5   Conclusions

Liberalizing telecoms later allows a country to profit from the lessons of experience of other countries and, when seeking international partners, to have a wider choice and therefore possibly more competitive bidding. The main pitfall to avoid is allowing the considerable benefits from modern telecoms networks to be inefficiently extracted in monopoly rents rather than assisting the country improve its competitive position and the welfare of its consumers. Designing good regulation to encourage technical innovation and competition without excessive litigation and delays remains a challenging task, especially in countries with poorly developed regulatory institutions. Maintaining free entry, keeping access charges low, but otherwise regulating with a light touch may not prevent abuses of dominant position. Nevertheless, such market failures are probably less costly than the likely costs of overambitious regulation.

Appendix: Telecoms Costs and TELRIC

As the telecoms industry is being forced to unbundle and price different services, so there is increasing emphasis on determining the costs
of each component, and it is become slightly easier to discover what
these are. For economic (and therefore regulatory) purposes, what is
needed are costs based on the modern equivalent asset value (MEA,
i.e., the cost of providing any given service using the currently least-
cost option). There are two immediate and related problems. As technology is evolving so rapidly, these costs soon become out of date (and
Moore's Law applied to switches suggests that these prices could be
halving every two years), and the depreciation element begins to dom-
inate the capital cost calculation. An example may clarify this. Suppose
that a switch costs 100 now but is halving in cost every two years.
The rate of interest is 10 percent, so the cost in the first year is interest
of 10, and depreciation of 30, with a second hand value of 70. In
the second year the interest cost will be 7 (10 percent of 70), and depreciation will be 20, giving a secondhand value of 50 (assuming no
deterioration in quality), equal to the MEA value. The annual capital
cost has therefore fallen from 40 to 27 (and will continue to fall). If the
equipment was assumed to experience no technical progress but to
become valueless after 10 years, and if it were subject to straight-line
depreciation, the first-year cost would be measured as only 20 (or
half the correct value), the second year 19, and so on. At the end of
four years the book value would be 60 but the MEA value would only
be 25.

The consequence of rapid technical progress is that historic costs tend
to overstate the value of the assets, but conventional rules of depreciation tend to underestimate the annual capital costs. In the present
example, if the average age of equipment were slightly more than two
years, the two effects would approximately balance out (assuming no
normal inflation), but this would represent an extraordinarily young
capital stock. Shifting from historic cost accounting to current cost (i.e.,
MEA) accounting and applying a TELRIC methodology therefore risks
stranding assets, as BT complained to Oftel (Oftel 1997a). Much then
depends whether parts of the network have been written down to less
than MEA (by inflation, or because they are more durable and less
prone to technical change).

The local loop has in the past been far less subject to this rapid technical progress (and real costs may have been rising as real labor costs

rise), though this may change if the twisted copper pair is superseded by lines with higher bandwidth, and the fraction of the cost allocable to voice decreases with new services supplied over the line.

The preferred concept of cost for regulating prices in the United Kingdom and the United States, and increasingly elsewhere, is (forward-looking) total element long-run incremental cost (TELRIC), where costs are based on the *elements* of the system needed to provide the service and include the *total* attributable costs of that element, calculated as the *incremental* cost incurred to provide an extra unit of the service over the *long run* during which all costs can be varied and are forward looking in determining the proper capital cost based on MEA values and depreciation. Oftel (1998) sets out their interpretation which stresses that it is the whole output of the relevant service that is the relevant increment, which they describe as the total service long-run incremental cost approach. In the United States only the existing location of switches is held constant in constructing and costing notional networks designed to determine the costs when providing a service and when not (to determine the incremental cost of that service), therefore making all capital costs variable, though common costs could be recovered by a suitable markup on these incremental costs (FCC Order August 1996, §§672–802). The European Commission's recommendation of January 8, 1998, on interconnection in a liberalized telecommunication market (98/195/EC) states that "the most appropriate approach to interconnection pricing is one based on forward-looking long-run incremental costs since this is most compatible with a competitive market."

The TELRIC methodology has been criticized by Harris and Kraft (1997, p. 106) for assuming that networks "can be instantaneously and entirely reconstructed with the best-available forward-looking technology. Clearly, these assumptions fail to mimic the actual functioning of competitive markets, which is the explicit intention of TELRIC." This may be a valid criticism of the way TELRIC is computed in the United States, but it is not a criticism of the concept. Indeed, if a current technology were cheaper to install and operate, earning an adequate (presumably high) return on the risky investment (which has to face similar threats from later competitors) and depreciating its equipment correctly to reflect the changing MEA value of its assets, then in a competitive market entry would occur until prices were driven down to these TELRIC costs. What is not clear is whether attempts to measure TELRIC use a sensible risk-adjusted rate of return on assets and appropriate economic measures of depreciation. There is a risk they will understate the true cost.

Oftel in the United Kingdom and the FCC in the United States attempt to apply the TELRIC concept (though whether they use the right rates of interest and depreciation is not clear), but many other costs to be found in the literature are some way from this ideal. Mason (1998) summarizes data for the PSTN (to compare it with the costs of internet telephony) as it stood in 1997, based on Oftel (1997), FCC (1997), and industry data. OFTEL estimates the annualized costs of access to the local loop as £120 (1996) values (or U.S.$187), compared to the annual line rental of £100 (U.S.$155), where the local loop includes the local switch. If this cost were allocated yearly to the average 6,000 called minutes, the average access cost would be 2.1 p/min, (3.3¢/min), and the marginal access cost might be 0.53¢/min. The U.S. figures are $120 to $216/year (and the line rental for flat rate service in 1995 was $163/year) giving an average of 1.7¢ to 3¢/min (for more called minutes) and the marginal access cost probably rather similar to that in the United Kingdom (0.5¢/min).[24] The U.K. national (long-distance) link is estimated at 0.31p/min (0.48¢/min) whereas the U.S. equivalent is 0.35¢ to 0.55¢/min. The costs of an international link is the switch cost (0.14¢/min) and the undersea link, which from the United Kingdom to the United States is estimated at 0.625¢/min. Thus the cost of an end-to-end call from the United Kingdom to the United States is the sum of local access, U.K. long-distance to an international switch, the undersea link, and the same again at the U.S. end, or 3.3 + 0.48 + 0.14 + 0.625 + 0.14 + 0.55 + 3.0 = 8.24¢/min. The marginal cost where fixed costs are properly collected through fixed charges would be less at about 3¢/min. In computing the deadweight losses both the collection charge and the costs include the annual line rental spread over the number of called minutes, and as it is the *difference* between the collection charge and the cost that matters, effectively we are working with marginal not average access charges.

There is an additional problem with the TELRIC methodology for setting the floor price in the U.K. system of regulation for preventing predation, if a high fraction of costs is related to capacity rather than use, and there is excess capacity in some components of the network (notably, the local loop). This might suggest that it should be the time-averaged charge including the fixed element that is subject to a floor. The main problem then is that the incumbent can undercut rivals by effectively charging itself a lower access price than its rivals at certain times (e.g., weekends, when BT's long-distance rates have sometimes been less than the access charge it levels on its rivals). This problem is likely to be less severe for other parts of the network, which are sized for peak flows, where these other parts might cost several times the average amount at the peak, and essentially zero in the off-peak. Time-of-use pricing and suitable averaging ought to deal with much of the problem. As delay-tolerant data traffic increases, the time variability of demand may reduce and make average costs a better measure of opportunity cost, but that will only affect a small part of the total cost until the local access charge is rebalanced more toward a fixed charge (as with the free local calls in many countries, or with some calling options).

The conflict will be between efficient discriminatory pricing and inefficient uniform pricing leading to excess inefficient entry. One theoretically attractive solution is for subscribers to pay for and own the local loop to the nearest switch, leaving them free to decide whether to replace, upgrade, or duplicate the connection (Schecter 1996).[25] The marginal price of calling could then fall substantially (and closer to marginal cost), since the fixed cost of the local loop would no longer need to be recovered through an inefficient tax on calls and customers would have access to a wider range of competing carriers once they have control of the bottleneck of the local loop.

8 Deregulation and Restructuring in Gas

Electricity, telecoms, and gas are alike in that they were once all thought to require vertical integration because of their natural monopoly properties and public service obligations. All three utilities are being liberalized and restructured in various ways in the United States and the United Kingdom, and in all cases the aim is to introduce competition to reap efficiency gains. The sources and extent of the inefficiencies in the traditional integrated structure differ between these three utilities. One reason is that their cost structures differ in important respects. In electricity generation, costs and technology are transparent and moderately stable so that it is not difficult to set efficient prices. National grids have a more complex cost structure, but in densely populated mature countries account for a relatively small fraction of the total cost.

Telecoms cost structures by contrast are opaque, subject to rapid technical progress, with a large share of costs that are fixed and/or common, making the design of tariffs problematic. Nevertheless, as technology converges, it is increasingly possible to define a reasonable cost for a network in a given country, which is likely to be similar to comparable systems elsewhere. Transparency is thus gradually improving. In contrast, gas production has opaque and ill-defined costs. Gas production properly ought to include a resource rent that is site specific, heavily dependent on the market into which the gas is sold, and thus its costs are hard to compute. Whereas electricity generation and telecoms systems are not tied to particular sites, provided that they are connected to consumers, gas production sites are fixed by geology and unevenly distributed across countries.

These differing cost characteristics have important implications for the benefits of liberalization. At least in advanced countries, electricity prices are usually not very different from costs, and the costs of inefficient pricing are modest. The main gains come from improving investment performance and breaking the influence of fuel-based interest groups on investment and energy policy. Telecoms prices often bear little relation to costs, and pricing and regulatory inefficiencies are hugely costly. The particular resource characteristics of gas create a new set of pricing and regulatory inefficiencies. If gas is to be exploited and delivered to customers, large investments in exploration, production, and gas pipeline systems are needed before any gas can flow. These production and delivery systems are inflexible and durable, and at least in the early stages of development, they lock the producer and consumer into a bilateral relationship. The cost of producing gas includes a resource rent whose size depends on the value placed upon the gas by the consumer. This in turn depends on competition from alternative fuels and, critically, on the rate of supply of gas. Gas not produced today can be sold tomorrow, and its future value is therefore important in determining its present opportunity cost.

The result is that gas producers have been unwilling to invest without a secure long-term contract with a pipeline company, while the pipeline company is unwilling to invest without either a long-term contract to sell to final consumers, or a guaranteed franchise market from which contract costs can be recovered. The resource rents, which are available to the producers to cover costs of exploration, and to governments in the form of various taxes, depend on the price and volume sold in the final market, exactly as in the case of oil. The contrast with oil is striking, however. Oil is easily transported to any market, where it is competitively priced and highly liquid (in the sense that oil of a particular characteristic readily substitutes for similar oil and receives the same price). Gas cannot be readily moved between markets unless there is a mature pipeline system with spare capacity, and its price therefore depends on its scarcity value in the particular market to which it is delivered. The resulting equilibrium, at least in the initial stages of development, is one in which gas is limited in supply to high-value users, and supply is carefully adjusted and expanded in line with demand to sustain those prices. This strategy ensures high rents to finance exploration and production, and secure revenues to finance the heavy investment in infrastructure. The high cost of gas delivered into the pipeline and the heavy cost of the pipeline in turn justify the high regulated prices to charge in the final market.

The fact that gas is often priced against competing fuels provides another interesting contrast with telecoms and electricity, neither of which face competition from close substitutes. Despite this competition with other fuels, gas has typically been treated as a monopoly, and preserving this monopoly against competition from other supplies of gas has been a major motivating factor behind regulation and ownership structures. Mispricing and regulatory inefficiencies were very large in the United States, and were resolved by liberalization. The main inefficiencies on the continent are that gas is overpriced, and as a result demand has been suppressed. The dominance of the incumbents restricts access to new supplies of cheap gas that could transform the market and also transform the electricity industry. U.S. levels of gas penetration may be delayed in some countries because gas pipeline companies control the bottleneck of gas transport and are reluctant to let new players into the market.

The benefits from liberalizing gas have very much to do with disturbing this equilibrium in which supply is restricted to raise prices above their competitive equilibrium level. If gas producers could be sure that any additional gas found could be delivered and sold in the most valuable market, and if consumers could choose between different sources of supply with confidence that enough gas was always available at a reasonable price, then gas spot markets could develop and provide the assurance that previously could only be guaranteed by long-term contracts and vertical integration.

Gas on gas competition typically lowers the price of gas, both because it reduces the market power of those who control supplies to the final market and because the creation of a liquid spot market makes it less risky to develop new reserves and build new pipelines in the expectation of profit. Given the huge profitability of many fields and pipeline links, this process can feed upon itself to extend the market, increase liquidity in the market, and in turn provide assurance for further investment. The benefits of gas liberalization are thus to reduce monopoly power that regulation was unable or unwilling to address, partly because of the opacity of the cost structure and the endogeneity of the rent element of those costs. The fact that governments, who benefit from some of the resource rents, conspired to support this high-price equilibrium may explain some of the resistance to liberalization.

There is an additional dimension to the problem of designing regulation to support liberalization. While electricity regulation is primarily a domestic matter, both gas and telecoms need access to other countries on fair terms to gain the full benefits of trade. The counterpart to the General Agreement on Trade in Services for telecoms is the

Energy Charter Treaty (ratified in April 1998) which grants GATT-like trading protection for a wider range of countries than have signed up to all the provisions of the GATT and WTO (notably in Eastern Europe, though not yet in the Ukraine and the Russian Federation, through which the major transit pipelines from Russia pass). Within the EU, the Gas Directive attempts to ensure access through other member states, but it lacks adequate mechanisms to resolve regulatory conflicts between member states. Gas liberalization therefore raises new issues and the lessons from electricity and telecoms cannot be simply transferred to the gas industry.

8.1 Similarities and Differences between Gas and Electricity

Gas and electricity are often discussed as though they can be treated similarly. They are both forms of energy, they require a high-pressure pipeline system or high-tension grid to bring the energy from producers to the local distribution networks, and gas molecules, like electrons, are indistinguishable and can therefore be marketed anonymously in a bulk supply market. Both industries require large investments in a network that is readily financed from monopoly franchises but, once mature, faces the problem that consumers want to escape from the regulatory compact that created these networks. In electricity, new technology, the excessive expense of past nuclear investment, and excess capacity caused by the failure of demand to continue to grow at past rates all offer the prospect of cheaper electricity if the old regime could be liberalized. In gas, regulatory failures in the United States have precipitated liberalization. In Europe, high prices for gas combined with increasing success in tapping offshore gas fields and creating pipeline links to other countries, have caused a weakening of spot and new contract prices compared to older contract prices, again putting pressure on the old regulatory structures.

The development of CCGT created a large new market for gas for new gas traders who could gain access to the pipeline network. The end of the cold war and the collapse of energy demand in Russia and Central Europe made gas imports from Russia seem less insecure and released large volumes at competitive prices. Although in 1997, the EU-15 countries still consumed only just over half the amount of gas of the United States (and its share of gas in primary energy consumption was also about half), its rate of growth of consumption from 1990 to 1996 was 5.2 percent per year—more than twice that of the

United States at 2.4 percent per year. At last Europe looked set to enjoy the market penetration and low gas prices previously associated with North America, and it also looked set to follow a similar move to liberalization.

Although there are similarities in the issues raised by competition in gas and electricity, there are also important differences. European countries are almost all self-sufficient in electricity production, and international trade is minor (though important for countries with surplus low-cost electricity). In contrast, many European countries are heavily dependent on imports for their gas, while some (Norway, the Netherlands) are major exporters. Russia is a major supplier to Europe, as are the politically unstable countries of North Africa and the Middle East. Countries that import by pipelines are locked into supply relationships that raise issues of security and dependence in a more acute form than oil, where most countries can rapidly switch between a variety of suppliers. Liquified natural gas (LNG) might seem more like oil in providing more flexible supply links, though until recently, the need to coordinate the facilities required to liquefy, transport and regasify meant that most such trade was on long-term contract between dedicated facilities and almost as inflexible as pipeline trade.

Creating a competitive market in electricity generation is fairly simple in most countries, as the minimum efficient scale of generation is normally small compared to the size of the market. CCGT stations with a capacity of 70 to 150 MW are viable where gas is available, so a country with a population of 10 million and demand of 10,000 MW can clearly sustain a large number of competing generators. Argentina, with capacity of 16,000 MW, had 40 generating companies in 1997 with none larger than 8 percent of the total, and a correspondingly competitive wholesale market (as described in chapter 6, section 6.5.2). Generating stations (except for hydro) have considerable freedom of choice of location, though access to cheap fuel may make some locations more attractive than others (e.g., at a port, on a rail link or near a coal field). Since electricity fuel prices tend to be moderately similar in neighboring countries, and electricity is expensive to transmit over long distances, electricity trade tends to be restricted to peak shaving or providing access to cheap hydro power.

Gas production, on the other hand, is tied to gas fields, which are unevenly distributed across countries, and often under concentrated ownership. Gas producers face the problem that gas at the field has no value unless it can be delivered to a market. A pipeline may only give access to a limited market, or even a single buyer. To overcome the risks of holdup and ex post opportunism, fields and pipelines were at least initially developed on the back of long-term contracts, fifteen years being a typical length. If a country like Britain faces a small number of large multinational oil companies developing gas reserves offshore, then it is natural for the government to insist on bilateral bargaining over the terms of supply, in order to redress the perceived imbalance in bargaining power. Granting a domestic monopoly to British Gas offered the prospect of sharing the rents with the gas producers, rather than allowing the producers to capture the entire rent if they were free to price discriminate in the final market.

This concern was almost certainly misplaced in Britain, where a reasonably large number of different fields offered the prospect of competitive gas supply, but it is a very real concern where a country with few indigenous supplies faces a single monopoly foreign supplier. Most countries of Central and Eastern Europe are almost entirely dependent on Russia for pipeline imports, and in such cases a competitive downstream market allows the producing country to capture most of the rent, unless there is a credible threat to sign long-term contracts with other suppliers with independent access to the country.

European countries started the decade with very concentrated ownership of pipelines, production and supply, and well-entrenched companies who argued convincingly that security and safety required integrated management of operations from the entry point into the pipeline system right to the burner tip. For a country to contemplate liberalizing its gas market, it first has to be assured that the producers or external suppliers lack excessive market power. Some countries are well placed to connect directly to new sources of supply. Spain has now three LNG terminals on the coast as well as a pipeline direct to North Africa giving it access to Algerian production. It also has a pipeline connection to France, which lacks adequate domestic supplies. That pipeline connects to the West European gas grid, but for that to translate into access to other producers, Spain must be able to negotiate transport rights to pipelines through a number of countries.

The importance of assuring countries of a diversity of possible suppliers to reduce the market power of any single producer has been an important force behind the EU Gas Directive which was finally agreed in 1998, and which is discussed below. Removing external market power in turn removes the case for countervailing market power on the part of the domestic gas company that has to secure supplies to deliver to domestic customers.

Creating a competitive internal market in gas requires that consumers have access to a sufficient number of competing suppliers, each of whom can deliver gas in variable amounts to that consumer. Consumers and/or traders therefore need access to the transport services of the domestic pipeline owner, or have to be able to request delivery of equivalent gas at prices equal to the input price of gas plus a nondiscriminatory transport cost. Until recently this was not possible in most European countries, but the intention behind the 1998 European Gas Directive is to ensure such third party access to pipelines within and between EU member countries.

It is hard to judge how competitive the gas market has been over this period. Figure 8.1 shows the evolution of pretax industrial gas prices

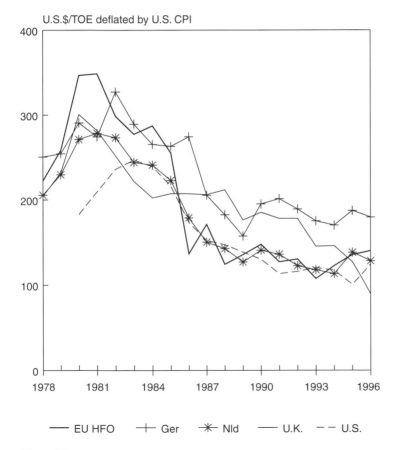

Figure 8.1
Industrial gas prices in 1995 U.S.$/TOE (GCV) before tax.
Source: IEA (1997).

in Europe and the United States over the period 1979 to 1996 compared with the pretax price of heavy fuel oil, HFO (averaged over EU countries). The graph of border prices of gas in Europe follows a similar and if anything tighter pattern, consistent with a competitive international market in gas. European industrial gas prices track HFO reasonably closely (including those not shown on the graph); this may reflect the contract provisions for international (and national) gas supply, which are normally indexed to the price of oil, which in turn moves closely with the price of HFO. What is more surprising is that gas prices in the United States also track HFO prices and hence European gas prices, even though they are not connected by pipeline, and LNG trade into the United States has little influence on price setting there.

It may also reflect the pricing policy of the domestic monopoly supplier pricing gas against the competitive fuel (for heat raising), which would indicate market power constrained by competing fuels. Gas on gas competition (i.e., competition between gas producers unconstrained by the prices of other fuels) ought not to lead to such a close link to the price of oil, but it would probably require a shift from selling most gas on contract to an active spot and futures market; that would then guide the setting of contract prices and allow them to be delinked from the price of competing fuels. There is some evidence of this happening in Britain since 1996 when the gas spot market began to play an active role in price setting. Gas on gas competition in the United States predates that in Europe, and it may be that the gas and HFO markets are so substitutable there that they are both competitively priced.

The result of these pressures for increased access and competition in European gas and electricity markets (where there is a comparable EU Electricity Directive) is of growing convergence of the two industries, in their structure, markets, and regulation. The incoming British Labour government has decided to combine the two regulatory agencies, Ofgas and Offer, following the example of several other countries. The two fuels are increasingly substitutable in production and consumption, as combined cycle gas turbines offer generators the option of turning gas into electricity if its value as electricity exceeds that as gas, or selling into the spot gas market if the converse is true. Britain now quotes the price of gas in pence/kWh, the same units as electricity, making this comparison easy to make.[1] The spot markets for electricity and gas are thus interlinked, and actions of traders in one market have repercussions in the other. High spot prices for gas have on occasion created unanticipated supply withdrawals from the pool and caused supply security problems that required regulatory changes.

The two markets interact over longer time periods as well, for gas can be more easily stored than electricity, especially over short time periods, and this should put a floor on the price of electricity. Conversely, coal (and oil) can be more cheaply stored from summer to winter than gas, which may reduce the seasonal swing in gas consumption if gas displaces coal in the summer and conversely in the winter. The seasonal variation in demand for gas in Britain was running at six to one, creating a need for expensive storage and a marked seasonal pattern to gas prices which fuel switching in generation can alleviate. Since gas can be replaced by gasoil in CCGT (as well as coal in conventional stations), the electricity sector provides additional security of gas supply to the domestic market. CCGT stations can sign cheaper interruptible gas contracts, reducing the need for additional storage and/or reducing the risk of interrupting the domestic market, which is very costly. These market interactions spill over into the coal and oil product markets. Indeed, there is a chain of possible substitutions that allows one increasingly to talk of fuels in terms of their energy and attributes (storability, ease of transport, etc.), so the rapid growth of demand for gas for use in power generation has an effect on the price of coal and HFO which are also used in generation.

Regulatory convergence is not only impelled by the need to ensure that the gas and electric spot market work compatibly but also by the belief that lessons for network regulation learned from one industry can usefully be applied to the other. In the United Kingdom, electricity transmission services are handled through the Pooling and Settlement Agreement. This has generated considerable dissatisfaction because it has proved hard to agree changes. When the gas Network Code for handling shippers obligations and rights was developed between 1996 and 1998, there was a conscious attempt to avoid the problems created by the unsatisfactory governance structure of the electricity pool. In the 1998 electricity pool review, U.K. gas-trading arrangements were held up as a suitable model for electricity trading arrangements, and they appear to have been influential in Offer's final proposals (Offer 1998c).

Transmission pricing for both gas and electricity affect the choice of location for CCGT stations, and if not set at efficient levels, it can give rise to costly mistakes that endure for decades. The methodologies for setting electricity and gas transmission prices have both changed since

1990, and neither is yet completely satisfactory. If either or both are to be changed, the regulators will need to ensure that the locational signals are set sensibly. It is more important that the locational price differentials for gas and electricity are sensible relative to each other than that either set of prices by itself is "correct."

Gas and electricity are also substitutable in demand, for cooking, heating, and even air conditioning. Domestic gas prices are typically one-third off-peak electricity prices in the United Kingdom. While gas may be only 70 percent efficient compared to 100 percent efficient for electricity, gas is still cheaper for heating (though the capital cost of electric heating is less than that of gas-fired central heating).[2] In the days when domestic electricity and gas were supplied by different franchise holders, the RECs marketed electric heating very aggressively. The two fuels were certainly in competition, though after 1998 suppliers can (and often do) offer both fuels with a discount for taking both from the same supplier. In some countries (e.g., Germany) the same company has had a local franchise to offer both fuels. The evidence in such cases is that interfuel competition is muted and prices tend to be higher than when they are supplied by competing franchise holders, though if both markets are completely liberalized bundling should not raise such anticompetitive concerns.

In the past, gas penetration in different European countries varied considerably, depending on whether they had indigenous gas and how well placed they were for imports. Countries that are connected to the main European pipelines face similar import prices. As figure 8.1 shows, industrial gas prices in each country have tended to follow a similar downward trend in real prices, though with a considerable spread across countries. Tax regimes differ considerably across EU countries, so final prices can still differ, even in a competitive market. Industrial gas prices are normally untaxed, except in Germany (where the tax rate is 14 percent of the final price), but HFO is heavily taxed in Britain, Denmark, France, Germany, Italy, and Austria, typically at rates above 15 percent and usually at specific rather than ad valorem rates. Competitive markets will have arrived when gas prices to final consumers are linked to the spot prices of gas at various hubs in Europe by the cost of transport and the prevailing tax rates, and not by the exercise of market power by price-discriminating domestic monopolies. The success of the EU Gas Directive will be measured by the speed with which this happens.

8.1.1   Technical Characteristics of Gas

Gas differs from electricity in a number of important ways that affect the way the industry can be organized. Perhaps the most important is that while electricity fails to safety, gas fails to danger. If the gas supply to consumers is interrupted even briefly, and then re-established, unburned gas can escape and cause fire and explosion risks. If air enters the gas pipeline, an explosive mixture of air and gas may result. Continuity and integrity of supply are therefore critical, and although large customers may contract for interruptible supply, the supplier and consumer have to ensure that supply is turned off safely at the consumer end.

Supply and demand therefore have to be kept in balance, though modern high-pressure systems allow this balancing to be handled over periods of a day by diurnal (daily) storage (from gas holders located near demand centers and variations in line pressure). In Britain, the daily peak demand is typically 1.5 the average demand and 4 times the minimum; 15 percent of the peak demand is met from diurnal storage. Seasonal variations (which in Britain are large, with the peak demand 2.2 times the average daily demand and 5 to 6 times the trough) are handled by peak and seasonal storage or by varying the rate of extraction from the wells, and by interruptible contracts. Swing (the ratio of the peak to average supply) is expensive for offshore deep water wells, since the capital cost of the well and pipeline delivery to the beach depend on the peak flow. Therefore high utilization rates (with little variation in flow rates) are desirable. In Britain the deeper northern basin has a swing of 1.1 (corresponding to a load factor of 91 percent), while the shallower and closer inshore southern basin has a swing factor of 1.67, giving an average swing of 1.5 compared to the demand swing of 2.3 on average (a 45 percent load factor).[3] The tariff market below 2,500 therms (250 MBTU, 73 MWh) per year has a load factor of 35 percent, while the contract market above 25,000 therms (731 MWh) per year has a load factor of 47 percent, with industrial users having higher load factors (53 percent).[4]

Large onshore fields like the Groningen field in the Netherlands may be able to provide extra delivery capacity at lower cost and hence offer swing more cheaply. Storage in salt caverns or nearly depleted fields on or close to the shore can be equipped with compression facilities to reinject gas in offpeak months and make it available at the peak. LNG can be stored for short-term rapid release over periods of days and can be used to increase supply security at the ends of the network to avoid unacceptable pressure drops in periods of high demand. The LNG can be replaced (at a cost) by liquifying gas delivered by pipeline or from deliveries by LNG tankers. The transmission and storage system needs to be sized for the level and variability of demand and adapted for new sources of supply and demand. In Britain, peak shaving storage from LNG and seasonal storage accounts for only 5 percent of total annual demand but 30 percent of peak demand. Most (80 percent) of the seasonal storage comes from a single depleted gas field (Rough) 16 miles offshore.

Security of supply is provided by selecting a probability of failing to meet demand, and then providing sufficient transmission and storage capacity to meet that standard. Thus British Gas (and its successor, TransCo) sets the standard at 1 in 20 peak days, meaning that only on average once every 20 years would supply be inadequate to meet demand (on the peak day). There is an additional requirement that only once in 50 years would the cumulative supply, including that from storage, be inadequate to meet cumulative demand over a winter, for example, if there were a sustained run of very cold weather that depleted all storage.

Demand can be adjusted to supply through interruptible contracts. In 1992, 3.3 billion therms were sold on interruptible contracts (which can be interrupted for up to 45 days per year) out of a total of 19 billion therms, or 17 percent, more than three times the volume of storage. The number of days on which interruptions were invoked has varied from zero (e.g., in 1992–93, which was a warm winter) to 51 days in 1985–86 (of which 7 days were because of a strike in the Frigg field).

Britain is fortunate in being effectively self-sufficient in gas, so security can be determined primarily from weather patterns and the risks of equipment failure. Strikes, though rare, have interrupted supply occasionally, but they do not loom large in planning adequate storage. The situation is very different in importing countries that perceive a political risk in their dependence on pipeline supplies. Until the new pipelines through Poland are complete, all Russian gas reached the West through the Ukraine, which was in long-term default in paying for its gas imports from Russia. There were concerns in the West that Russia might suspend gas deliveries to the Ukraine in order to force payment, and that the Ukraine might retaliate by diverting transit gas to its own use, thus disrupting deliveries. In 1992 nearly 20 percent of total West European gas supply came through the Ukraine, with France, Germany, and Italy nearly one-third dependent on Russia, and Austria 74 percent dependent. Such countries normally adopt a combination of interruptible contracts and storage to provide the ability to withstand a considerable period of disruption, and the IEA monitors their dependence on Russia and their ability to cope with disruptions. While Britain had only 20 days storage in 1992 (and this has since fallen), Austria had 120 days storage, Italy had 96 days, France had 91 days, and Germany had 48 days (IEA 1994). Some countries like Finland have no storage (because of the unfavorable geology of the country) but insist that consumers can be interrupted and have alternative backup fuels.

Gas pipelines experience considerable apparent economies of scale in that pipeline cost per unit of capacity falls as the diameter of the pipeline increases. Thus the cost of per billion cubic meters (bcm) per year of transport capacity falls from about $270,000/mile for a 15 inch pipeline to about $100,000/mile for 36 inch capacity (1991 prices; IEA 1994). Pipelines therefore appear to be natural monopolies, but in practice, the high-pressure transmission system is normally built to a standard (large) size (in the United Kingdom, 900 or 1,200 mm). The capacity of links in a network can be fairly smoothly varied by installing additional compressors or doubling sections of the pipeline. The latter arrangement reduces the pressure drop for a given throughput and allows the pressure delivered to the subsequent single pipe section to be increased, which in turn increases the pressure drop and hence throughput to the next compressor station. The net effect of the variety of ways of increasing capacity along a route is that unit transport costs are more uniform and less volume dependent, and more distance related than simple pipeline cost comparisons might suggest. The argument for integrated management of pipeline development is then more one of optimizing expansion by taking advantage of the capacity of the whole network rather than confining attention to capacity on a particular pipeline connecting the entry and exit points.

8.1.2   Market Structures and Access Arrangements in Gas

The traditional structure of gas industry is that of a merchant pipeline operator, in which the company owning the pipeline buys gas from producers, transports it through the high-pressure pipeline system which it owns, operates and maintains, and delivers it to large customers and local distribution companies (LDCs). In some countries such as the United Kingdom before the breakup of British Gas the LDCs are owned by the monopoly merchant pipeline company, and in some cases the merchant pipeline company also owns production wells. Until recently LDCs invariably had a local franchise, but pipeline companies did not necessary have a monopoly in supply.

Pipelines may operate as private carriers, in which case they are typically owned by the producers of the fields supplying the pipeline and the gas is owned by the pipeline owner. The pipeline may act as a contract carrier where it contracts with gas owners to transport gas but is free to determine whether or not to accept contracts, or it may act as a common carrier, in which case it is required to offer transport services on a nondiscriminatory basis. Common carriage often requires the pipelines to allocate space in proportion to the amounts tendered, which could exceed the capacity of the pipeline. Given that transport rates are invariably regulated, this poses an obvious problem in the design of mechanisms to allocate space efficiently.

Common carriage or open access must be distinguished from third-party access (TPA), which is defined by the European Commission as "a regime providing for an obligation, to the extent that there is capacity available, on companies operating transmission and distribution networks for . . . gas to offer terms for the use of their grid, in particular to individual consumers or to distribution companies" (EC 1992). TPA thus imposes no obligations on the pipeline owner to provide access if the capacity has been already allocated. Under Article 17 of the 1998 Gas Directive, pipeline owners may also refuse access where this would prevent them from carrying out public-service obligations or on the basis of serious economic and financial difficulties with take-or-pay contracts, though in both cases "duly substantiated reasons shall be given for such a refusal."

The arrangements for trading gas between countries are quite varied, with the ownership of the gas changing hands at different points. In some cases, the exporting country owns the gas to the border of the importing country; in other cases, the buyer may own the gas while it transits through third countries in pipelines owned by other parties. A number of international pipelines are jointly owned by importing and exporting countries, whose ownership shares gives them entitlements to shares in the capacity of the pipeline, and they may transport gas on their own behalf or acting as a carrier for another owner. Most onshore pipelines in Europe are owned by state enterprises with de jure or de facto transportation monopolies. Thus SNAM is a state-owned Italian gas company that imports gas from the Netherlands, Russia, and Algeria. SNAM has joint ventures with gas companies in the transit countries involved. For example, Russian gas arrives at the Austrian border and transits through the TAG pipeline, which is jointly owned by the Austrian gas company and SNAM, while Dutch gas comes through Germany in the TENP pipeline jointly owned with Ruhrgas, and imports from Algeria cross the Mediterranean in a pipeline jointly owned with the state-owned Algerian gas company Sonatrach.

8.1.3 Requirements for Liberalization

The principle questions to ask when liberalizing the gas market are which of the services of transmission, storage, meter reading, and investment in pipelines can be made competitive, and how to manage the interface between the regulated natural monopoly and competitive services. The overriding importance of supply security and integrity argue for allocating responsibility to a single operator, while the ability of the system to accommodate short-term fluctuations over periods of up to a day offers the prospect of greater unbundling. Gas moves at less than 50 kph rather than at the speed of light, and variations in pressure in the high-pressure system are acceptable in a way that voltage fluctuations are not. Therefore response times do not need to be so fast; they are better suited to the speed with which markets can operate. The debate over liberalization is partly one of finding the right balance between these two opposing arguments, as well as the normal arguments over the financing of a highly capital-intensive durable and immovable network without a franchise or long-term contracts that are inimicable to spot markets, entry and exit.

Storage provides insurance against costly disruptions and the amount to provide is either a statistical calculation (as in Britain with control over its own supply) or a strategic geopolitical decision for import-dependent countries. It is also a public good for consumers who are not on interruptible contracts (which are only feasible for large sites that are daily metered and in communication with the gas company). The level of security supplied to any one of these consumers is automatically supplied to all others, whether or not they are willing to pay. This public good feature presents obvious problems when it comes to replacing a centrally planned determination of supply security with decentralized market choices and is bound up with the question of who acts as supplier of last resort, or who is required to offer universal service. In practice, this aspect of supply is almost certain to require regulatory oversight. One of the tests of successful liberalization is whether adequate but not excessive storage can be provided with low transaction costs by market mechanisms, and whether this will meet the various supply and security obligations met in the past by the franchise holder.

The resistance to liberalizing the continental gas market comes from the integrated gas companies, whose criticisms include the following:

· TPA will lead to stranded contracts as existing producers continue to buy old gas at the old contract prices and entrants obtain additional new gas at lower prices, and compete down final sales prices.

· TPA will make it difficult to finance new pipelines which require long-term contracts and are put in jeopardy by TPA.

· Liberalizing the downstream gas market will increase producer power and reduce the security of supply as trading arrangements will necessarily become of shorter duration.

· Liberalization will benefit large consumers at the expense of small consumers.

· Liberalization may jeapardize public-service obligations to ensure security of supply and consumer protection which free competition cannot necessarily guarantee.

· TPA will replace commercial contractual relationships with intrusive and burdensome regulatory oversight.

These fears can be seen very clearly in the safeguards placed in the European Gas Directive, and they are nontrivial. The inflexibility of the gas pipeline system and Europe's heavy dependence on a small number of oligopolistic gas producers creates quite a different market environment for liberalization than in the electricity industry, or even in the very much more fragmented and domestically self-sufficient U.S. market.

The 1998 European Gas Directive was the outcome of nine years of painful negotiations between countries, some of which were highly protective of their present arrangements. They have succeeded in inserting various exemptions for public-service obligations, consumer and enviornmental protection, and for stranded investments and contracts. None of these terms are clearly defined which therefore gives the countries opposed to change the opportunity to delay reform.

Indeed, the Directive states that "these rules are no more than general principles providing a framework, the detailed implementation of which should be left to Member States, ..." Nevertheless, the Directive clearly signals the intention of creating competitive markets. It therefore encourages the emerging pressures for competition created by surplus pipeline capacity, falling gas prices, and the demands of independent power producers for access to cheap gas. An optimistic view is that countries will increasingly recognize that their competitive position is not improved by resisting the liberalization of the gas market. The internal balance of interest groups will have been upset by the increased flexibility in the international gas markets, as well as pressure from other domestic interests.

The most important step to liberalize gas markets is the legal unbundling of transmission from supply or marketing, yet this is not required by the Gas Directive. Since there are no European regulatory agencies nor any agreement on the methodology for determining access prices, it will be difficult for competitors to demonstrate the abuse of incumbent market power. Gas companies are, however, required to unbundle the functions and management of transmission and marketing. An aggressive pro-competitive regulator can use this to encourage legal unbundling, as happened in the case of AT&T and British Gas, and there is some evidence that countries are learning from the experience of others on how best to liberalize the sector. The fact that regulators meet on a regular basis and compare and benchmark the performance of each company will hasten convergence. The main inducement to the companies to accept liberalization is the threat that if they do not do it themselves, the Commission may impose less satisfactory alternatives, or pursue them under other Articles of the Treaty of Rome for abuse of market power. Individual companies wishing to dispute terms of access and unable to appeal to an adequately energetic regulatory authority within the country face a lengthy and legalistic route through the European Court. The European Court is reluctant to become involved in political issues affecting national security, and is thus likely to be relatively ineffective for forcing access against the wishes of member states.

The Directive offers two alternative forms of TPA: negotiated and regulated TPA. Negotiated TPA under Article 15 requires countries to allow eligible customers and other gas undertakings inside and outside the country to negotiate voluntary commercial agreements "in good faith," and under published commercial conditions. Regulated TPA

(Article 16) requires gas undertakings to publish "tariffs and/or other terms and obligations of use," though as mentioned above, Article 17 allows access to be denied in specified cases (public service obligations, stranded assets, etc.).

The trend appears to be away from negotiated TPA to regulated TPA, while the rate of market opening appears to be faster than that required by the Directive. Spain presents an interesting example of a country with little indigenous gas, heavily dependent upon external unstable suppliers, most of which are monopolies. Nevertheless, Spain has aggressively pursued a liberalized and competitive gas market and has already opened the market to direct purchase for buyers taking above 20 million cubic meters (38 percent of total volume) under regulated tariffs for transport. The safeguards chosen are that no single supplier should have more than 60 percent of supply to those with a significant market share, and buyers must provide 35 day storage unless they have an alternative fuel to which they can switch and interrupt. With three LNG plants and two pipelines (one from France and one from the Magreb), Spain has diversified her potential sources of supply as rapid domestic demand growth removes the problems that might otherwise be created by take-or-pay contracts.

France, in contrast, holds firmly to a traditional energy policy with the additional French preference for defending the power of the French state which is done under the public-service provision of the Directive. This defense has worked in the past where the onus is upon those bringing suit against the French government to demonstrate that public-service obligations are invalid.

Given the fears of different countries, and the hopes of those wishing to press ahead with liberalization, it is worth looking at the experience of the two countries most advanced in the process, the United States and the United Kingdom, to see what problems have been encountered. The two countries are alike in being largely self-sufficient in gas, and they have similar reserve to production ratios of about 8.8. They have similar shares of gas in total final energy (29 percent for the United Kingdom, 24 percent for the United States), though the share in the United Kingdom is rising rapidly with the collapse of its coal demand, while that in the United States is fairly stable. Both countries are gas intensive compared to OECD Europe with its gas share of 15 percent. Nevertheless, several other European countries (the Netherlands, Austria, and Italy) had higher gas shares in total final energy consumption than the United States, with Germany and Belgium close behind. Lessons drawn from these two countries will therefore need to be interpreted in the light of the differing degrees of market penetration and import dependence in other countries.

8.2 Experience of Liberalization in the United States

The United States gas market is quantitatively and qualitatively different from that anywhere else in its maturity and market structure. Whereas continental Europe was dominated by a small number of mainly state-owned enterprises, the United States had over 8,000 producers, with the 40 largest accounting for 57 percent of 1990 gas production. They were connected to more than 1,600 LDCs through 44 major interstate pipeline systems and hundreds of smaller pipeline companies (IEA 1994).

The problems that ultimately led to gas deregulation started with the passing of the Natural Gas Act of 1938. This followed a report by the Federal Trade Commission demonstrating that unregulated interstate pipelines used their monopoly position to extract rents from both producers and distributors. Congress had dealt with a similar problem with oil pipelines in 1906 by regulating the transport function, but the gas pipeline owners wished to protect their monopoly privileges by treating the whole industry as a public utility, rather than restricting regulation to the natural monopoly component of pipeline transport. The 1954 Supreme Court opinion on the Phillips petroleum case gave the Federal Power Commission the right to regulate the well-head sales price of gas, despite evidence of substantial potential competition between producers, and, worse, based this price on the historic cost of finding and producing gas, ignoring the concept of economic rent. Regulating well-head prices led to an acute gas shortage in the 1970s in the wake of the oil shocks and the oil embargo. It is estimated that consumers lost between $2.5 and $5 billion per year through higher energy costs and lost production as a result of regulatory-induced gas shortages (Pierce 1988; Ellig 1991).

The chaos caused by charging different prices for different vintages of gas and the fivefold increase in the price of "new" gas compared to the old area rates precipitated the Natural Gas Policy Act of 1978 which proposed a gradual deregulation of producer prices. The gas shortage was addressed by raising gas prices to industrial customers and prohibiting gas use in electricity generation and many other industrial uses, both of which dramatically reduced demand. Gas curtailments in a severe winter of 1976–77 reduced consumer confidence in the reliability of supply and further reduced demand, while the system of averaging transport costs meant that transport charges rose as demand fell, amplifying the impact of the initial gas price rises.

All these regulatory interventions in the gas market made it extremely difficult for consumers and pipeline operators to predict the market equilibrium price, and in the late 1970s, faced with continuing rises in the price of oil which were projected to continue into the indefinite future, merchant pipeline companies signed long-term take-or-pay contracts. These were struck at a high level without the precaution of linking prices to those of oil, and as oil prices fell, the contracts were rapidly revealed to be above equilibrium gas market prices. Between 1972 and 1986 gas demand dropped by 20 percent, creating excess capacity in pipeline networks, ideal conditions for the introduction of competition (IEA 1994), but creating conflicts between the pipelines and their customers. The LDCs argued that the take-or-pay contracts had been imprudently negotiated, which prompted the passing of FERC Order 380 of 1984. This prevented the merchant pipeline companies from imposing "minimum bills" on their customers, released LDCs from their take-or-pay obligations, and immediately stranded the pipeline contracts. The U.S. gas industry illustrates very clearly the problems of sustaining a regulatory compact in a period of high prices and falling demand, but the resulting reaction of the pipeline companies demonstrates the power of the courts in upholding the rights of regulated utilities in the United States.

In 1985 FERC passed Order 436 which provided for nondiscriminatory open access to transport at regulated rates. Transport rates had to lie between variable costs and the fully allocated cost of transport. Order 436 did not deal with the problem of stranded take-or-pay contracts, and a 1987 court ruling vacated the Order, prompting FERC to issue Order 500 which provided for mechanisms to recover the stranded contracts. A series of court decisions and revised orders eventually led in 1992 to Order 636 which finally completed the restructuring of pipelines' transport services. It required pipeline companies to provided unbundled transportation, unbundled storage and equal treatment of third-party users and pipeline affiliate users, and to provide open access with firm transportation service on demand. This allowed competitors to compete in final markets, and in turn created a liquid spot market with prices at different locations moving together, suggesting that competitive market forces were operating over wide areas. The subsequent fall in gas prices was fed back to producers, who were the main losers in the process of deregulation, since the pipeline companies had been at least partially protected from the full consequences of their initial imprudent take-or-pay contracts. Gas on gas competition lowered the price of gas, shortened the time horizon of contracting, and, on some views, reduced the reliability of delivery and the predictability of future contract terms (Spring 1995).

Pierce (1994) points to another important power that FERC has exercised in creating a competitive market. In contrast to the electricity industry, where the states have sole jurisdiction over building and extending electricity transmission grids, FERC has plenary and preemptive power to authorize construction or expansion of gas pipelines and has used this power to ease bottlenecks that protect the market power of producers in certain areas. Here the difference between gas and electricity is important, since a failure to build electricity transmission can be countered by siting a power station near the demand center, but gas can only be produced from gas wells that may be inconveniently located. The ability to ensure that producers within an area do not restrict additional supplies by preventing the construction of further pipelines is therefore important for creating a competitive gas market.

8.3   Restructuring British Gas

Gas utilities emerged in the nineteenth century as one of the first public utilities, though the gas was originally locally manufactured from coal and distributed to the customers in the town through a local distribution company (hence the name coal gas or town gas). In the 1930s there were about 11 million customers in Britain supplied by private companies and municipal undertakings. These were all nationalized in 1949 and amalgamated into twelve area boards as separate statutory bodies. In 1965 large volumes of natural gas were discovered in the North Sea, and it was decided to build a national high-pressure gas transmission system linking all consumers to the new supplies. The different properties of natural gas meant that gas appliances had to be replaced or converted to burn natural gas instead of coal gas, a process carried out between 1967 and 1977. Whereas town gas had been a local or regional business, the new national transmission system created a single industry. The new structure was recognized in the Gas Act of 1972 which created the British Gas Corporation (BGC). BGC took over the twelve area boards while retaining the same regions in its organizational structure.

The first tentative steps toward liberalization took place with the Oil and Gas Enterprise Act of 1982, which removed BGC's statutory monopoly on the pipeline system, but left the terms on which access would be granted unspecified. No entry occurred, and BGC was free to foreclose any downstream competition by specifying uneconomic access charges. This unsatisfactory state of affairs, and the success of privatizing BT in 1984, led the government in May 1985 to announce its intention to privatize BGC. The Gas Act of 1986 transferred the business of BGC to British Gas (BG) and established the regulatory framework, the key part of which was the Office of Gas Regulation (Ofgas). The secretary of state appoints the director general of gas supply (DGGS) for periods not exceeding five years at a time. The duties of the secretary of state and the director general (conveniently summarized in MMC 1993c) are to ensure the following:

1. That authorized gas suppliers satisfy, "so far as it economical to do so, all reasonable demands for gas in Great Britain."

2. That such suppliers are "able to finance the provision of gas supply services."

3. That, in relation to the conveyance and storage of gas, gas suppliers "secure effective competition."

Gas suppliers were also obligated to protect consumer interests "in respect of the prices charged and the other terms of supply, the continuity of supply, and the quality of gas supply services provided"; to "promote efficiency and economy" on the part of authorized gas suppliers; to protect the public from danger; and to enable effective competition and the supply of gas to premises taking more than 25,000 therms a year (i.e., about one-third of the market by volume).[5]

BG was given an authorization as a public gas supplier in July 1986 with a franchise that covered any premise within Great Britain with a duration of at least twenty-five years. The franchise could be revoked at thirty days' notice with the agreement of BG if it failed to meet the conditions of the authorization, or if it failed to comply with an order relating to the gas supply business under the Fair Trading Act of 1973 or the Competition Act of 1980, or if it ceased business or went bankrupt. As with BT, BG was privatized intact, with a franchise monopoly that covered two-thirds of total gas and the vast majority of the 19 million customers. BG owned transmission, distribution, supply, and bought gas on long-term contracts from North Sea producers and Norway, in addition to owning some of its own gas fields.

The regulatory regime had a number of flaws that soon became apparent. It was confined to the franchise market, and there was no requirement or ability to separately regulate the natural monopoly elements of transport and distribution. Not only were the competitive and natural monopoly elements not clearly distinguished, but there was no requirement to produce separate accounts for the regulated franchise market and the unregulated contract market. Worse still, the cost of gas for the regulated market was taken as the average cost of all gas bought by BG, so, as Yarrow (1991) has pointed out, any new purchases from the more costly fields of the northern North Sea for sale in the contract market would be cross-subsidized by the existing contracts. Since BG had inherited cheap early contracts from the southern North Sea basin, it had a competitive advantage against new entrants, while imposing extra costs on its captive franchise customers.

Not surprisingly, BG was able to exercise considerable market power, particularly in the unregulated contract market, and in 1987 the director general of fair trading (DGFT) referred the supply of nontariff gas to the MMC (MMC 1988). The MMC found extensive discrimination in the pricing and supply of gas to contract customers. Prices were inversely related to the ease with which customers could use alternative fuels. BG could selectively undercut potentially competitive gas suppliers, which deterred entry and inhibited competition. The MMC also found that BG was acting against the public interest through a lack of transparency in prices, a refusal to supply interruptible gas to some customers, the use of contract terms which restricted the use of gas or other forms of energy by the contract customers, by its failure to provide adequate information on the costs of common carriage, by its ability to use information obtained during negotiations to identity potential customers of competing suppliers, and by using its dominant position as the de facto sole purchaser of gas in Britain (MMC 1993c, §1.49).

The MMC recommended that BG should publish price schedules for firm and interruptible gas, that it should not discriminate in pricing or supply, that it should not refuse to supply interruptible gas on the basis of the use made of the gas or the alternative fuel available, and that it should publish information on common carriage terms. In addition BG should not contract initially for more than 90 percent of any new gas field in order to release gas for potential entrants. The MMC also concluded that if competition failed to develop over the following five years then the question of restructuring the gas industry to ensure competition should be considered.

The Minister accepted the recommendations, which were embodied in modifications to BG's authorization and undertakings with the Office of Fair Trading (OFT). The Minister asked the OFT to conduct a review after two years, which was completed in October 1991. The OFT Review concluded that the remedies introduced had been ineffective in encouraging self-sustaining competition because of the lack of available gas for competing suppliers and BG's monopoly supply to tariff customers together with its control of transmission, distribution, and storage. BG was exercising its power to cross-subsidize and set the prices in the interruptible market that its competitors could not match.

The behavior of privatized monopolies like BT and BG prompted the government to pass the Competition and Service (Utilities) Act of 1992 which strengthened the powers of the regulators over quality of customer service. The Act also allowed the Minister to vary the threshold level for the gas franchise, and in 1992 the Minister issued an order to reduce the limit of the franchise to 2,500 therms (covering 86 percent of the previous franchise volume but still 98.5 percent of the number of customers). On the same day BG started discussions with the OFT about undertakings needed to avoid a further MMC reference. BG undertook to ensure that other suppliers would be able to supply at least 60 percent of gas to contract customers by 1995, and to use its best endeavours to create self-sustaining competition in the contract market. The 1992 Act gave Ofgas new powers to regulate transportation and storage, and BG undertook to set up a separate gas transportation and storage unit within BG from 1994 (BG T&S, later to be called Transco). It agreed to publish transport tariffs on 1 September 1992 which would apply equally to all shippers, including BG Trading. These undertakings would not have statutory force, but if breached would lead to a reference to the MMC.

BG published consultation documents on the pricing methodology of transmission and storage in 1992. From BG's point of view, its best strategy would be to place as large a part of its total costs as possible within the regulated bottleneck facility of transport, leaving it with lower costs in the competitive parts of the business, both of which it still owned. This was bound to lead to a clash with the regulator, and the resulting conflict required two references to the MMC to resolve.

Initially the issue was one of defending the right to the maximum revenues from the regulated core, though later the dispute evolved into where the boundary should be drawn between the regulated monopoly parts and the potentially competitive parts, and how costs should be allocated between them.

BG opened its case for high transport tariffs by claiming that these should be sufficient to earn a higher return than the 4.5 percent used in the consultation document, but Ofgas argued that transportation and storage were low-risk businesses that did not justify a higher rate of return. BG had no incentive to develop accounting systems that accurately apportioned costs to different parts of the business, and doubtless benefited, not from asymmetric information, but from symmetric ignorance.[6] Ofgas was consequently frustrated by the difficulty of obtaining prompt responses to questions and access to data (much of which may not have been readily available, if at all). As it became increasingly unlikely that they would reach agreement by the October 1, 1992, deadline, Ofgas decided that the only solution was a reference to the MMC.

Ofgas was also concerned at the failure of BG's proposals to encourage competition while BG remained vertically integrated, with the potential to cross-subsidize competitive activities from the regulated business. BG was unwilling to divest its transport and storage business, although that in Ofgas's view was the only viable long-term solution. Progress on this was difficult, since under the 1986 Gas Act the MMC could only recommend remedies involving a modification of BG's authorization, which did not allow for breaking up BG. For that the Minister would have to refer BG to the MMC under the Fair Trading Act. The upshot was that Ofgas made a reference to the MMC asking it to investigate "whether the operation of its pipeline system and other facilities for transportation and storage operated, or may be expected to operate, against the public interest." At the same time the secretary of state referred BG under the Fair Trading Act, and in August 1993 the MMC published two (largely identical) reports, dealing with the two references.

The MMC found that competition in the contract market had improved but had not been extended to interruptible gas. Competition was weak for large-volume customers and was based on BG's temporary and voluntary restriction of its share of the contract market. Because BG both owned the transportation system which was used both to supply BG's own customers and those of its competitors on terms and conditions that BG chose to specify, there was an inherent conflict of interest which made it impossible to provide the necessary conditions for self-sustaining competition (MMC 1993a, p. 2).

The reports also argued that the franchise should be reduced to 1,500 therms in 1997 and eventually removed (probably by 2000 or 2002), but that the timing of complete removal should be delayed until the neutrality of the transportation and storage system was ensured as this was seen as the critical condition for effective competition. The report under the Gas Act recommended that BG's authorization be modified to create BG Trading and BG T&S as separate units, while also giving the DGGS "full concurrent jurisdiction with the DGFT, including the power to make references to the MMC under the Fair Trading Act relating to the supply of gas to the non-tariff market." (MMC 1993a, §1.17)

The report under the Fair Trading Act recommended that BG's trading activities be divested before April 1997. The Department of Trade and Industry rejected this recommendation in favor of full accounting separation, mainly because of the government's desire to introduce competition into the domestic market as soon as possible, which complex restructuring would impede (Stern 1994; Spring 1995).

One of the central issues that the MMC had to address was the setting of transportation charges, which required taking a view on the value of the regulatory asset base (RAB) and the rate of return that could be earned on this base. The problem, not peculiar to BG, was that the assets had been sold for less than their current cost accounting (CCA) book value.[7] The ratio of the stock market's valuation of BG to BG's CCA net asset value, known as the market to assets ratio (MAR), was some 41 percent at the date of privatization, some 62 percent at the end of 1991, and 68 percent at the end of 1992. Ofgas and BG had agreed on the need to make some allowance for the MAR, for otherwise "shareholders would enjoy significant and excessive gains at the expense of BG's customers" (MMC 1993a, §2.149).

BG argued strongly for using the full CCA net book value, and argued that it needed a real rate of return (ROR) of 10.8 percent on its new investment. It was prepared to accept a lower rate of return on its existing assets, equal to the MAR applied to the ROR, or 6.7 percent. The MMC argued that the appropriate real ROR was between 6.5 and 7.5 percent, but unfortunately accepted the principle of applying the MAR to this to give a rate of return of between 4 and 4.5 percent on old assets. Their argument for discounting the ROR by the MAR was that "allowing a full ROR (equal to the market cost of capital) would lead to a substantial windfall gain to BG's shareholders, at the expense of its customers." They went on to claim that "It would be possible to apply this reasoning to the depreciation charge as well as to the profit measure, . . . However, making arcane adjustments of this type may make the calculations unduly complicated and give a spurious aura of precision to what are essentially subjective estimates" (MMC 1993c, §§7.78–80).

The effect was to set a price-cap that would allow BG to earn $mrV + D + C$, where V is the CCA asset value, r is the ROR, m is the MAR, D is the full depreciation of the CCA asset value, and C are the operating costs. To simplify matters, there is assumed in this expression to be no new investment (yet). While it makes no difference whether the first term is interpreted as applying mr to the full asset value V, or the full r to the written-down asset value mV, it does make a difference for depreciation. If full depreciation is given, then shareholders will eventually be repaid V, which is more than their payment of mV to acquire the assets. Newbery (1997) has argued that the correct procedure was to write down the original CCA net book value by the MAR, and allow the full ROR on inherited assets and new investment. This way the RAB would be incremented by investment, and the MAR applied to any depreciation of old assets when writing down the RAB. Then BG would have a price-cap set to produce revenue $mrV + mD + C = m(rV + D) + C$. This is equivalent to writing down the old assets *and* their associated depreciation stream so that over the remaining life of those assets the revised depreciation recovers no more than the opening RAB; otherwise, shareholders will have a greater value returned to them than they paid for.

It took another MMC reference to straighten this out (as part of a larger inquiry into Transco's price-cap), but the principle now appears to have been accepted by all the regulators. The problem of setting price-caps for assets sold at a discount is most acute for the water companies, where the MAR was less than 10 percent. This implies that the long-run marginal cost (LRMC) of expanding the water system is considerably higher that the average cost of existing supplies. Pricing at LRMC would transfer huge rents to the water companies, while pricing at average cost overstimulates demand for expansion. One solution, under discussion, is to charge existing water consumers the average cost for a specified volume, and to charge LRMC for amounts above this level. However, there are obvious difficulties with new domestic customers, and in setting the fixed and variable parts of the tariff appropriately. Fortunately, none of this matters in the case of Transco, where the LRMC is less than the average cost based on full CCA asset value but rather close to the average cost based on the discounted value.

8.3.1   Restructuring and Competition

The MMC reports prompted the minister to announce new legislation to introduce competition in the franchise market, starting in the southwest in 1996 and extended to the whole country by 1998. By this time all customers were able to choose their suppliers. In order to ensure that suppliers would have satisfactory access both to gas and to the transmission network, the Gas Act of 1995 replaced the original system of authorizing public gas suppliers with three new types of license. The first type of license is a public gas transporter's (PGT) license, required for transporting gas. The regulator can only grant a license or license extension to another transporter within 23 meters of a PGT's main with the existing PGT's consent, or if there are no connected premises in the area. By 1998 six other PGT licenses had been issued and these transporters can also be required to connect customers to their pipeline. The new license holders typically extend the low-pressure system into new housing estates, though as 89 percent of households were within 23 meters of BG's gas mains in 1993 (of which 92 percent used gas) the scope for new pipelines is modest. The larger number of licenses are for gas suppliers, who are required to have a gas supplier's license, and for shippers who contract with a PGT for gas to be transported through its pipeline and are required to have a gas shipper's license.

The process of unbundling different services is written into the Gas Act of 1995, which does not permit a PGT to hold a gas supplier's or shipper's license. In 1996, when the Act came into force, the assets and liabilities of BG's supply business were transferred to British Gas Trading, which was granted a shipper's and supplier's license, while BG was granted a PGT license. The duties and obligations of Transco as the major PGT were set out in the Network Code launched (without the full rigours of financial penalties for the first six months) on March 1, 1996. In the new unbundled structure Transco has to arrange for daily balancing of inputs and off takes by each gas supplier and provides a "flexibility mechanism" to maintain overall system balance when individual shippers are out of balance. Transco accepts bids to supply for the balancing process and establishes a price at which imbalances are charged. As with the electricity pool, there have been allegations of gaming, but in contrast to the pool, the regulator has the power to impose changes in the code after consultation with the industry. A large number of modifications have already been agreed and/or imposed.

BG had a large portfolio of long-term take-or-pay contracts when it was privatized, and the prospectus on which it was sold claimed that BG had a twenty-five-year authorization as sole supplier to about two-thirds of the market by volume, until 2009. The development of CCGTs created a potentially strong demand growth for gas, but BG was initially reluctant to supply cheap gas for electricity generation, which was seen as a strong competitor in the consumer market. The regulator insisted that BG offered interruptible contracts to the new IPPs on the same terms that it offered them to large industrial customers (on terms that were more favorable than appeared, since they were in practice not interrupted as much as might be expected). The regulator also insisted that interruptible contracts should be interrupted for a minimum of seven days a year, again to ensure nondiscrimination. BG then offered a series of long-term interruptible (LTI) tariffs at a time when the North Sea appeared to have matured, with all the major fields already discovered and the prospect of scarcer and more expensive future gas.

The IPPs therefore eagerly signed up to LTI2 contracts for fifteen years at 16 to 17 p/therm. LTI2 was then withdrawn in 1994 after 4,185 MW of CCGT had signed contracts and replaced by LTI3 at 19 to 20 p/therm. The forced opening of the contract market and the continued growth in power station demand for gas opened up an attractive new market for gas producers, who no longer faced a monopsony buyer in BG, and they responded with a considerable expansion in supply. BG had been aggressively signing contracts for new gas, both because it expected gas prices to rise and to forestall entry. Nevertheless, after its negotiations with the DTI, it agreed to reduce its contract market share to 40 percent. The difference between the contracted supplies and reduced contract demand forced BG to sell surplus gas into the spot market just as substantial new supplies were coming on stream. In addition technical progress in developing ever more efficient

CCGT plant lead to the rapid introduction of relatively unproved designs, some of which experienced commissioning difficulties and delays. Their operators were also forced to dump their contracted gas in the spot market, causing the spot price to drop from over 18 p/therm to less than 10 p/therm during 1995, with contract prices (presumably the best estimate of the medium-term future price) hovering around 15 p/therm, compared with over 20 p/therm in 1993. From 1995 to 1998 spot prices did not rise much above 12 p/therm, except for short periods.[8]

The development of increasingly liquid spot and futures markets created a serious alternative to long-term contracts for producers and suppliers, and dramatically changed the structure of the industry, just as it had done earlier in the United States. Contract lengths shortened, producers were encouraged to release supplies, and prices dropped, stranding many of the contracts that BG had signed in the expectation of continuing to sell on a short-term basis at prices related to long-term contracts. Of course, the LTI contracts that BG had signed with the IPPs survived, much to the distress of the RECs who owned the IPPs and had signed long-term power purchase agreements with the IPPs. They had to make provisions for losses on these IPP contracts once the electricity franchise market ended in 1998, when they were no longer able to pass through their overpriced electricity contracts.

Although the Minister had not required BG to divest transport and storage, the functional unbundling, close regulatory scrutiny, and the need for different parts of the business to focus on very different activities, induced British Gas to separate its trading activities (now named Centrica plc) from the rest of the company, BG, plc. The shareholders accepted the demerger in February 1997. Centrica owns British Gas Trading, British Gas Services, Energy Centres (i.e., shops), the North and South Morecombe gas fields (which have high swing, and accounted for 10 percent of total U.K. production in 1997 and about the same share of reserves), and 51 percent of Acord Gas. Centrica inherited the stranded contracts, and had few other assets, hence the need to add the large gas producing fields of Morecombe to ensure a positive market value for the company. Placing both the upstream gas production business and the downstream supply business in the same company also reduces risks and some of the need for contracting. Indeed, when wholesale gas prices rise, upstream profits rise and downstream profits are squeezed, and vice versa. The other company retained the name, BG plc, and owned the remaining businesses:

Transco (which owns the transmission system and storage), Exploration and Production (which lost the Morecombe fields), and various other service companies.

The first phase of competition started in April 1996 in the southwest of England with ten competing licensed gas suppliers (including BG). Customers who switched away from BG to one of the new suppliers initially were offered discounts of up to 25 percent, or about £60 to £80 (U.S.$100) per year. Initially about 7 percent of customers switched, building to rather less than 20 percent in the first year, with a plateau at about 25 percent, suggesting that Centrica retained substantial market power and would be able to recover more of its stranded assets than might be expected. Later zones when opened to competition experienced a faster rate of growth of competitors penetration, again stabilizing at about 25 percent. By the end of 1998, when the whole market was open to competition, 20 percent of customers in the whole market had switched, and this was expected to rise somewhat further. However, the discounts are concentrated on those customers who pay quarterly or by direct debit from their bank accounts (and have narrowed somewhat as Centrica increasingly needs to respond to competition in the whole market), while those with prepay meters have been offered essentially no discounts by new competitors, and only about £10/year from Centrica. This may reflect the higher costs of servicing them and be a further example of liberalization driving prices into line with costs. However, it has raised concerns over social equity and fuel poverty. Prepay meters are used where customers have been unable or reluctant to pay their bills on time, and the meters allow the customer effectively to self-disconnect. The poor thus now pay even higher prices per unit of gas than the rich, and they have hardly benefited from the fall in the wholesale price of gas.

The lower prices available to the other customers were entirely the result of lower spot and contract prices for the new entrants, rather than any efficiency improvements. But they undoubtably put pressure on Centrica to reduce its costs, compared to the earlier situation in which average gas purchase costs can be passed right through to the franchise market. In the future, domestic prices can be expected to track short-term (annual) contract prices, since customers can switch supplier at almost any time with little notice. This is fine while prices fall as the market adjusts to its new competitive equilibrium. This is more favorable for bringing on stream new supplies, and possibly also increasing depletion rates of existing fields, but it may become problematic if spot prices were to rise sharply (which they might after the Interconnector links the U.K. market to the continental market).[9]

Liberalization raises the question of how risks are to be shared in the future between gas producers, gas utilities, and gas consumers. The obvious solution is that gas producers will shoulder more of the risk, in the same way that oil producers (who are often the same company) bear the risk of oil price fluctuations. In the past the lack of a competitive market for gas has meant that gas development faced the same problems of opportunism as other capital-intensive sunk investments tied to a single market, which they managed by signing long-term contracts. If there is a genuinely competitive gas market with a sufficiently large number of buyers and sellers, and if final gas prices are not regulated (though their transport may be), then these problems of opportunism are reduced, and only commercial risks remain. Oil companies are familiar with these potential problems, and manage them with rather shorter-lived contracts, futures, and by shifting the remaining risks onto their shareholders who can hold diversified portfolios.

In the oil market the effects of the fall in the price of oil in the mid-1980s has been to put tremendous downward pressure on the costs of developing new fields, and this has forced technological innovation at a rapid pace. If the same happens in the gas market, then gas might begin to make the same inroads into the European energy market that it made two decades earlier in the United States. Given the environmental advantages of gas compared to other fuels, this would have additional attractions.

8.3.2   Regulating Transmission and Further Unbundling

The 1993 MMC reports achieved their major objective of unbundling BG, but left the question of the return on the regulatory asset base of Transco in an unsatisfactory state. As the next periodic review for setting prices for transmission and storage from April 1997 approached, Transco argued strongly for maintaining the full CCA asset value and full CCA depreciation. The regulator rejected this argument, and proposed a 20 percent reduction in transportation charges in 1997–98 and thereafter a price cap of RPI − 2.5 percent. BG (as it still was) rejected these proposals, and Ofgas referred them to the MMC, who had to decide whether continuing with the old price formula would be against the public interest. The MMC revisited its earlier views on determining the regulatory asset base and rate of return (ROR), and decided that a 7 percent ROR was reasonable, but that pre-1992 assets should have their depreciation adjusted by the market to asset ratio, and that regulatory asset values should be rolled forward by reference to the RPI rather than CCA replacement cost. The final result was that Transco's charges would be cut by 21 percent, but prices would be capped at RPI – 2 percent (equivalent to Ofgas's proposal of RPI – 2.5 percent when revised volume forecasts were taken into account) and that there should be separate charging conditions for transportation and storage.

The MMC also considered that if competition developed in the storage market then price regulation might end, possibly as quickly as within three years. The main problem in introducing competition in storage is the dominant position of the Rough field, which is a depleted gas field near the Yorkshire coast capable of meeting over 10 percent of current peak day demands with a delivery rate that can be sustained for more than two months. The only other storage facilities are an underground salt cavity at Hornsea with a capacity about one-sixth that of Rough but a deliverability 43 percent as large, and five LNG sites that have high rates of deliverability for up to five days and are located near to demand to relieve transmission capacity constraints during peak demand periods. Shippers pay separately for deliverability and space (i.e., the total volume of gas), and they can reinject gas to top up their space after they have drawn it down within the season.

With only two significant storage facilities available for seasonal storage, both owned by Transco, and the overwhelming proportion of the demand for storage services still required by Centrica for meeting its obligations to the over 75 percent of the domestic market with its large seasonal variation, the prospects for competition did not look especially attractive. It amounted almost to bilateral monopoly. The shippers were very anxious to force Transco to put all storage on the market and let it determine its own price, and to auction any unused deliverability on the day to those with adequate volumes in store. Doubtless they were relying on Centrica to exercise monopsony power to drive down the price of storage, while Centrica's ownership of considerable swing in the Morecombe fields gave the company a substitute for storage, which might further distort storage and peak gas prices.

The solution, reached in September 1988, was that BG storage's rights in Rough and Hornsea would be auctioned, with capacity rights available for up to five years ahead but with no bidder or associated group of bidders able to buy more than 20 percent of capacity in the auctions. As a result the storage prices from Rough and Hornsea are no longer to be regulated by Ofgas, though the five LNG storage facilities, which are better considered as part of the transmission services business, continue to have regulated prices. This agreement avoided the need to refer the storage issue to the MMC, and marks almost the end of a long process of narrowing down the definition of the core natural monopoly to the pipeline system.

Even this apparent natural monopoly is questioned. If rights in the capacity of a single large storage facility can be auctioned and then traded, why should not capacity rights in the national transmission system (NTS) be similarly auctioned and then traded? These capacity rights would define market-based prices for transport to replace the present rather complex system of calculations of the long-run marginal cost of providing additional transport capacity, which are then scaled to generate a revenue that meets the price-cap formula set by the regulator.

There are two problems with this approach, one possibly surmountable, but one that is both subtle and sometimes difficult to resolve. The obvious problem is that a market in a bottleneck facility like a link in the transport network might profitably be monopolised and all of the rents upstream and downstream captured by the owner. The solution would be to deny any single company or consortium rights to more than 20 percent of the capacity on any link or bottleneck (with exceptions for those parts of the system that are dedicated to delivering gas from a beach head with few suppliers into the main system, where the shares could be capped at the entry shares). The more subtle problem is that it may be hard to define the capacity of a part of a network, as this can vary with the pattern and level of flows elsewhere. If it is hard to define capacity, then it is not clear what trading in capacity rights means.

Some pipeline configurations lend themselves to both defining capacity and trading that capacity. This is the case for simple links between two points where there are no alternative connections (or their access is restricted). The Interconnector from Bacton in England to Zeebrugge in Belgium is an excellent example, and trading arrangements are already developing. Canada has an active secondary market in pipeline capacity that is unregulated. In 1998 the demand price for transport exceeded the cost of construction, since there was too little capacity and the price provided useful investment signals (as well as the means of financing construction of additional capacity). Given the economies of scale in pipeline expansion, there is no guarantee that the market will provide the efficient level of additional capacity, but it may be better than administrative alternatives. There is an interesting contrast with the United States where the market in released pipeline capacity remains under the jurisdiction of FERC. The Natural Gas Act requires that such capacity be subject to a price-cap. There are discussions underway to relax these regulatory impediments to creating an active market in capacity, but fears over the possible exercise of market power will doubtless slow this process down.

The contrast between simple pipeline links and the U.K. NTS is that there are two and often more routes to almost every node, while the multiple branching points means that there may be a large number of possible routes between entry and exit points. If capacity is tight on one route, it is possible to route gas by another route, unless that is already at capacity because of other flows. It is therefore difficult to define the capacity of a route without knowing all the other demands made on the system.

The British approach to date has been to operate as though there is a single pool of gas inside the country, into which gas can be delivered at the entry points, and from which it can be withdrawn at exit points. Although the capacity at these entry and exit points has an obvious upper limit, it may not be possible to fully use that capacity if there are transmission constraints on the links connecting them. The same problem of dealing with transmission constraints confronts those designing bulk electricity markets, where the tension is between a single wide area pool and nodal pricing. As with gas, the ideal is to have a deep liquid market with as many competitors as possible to reduce market power, but the reality is that gas in different locations, like electricity, may not be easily substitutable at short notice.

The initial approach in creating a spot market was to define a national balancing point (NBP) and to set transport tariffs t_{ij} between entry point i and exit point j as the sum of an entry price, b_i, and an exit price, p_j (so $t_{ij} = b_i + p_j$). These tariffs are per peak volume demanded rather than capacity actually used, and they support the fiction that gas that has paid the entry price is all the same gas (and notionally available at the NBP). The values of entry and exit prices are derived from the long-run marginal costs of expanding the system to deliver an increment of gas from i to j by simple regression analysis, with an inevitable blurring of the detailed information contained in the LRMCs.[10] In order to encourage liquidity, there are no constraints on the amounts of capacity for entry and exit that can be booked, though in the event of excess demand or supply, actual capacity is allocated proportionately to capacity purchased. Such capacity rights can be and are traded, but they are not firm. Firm rights would require limiting the volumes that could be sold, with variable amounts of excess capacity left available in most (but not all) states of the network flows, which might result in a less efficient utilization of the system. Various schemes involving several balancing points with the need to buy capacity to and between them have been proposed. These schemes increase the amount of firm capacity that can be defined but reduce liquidity by spreading trade over more spot markets, and they create more bottlenecks where market power may be an issue.

The industry seems confident that better market solutions will emerge for two reasons. Gas is a more forgiving commodity than electricity, since it can be stored over short periods quite easily, relaxing the tolerances on supply-demand balancing over short periods of time or within small areas. Second, the governance structure for changing the network code is more responsive and gives greater powers to Ofgas to resolve disputes and settle rule changes than the Pooling and Settlement Agreement for electricity, which has impeded market solutions. The true test of the market will doubtless come in a severe winter, or if there is a major supply disruption (in the North Sea, or on the continent now that we are interconnected), when market prices might move dramatically and may lead to bankruptcies, failure to honor contracts, and possibly more confusion just when the system needs to respond in a coordinated way. Transco retains considerable powers to intervene and ensure system integrity; it can require the system as whole to provide adequate reserve storage, at present by central control, which is somewhat at odds with decentralized market solutions.

Finding the most market-friendly way of providing insurance against the various possible disruptions while preserving the efficiency of the whole system remains a challenging task. There are further challenges in ensuring efficient long-term development of the NTS under a regime in which shippers book capacity only one year at a time while pipelines last for thirty years or more (though new pipeline investment to meet large loads, such as those required by power stations, are subject to long-term agreements to pay for that capacity).

8.4   Gas Liberalization on the Continent

The same debate on liberalization that started in the United States and has been pursued almost to its logical conclusion in Britain is now being cautiously raised on the continent, partly in response to pressure from the European Commission and the Gas Directive. It is not yet widely accepted that there are considerable gains from liberalizing access. This reduces the need for complex contractual negotiations, thereby increasing supplies and moving prices closer to opportunity costs and away from averaged contractual costs. As we have seen, the view of competition and regulatory authorities is that liberalization requires separating pipeline ownership from trading. The argument for separation is to avoid foreclosure: There is no alternative open to competing traders in Britain to Transco's transmission system, and the same is true in most other European countries. If Transco remained part of BG, and had some discretion over the structure of charges for use, and if it were encouraged to maximize the profits of BG as a whole, then raising its rivals' costs in the downstream market would increase BG profits (Armstrong, Cowan, and Vickers 1994, ch. 5).

The main argument against vertical unbundling, third-party access, and competition is that they shorten the time horizon over which agents are willing to contract. Investments in offshore gas fields and long-distance pipelines to access new supplies on the continent are expensive, long-lived, and in the past have been protected either by credible long-term contracts or by protected downstream franchises. If these investments become significantly riskier with the loss of credible future earnings guarantees, then supply costs may rise. Whether this will be at the expense of producer rent or consumer surplus depends on the intensity of interfuel (and gas-to-gas) competition, which in turn depends on the degree of spare capacity and flexibility in the supply systems and the number of competing producers.

Continental gas companies have opposed liberalization, arguing that capacity is scarce, producers are few in number, and that security of supply, both at the country level and for the individual consumer, is critical. There is a qualitative difference in the capital costs and risks of bringing new supplies on stream on the continent compared to the United Kingdom. There, gas will have to come from Russia (over pipelines of 6,000 km), Algeria (LNG, and/or undersea pipelines), Nigeria (LNG), the Gulf states (LNG, or new very long distance pipelines), Turkmenistan/Iran or the northern North Sea. The capital costs of these pipelines or LNG trains are huge per unit of energy capacity. Most of the pipelines transit several countries of doubtful political stability, while the more secure North Sea is high cost and distant from many of the major consumers. Improving supply security requires more storage, more interconnection in the pipeline system, and more up-front investment, all of which require strong assurances of the ability to recoup these initial costs from later charges. For this the greatest assurance is a guaranteed monopoly position in a captive market. In Britain, in contrast, the "dash for gas" in electricity genera-tion created the potential swing consumer that would support a more competitive gas spot market, and with a mature pipeline system in place and already paid for, the benefits of competition clearly out-weighed the cost of increased risks to gas producers.

Thus one can see in action the dynamics of regulatory reform. During the initial heavy investment phase of creating the network, investor protection requires a guaranteed monopoly position, either regulated or state-enforced by ownership. In the mature phase of low investment, competition no longer threatens investment security (and may enhance it by replacing regulatory risk by commercial risk) while delivering effi-ciency gains. Britain, with its fortunate access to secure gas reserves at an early stage has moved through to this last stage, while the conti-nent, lacking adequate indigenous or close sources, continues to need large investments to secure its requirements.

The old continental argument is now beginning to look less con-vincing. The high profits to be made from selling gas has encouraged possibly excess pipeline development, so there is now a fairly mature network of pipelines with spare capacity. The collapse of Russia has released large supplies of gas to the West, and these are having to compete ever more aggressively with additional supplies from many other producers—Norway, North Africa, and now Britain through the Interconnector. Oil prices in 1998 had fallen to their lowest level in real terms since 1973, encouraging oil and gas companies to seek new markets for their gas reserves. Falling oil prices puts downward pres-sure on gas prices and encourages new traders to enter the market as demand increases. The Electricity Directive will enable new entrants in the electricity market, who will demand access to gas at competitive prices. The Gas Directive holds out the prospect, if not the promise, that this can be delivered.

Different countries on the continent are very differently placed for supporting or benefiting from gas liberalization. The country with the greatest apparent stake in liberalization would seem to be the Netherlands, which not only is a net exporter seeking markets elsewhere on the continent but has large volumes of onshore gas that can provide both swing and emergency supplies in the event of disruptions elsewhere. While guarantees for backup gas can be negotiated with companies in other countries, a liberalized continental gas market would seem to offer the Netherlands the chance of striking a larger number of more profitable spot transactions, while its position as a hub for many pipelines in northwest Europe makes it the natural place for a spot market to develop. The main obstacles to liberalization are the usual ones that the producers fear losing the attractive and substantial rents they enjoy, while the government, as a major beneficiary of these rents, initially considered their value higher than the benefits of improved competitiveness to the economy.

In 1995 the Dutch government changed its views on the benefit of energy liberalization with the publication of a White Paper in which it signaled its intention to disengage network functions from production and supply (except for gas where transmission and supply remain under Gasunie control) with the intention of promoting nondiscriminatory access to the network and competition within the country. Exports and imports would be freed so that producers could export rather than being required to sell to Gasunie for the domestic market, though the requirement to retain twenty-five years' reserve for internal demand would be retained. The details of regulation were not spelled out, nor was it clear whether it would remain within the Ministry of Economic Affairs or be independent. Only large consumers would initially be allowed access to networks and alternative suppliers, and they would have to negotiate the terms of access. Stern (1998) draws the rather cautious conclusion that Dutch liberalization could easily be reversed by a change of government, and has been made contingent upon reciprocal measures by other EU member countries, either of which could slow the rate of liberalization within the Netherlands. Nevertheless, as the major EU gas producer on the continent, the Netherlands clearly plays a critical role in increasing the supply and demand of gas on the continent and liberalizing markets.

If the Netherlands is cautiously in favor of liberalization, France remains implacably opposed, while Germany exhibits its normal tension between the energy cartels and the Competition Authority or Cartel Office. Attempts at liberalization have been resisted, and are subject to lengthy legal proceedings which have slowed progress. German gas companies, as with the electricity companies, operate regional monopolies with private law and demarkation agreements that date back to the 1930s and were the quid pro quo for building the infrastructure network. There is no monopoly high-pressure pipeline company covering the whole of Germany, and in practice, competition between different pipeline companies has increased. Gazprom, the Russian monopoly gas producer and transmission company, has been aggressively extending its operations downstream by forming joint ventures in consuming countries to finance pipelines. Wingas, one of these joint ventures, has been actively building pipelines to market Russian gas, but other pipelines to deliver Norwegian or British gas have already entered the market to compete with the highly profitable incumbent gas companies such as Ruhrgas.

The German government has been actively trying to overturn the demarkation and concession agreements that restrict competition in the electricity and gas industries since 1993. The Law against Restrictions on Competition of 1989 was amended to restrict demarkation agreements to no more than twenty years, and to end any existing agreements older than twenty years by 1995, but this provoked not only litigation but attempts by transmission companies to integrate into distribution companies as an alternative route to preserve market power (Stern 1998).

The levels of profit are so high in German gas transmission systems that competition has taken the form of duplicating pipelines to gain access to customers, rather than the more socially desirable alterantive of obtaining access to use existing pipelines and coordinating their expansion to produce an efficient and dense pipeline network. The end result of this facilities competition may be more market-driven transport tariffs, though the intent is clearly to thwart competition as long as possible by raising entry costs. Germany is well placed to receive both Russian and Norwegian gas, and it is also well connected to the south and hence to the Mediterranean sources of gas. High coal prices make electricity generation from gas extremely attractive, so Germany ought to gain considerable benefits from more extensive liberalization.

Nevertheless, progress has been slow and litigious, as in that other federal country, the United States, with the Cartel Office playing a similar role to FERC in pressing for more rapid progress than the states and certainly the companies wish to see.

8.5 Conclusions

Gas liberalization, like telecoms liberalization, started in the United States, has been aggressively pursued in the United Kingdom and is now gnawing away at the gas monopolies of the continent. While one should not underestimate the geopolitical concerns of import-dependent continental countries, the ending of the cold war and the weakening of the OPEC cartel has reduced their prominence. The single market and even more the single currency, which started for the main EU members on January 1, 1999, will put greater pressure on large gas consumers who export to secure advantageous prices for their gas. They will monitor gas prices in competitor countries closely, and lobby for the effective implementation of the EU Gas Directive.

The 1998 collapse in oil prices, the emerging European gas bubble, and spare capacity in the pipeline system will give new entrants access to cheap gas (compared to old contracted gas). Provided that they are not prevented from gaining access to the pipelines on reasonable terms (by stranded contracts, by protracted negotiations, or unreasonable charges), EU countries have the potential to introduce effective competition rapidly and to demonstrate the advantages of liberalization. The gas monopolies will then be under threat, and it may even become thinkable to adopt Anglo-Saxon regulatory and restructuring solutions in the ensuing Darwinian struggle.

Compared to the services provided by the other network utilities considered in this book, gas is most like a commodity and least like a service, particularly when the network matures and develops adequate capacity and flexibility. The high-pressure pipeline system is a relatively simple piece of infrastructure, more like a railway than a telephone or electricity grid. Gas itself is more like oil than electricity. The local distribution companies raise few regulatory issues that have not already been addressed and resolved. The decisive regulatory innovation is the creation of spot and futures markets for gas and gas storage to supplement (and partly substitute for) the less flexible system of long-term contracts. Provided there are a sufficient number of competing producers (which has been assisted by interconnecting and extending the European gas grid), competition can replace the system of regulated access that led to high prices and considerable inefficiency. Once that stage is reached, the remaining regulatory issues seem minor, and the sustainability of the new equilibrium looks relatively unprob-lematic. But just because liberalization may be both irreversible and obviously superior for consumers, it is likely to be most fiercely resisted by incumbent gas companies.

9   Conclusions

The year 1984 was in many ways a watershed. Far from the Orwellian vision of the all-controlling state, it provided key examples that questioned the legitimate role of the state in economic activity. British Telecom was privatized as the largest share offering to that date. The United States liberalized access to gas pipelines and dismantled AT&T, making long-distance calls competitive. Chile had started returning nationalized but previously private companies to private ownership almost as soon as Allende was overthrown in 1973, but the significance of the British Telecom privatization was that it was the first network utility to be privatized. Chile moved to the more significant stage of privatizing network utilities shortly after, and Britain gradually privatized all the remaining network utilities of gas, water, electricity and finally railways over the following twelve years.

The balance between state and market experienced a seismic shift with the fall of the Berlin wall in 1989. The economies of Central and Eastern Europe began the difficult transition from state-socialism to the market. By then, network utilities were considered legitimate (and valuable) assets for the state to sell. The boundary between state and market is not just a matter of public versus private ownership but a contrast between modes of control—between political control exercised directly though ownership or indirectly through regulation compared with decentralized market forces. The United States did not privatize gas or telecoms, for almost all utilities were already in the private sector. The significance of deregulation and liberalization was that they questioned the legitimacy of state control by regulation and attempted to reduce its scope.

Privatizing public utilities is primarily about ownership rather than control, since utilities can face remarkably similar regulation under public or private ownership. Liberalization, in contrast, subjects utilities to market forces; it can induce more dramatic changes in performance than privatization alone. Before 1984 it was accepted that the network utilities of gas, telecoms, and electricity should be organized as vertically integrated monopolies centered on, and justified by, the natural monopoly of the network. When British Telecom was privatized in that year, its sole licensed competitor, Mercury, was granted access to its network, with the prospect of further entry in 1991. The pressure to create competition was increasing, so that by the time Britain came to privatize electricity in 1990, generation was separated from transmission in order to confine regulation to the network and allow competition in generation and supply. Competition is difficult to achieve within the public sector, so there is a natural complementarity between liberalization and privatization.

The central argument of this book is that introducing competition into previously monopolized and regulated network utilities is the key to achieving the full benefits of privatization. Privatization seems to be necessary but is not sufficient. Regulation is inevitably inefficient, suggesting that it be confined to the core natural monopoly of the network. Provided that competition is effective, it can replace regulation for network services and thereby increase efficiency. But liberalization also redistributes rents and raises new regulatory problems in managing the interface between the regulated and competitive parts of the utility. In response, economists have developed new theories to analyze competition over and between networks, and have made the study of regulation one of the most exciting branches of microeconomics.

The intensity of competition is strongly influenced by technology and initial endowments; it may not be sustainable in every utility, nor in all circumstances. Economists can play a key role in clarifying the determinants of successful liberalization, and the risks of inappropriate restructuring. Opportunities for restructuring are rare and hard to reverse, so such choices need to be well informed. We need good analytical models of network competition, informed by historical studies of regulatory institutions, and backed by empirical studies of the consequences of liberalization. The last three chapters have demonstrated some of the distinctive features of market behavior in three different network utilities. They discussed some of the techniques that have been developed to analyze issues of market power. Bidding models and the concept of supply function equilibrium proved useful for electricity, while access pricing issues arise for all three utilities. International comparisons proved useful, particularly for electricity where the range of possible designs for the bulk wholesale market is now quite large. These and earlier chapters also surveyed the gradually accumulating empirical evidence.

Although the evidence suggests that market forces can bring efficiency gains, the first chapter observed that the early network utilities were born of the free market but everywhere were placed in the chains of regulation or public ownership. The reason, and the central problem to address, was set out in chapter 2. The networks of these utilities are classic natural monopolies that create rents that will be fought over. The networks are durable and fixed, so the rents will persist. The capital of the network of the utility is large and sunk; once created, the balance of bargaining advantage shifts from investor to consumer. Finally, the networks of gas, water, electricity, and telecoms are directly linked to the consumer, giving their owner potentially large exploitative power. Their consumers are numerous, politically important, and have no choice of network. Once the mass of the population is wealthy enough to enjoy the services of these utilities, and politically powerful enough to demand some say in their operation, regulation or public ownership is inevitable.

The problem facing investors and consumers is to devise an institution that will balance these interests and powers. The tension between the investor and consumer can be side-stepped by state ownership, which has the coercive power to finance the sunk capital without requiring the assurance of a future return from the utility. Alternatively, it can attempt to reconcile private ownership with consumers' political power through regulation. Either way, network utilities operate under terms set by the state.

Institutions had to evolve to ensure that investment could be financed and the rents distributed to various claimants. Creating durable regulatory institutions was more difficult under private ownership, where the owners needed reassurance that their investment would be adequately rewarded. If profits were too high, regulators would come under political pressure to transfer them to other claimants, but if too much were redistributed, investment might become unattractive. The result in the United States was rate-of-return regulation protected by the constitution against expropriation.

Whether private ownership was viable depended on the availability of reliable institutions to uphold long-term agreements, as well as the transaction costs of monitoring performance and quality. Britain, with its powerful capitalist class, strong but provincial municipalities, and deep-seated class antagonisms, may have found the least satisfactory balance of interests, compared to which state-ownership after the war may well have been preferable. Other continental countries either moved directly to more efficient state ownership or managed to achieve a better balance between public and private interests, often by cartels operating under loose regulation. Some evolved a more satisfactory and durable system of municipal ownership in partnership with the state for statewide networks, as with the Scandinavian electricity grids. The United States, with its open frontier, federal structure, and a balance of powers, evolved a system of investor-owned utilities under state and federal regulation that was remarkably durable.

The historical record and empirical studies suggest that a variety of regulatory institutions emerged to handle the conflicting claims of various interest groups on the natural monopoly rents. These institutions continued to evolve until they reached a local equilibrium from which further change could be successfully blocked by these interest groups. This *interest group theory of regulation* has a number of important implications. The most relevant is that bargaining over the rent will be inefficient, since it provides incentives to conceal information. The obvious analogy is with public finance where taxes to transfer income from one group to another are inevitably distortionary. The theory predicts important similarities and differences between public ownership and regulated private ownership. Under public ownership, interest groups will compete in the political market place for benefits, while under private ownership, the regulator will represent the interests of the non-owning groups. This was demonstrated in chapter 4 by comparing the electricity industries in Britain under public ownership with private integrated electricity companies in Germany and Spain. Regardless of ownership, all three countries evolved systems of protecting high-cost domestic coal producers and recovering these costs from electricity consumers. It required privatization and liberalization to cut British coal subsidies, though they survived in the vesting contracts for a further three years, and with coal contracts passed through to the franchise market for the following five years. The United States has managed to impose what is effectively a very distortionary tax on long-distance telephone rates to finance various interest group objectives, from locally subsidized service to internet connections to schools.

The best way to create and protect rents for distribution to the incumbent interest groups is to maximize the horizontal and vertical extent of the utility's monopoly. The best way to shift the balance of bargaining advantage toward consumers is to minimize both extensions of monopoly. The fact that these industries were in the past almost invariably vertically and horizontally integrated suggests that well-organized groups have succeeded in capturing the rents at the expense of consumers. The reasons were set out in section 4.1.2. Crucially, vertical integration enhances the utility's ability to control information to defend its interests. The remaining arguments are deployed to justify this desirable position—that economies of scale and scope make integration efficient, unbundling creates unnecessary price risks, while the loss of the captive franchise market makes it harder to finance investment. The bribe offered to politicians is that they will be able to provide political patronage in the shape of rent reallocations (and possibly jobs). Politically desirable cross-subsidies can be financed by implicit rather than explicit taxation. Cross-subsidies thus buy political support to protect the franchise, making for a durable politico-economic equilibrium.

Utilities in each country evolved along their differing history-dependent paths, and they achieved differing levels of efficiency. Nevertheless, they had acquired a remarkable similarity in their structure and system of regulation. Almost all evolved toward vertically integrated franchise monopolies subject to cost-based regulation, in which there was essentially no alternative to buying from the incumbent monopoly (except for autogeneration in electricity, which was only feasible for large industrial producers). Given this degree of convergence, perhaps it was not surprising that it was hard to detect systematic differences in efficiency between public and privately owned utilities.

9.1   Restructuring Network Utilities

Liberalization in the United States, and privatization in Britain and elsewhere, have demonstrated the importance of structural reforms that either allow entrants to compete with the incumbent integrated utility or separate the potentially competitive parts from the natural monopoly core of the network utility. Such reforms provide one of the major reasons for privatization, at least of the competitive services. Whether they also create a case for privatizing the core network is less clear, and the evidence from Britain suggests that even if privatization is ultimately desired, it should be delayed until the problems of access pricing have been resolved and the network can be properly valued.

The case for privatizing the network is to ensure that it is properly regulated and hence provides credible pricing for the network service providers, and does not subject them to covert taxation or additional state intervention. The case for retaining the core network in public ownership is primarily the difficulty of valuing it and/or regulating it to achieve the desired coordination benefits, particularly of expansion. That case looks strongest for electricity grids, less strong for gas pipelines (where loop flows are not an issue), and least convincing for telecoms networks, where service and network are hardest to separate. This final chapter summarizes the lessons from regulatory reform and discusses the various regulatory issues that need to be addressed when liberalizing network utilities.

Privatization offers the advantage that the structure of the competitive part of the industry can be designed, whereas liberalizing an already private but regulated utility can at best precipitate structural changes whose final form is unpredictable. Antitrust suits, MMC investigations, regulatory pressures on access pricing, demands for accounting separation, and "Chinese walls" can persuade integrated utilities that life would be simpler and even more profitable if they voluntarily unbundled—British Gas is a good example. Entry and competition may force changes, though this will depend on the relative costs of the entrant and the incumbents, regulatory constraints placed on the incumbent, and their skill in market strategy. The process, as we saw with AT&T, is largely out of control, with no guarantee that the final industry structure will necessarily be the best.

Privatization, in contrast, appears to offer the chance to create an optimal industrial structure. Unfortunately, the political realities of privatization rarely allow carefully planned industrial restructuring. Privatization is normally an ideological as well as economic policy, and in Britain was based on the view that the business of government is not the government of business. Politicians pressing for privatization are unlikely to believe in the government's ability to carefully design the postprivatization industry. Second, at least in Britain, privatization was the policy of the governing Conservative party and strongly resisted by the opposition party, who threatened to stop any privatizations if elected. This put pressure on the government to complete each privatization within the term of the current parliament, but haste is the enemy of careful restructuring.

If an industry is to be broken into potentially competitive firms, then a great deal of additional work is required. The assets need to be identified and allocated, as do contracts, liabilities, employment, pension assets, and the like. The financial structure must be designed and tested for robustness, pro-forma accounts prepared, and a past history of accounts relating to the assets of the new firm created to convince financial analysts of the commercial viability of each proposed firm. Even if the managers of the original monopoly are completely convinced of the desirability of reform, these tasks are inevitably time-consuming. It took AT&T two years to agree to the divestiture of the already financially separate Bell operating companies, with strong internal management support for the restructuring, an existing history of accounts, profits, and share prices, and no need to raise additional finance. Most public utilities in Britain were very hostile to any restructuring and competition, which they feared would force them to reduce costs and sack workers, as well as reducing managerial power, and were thus inevitably uncooperative. Alan Walters (1988), who acted as an advisor to Mrs. Thatcher during the early privatization period, claimed that the relevant ministers were anxious to break up BT and introduce competition.[1] They were persuaded that it might take three years to implement this decision, which was longer than the government had left to run. It was felt instead that it was more important to establish the possibility of privatizing a monopoly than to risk losing possibly their only chance.

Later, as the early privatizations proved successful, but after British Gas was sold as a monopoly, the idea of transforming public monopolies into unchanged private monolithic monopolies was abandoned. The water companies were sold as regional utilities, as were the electricity distribution companies (the RECs), though these had both existed before in a regional form. The first serious restructuring that involved breaking up an existing corporation was that of the CEGB, and even here the pressure of time prevented a fully satisfactory solution. Nuclear power stations were thought to need the strong balance sheet (and market power) of a large generating company. National Power was therefore created, but by the time nuclear power had proved unsalable to the City, it was too late to break National Power into smaller companies. Similar political pressures undoubtedly hinder restructuring in other countries.

In the case of electricity privatization in Britain, although the initial structure was insufficiently competitive, entry was unregulated, and the duties of the regulator required him to encourage further competition. If it is not politically practical to restructure industries before privatization, is it sufficient to liberalize entry and await the gradual development of competition? This policy raises a number of important questions. First, is entry desirable or should it be limited? Second, should the utility continue to be regulated until adequate competition has developed? If so, how is it possible to balance the requirements that the price should be kept low enough to prevent the abuse of market power but high enough to attract additional entry and competition? Finally, if the future shareholders in the privatized company expect liberalization and entry, how will they value the incumbent monopoly? If liberalization benefits customers, then there will be strong pressure to allow it to happen. In this case it becomes even less sensible for the government to privatize the utility as a monopoly, since shareholders expect future entry and will value the company accordingly. This undermines one of the arguments for selling utilities as monopolies, namely that they are then worth more and thus reduce public debt by a larger amount.[2]

The first set of questions is whether entry into a monopolized industry is necessarily desirable, whether it makes much difference to the social value of privatizing a utility as a monopoly subject to entry, or whether there really are large costs in not creating competition before privatization but allowing it to develop later.

9.2   Entry

It is a striking fact that in almost all cases of liberalization, regulatory reform has been followed by entry and increased competition, except for a limited period of protected duopoly in the British telecoms market, where no further entry was allowed until after 1991. Electricity liberalization in Victoria provides another important counterexample, discussed below. To judge whether entry is beneficial, it is important to distinguish the reasons why it occurs. There are three quite different reasons for entry, though there may be several compounding factors in any individual case. The first reason, most evident in the case of AT&T, is that the incumbent firm may be regulated in a way that distorts prices and leads to cross-subsidies, and entry occurs into the overpriced segments—"cream skimming" or "cherry picking." There is no guarantee that the entrant has lower costs than the incumbent, and hence no guarantee that industry costs will be reduced, though greater competition may lower prices to the benefit of consumers and may force a realignment of prices to costs, which will yield allocative gains.

The second reason is that the incumbent may be exercising market power, and keeping prices and profits high enough to induce entry. If entry occurs in a homogeneous goods oligopoly context, then the standard result is that there will be "excess entry"; that is, the equilibrium number of entrants will lead to lower total welfare than if entry were restricted. As more entry occurs, prices fall, lowering profits and raising consumer welfare. Each additional entrant steals part of the market (and profits) from existing firms in the industry but does not balance this loss against the extra costs of entry. This business stealing externality is the source of the excessive entry. There is a considerable literature on this effect, usefully summarized in Armstrong, Cowan, and Vickers (1994, p. 107) and set out in the appendix to this chapter.

The excess entry theorem might not seem relevant to deregulating a previously regulated monopoly, for if the regulated price were related to the cost of efficient operation, then removing price controls should not have adverse effects. If the incumbent is more efficient that potential entrants, it should find it more profitable to price to deter entry; otherwise, it risks losing profitable sales for no sustainable increase in price. If it is less efficient than entrants, they should enter anyway. Nevertheless, the incumbent may believe that raising profit margins may generate sufficient short-run profits to outweigh the longer-run losses, and may also believe that its position would be more secure against regulatory scrutiny if the industry were shared with new entrants. The theorem does, however, serve as a warning that the socially optimum number of competing oligopolists created by breaking up a previously state-owned utility may not be able to deter excessive subsequent entry where there continue to be economies of scale.

The English ESI offers an interesting example, where only two price-setting generators were created from the unbundling of the CEGB, inducing substantial and arguably excessive subsequent entry. The argument of chapter 6 was that two price-setting generators was too few, and that five would have resulted in more competition and possibly little additional entry. The required replacement investment in CCGTs could have been undertaken by the incumbent firms, though equally it could have been done by new entrants. Excess entry was not inevitable, since the five firms could have realized all available economies of scale. The excess entry theorem, which points to the unsustainability of the social optimum with economies of scale (involving prices below average costs) was not relevant. Instead the market was contestable and would have behaved competitively. When the state of Victoria restructured its ESI by creating five generation companies, competition was intense, and no entry occurred, illustrating this point.

Radical restructuring to create sufficient competing firms out of an existing monopoly is not a readily available option when the regulated utility is already private, and in that case entry is the natural solution. If this is to make any sense, then it cannot be the case that the incumbent's costs or prices are independent of the entry; otherwise, there would be no social benefit at all from liberalization. There are several obvious advantages to allowing entry, even if the incumbent firm remains dominant (and regulated), for increasing the number of firms improves the cost information available to regulators. In the simplest version of this, observing a larger number of firms allows the regulator to disentangle the effects of common shocks to the industry (cyclical demand factors, input price changes, etc.) from firm-specific events that can more reasonably be attributed to managerial competence. Yardstick regulation has a better mixture of incentives and (partial) risk sharing than regulation based on the information from a single firm (Shleifer 1985; Laffont and Tirole 1993; Armstrong, Cowan, and Vickers 1994).[3]

The third reason for entry is that lack of competition causes the incumbent's costs to be higher than they might otherwise have been (because of X-inefficiency, or rent sharing with unionized workers), and above the costs of potential entrants, who view the prospect of competing with an inefficient incumbent as attractive. Airline deregulation in the United States encouraged new entrants with lower-wage rates and operating costs to compete against the heavily unionized incumbents. The effect of competition in reducing X-inefficiency is potentially the most important reason to liberalize markets, and it offers the prospect that even entry that increases spare capacity may still bring benefits. The existence of spare capacity means that incumbents need only cover their variable costs to survive, while entrants need to earn a return on any sunk capital. This will act to reduce entry, and possibly avoid some of the costs of duplicating capacity. If entry causes operating costs to fall, then the excess entry theorem may be overturned.

Whether liberalization will lead to excess entry with economies of scale becomes an empirical matter, resting on the difficult issue of the responsiveness of costs to competition. The implications for restructuring before privatization are also not clear cut. Provided that entry is not impeded by incumbent control over the network, then restructuring is less important if the market is growing rapidly (for then any idle capacity caused by duplication will be needed soon after in any case). Restructuring is less important if economies of scale and scope are low (e.g., in generation, in long-distance telephone markets, and possibly in high-density local telephony). In the British telephone case, the incumbent BT was restricted from entering the local cable TV market to ensure that all expansion of that service was by competitors, thus maximizing the rate of introduction of competition while reducing the tendency to excess capacity. The cost of this policy was the possible loss of economies of scope with the existing BT network. In the electricity case about half the new investment in CCGT generation was by the incumbents. Although more competition and possibly less excess capacity might have been created if the incumbents had been prevented from similar investments, it is hard to see how this could reasonably be done, since it is not a new kind of service, nor do the incumbents have the power to impede entry that BT possessed.

9.3   Institutional Innovations Needed for Liberalization

Two key innovations have contributed to transform the earlier convergence of structure and performance of public and private network utilities, and to shift the argument decisively in favor of private ownership. The first was the invention of price-cap regulation to better mimic the effects of a competitive market for the core network where competition is not feasible. The second was to create markets in the services offered over the networks, replacing regulation by genuine markets. Price-cap regulation is a high-powered incentive scheme, whereas cost-of-service or rate-of-return regulation is low-powered, providing poor incentives for efficiency, unless costs can be cut fast enough to permit the utility to retain the increased profits before tariffs are reset. High-powered incentives increase risk and are only attractive if they deliver enough efficiency gains to offset the higher costs of risky finance. For these gains to be realized, the regulator must be held to the regulatory compact, and the state must be able to ensure that the regulator is not unreasonably overruled.

The British solution enshrines the price-cap $(RPI - X)$ in a legally enforceable contract set for a fixed period. At the end of this period, prices can be reset to reflect continuing cost reductions, on the understanding that past profits are not clawed back. This understanding was threatened when the newly elected Labour party carried out its manifesto promise to impose a retrospective windfall profits tax to recoup "excessive" postprivatization profits in 1997. This demonstrates the difficulty of creating the necessary legislative commitment to high-powered regulation in an adversarial parliamentary democracy, and it is one reason why cost-of-service regulation is a more durable if less efficient equilibrium. Nevertheless, price-cap regulation, with its explicit indexation against inflation, and the flexibility to allow rapid tariff rebalancing, represents a genuine innovation that is increasingly copied elsewhere.

Price caps are particularly well suited to the transition to unregulated markets as competition reaches critical intensity. Price-cap regulation was indeed originally devised as a transitional arrangement. Price caps have therefore been adopted by the FCC in regulating AT&T's long-distance charges. But they have also evolved to apply to core network monopolies like transmission and distribution of gas and electricity. Britain has developed a set of procedures for periodic regulatory reviews of the price-caps for these network monopolies through a series of references to the Monopolies and Mergers Commission. The experience of these periodic reviews demonstrates the importance of good dispute resolution procedures, which enable regulation to be adapted to changing circumstances without undermining its credibility.

This new and more efficient system of regulation was necessary to reap potential efficiency gains, but it is more demanding than the former equilibrium system that had evolved in the United States. The British system of price-caps has still to demonstrate its robustness in the more fragile institutional environment of Eastern Europe. Hungary privatized the regional electricity companies with price-cap regulation, but the first few years were marked by disagreements over its implementation and complaints that the companies were not granted the return promised in the legislation. For the first period of the price-cap, this may not matter too much, since the companies submit bids in the privatization auction that reflect their judgments about likely political and regulatory developments. The real test comes once the price-caps are reset, after the companies have become locked in to their purchases. The prospect of joining the EU and meeting the required Directives on gas and electricity offers some comfort that Hungary and similar countries can benefit from the regulatory credibility of the EU and sustain price-cap regulation. It will be interesting to see if Asian countries can evolve comparably efficient and credible regulation if they choose to privatize their networks.

The second major innovation was liberalization, which on the face of it seems to offer unambiguous gains that are not dependent on the institutional maturity of the country. The evidence presented in this book shows that interpretation to be simplistic. Creating competitive and efficient markets for network services paradoxically requires sophisticated regulatory institutions, more so for some utilities than others. Networks offer many potential bottlenecks that can be exploited unless there is good regulatory oversight, sufficient competition, and/or enough spare capacity. If pipelines and transmission grids have spare capacity at the peak, and if there are sufficiently many service providers, there may not be much problem.

The argument of chapter 2 was that it is politically attractive to liberalize network utilities when the network is both mature (in terms of coverage) and has spare capacity. This configuration of demand and supply tends to undermine the previous politicoeconomic equilibrium of vertical integration. For private regulated utilities, the gains from changing the earlier regulatory compact may outweigh the loss of credibility. For state-owned utilities, fiscal problems caused by weak prices and excess capacity, combined with potential efficiency gains from restructuring, may combine to overcome opposition to privatization. Spare capacity also reduces the risks of politically damaging demand-led price rises, though it does not completely resolve the problems of systematic underpricing found in Eastern Europe.

If major shifts to liberalization are more likely to occur in periods of excess capacity, as borne out by recent history, there may be a breathing space during which policy toward bottlenecks and essential facilities can be refined. This breathing space may be distinctly time limited. Efficient network management would aim to reduce excessive spare capacity. Certainly private owners are more likely to underestimate the social value of excess capacity and appreciate the market power that undersupply offers. The evolution of networks may therefore proceed from excess to deficient capacity unless security standards are carefully specified and enforced.

One sign that regulators and lawmakers appreciate the need for new tools to deal with the wider range of abuses of market power that networks offer is the shift to penalties and prohibitions. Articles 81 and 82 (ex Articles 85 and 86) of the Treaty of Rome (which deal with multicountry anticompetitive behavior) are increasingly being written into domestic competition laws. In Britain, the Competition Act reached the statute books at the end of 1998, and jointly empowered the regulators with the director general of fair trading to impose fines for abusive behavior. The emphasis may shift from economic analysis, followed by license amendments or further restructuring, to a more legalistic interpretation of whether the rules were followed regardless of economic logic. The hope in Britain is that the new powers will allow the regulators to enforce competitive behavior more swiftly. The fear is that enforcement costs will rise, that courts will be used to delay resolution excessively, and that the result will reflect narrow legalisms rather than economic rationality.

If markets are to be sustained as adequately competitive, they will require effective antimonopoly agencies. Countries vary widely in the maturity, power, and independence of such agencies, and will consequently vary in their ability to sustain truly liberalized network utilities. One of the questions invariably asked by countries contemplating network liberalization is what kind of institutions need to be set up. Should they adopt the New Zealand approach of relying on the general competition authority, should they follow the British approach of setting up a separate regulatory body for each network industry, or should they compromise and set up one (or perhaps just a few) agencies to cover all (or some) of the utilities? Britain has decided to combine Offer and Ofgas into one energy regulatory body, though there is no suggestion that it should also deal with water, telecoms, and rail.

The argument for no specialized regulatory agencies has two sides. It is cheaper, and it reduces the risk of regulatory capture. The pessimistic Chicago theory of regulation is that regulation is designed to protect monopolies against competition, rather than consumers against exploitation. The U.S. evidence shows that the interest group theory of regulation is alive and well. On this view it is better to allow firms to exploit their market power rather than attempt to regulate it. Market power leads to high prices that provoke entry and lead to greater competition, which will be its eventual undoing. The English electricity market is a good example where entry has been massive and arguably excessive. Attempts to regulate that market power are more likely to lead to entry barriers, favoring incumbents and preserving potential market power, which, over time, will lead to higher prices than the alternative.

The argument for specialized regulators is that each network industry has very different cost structures, bottleneck possibilities, and market behavior. If the regulators can be relied upon to be competent, upright, and independent, they will be better placed to identify abuses and deal with them in a timely fashion. The contrast is with the Clear case in New Zealand (concerning the terms of telecom interconnection), where the dispute moved through successively higher courts until it was appealed to the final arbiter, the U.K. Privy Council (Whish 1995). The dispute was settled on a narrow legal reading of the original Act after a delay of four years. In Britain, disputes are normally resolved in a matter of months provided that the regulator has standing to act. This last proviso is important, for the major obstacle to reforming electricity trading arrangements has been the Pooling and Settlement Agreement, an unlimited duration contract that can only be altered with the agreement of a large number of cosignatories.

9.4 Dispute Resolution

The most difficult part of the design of any system of regulation is deciding how to deal with changes, new circumstances, or unanticipated events. It would be impossible to specify what the regulator should do in all possible contingencies in the initial Act, and there must therefore be a mechanism for dealing with unforseen events as they arise. In the British system, the regulator can either use his discretion where the Act provides flexibility, or it may be necessary to negotiate a change in the license. But what constrains the regulator to ensure that he does not behave unreasonably? Who regulates the regulator? (Whish 1995).

The regulated utility has two options open in the event of a disagreement with the regulator—a reference to the Monopolies and Mergers Commission (MMC, now the Competition Commission) or an appeal for judicial review. If the regulator is empowered to make a license change (at the periodic review, when the price controls can be reset), but the utility does not consider the change fair or reasonable, then the utility can appeal the change to the MMC. Similarly, if the regulator requires the agreement of the utility to make a license change, and if the utility cannot be persuaded to make that change, the regulator can refer the conduct in question to the MMC. Either way, the regulator will then draft the terms of the reference, and might widen the scope of the enquiry beyond that of the original dispute to ask more searching questions of the structure and conduct of the industry.

The MMC first determines whether the conduct in question is against the public interest. If not, the dispute ends there and then. If the MMC finds that the conduct is against the public interest, it will propose remedies (which are typically of the same general form that the regulator proposed but may differ in details, such as the size of the regulatory asset base, the allowed rate of return, the initial price level, and/or the rate of change of real prices in the price-cap, i.e., the value of X in $RPI - X$). The MMC reports to the regulator who normally takes regard of their recommendations, but may argue that circumstances have changed since the reference, requiring some different action. If the case was brought to the MMC under other legislation than the relevant utility act, the MMC reports to the Minister of Industry and Trade, who may accept, reject, or modify the recommendations (see chapter 2, appendix B).

Recourse to the MMC can be enormously costly for the utility as it ties up scarce managerial time for an extended period, prejudices any negotiations between the company and other companies, while the outcome of the team of economists and lawyers recruited to adjudicate may be hard to predict. It is also costly for the regulator, for it suggests that he or she is not able to reach agreement by negotiation, and exposes the regulator's arguments to searching scrutiny. If these arguments are found flawed, then the regulator's credibility is weakened, as is his or her chance of reappointment and/or an honor in the periodic distribution of honors (knighthoods, etc.).

If the regulator used his discretion arbitrarily or unreasonably (particularly in responding to a recommendation of the MMC after an earlier dispute reference), then the utility can request a judicial review. This may not be very satisfactory, since a review can only adjudicate on a very narrow interpretation of whether the regulator acted reasonably; it cannot comment on the actual decision nor replace it by an alternative. Nevertheless, the threat of judicial review hangs over regulators and the MMC and acts to encourage consistency and due process. When the Northern Ireland regulator, whose relations with Northern Ireland Electricity (NIE) were quite remarkably acrimonious, imposed a more severe price-cap than the MMC had recommended (in March 1997) after NIE had requested a referral in response to the first price-cap, NIE took the regulator to judicial appeal. The Belfast High Court heard the case in December 1997 and ruled in June 1998 on a narrow technical point. The judge ruled that because the MMC had not stated explicitly that the £575 million revenue was a floor for the required revenues, it was open to the regulator to propose a lower figure. NIE appealed, and in October 1998 the judge ruled that reading the MMC report as a whole led to the interpretation that any lesser amount than the proposed revenue of £575 million would be insufficient for the conduct of NIE's business. The judge also awarded costs against the regulator and denied leave to appeal to the House of Lords.

This rather bizarre train of events shows that judicial review is slow, that it can produce rather perverse and legalistic findings, but that with luck common sense about interpreting MMC rulings should prevail. It clarified the sense in which MMC recommendations should be taken account of by the regulator, who can only depart from them with good reason. While the case was under appeal, the government published its response to the Green Paper on Utility Regulation stating that it intended to legislate "to require regulators to seek final endorsement from the MMC that any license modification following a reference to the MMC are requisite to remedy or prevent the adverse effects identified by the MMC" (DTI 1999c, conclusion 7.14).

In extreme cases, where there is deep-seated dissatisfaction with the way utility regulation is working, the government may initiate an inquiry, issue a White Paper, and ultimately enact new legislation to remedy the defect. The earlier 1986 Gas Act has been replaced by the 1995 Gas Act to introduce competition into the franchise market and deal with the earlier unbundling of the industry. The new Labour government undertook a review of utilities shortly after coming to office and has issued a White Paper in 1998 foreshadowing new legislation, but at that time there was no legislative time available in the next Parliament, so the proposals await discussion and enactment. The pool review has proposed major changes to electricity trading arrangements (see section 6.6). If all parties agree, no legislation will be needed, but if not, progress may be delayed. If the pool is abolished, the Pooling and Settlement Agreement will automatically lapse, but it is not clear whether the pool can be abolished against the wishes of major players who may be disadvantaged, such as the nuclear generators.

Is this a satisfactory way to handle disputes? Clearly, there must be some cost and disincentive to the regulated industry in appealing against decisions of the regulator; otherwise, the appeal body itself acts as the regulatory agency. The present British system has this property. It is not clear that all disagreements should require an equally costly appeal procedure, and there is a danger that the regulator can use the threat of a breakdown in negotiations and a reference to the MMC to enforce agreement with the industry that would not be accepted if appeals were less costly. The trend, however, is toward a more rule-based approach that may constrain regulatory discretion and penalties that may restrain utility opportunism, so the problems of unreasonable discretion may become less severe as case law accumulates.

The alternative in which appeals are made to the Minister or Parliament has the drawback of politicizing decisions so that appeals are judged on the basis of popular support rather than economic logic. One of the most severe tests to which electricity regulation has been exposed to date was the 1992 House of Commons inquiry into the market for coal, described in section 6.3.2. At vesting, British Coal had three-year take-or-pay contracts with the generators for 65 million tons of coal at prices substantially above import parity. At these prices for coal, and the 1991 price for gas, it was cheaper to build and operate CCGT plant than to incur the avoidable costs of existing coal-fired stations. Within a remarkably short space of time, some 9 GW of CCGT plant was contracted (about one-sixth of existing total capacity), together with back-to-back fifteen-year contracts for gas and the sale of electricity. This would displace nearly 30 million tons of coal, and on October 13, 1992, British Coal announced that it had been unable to renegotiate the 65 million ton coal contract and that within two years its sales to the generators would fall to 30 million tons. It therefore proposed to close 31 of its 50 remaining pits, with a loss of over 30,000 jobs.

The public outcry reflected in the House of Commons resulted in referring the matter to the Trade and Industry Select Committee of the House of Commons. The Select Committee called witnesses and received submissions, many of which argued that the regulator had failed in his duty to ensure efficient electricity supply. The secretary of state of the DTI explained that he had no powers to intervene or override the contracts drawn up between privately owned companies in the industry, in contrast to the days of public ownership (DTI 1993). Nevertheless, the two coal-fired generators were persuaded to sign five-year contracts for coal at above world market prices, backed by five-year coal contracts with the RECs, who were allowed to pass the extra costs through to the franchise market. Electricity prices in the nonfranchise market then fell relative to those to domestic consumers. The hope was that British Coal would be able to cut costs fast enough to meet international prices during the transition period. To provide the necessary incentive to cut costs, the government privatized the coal industry.

The final outcome of an intense period of public and political scrutiny was a new kind of politicoeconomic bargain in which players had to be persuaded to reach satisfactory compromises, rather than being instructed by the government as owner. Persuasion requires inducements, and the cost of subsidizing British coal was visited upon the domestic consumers, trapped by their franchise and poorly represented in the political discussions. The industry was allowed to continue operating in a moderately free market, with all of the fixes written into contracts that did not unduly disturb the spot market price. In that sense the principles of free competition were upheld and the privatized structure emerged remarkably intact, as did the system of regulation.

It is interesting to contrast the political response to the first coal crisis with the second, that followed almost with predictable inevitability as the five-year coal contracts matured, and British coal costs remained stubbornly above international coal prices. This time the coal industry was under private ownership, and the country was under the new Labour government. In a decisive break with the past, the Labour party, which described itself as New Labour in contrast to Old Labour, abolished Clause Four of its constitution that committed the party to national ownership of the commanding heights of the economy. Less than two years earlier a Conservative government had to warn prospective buyers of the opposition Labour party's threat to renationalize the industry, but now, renationalization was off the political agenda, even for rail. New Labour would be business friendly, actively seeking public-private partnerships, and intent on improving the competitiveness of the British economy.

Everything therefore seemed set for allowing the market to resolve the impending coal crisis, once again associated with another "dash for gas." Gas liberalization had halved the spot price of gas, CCGT technology had evolved with more efficient turbines, and the Environment Agency was exercising its considerable autonomy to impose ever more unreasonable sulphur emission targets on coal-fired power stations. Faced with a limited life expectancy for much of their plant, National Power and PowerGen ignored a presumed inevitable threat of entry by further CCGT IPPs and used their market power to raise prices considerably in the 1997–8 winter (Offer 1998d). This further encouraged

IPPs to seek Section 36 consent to build new power stations, and worsened the already rather dismal prospects for British coal.

Even though the number of coal miners was now down to less than 10,000, and the industry was in private ownership, this insult to the traditional heart of the Labour party was too much to take. The government imposed a moratorium on new gas-fired generation, and undertook to review energy sources for power generation (DTI 1998b). The House of Commons Trade and Industry Committee also visited the question of fuel choice in March 1998 in its *Coal Report*, criticizing the gas moratorium and also the behavior of the Environment Agency for poor policy making on emission limits (House of Commons 1998a).

What do we learn from this second test of allowing market forces to substitute for traditional energy policy? Arguably that the reasons for political intervention remain intact, but their implementation has become more complex, public, and messy. Too many confusing strands had become intertwined for a simple solution. The coal-fired generators had too much market power, which they exercised by restricting output and keeping prices high, reducing the coal burn, and excessively encouraging gas entry. But the reason why they invited entry rather than resisting it by entry-deterring pricing was the malign influence of the Environment Agency, making coal-fired power stations wasting rather than valuable assets. The electricity regulator had no jurisdiction over environmental issues and was therefore relatively powerless to act. The government clearly believed that most faults could be laid at the door of the flawed design of the electricity pool. They claimed that the flexibility of coal-fired generation was underrewarded, that gas-fired generation could bid zero and still be paid the pool price, and hence the market was biased against coal. The pool inquiry was therefore instructed to find remedies, but it was prevented from addressing the fundamental problem of market power (see chapter 6.6).

At a relatively late stage the team at the Department of Trade and Industry managed to make sense of this highly confused situation, but by then the die was cast. The government was committed to the kinds of electricity trading reforms announced by Offer in July 1998 while recognizing that they would not adequately address issues of market power, and it was silent on the problems of environmental emissions. The DTI's very sensible strategy was to encourage more competition among price-setting generators by further divestiture of coal-fired plant. Powergen agreed to sell two large power stations with 4,000 MW by April 30, 1999, in return for regulatory clearance (granted on November 25, 1998) to buy the U.S.-owned English REC, East Midlands. National Power sold Drax, the largest coal-fired power station in Europe, with 4,000 MW fitted with Flue Gas Desulphurisation (FGD) and hence meeting stringent environmental standards, possibly as part of a deal in which National Power acquired Midlands Electricity's supply business. Eastern Group, which had bought the 6,000 MW of coal-fired stations in the earlier divestiture (see section 6.3.2), agreed to install FGD and to stop paying the £6/MWh earnout to the former owners, National Power and PowerGen (see section 6.6), thus easing emissions constraints and encouraging them to bid in their stations at lower prices.

The DTI appears willing to allow vertical integration as a price for increased horizontal competition, and to allow a restructuring of the pool into a more opaque commodity market that will favor such vertical arrangements. If the major power generators have been persuaded to sacrifice market power to save the coal industry (and improve the efficiency of investment decisions and fuel choices), one must wonder who is going to bear the cost of the compensation they required. The answer, almost inevitably, will be domestic consumers through higher prices. Although the domestic franchise has ended, the earlier and simpler coal contract fix is not readily available. Incumbent REC suppliers, many of which are vertically integrated, will probably be able to pass on higher costs to their less mobile customers, to the benefit of their generation business. Larger and more agile industrial customers may believe they can avoid at least some of the costs of the deal and hence will not oppose it. The dynamics of regulatory change continue to be shaped by interest groups, though now they have to play on the more complex market stage. Fortunately for such groups, the scenery can still be shifted around, for markets can be redesigned to shift rents in desired directions. The hope is that markets will constrain inefficiencies better than the old smoke-filled rooms of political fixing.

The British experience shows that at moments of crisis which occur periodically, the energy industries will be inevitably attract political concern. Any regulatory system that is to command credibility from investors must have some resilience against these pressures. The British structure operating though licenses that can only be altered by a complex, costly, and lengthy procedure provides considerable political insulation. The autonomy of the regulator has been demonstrated, provided that he or she in turn acts within his or her mandate. The legislative power of the House of Commons, which may be able to remedy sufficiently unsatisfactory outcomes, clearly cannot be used for minor reforms or arbitrary interference. Political fixes can still be constructed, but only by devising some way to generate rents to compensate those who would otherwise lose, and as always, domestic consumers are likely to be stuck with the bill. The more competitive is the final market, the harder this is to engineer, providing the main argument for the costly final step to franchise liberalization.

9.5   Differences between the Network Utilities

Part of the argument for specialized regulatory agencies is that each utility presents different regulatory challenges. Even where they share common problems, there are advantages in regulatory experiment and competition, at least in the early stages of regulatory learning. One good example is the debate over how to value the regulatory asset base of the core network. This question arises when resetting price-caps at the first periodic review. Each regulator has learned from the experiences of his or her counterparts, informed both by a public debate conducted at a remarkable number of industry seminars, and subject to critical revision by the MMC. The main case for separate regulatory agencies is that telecoms, electricity, and gas differ in important ways, as chapters 6 through 8 have demonstrated. Each utility presents differing regulatory challenges in introducing and sustaining effective competition.

9.5.1   Liberalizing Telecoms

Telecoms offers the greatest advantages from competition and yet poses some of the most challenging regulatory problems. Telecoms costs are both low and falling rapidly, but the industry cost and tariff structures are kept remarkably opaque. As a result too many tariffs in price-elastic market segments remain excessively high. The dead-weight losses of excessively high prices are truly enormous—directly in discouraging such a cheap and efficient means of communication and indirectly in stifling innovative uses of the network, whether it be internet access, wider mobile penetration, or spreading the advantages of high bandwidth. High profits may stimulate vigorous technical development by the phone companies and equipment suppliers, but high prices have highly adverse effects on the business competitiveness in an increasingly global and interconnected world. Countries that discourage cheap communications risk reducing their innovativeness and future prosperity.

There seems little reason to trade off high prices in return for high rates of investment, given the attractions of entering the industry and capturing customers, coupled with the large number of telecoms companies willing to enter markets. As a result, and because of the rapid rates of growth of demand, rapidly falling costs and the power of telecoms companies to retaliate against unreasonable regulatory intervention, privatizing telecoms is relatively easy in most countries. Regulating privatized telecoms companies to transfer the massive potential gains of technical progress to consumers is, however, considerably more difficult. One useful and important lesson is that protection against entry (like the U.K. duopoly) has little to recommend it.

The main regulatory challenge is to set efficient access prices to the bottleneck elements, especially the final mile to each customer, so that different service providers can compete with undistorted cost-related prices. But entry may not be enough to drive prices down to cost without further regulatory action. The U.K. and U.S. evidence is that duopolies are able to sustain nearly collusive price levels, while a triopoly of long-distance providers in the United States has allowed price-cost margins to widen. This has been concealed by the rapid fall in costs that allows prices to be cut without harming profits, and market behavior suggests that over time competition does put downward pressure on prices.

Regulators can encourage price competition by easing the costs of choosing the cheapest provider. Number portability and carrier preselection choice both enable consumers to choose the cheapest provider of each type of service, without being forced to buy all services from a single company. Certainly in Britain many domestic customers use three or more different companies to handle each of local, long-distance and various international calls, even though the incumbent BT offers all three services. Incumbents have responded by devising ever changing and complex packages. BT offers "Friends and Family," in which certain numbers are cheaper, and a variety of "ValuePlans," which are nonlinear tariffs with higher line rentals and lower charges. As a result most subscribers appear to have no idea what telephone calls cost and are poorly placed to shop around.

Facilities-based competition may be slow to develop (and Mercury gained less than 5 percent of the market during six years of investment), while ensuring efficient sharing of facilities requires complex cost modeling to set access charges that may take years to develop. Aggressive price-cap regulation therefore offers an attractive transitional way of simulating the competitive market and restraining what appear to be very powerful tendencies to monopoly pricing in the industry. If competitive forces are not very strong, consumers benefit from them operating on a set of prices that is low rather than high. Competition is then less likely to induce inefficient or excessive entry and more likely to lead to cost cutting, innovative services, and further price reductions.

The key analytical developments in analyzing telecoms networks have been progress in understanding how access prices should be set, whether competition will allow access pricing ever to be liberalized, and whether vertical separation may be desirable. The first two issues have been discussed in section 7.4.5, and are discussed further in Armstrong, Doyle, and Vickers (1996) and elsewhere (Bergman et al. 1998, Armstrong, Cowan, and Vickers 1994). The last question raises rather different issues.

9.5.2 Access Pricing and Vertical Integration

The most difficult regulatory issues have to do with pricing access to the bottleneck when the bottleneck owner is also competing in one of the markets served by the network. In our three network utilities, this would happen if the grid operator also owned generation which competed with stand-alone generation, if the gas pipeline operator was free to sell gas to final customers, or if the owner of the local telephone loop also owned long-distance lines that competed with other carriers. In each case the supplier of a competitive good or service (gas, electricity, long-distance carriage) needs access to the bottleneck (the pipeline, grid, or local loop) owned by a rival. Since the synergies between distribution and production appear modest in electricity and gas, there are strong reasons for vertical separation. In telecoms the synergies may be so large as to make this too costly an option, at least for some parts of the network, so the question is most relevant for telecoms networks (though it arises in the single buyer model of electricity, discussed below). Clearly, the access price to this bottleneck will need to be regulated, but how should it be set, and how should the access price depend on the nature of competition in the unregulated market?

If the regulator has good information about the costs of the bottleneck, then the answer depends on whether competition in the unregulated market is price taking (competitive, or Bertrand competition) or imperfect. In the price-taking case, the bottleneck owner has no influence on the final price, so the bottleneck should be priced at average cost (assuming that the owner cannot be subsidized) whether the bottleneck owner is separate or integrated. In the imperfectly competitive case, a separate bottleneck owner must again be paid average cost, but an integrated owner will make profits downstream. It is tempting to argue that these profits should be partly used to defray the difference between the average and marginal cost of the bottleneck (which, being a natural monopoly, experiences lower marginal than average cost), thus moving the price closer to the efficient level. If the number of entrants in the imperfectly competitive market is not affected by the access price, then this argument holds. If, however, entry is affected by the access price, then one must be careful, for the access price will then depend on whether there is too much or too little entry in equilibrium.

Vickers (1995) addresses this question in a model in which there will be too much entry (of the kind set out in the appendix). He also looks at the larger structural question of whether it is desirable to allow the network natural monopoly to compete in the deregulated competitive sector, given optimal regulated access pricing but asymmetric information by the regulator about costs. He shows that the answer to this structural question is ambiguous. Vertical integration allows the network owner to raise his rivals' costs to secure competitive advantage in the deregulated market, and this has both costs (inefficient pricing through higher prices) and benefits in reducing the number of entrants into the deregulated market and thus diminishing excess entry. Depending on the nature of the demand schedule for the final product, it may be desirable or undesirable to permit integration. However, given the structure of the model, if vertical integration is allowed, the access price should be higher than if not, since a higher access price allows the integrated firm to increase its market share and reduce the amount of excessive entry. (The reason that the integrated firm increases its market share is that it faces only the marginal cost of access, which does not change, but increasing the access price raises the rivals' costs further.) As is so often the case, a slight change of the model to allow the network operator to reduce costs by unobserved effort reverses this finding; it argues for lower access charges under integration.[4]

Finally, if there is too little entry, because of undesirable entry barriers and/or because entry creates sufficient extra benefits by reducing X-inefficiency or encouraging faster technical innovation, then access prices should be lower with vertical integration than without. Many telephone companies subsidize the fixed or nontraffic sensitive cost of providing access to the local loop out of higher prices for calls, particularly long-distance and international calls. In Britain, the extra charges made on the local part of any call is termed the *access deficit charge*, and at privatization BT was restricted in the rate it could rebalance the line rental charge and reduce this cross-subsidy. In the United States, with separation between the local operating companies and the long-distance carriers, a similar access deficit charge (at a constant rate per minute) was levied on all long-distance carriers to preserve the cross-subsidy after the breakup of AT&T. In Britain, where BT is vertically integrated, Oftel decided that entrants would not have to pay this access deficit charge until their market share reached a certain level, thus effectively subsidizing (and encouraging) entry. Once BT faced adequate competition, it was allowed to rebalance its charges, removing the need either for the charge or the subsidy. Thereafter any social case for providing subsidized access to telephones (for universal access) should be financed out of general taxation, or as a second best, on the fixed charges (line rentals) of all telecoms operators. In the spirit of market provision, the FCC is considering competitive tendering or auctions as ways of providing loss-making services at least subsidy.

9.5.3 Introducing Competition into Electricity

If telecoms privatization is relatively simple, even in transitional and developing countries with fragile or underdeveloped regulatory institutions, electricity privatization is considerably harder, and it has made far less rapid progress. The evidence of electricity privatizations to date is that it is often fiscally costly (at least in present value terms, even if it temporarily eases the public sector budget constraint). The efficiency gains are typically an order of magnitude smaller than with telecoms privatizations, and they appear to derive mainly from restructuring rather than ownership changes. Furthermore it is harder to ensure that consumers, rather than shareholders, capture these efficiency gains, though indirectly they may benefit from the effect electricity restructuring has on other fuel industries.

Britain enjoyed dramatic cuts in fuel costs after electricity privatization, and even though profit margins widened considerably, consumers saw real prices (eventually) fall. Arguably some of the fall in fuel costs derived from the general atmosphere of liberalization, of which electricity privatization was a leading element. Gas prices fell with gas on gas competition, and that was greatly facilitated by creating a new and substantial extra demand for gas use in CCGT. Some of the major supply shocks undermining prices in the gas spot market were directly or indirectly caused by the liberalized electricity supply industry (ESI). The dash for gas encouraged (and perhaps overencouraged) further gas exploration and exploitation. The ability to back out a spot price of gas from the Electricity Pool encouraged gas trading, which increased liquidity and reduced the need for long-term gas contracts, making gas development easier. The failure of some CCGTs to perform on time created a gas surplus which eroded the implicit gas price-setting quasi-cartel. Falling gas prices may have put downward pressure on domestic coal prices, while allowing generators to import coal certainly did. Fossil fuel costs per kWh of electricity fell 45 percent in real terms in the five years after 1990, to the immediate benefit of medium-sized customers and eventually for other customers as well (see section 6.4).

The British experience shows that competition can take several forms, some of which are more efficiency enhancing than others. In Scotland, competition between vertically integrated utilities has had little detectable effect on productivity growth, compared to the unbundling of generation in England and Wales, and Northern Ireland. The latter example is especially instructive as it is a small system more like that of many developing countries than the mature and large system of England and Wales. Northern Ireland corresponds to the EU Electricity Directive concept of a single buyer, and NIE buys electricity on long-term power purchase agreements (PPAs) from three independent power stations. Section 6.4.1 showed how these PPAs dramatically increased availability and provided strong incentives for the generators to cut costs, though the gains were not passed through to customers without further regulatory action.

The single-buyer model (SBM) is one of the options offered under the EC Electricity Directive and potentially attractive for smaller-sized countries, so it is worth considering in greater detail. Under the EC Directive, the single buyer (SB) must publish a nondiscriminatory transmission and distribution tariff, and stand willing to buy on behalf of any eligible customer from any designated seller at the price equal to the buyer's price *less* the published transmission and distribution tariff. The intention is that the result will be exactly as though the buyer and seller had negotiated a contract and had then subcontracted for transmission with the transmission operator.

The SB must be quite separate (in both accounting and information terms) from the transmission, distribution, and generation activities of the vertically integrated enterprise. Buyers can contract with sellers outside the system (within the EU) on the same terms as within the system, thus creating the desired single market in electricity. Finally, eligibility to contract is defined in terms of annual consumption on a single site, and starts at the rather high level of 40 GWh/yr (or less) (from February 1999 for the core signatories), reducing to 20 GWh/yr (or less) one year later, and finally to 9 GWh/yr (or less) after a further three years (in 2003). This last state is more restrictive than the original step in Britain of allowing all with demands of more than 1 MW the right to a choice of supplier or freedom to buy in the pool.

9.5.4   Liberalizing Electricity: Pools versus the Single-Buyer Model

The SBM is an attempt to make generation contestable and to improve the efficiency of investment in and operation of power stations. The SB prepares forecasts of demand and the associated costs of meeting that demand each year from the existing plant (which will depend on the terms of the PPAs in place and on the cost of ancillary services). Given these forecasts, it can estimate when new plant or new transmission would reduce the total systems cost of meeting the forecast demand; it may then invite periodic tenders. Generation tenders would specify the variable and fixed costs and duration of the power purchase agreement (PPA) required by the bidder, and the SB can then select the least cost bid. Under the PPA the generator would be paid a daily amount if available for dispatch and the variable bid per unit generated. The availability payments might be varied depending on system maximum demand, to encourage plant to schedule maintenance in periods of lower demand, but are intended to provide incentives for plant availability. The evidence from systems with such availability payments is that they can dramatically improve plant availability (Argentina, Northern Ireland).

The bidder will be motivated to bid the actual variable cost (or its best prediction of that cost, possibly as a formula specifying a heat rate to be used with a fuel price) and to make all additional profits through the fixed element. The reason why truthful revelation of variable costs is a dominant strategy is that there would be gains from moving from any inefficient marginal price to the efficient price which can partly or wholly be captured through variations in the agreed annual fixed charge. One appealing consequence of this result is that the generator remains motivated to seek profitable cost-reducing investments which it can propose to the SB, and which are then passed on as lower marginal bids. The SB can now compute the system marginal price (the marginal bid of the highest cost generator required to meet instantaneous demand) and can use this to set a spot wholesale price, and the benchmark for determining any contract prices offered to downstream buyers. Finally, any unrecovered fixed costs from generation (which will be small if forecasts were correct),[5] and the fixed costs of transmission, can be recovered by additional fixed charges from the final consumers. These fixed charges are best recovered in proportion to demand at the system peak, since this will determine the amount of capacity in generation and transmission required.

The advantages of this model are that it provides incentives for efficient investment and operation, both by the station operator, and by the SB, who can minimize total costs be dispatching plant in merit order. The disadvantages vary, depending on whether the SB also owns generation, and how the SB is in turn regulated. If the SB is allowed to own generation, then it may favor bids from its own company, even where the bids are not least cost, since it may be able to transfer income from its distribution business to its own generating subsidiary, assuming that the regulator allows the SB to pass through the costs of generation to final consumers. Of course, a vigilant regulator will wish to inspect the bids, but the SB may be able to argue that the apparently cheaper generation bids require extra transmission investments that make them more expensive. This suggests that bids should include the costs of any transmission reinforcement required, and an independent consultant will be required to establish that each expansion proposal meets the required security standards. The SB probably has a comparative advantage in identifying least cost locations and may be able to exploit these informational rents to win the bids for new plant.

More generally, the SB competes with potential entrants and has an incentive to raise their costs (Salop and Scheffman 1983) to favor its own competitive generating subsidiary, and it may be able to do this in a variety of ways that are hard for the regulator to detect. Transmission pricing is a sufficiently complex issue that it may be enough to devise a set of transmission charges that discourage new entrants and favor the incumbent. There are certainly examples in Britain and the United States from earlier periods in which new entrants were allowed to negotiate access to customers over the incumbent's grid, but they found that there were no commercially acceptable deals to be struck. The EC Directive recognizes this danger by requiring the transmission operator to act as an independent system operator (ISO), through the device of "Chinese walls" if there is not actual independence.

A possibly more worrying aspect of the SBM is that part of the problem of a vertically integrated structure is that there was a bias toward capital-intensive and/or overengineered technologically sophisticated plant, reflecting the ambitions of the technical managers and encouraged by cost-of-service regulation. If the SB (or transmission operator) uses its own criteria to select plant, even if it is disbarred from owning competitive generation, it may exhibit the same bias as before. This incentive will be reduced by price-cap regulation, but at the (possibly small) cost of not passing through the benefits of reduced costs from more competitive bidding until the next regulatory review.

In contrast, the unbundled model in which generators bid against each other in a pool and accept the full risks of making the entry decision allows for a faster transfer of these cost reductions, provided that the pool is adequately competitive. The practical question is then whether it is possible to create a wholesale market that is adequately competitive to avoid inefficient dispatch, excess entry, and excessive prices, all of which are more likely with too few competing generators. This in turn will depend on the size of the market compared to the minimum efficient scale of generation.

An additional advantage of the pool model is that facilitates supply competition, which in turn aligns prices with costs and encourages cost reductions in metering and billing. Suppliers are free to buy from generators or in the pool at the pool or pool-related contract price, whereas in the SBM, each power station will be paid a different amount at the margin, and must be prevented from contracting for marginal sales with final consumers unless they can somehow be charged for the fixed costs. The consequence is that the SB takes all the risks of plant choice; it may find that it has inherited a set of stranded assets if at some later date a pool is introduced and consumers can contract directly with power stations.

What are the drawbacks of the pool model? First, prices would move up to the SMP, which might give windfall gains to existing generators and raise prices to consumers, especially to domestic consumers. This can be avoided by ensuring that existing generators continue to honor existing PPAs, which could be transferred to a holding company that receives the profits of bidding these plants into the pool and paying the agreed PPA terms. Such a company might in turn be jointly owned by the RECs in proportion to the number of domestic customers, and the profits could be used (as before) to subsidize the first block of domestic tariffs, via the setting of price-caps, again as at present. Second, competitive pools seem to find difficulty in ensuring adequate margins of infrequently run plant, judging from the Victorian case discussed in chapter 6. This again can be avoided by charging the ISO to contract for such plant and include the costs with other ancillary charges.

Third, a pool may or may not be perceived as more risky than contracting with the SB. If the contracts with the SB are considered secure and enforceable, then the risks should be less than a pool, which, as a competitive market, suffers both from price and demand uncertainty, and also regulatory risk from possible intervention. Finally, how would the pool model allow security of supply issues and environmental considerations to be taken into account? The latter are the more simple, since any generator wishing to enter would have to secure a license and would therefore have to meet any environmental standards that the law or the licenses require. Security of supply issues can be taken into account in a variety of ways, requiring dual fuel capability for gas-fired generation being the most straightforward. The British Fossil Fuel Levy is a means of raising revenue from fossil generation to fund renewables and nuclear power, and it operates within the pool context. Similar mechanisms can be used to ensure adequate diversity of supply, though are institutionally more demanding (but perhaps less prone to manipulation) than giving the SB the power to choose the fuel mix.

The private sector is increasingly involved in the electricity sector in developing countries, but mainly under PPAs with a single buyer, except for a few important examples in Latin America. Izaguirre (1998), drawing on data from the World Bank PPI Project Database, finds that 62 developing countries have involved the private sector in the ESI to some extent between 1990 and 1997.[6] Between 1990 and 1997 total investment in private sector electricity projects was U.S.$ 131 billions (at 1997 prices), of which over $40 billion took place in 1997 alone. East Asia accounted for about $50 billion, followed by Latin America and Caribbean with $45 billion, South Asia with $16 billion, with the rest of the world, including Eastern Europe, accounting for only $19 billion. The top ten countries accounted for three-quarters of total investment, lead by Brazil ($18b), China ($15b), Argentina ($12b), Philippines ($11b), Indonesia ($10b), India ($10b), Pakistan ($7b), Malaysia ($6b), Colombia ($6b), and Thailand ($6b). Chile (with $5b total and $347 per capita) and Argentina ($341 per capita) had the two highest levels of private investment per head of population.

Three-quarters of total investment went into stand-alone generation projects, with only 1 percent going into transmission projects and 11 percent into integrated utilities. Over half total investment went into green-field sites, and 40 percent into divestitures concentrated in Latin America and transitional countries. Asian countries have been reluctant to privatize the ESI and instead have favored single buyers contracting with IPPs under power purchase agreements (PPAs). Eight-four percent of private electricity investment in Asia went into IPPs, and 93 percent in South Asia. Asian countries, faced with high predicted rates of demand growth and poor revenue recovery from underpriced electricity, were anxious to involve the private sector to relax the investment constraint.

Izaguirre (1998) comments that failing to address the fundamental structural problems leading to underpricing made this private sector involvement problematic. The poor credit worthiness of the electricity companies and their inability to set cost-recovering tariffs made investors seek government guarantees to underwrite the PPAs. As such, the investment was effectively public sector borrowing (akin to earlier loans from the World Bank for infrastructure investment) but on more onerous private financial terms. Worse, by relaxing the investment constraint, it reduced the pressure to address the fundamental problems and stored up future difficulties. With the Asian currency crises of 1997–98 and a collapse in the demand for electricity at prices set in U.S.$, companies and governments attempted with varying degrees of success to renege on their contractual obligations, often arguing that previous governments had acted corruptly in signing the original contracts. This is likely to have a chilling effect on the willingness of private investors to build IPPs, and to make it harder for governments to persuade them to take more of the demand forecasting and price risk.

It became painfully clear that this form of private investment in power generation is equivalent to expensive foreign debt borrowed by the government. The true cost of the debt may be concealed by the terms of the PPAs, but the interest rates are inevitably high because of risk and the source of finance. Private investors inevitably borrow at higher rates of interest than institutions like the World Bank, even in stable markets, but the risk of lending to state enterprises in corrupt economies is perceived by the foreign investor to be high, particularly given attempts by governments to repudiate the debts entered into by their predecessors. Nor has this form of private involvement led to much restructuring of the sector. It has not addressed the underlying problem of non-cost-reflective tariffs set at nonremunerative levels—if anything, the currency crisis seems to have made this worse.

Contrast the effects of a currency crisis under the SBM with that under a liberalized electricity market in which IPPs sell electricity spot and under contract to final consumers. If the IPPs have confidence in the continued competitiveness of the wholesale electricity market, and the liquidity of the contract market, they will not feel the need to sign long-term contracts in order to protect their investment. Of course, they may choose to contract some part of their generation under longer-term contracts to the supply companies covering any franchise market within the distribution company's area. If so, they will doubtless take due account of the credit worthiness of the supply company (which may be backed by the assets of a distribution company) and of the general macroeconomic and financial risks facing the economy. In the event of a financial crisis with a collapse in demand and of the exchange rate, much will then depend on how the IPP is financed. If the local capital market is reasonably well developed, and the IPP has issued local debt and purchases domestically produced fuel, it will be insulated against the currency change (though not fully if the fuel is internationally traded). A collapse in electricity demand will almost certainly lead to a fall in the (dollar) spot price of electricity, reducing the profits to the IPP, and possibly leading to attempts by suppliers to renegotiate contracts. If some suppliers declare bankruptcy, the financial plight of the IPP will be adversely affected, but there is no obvious reason why the government need guarantee the terms under which the IPP chose to enter the market. The fall in spot electricity prices will be beneficial to eligible customers buying on short-term contracts, and this will reduce the deflationary effect on electricity demand. The natural monopoly transmission and distribution companies should not be particularly adversely affected by the shock. There the revenue will be indexed to inflation, and any fall in demand should be matched by a comparable fall in operating costs. Although the competitive elements of generation and supply may face financial difficulties and even bankruptcy, the plant will remain after creditors have sorted out claims, while new suppliers can enter the industry and ensure the continued viability of the ESI as a whole.

The SBM thus misallocates risks between foreign investors and the domestic electricity company where the latter remains in state ownership, and it is a poor substitute for traditional forms of financing electricity investment from multilateral sources. It risks stranding contracts that complicate further restructuring, and creates heavy debts instead of resolving the financial problems of the sector.

Some of the experiences were happier, though. The Philippines, after a long period of gross mismanagement, faced daily brownouts caused by inadequate capacity. In the haste to remedy the shortages, the first private power projects were commissioned in considerable haste under PPAs of more than 13 U.S.¢/kWh. Subsequent PPAs were put out to competitive tender and were secured at prices of 5¢ to 8¢/kWh, showing the benefits of competitive bidding. The only defense of the early procedure was that power was needed immediately, since the cost of power shortages was estimated at over 50¢/kWh. The fast-track approach of directly commissioned projects avoided delaying until a competitive auction could be designed (Klein 1998), though a limited auction might have been almost as fast and considerably cheaper.[7]

The case for privatization in developing countries is therefore strong in principle, but clearly difficult in practice in many countries. Privatization of the entire ESI forces tariffs to cost-reflective levels (at least on average) and puts pressure on the government to develop the required regulatory institutions. If investors can be convinced that the price of power is and will continue to be set by market forces rather than administrative fiat, they may require lower returns or fewer guarantees before investing. Izaguirre (1998) argues that the evidence, especially from Latin America, is that private investment is feasible in competitive electricity markets, provided that the business environment is sound. This requires politicians to abandon the patronage and redistributive policies associated with state-owned ESIs, and that they seem reluctant to do. Compared to telecoms, where the rents available are so large and where it is therefore simpler to construct deals in which almost everyone gains, serious electricity restructuring and privatization almost always results in losers as well as gainers, and it is therefore politically harder. Privatizing the distribution companies, placing them under regulatory control, and giving them the right to contract directly for power as eligible customers, removes a large part of the ability of the SB transmission company to bear the risk of long-term PPAs, and hence prompts a beneficial restructuring of the wholesale electricity market and the terms of entry into that market. It reduces the financial risk and cost to the government as lender of last resort, and hence addresses one of the fundamental problems facing the sector.

9.5.5   Gas Liberalization

Gas liberalization follows telecoms and electricity as a poor third in the speed of liberalization, largely confined to the United States and the United Kingdom, with the continent only recently galvanized by the final passage of the EC Gas Directive. In some ways this is surprising, for gas liberalization offers apparently larger efficiency gains that would benefit a wider section of the population than electricity. Whereas electricity prices are normally close to (or even below) cost (though those costs may be inflated), gas prices seem far too high in unliberalized markets. At least in advanced market economies, both industries are operated moderately efficiently (and the overmanning has a proportionately modest cost as labor costs are a small fraction of the delivered price of energy). The main gains to be reaped in gas liberalization all stem from lowering prices and creating liquid markets, which relaxes the inflexibilities in developing the system and provides incentives to deliver more gas to market more quickly.

While this apparent energy profligacy may be anathema to resource pessimists, it cannot be readily faulted on efficiency grounds and has compensating environmental attractions. Gas releases less CO_2 per useful unit of heat than other fossil fuels, so displacing coal is good for global warming. Global warming is in any case best addressed by global carbon taxes at uniform rates per ton of carbon content of fuel, and in such a fiscal regime gas would be even more attractive than it is at present in liberalized markets.

The reasons for slow liberalization were set out in chapter 8, and reflect the successful exploitation of (plausible) geopolitical concerns by incumbent gas companies. There would seem to be two possible equilibria, with the second harder to reach. In the first, as the network is built up, long-term contracts hedge risks, while supply security is ensured by keeping gas penetration low, building storage and, as networks become denser, arranging swap arrangements with other suppliers. The second, more attractive equilibrium relies on densely interconnected networks and spot markets to create something closer to a pool of gas, while electricity generation allows interruptible contracts (when CCGTs switch to gas-oil, or other generators burning different fuels change their position in the merit order).

Gas then becomes more like oil, and just as the old vertically integrated oil majors lost market share to independents with the emergence of oil spot markets in the 1970s, so gas supply industries could become less integrated and dominant. The trick is to believe that supply security is not threatened in the shift between these two patterns. Britain, admittedly with the advantage of gas self-sufficiency and numerous different producing wells and regions, could make this shift at low risk, though not without entrenched resistance from the incumbent British Gas. The Netherlands is similarly self-sufficient, and though it has fewer producers, it is well-placed as a hub of the European gas grid. Spain has adopted an aggressively liberalized approach. The evidence that the risks are not excessive is mounting.

The interesting regulatory issues to do with competition are how far market solutions can be used for the network and its key ancillary service of storage, and how extensively market solutions should be sought elsewhere. Supply, meter reading, and seasonal storage (perhaps in that order) seem well placed for unregulated competition, but trading transmission rights will require close monitoring to prevent antimonopoly abuses, since bottlenecks can be created almost anywhere in the network. An efficient network would aim to be uniformly tight (i.e., have only the required margin of spare capacity) almost everywhere. Securing a dominant position on almost any section of the pipeline gives the chance of extracting either monopoly rents, or dissipating those rents in inefficient bilateral monopoly negotiations with similarly placed traders up or downstream of the bottleneck.

The other problem with allocating transmission rights is that capacity on a route is hard to define in an interconnected network, and that capacity expansions are considerably more durable than most trading needs or likely contract durations. Finally, security of supply, which requires adequate transmission and storage, is a quasi-public good that may require nonmarket solutions. Where national high-pressure networks were created under single ownership, as in Britain, there may be little benefit in moving from regulated natural monopoly to market solutions, but where different networks compete, as in Germany, it may be simpler to move to efficient trading rather than efficient regulation. The next few years may see experiments which throw more light on this regulatory choice.

Regulation itself is set to become simpler, as good cost models for transmission networks are developed, marketed, and used by regulatory agencies in more efficient ways. Already regulation increasingly accepts the advantages of capacity-based pricing systems, where the bulk of the transmission charge is levied on peak demand, rather than volume, while price-caps are increasingly based on sensible valuations of the asset base of the network, and benchmarked assessments of operating costs. Supply competition has required expensive IT investments, but has proceeded smoothly in Britain, and with considerably less difficulty than for electricity, so the prospects for gas liberalization have never looked better. Of course, another oil shock or gas embargo from Russia might shatter this complacent assessment, but it is worth remembering that competitive oil markets have managed considerable disruptions in the past. Most of the adverse effects arose from regulatory inefficiencies and macro impacts (which should not be so important for the less valuable and less traded fuel of gas).

9.6   End of Regulation?

Public ownership and traditional cost-of-service regulation of vertically integrated network utilities both run the risk of being trapped in an inefficient equilibrium that reflects the balance of power of the various interest groups. Privatization combined with restructuring, preferably involving vertical separation, of public utilities, and liberalizing access to private utilities, can disturb this inefficient equilibrium. Together they offer the twin attractions of enabling competition for network services and facilitating higher-powered regulatory incentive schemes such as price-cap regulation for the core network natural monopoly. Both reforms require that problems of regulatory commitment are solved, ideally by creating confidence that the services are supplied in a competitive market and by effective restraints on regulatory opportunism.

The evidence presented in this book suggests that the gains from solving this problem can be substantial, but that new regulatory challenges must be met and overcome. Competition over networks has distinctive features that distinguishes it from normal market competition, for networks are rich in bottlenecks and access problems. New analytical models have increased our understanding of the nature of competition, and the need for new forms of regulation. Regulation, however, is inevitably inefficient, and should be confined to those parts of the network where market power is particularly acute. The need for regulation is least where competition is naturally intense, and this is most likely if the incumbent is unbundled to give many competing service providers with access to a network with spare capacity. Such an industrial structure will be uncomfortable. Indeed, in capital-intensive industries like electricity generation, pricing at variable cost will fail to cover full costs, leading to underinvestment until scarce capacity causes prices to rise, perhaps to politically unsustainable levels. Restructuring that leads to an uncompetitive industry runs the opposite risk of encouraging excess entry, while failing to transfer the efficiency gains to consumers.

Liberalization where feasible looks attractive, but we are left with the list of questions posed in chapter 1: Will the forces that caused convergence to regulated vertical integration reassert themselves? Are we just witnessing a transient historical episode, or can the benefits of competition be protected against the pressure to reintegrate and monopolize? Is it possible to retain the benefits of competition in an equilibrium industrial structure—an equilibrium that balances the interests of the industry, the consumers, and the state through a stable set of institutions? The answers may not yet be obvious, but we can nevertheless draw some preliminary conclusions.

The pressures for horizontal integration are widely evident as constraints on mergers are removed by privatization and deregulation. Such mergers are often subject to more searching antimonopoly investigation than in other industries, given the sensitive political nature of the services supplied and the need to preserve benchmark competition. Pressures for vertical integration in unbundled electricity have been intense in Britain, while some countries have made cross-ownership of generation and transmission illegal in an attempt to restrict reintegration. In both horizonal and vertical integration there may be genuine synergies, but there are frequently greater dangers of increased market power that will require vigilance by the competition authorities to resist. Liberalization evidently does not mean the cessation of regulatory oversight needed to prevent the abuse of market power, which is arguably even more necessary for network utilities than other industries where entry is normally easier. The more difficult question of whether (and/or which) competitive and lightly regulated network utilities are politically sustainable remains to be answered by the test of time. The study of network utilities should continue to engage the interest of economists and policy makers for a good while to come.

Appendix: Excess Entry in Oligopolies

Firms are identical, so each produces the same amount $q(n)$ when there are n firms in the industry. Let $C(q)$ be the total per firm cost of producing output q, and consider the welfare of a representative agent who buys the product as a consumer and receives the profits as a shareholder. Let $V(p, y)$ be the indirect utility function for this consumer facing price p and receiving income y, which derives solely from profit, $\pi = n(pq - C(q))$, which free entry will reduce to zero in equilibrium. Differentiate welfare at this equilibrium:

$$\frac{d}{dn} V(p, \pi) = \frac{\partial V}{\partial p} \frac{dp}{dn} + \frac{\partial V}{\partial y} \frac{d\pi}{dn}$$

$$= V_y \left(-nq \frac{dp}{dn} + (pq - C) + n \left[(p - C') \frac{dq}{dn} + q \frac{dp}{dn} \right] \right)$$

$$= V_y n (p - C') \frac{dq}{dn}.$$

The second line follows from Roy's identity that consumer demand is $-V_p/V_y = nq$, where subscripts refer to partial derivatives, and V_y is the marginal utility of income y. The last line follows from noting that in equilibrium, profits $pq - C$ are zero. If there are entry costs that prevent unlimited entry so that firms retain market power, then prices will be above marginal cost, or $p > C'$. Then, as more firms enter output per firm will drop, or $dq/dn < 0$, so the whole expression will be negative. Thus at the free entry equilibrium, reducing the number of firms in the industry (and thereby economizing on the entry costs, or allowing each firm to operate at larger scale and lower average costs) will improve welfare.

This argument assumes that there are no beneficial distributional effects from entry, for all profits are equally divided among all consumers, so any fall in profits is felt as a fall in consumer income. If profits are received by the richer consumers, and the goods or services are relatively more important for poorer consumers, then entry that drives down prices and profits will have an advantageous distributional effect which may be enough to offset the loss in total money value added. The effect of the entry of identical firms on distributional equity can be addressed by the same techniques used for the social cost–benefit analysis of privatization in the appendix to chapter 3. Consider the impact of entry on a social welfare function, $W(V^1, \ldots, V^h, \ldots, V^H)$, defined over individual utility:

$$\frac{\partial W}{\partial n} = \sum_h \frac{\partial W}{\partial V^h}\left(V_p^h \frac{dp}{dn} + V_y^h \theta_h \frac{d\pi}{dn}\right) = \sum_h \beta^h\left(-q^h \frac{dp}{dn} + \theta^h \frac{d\pi}{dn}\right),$$

where q^h is demand for the good by household h and θ^h is its share in total profits, $\pi = n(pq - C(q))$, and where

$$\beta^h \equiv \frac{\partial W}{\partial V^h} \cdot \frac{\partial V^h}{\partial y}$$

is the social marginal utility of transferring £1 to agent h. As in the appendix to chapter 3, define the distributional characteristic of the good in consumption as d_c and of the profit shares as d_π:

$$d_c \equiv \frac{\sum_h \beta^h q^h}{\bar{\beta} n q}, \quad nq = \sum_h q_i^h, \quad \bar{\beta} \equiv \frac{1}{H}\sum_h \beta^h,$$

$$d_\pi \equiv \frac{\sum_h \beta^h \theta^h}{\bar{\beta}}, \quad \sum_h \theta^h = 1.$$

Here nq is aggregate consumption of the good and $\bar{\beta}$ is the average over the H agents of β^h, so d_c is a measure of how concentrated the consumption of good is on the socially deserving (those with high social marginal values of consumption, β^h), and d_π measures the extent to which profits go to the deserving. The derivative of social welfare with respect to the number of firms is now:

$$\frac{dW}{dn} = nq\frac{dp}{dn}(d_\pi - d_c) + d_\pi n(p - C')\frac{dq}{dn}.$$

As before, the second term is negative, and so is dp/dn as prices will fall with entry, but if profits are relatively less equally distributed than consumption, as one would expect, then $d_\pi < d_c$. The first term will be positive, and it may be sufficient to offset the second term, making entry a way of improving the income distribution.

Notes

Chapter 1

1. The data are taken from OECD (1996) *Historical Statistics*, tables 6.5 and 6.6, constructed backward taking most recent figures. The source gives EC or EU15 figures, but not on a consistent basis for the whole period. OECD-Europe tracks EU15 very closely over the past decade. The figures for the United Kingdom are from the same source to ensure comparability across countries.

2. The methodology is set out in *Economic Trends*, CSO (May 1987, pp. 92–119).

3. Jacobson and Tarr (n.d.) observe that electric output could be easily measured and the quality of public service aspects (street lighting) readily monitored, while neither was true for water (quality improvements, fire hydrant availability, and pressure). This made contracting costs higher for water thus favoring public ownership. Differences in transaction costs thus accounted for different institutional solutions for water and electricity.

Chapter 2

1. Railways, trams, post, and telecommunications, electricity, gas, and water supply.

2. Sharkey (1982) defines natural monopoly for a multiproduct firm by the property that the cost function be strictly globally subadditive, $C(\Sigma q^i) < \Sigma C(q^i)$, where q^i is the vector of outputs of the ith firm.

3. See, for example, Berg and Tschirhart (1988), Lowry (1973), and Sharkey (1982).

4. For a nontechnical introduction and guide to the more technical literature, see Gibbons (1997), or chapter 11 of Tirole (1988). Kreps (1990) sets out the uses and limitations of game theory well.

5. Some game theorists would not distinguish between actions and strategies, arguing that rationality and the information available will determine the rules for selecting actions, and similarly that rationality will lead to a natural choice of equilibrium. The aim here is to choose an inclusive approach that allows each step to be discussed.

6. Again, the model simplifies. In some regulatory regimes there is a well-defined regulatory period (typically five years in Britain), at the end of which the utility will present plans for investment to be undertaken in the next period. The critical issue is how large

is the new investment required compared to demand, and this will depend on the rate of growth of demand and the length of the regulatory period. In this simple model we just vary the length of the period, which can then be interpreted to cover a range of cases.

7. The story can be made more complicated, and would change if other potential entrants were waiting to see the outcome of entry in this particular market in order to judge whether to enter elsewhere. As we will see, strategies in repeated games can support a wide variety of outcomes.

8. Greenwald (1984) discusses the view that a fair rate of return might be one that equates the market to book value of the stock. In the 1960s the average ratio of the market to book value of regulated electric power utilities was greater than two.

9. Disallowing capital costs shrinks the utility's rate base and thus reduces the rate of return that the firm actually earns on its total investments, even if the firm's allowed rate of return is unchanged.

10. See, for example, Mitchell and Vogelsang (1991).

11. The FCC was able to change its system of regulation under the old 1934 Communications Act, which was sufficiently broad that it did not seriously constrain the form of regulation. The Chilean legislation is far more specific.

12. Why this was profitable will be explained in chapter 5, but briefly, generators are paid for capacity declared available, even if it is not required. These payments depend on the total level of capacity on the system relative to peak demand on the day. By declaring capacity unavailable the day before when the prices are computed, these payments can be driven up to very high levels, whereas redeclaring them available allows them to enjoy these high payments as the capacity payments were not recomputed to reflect actual availability on the day of dispatch.

13. Frydman et al. (1993a,b) document the progress in the CEE countries until roughly June 1992. Jarái (1993) and Mihályi (1993, 1995) give further details for Hungary. Mejstrik (1997) describes the Czech case.

14. The first section in this chapter noted that the response of Jamaica Telephone Co in 1962 to the Jamaican government's intention to renegotiate the terms of its license upon expiry in 1966 was to stop all investment.

15. Nevertheless, Spiller (1993) argues that Argentina failed to attract much foreign interest when it privatized its telephone companies precisely because of obscurities in the proposed regulation and tariff setting rules, and some countries have had to accept low sales prices and high rates of return earned by the foreign private operators who are anxious to recoup their investment before they are caught in a regulatory trap. Our model with the regulator as the single representative of the diverse interests of the politicians, the people, and other interest groups oversimplifies here, and conflicts between these groups may undermine the credibility of regulation even under the favorable circumstances apparently available to telecoms privatization.

16. The South West Hungarian Electricity Supply Company (ESC) was bought by Bayernwerke AG; the Budapest ESC, Northern Hungarian ESC, and Matra Power Plant all by RWE Energie AG/Energie-Versorgung Schwaben AG; the Eastern Hungarian ESC by Isar-Amperwerke AG; the Southern Hungarian ESC and North-West Hungarian ESC both by EdF International SA; and the Dunamenti Power Plant by Powerfin SA. The total sales proceeds for the ordinary shares together with options to buy 50 percent plus one

vote were $1.3 billion, accepted by the Board on December 6, 1995. Tenders for five power companies and MVM Rt were declared void at the same meeting.

Chapter 3

1. Detailed notes on the sources of and qualifications for the data are to be found in World Bank (1995).

2. The power sector would be able to finance all investment at an unchanged gearing ratio if the financial rate of return exceeded the rate of growth of capacity. The average annual rate of growth of power was about 7 percent p.a. for middle-income countries between 1960 and 1990, compared to an average *economic* (but not financial) rate of return on World Bank projects of 11 percent (World Bank 1994a, fig. 3, table 1.2). Had the financial rate of return been raised to the economic rate of return, financing should not have been a problem.

3. In the World Bank' classification, middle-income developing countries are those with a per capita GNP of between $750 and $9,000 (in 1994 U.S.$), ranging from Bolivia to Argentina and South Korea.

4. Even this is not invariably true. When British Rail was restructured and privatized, the train-operating companies submitted bids to operate services on designated routes specifying the level of subsidy they required to maintain the timetabled frequency of service, and to lease rolling stock and pay track access charges.

5. The proper written-down value is better estimated from the cost of replacement with a modern equivalent asset and the time remaining before the replacement is required. The United Kingdom attempted to do this in reaching a written-down current cost valuation of assets of the utilities before they were privatized.

6. Following Farrell (1957), technical efficiency is measured as the extent to which the utility reaches the technical production frontier, variously estimated, while cost efficiency is the extent to which the utility minimizes costs at prevailing input prices. A utility can be technically efficient but not minimize its costs. Even if it minimizes costs, unless it faces efficient input prices, the outcome will not be allocatively efficient.

7. If entry continues until firms make zero excess profit, the last entrant reduces the scale of each previous firm. As prices remain above marginal costs at the zero profit equilibrium, the social loss cause by entry is the excess of price over marginal cost times the fall in output of the existing firms (Armstrong, Cowan, and Vickers 1994, p. 107, and the appendix to chapter 9 below).

8. The city of Hull retained ownership of its local telephone company until 1999.

9. This is net of short-run transmission losses of $22 million p.a.; it does not include the return to the sunk cost of the transmission interconnectors. This is reasonable as the gains are additional to those already secured through any bilateral trading. It does, however, ignore transmission losses, which may be serious, and the question of the likely net gains is considered further in section 6.5.5.

10. The approximation is exact for linear demand schedules and zero income effects; this is remarkably accurate for small changes in price and cost.

11. Equal lump-sum transfers were used by the Czechoslovak government in 1990 when the government abolished food subsidies (Heady and Smith 1995). The point about

transferring revenue raised in proportion to expenditure and giving back equal amounts to all is that if expenditure increases with income (as it does for almost all goods) the transfer hands back more to the poorer half of the population than it takes, and thus protects them while benefiting a majority of consumers.

12. If, on the other hand, implausibly, the only distortion in an otherwise optimal system of taxation is the underpricing of the utility, social welfare will be equally advantaged by an equal lump-sum transfer as an equal diminution of indirect taxes, since at the optimum redistribution is best done by lump-sum transfers (mostly in kind as health, welfare, or education) which at the margin have to be balanced against the cost of increasing indirect (and direct) taxes.

13. Government revenue is taken as the numeraire, and a social-welfare maximizing government would value lump-sum transfers to consumers as equally valuable (if not, they could be increased or reduced). Consumer surplus is only equally valuable if the income elasticity of demand is zero; otherwise, richer consumers enjoy relatively higher surplus. In industrial countries like Britain, income elasticities for gas, water, telephones, and electricity are so low that this effect can be ignored, though not necessarily in developing or transitional countries.

14. All figures are December 1987 Chilean pesos, where Ch$238.14 = U.S.$1.

15. The government announced in late 1983 before privatization that only Mercury and BT would be licensed to operate a nationwide network. This "duopoly policy" was to be reviewed in 1990.

16. By 1989, CTC had 800,000 installed lines.

17. All amounts are in U.S.$.

18. Carso/Southwestern Bell/France Télecom paid U.S.$1.76 billion for 20.4 percent of 5.2 million lines in 1990.

19. The force of utilitarianism is that it is *individualistic*; that is, it respects individual well-being as measured by the individual utility function. It is also *consequentialist*, in confining attention to outcomes, rather than processes or rights (though these can be included by restrictions on either information or policy variables).

20. The higher weighted average distributional characteristic in Hungary reflects the very much more equal distribution of income and expenditure, and hence the lower variation in budget shares of different goods across the population, than in the United Kingdom.

21. Individual demand for good i is $q_i^h = \gamma_i + b_i \, (m^h + g - \Sigma \gamma_j p_j)/p_i$, and $\tau = \Sigma b_j t_j / p_j$, bearing in mind that $t_i = 0$. The linear expenditure system has strong implications for optimal commodity taxes; see, for example, Deaton (1987). However, the main purpose of this section is to place d_i in context.

22. Thus looking across different goods, including different utilities, the various factors ε_i, μ_i, and d_i all offset each other when $m_i = \tau$.

23. If consumers are essentially identical (except for observable and unalterable characteristics, such as age) and preferences are separable, then commodity taxes should be uniform (provided all goods can be taxed). See Atkinson and Stiglitz (1980, ch. 14) and, for extensions, Deaton and Stern (1986). Part of the argument for uniform commodity taxes is that it is hard to imagine constructing an empirically convincing case for differ-

ential taxes that would increase the efficiency of the tax system by encouraging more effort and less leisure (Deaton 1987).

Chapter 4

1. Initially the British Electricity Authority, then the Central Electricity Authority, and, from 1958 after a reorganization clarifying the independence of the area boards, the CEGB.

2. The CEGB covers only England and Wales, with Scotland and Northern Ireland under separate organizations. After privatization, the *Digest of U.K. Energy Statistics* only gives figures for the United Kingdom as a whole.

3. The contrast with the French approach to nuclear power is instructive. After exhaustive analysis that paid considerably more attention to operating experience than design optimism, the French standardized on the PWR and achieved an impressive indigenous manufacturing capability as well as substantial economies of scale by replication.

4. In Germany the fraction of autogeneration was nearly 40 percent (47 TWh) as late as 1961. Thereafter the amount increased slowly so the share fell to 13 percent by 1987, in response to financial disincentives of the utilities (Müller and Stahl 1996, pp. 284, 302). In the United States, bypass or self-generation that avoids the high costs of regulated electricity has been a potent force for liberalizing generation and transmission.

5. The increase in productivity in Nuclear Electric came largely from improving the previously dismal performance of the advanced gas-cooled reactors, though there were staff reductions at headquarters as well. Employment in nuclear power stations is heavily influenced by safety requirements—a form of regulation that is unavoidable even under private ownership.

6. In futures markets the contracts for delivery of a commodity at a future date are "marked to market" at the end of each trading session. The futures buyer deposits only a small margin of the agreed price, in exchange for a promise to pay the full amount at the delivery if the contract is not sold before. If the futures price falls, the temptation is for the buyer to renege on his contract and buy at the now lower price, so his account with the exchange is shown as have assets equal to the margin plus the value of the futures contract and liabilities equal to the original agreed futures price. The exchange will call for additional margin to ensure that the assets sufficiently exceed the liabilities, and the amount is determined by revaluing the futures contract, or marking it to market.

7. U.S. Department of Commerce *Statistical Abstract of the United States 1995*.

8. This joint allocation of regulatory responsibility with the attendant goal of universal service were set down in the Communications Act of 1934.

9. The "above 890 Mc" decision, 27 FCC 359.

10. It also filed against the monopoly in telecommunications equipment and sought the divestiture of Western Electric, but this by itself would probably not have been sufficient grounds for bringing a suit.

11. Concepts such as contestability, constrained market pricing, access pricing, and the efficient component pricing rule were directly applicable to problems of pricing

telephone services (and other network utilities), though much of this work was published after the breakup. See Mitchell and Vogelsang (1991) for a recent survey of the theory of pricing telecommunications.

Chapter 5

1. Relative productivity is defined as real output per person of the industry divided by output per person employed in U.K. manufacturing industry. CEGB productivity is an index of kWh per person employed in the CEGB or successor companies, taken from Newbery and Pollitt (1997). BT's productivity is measured as real turnover per person employed, deflating the value of turnover by the index of retail prices of domestic telephones (CSO 1996). (Turnover before 1984–85 is taken from Armstrong, Cowan, and Vickers 1994, and after from CRI 1995.) If, as seems likely, business prices fell faster than domestic prices, then productivity growth will be understated.

2. The macroeconomic crisis of 1984 in New Zealand precipitated both the election which returned a Labour government and the subsequent reform program. Their first priority was to improve the efficiency of state-owned enterprises, with privatization as a possible part of this. Nevertheless, the logic of privatization has been compelling in most cases, except for the electricity industry. Later governments found less popular support for electricity privatization, which remained the only significant state-owned enterprise in 1998.

3. Nor is this indefensible. It has been proposed in the United States that stranded assets in generation be recovered by a competition transition charge collected from users of transmission. If new technology such as combined cycle gas turbine generation makes older technology no longer competitive, there is a sound economic case for writing down the book value of older plant to the present value of the remaining profit stream, valuing the output at the cost of production by new technology. Views may reasonably differ about these as yet unknown future costs. Another technique is to transfer all head office and service functions to the core and make them available within the company at (short-run) marginal cost.

4. After deducting taxes, at both current exchange rates and PPP exchange rates (from IEA, *Energy Prices and Taxes*, 1997).

5. One of the problems the authors find in making comparisons before and after corporatization is the lack of good accounting information when the industry was in the Ministry of Energy, so the figures quoted should be treated with caution.

6. If managers were rewarded with a share of the increased profits, they may be persuaded to maximize profit in a more commercial fashion, but SOEs seems reluctant to espouse the high salaries that the private sector finds acceptable, perhaps because of greater fear of corruption (or the public perception of corruption) where state property is at stake.

7. The joint ownership model runs the risk of poor shareholder monitoring and the lack of credible takeover threats; it may prove even less efficient than subscale local utilities.

8. The counterargument that managers with share options may conspire to undervalue the company by delaying cost reductions until after flotation is less of a problem if managers have to compete with each other and run the risk of being sacked before their options are granted.

9. Different kinds of storage deal with imbalances between demand and supply over different time periods and for different reasons. Short-run imbalances within the day can be dealt with to some extent by varying the pressure in the high-pressure pipeline (line pack) which is clearly best managed by the pipeline operator. Short-term shortages caused by transmission constraints may be dealt with from storage close to the customers in the constrained region (in Britain, using old gasometers or LNG—liquefied natural gas—which can be regasified at short notice). Seasonal storage in Britain is supplied by a single large depleted gas field, and salt caverns. All might be separated and marketed, apart from possible fears of market power.

10. Modern equivalent asset costs for local loops were estimated at $700 on average in 1992, which is more than half the total cost per subscriber of providing the entire network service.

11. A therm is 100,000 BTU or 29.3 kWh. Thus 10 therms = 1 MBTU (million BTU), the standard unit in the United States and international gas markets. Gas in the United Kingdom is now denominated in kWh.

12. Thus entrants face more onerous connection terms, and while Hydro Electric's application for an additional 1,000 MW of capacity was unopposed and granted, Powergen's application to build a 300 MW plant was resisted by Scottish Power and referred to public inquiry. Finally the Scottish Grid Codes do not give adequate rules for the dispatch of independent generators, creating further uncertainty.

13. The cost of this residual risk should not be exaggerated, nor should the ingenuity of the traders in devising a variety of instruments (a whole range of options) to manage the remaining risk be underestimated. Indeed, it has been argued that the necessity of trading actively in the market and attempting to understand the nature of risks forces the supply companies to try and understand their customers' needs to the greater efficiency of the industry as a whole.

Chapter 6

1. More accurately, he asked the regulator to consider how a review of electricity trading arrangements might be undertaken and to draw up terms of reference, which lead to a consultation document published on November 5, 1997, and to a final report by the Office of Electricity Regulation in July 1998 (Offer 1998c).

2. It has been argued that if the grid is responsible for securing ancillary services through competitive bidding, then the same conflict of interest arises if it owns some suppliers of these ancillary services, so complete unbundling is still desirable.

3. One MW (megawatt) is 1 million watts, or 1,000 kW. The United Kingdom peak demand is roughly 1 kW/person. Electricity consumption is measured in kWh (the standard domestic unit), MWh (megawatt hour) = 1,000 kWh, the standard unit for bulk trading in electricity pools (so £10/kWh = 1 p/kWh, $10/MWh = 10 mills/kWh = 1 ¢/kWh). One GWh (gigawatt hour) = 1,000 MWh, and 1 TWh (terrawatt hours) = 1,000 GWh = 10 kWh. England and California each consume about 270 TWh/yr.

4. The Labour government elected in 1997 granted greater autonomy to Scotland, and accepted the wishes of the 50.1 percent of the voting residents in a referendum to create a separate Welsh assembly.

5. This uses turbines to pump water up to a reservoir at the top of a hill during off-peak periods, where it can be released to generate in peak periods or when called upon to meet a short-fall in generation.

6. A good example is the typical demand surge during the interval of popular TV programs like the World Cup, when large numbers of people simultaneously switch on electric kettles, creating sudden surges of 1,000 to 2,000 MW.

7. Henney (1994) gives the detailed background history, and notes that Merz and McLellan had been involved in the original design of the grid in the 1920s.

8. A generating set is the smallest generating unit, and each power station may have three or more such sets.

9. Offer (1998c, table 1) gives as an example Ferrybridge unit 2, which set SMP at £42.07/MWh in the period ending at 7.30 PM on November 27, 1997. The start-up price was £4,900, the no-load price was £9,790/h, and the three incremental prices were all set at the same level of £10.52/MWh. The set generated 1,707 MWh over five hours, so SMP = $((4{,}900 + (9{,}750*5))/1{,}707 + 10.52 = 42.07$. The start-up cost averaged over the five hours amounts to 7 percent of SMP, but the no-load cost paid each hour accounts for 68 percent of the SMP, and the incremental cost is only 25 percent of the SMP. There are additional subtleties that start-up and no-load costs are only spread over table A hours, which are defined as those hours in which there is less than 1,000 MW of spare scheduled capacity.

10. Measuring volatility by the standard deviation in U.S.$/MWh alone, Victoria went from $20 in 1995 to $55 in 1997, New Zealand remained at $8, Norway at $5, while England and Wales went from $75 to $24.

11. The deadweight losses vary with demand—at peak demand they are equal to the roughly triangular area DBX formed by dropping a vertical from D to meet the marginal cost line at a point X. As demand varies, it intersects the supply function and marginal cost function at different points to define smaller triangles, whose sum is total deadweight loss.

12. This result is reminiscent of, but more powerful than, the effect of varying the number of competing Nash-Cournot oligopolists, n, supplying a market with linear demand and constant marginal cost. In that case total deadweight loss falls as $1/(n+1)^2$.

13. Though not below the opportunity cost of the fuel, which was on take-or-pay terms and could only have been exported at a low price or stored expensively for several years.

14. In fact Electricité de France also benefited by an exemption from the fossil fuel levy which effectively allowed it to sell at the market price for generation *plus* the levy of a tenth of the *final* price of electricity—this was worth £95 million in 1991–92 but was phased out when all nuclear electricity became leviable from June 1998.

15. Connah's Quay, built in 1996, cost £368/kW and had 55 percent GCV efficiency. With gas at 15 p/therm (£1.5/mmBTU or U.S.$2.4/mmBTU), 80 percent load factor, and 75 percent debt finance over ten years, the levelized average cost is 2 p/kWh.

16. Pool prices were set by PSB the remainder of the time, but PSB buys from the pool at night and sells in the peak afternoon periods. NP and PG can arrange for the nighttime price to remain high, encouraging PSB to bid to support high afternoon prices, thus indirectly setting prices for this last 10 percent of the time.

17. The defense of the earn-out payments is that they reflect a (generous) assessment of the cost of fitting flue gas desulphurisation (FGD) equipment, which is taken as the value of the associated sulfur credits transferred with the stations, and which should ensure that stations with FGD will be dispatched ahead of these stations. In 1997–98 National Power's FGD station at Drax had a load factor of 77 percent (the highest of any of its coal stations), but PowerGen's FGD Ratcliffe station operated only at 48 percent, down from 81 percent in 1995–96 (Offer 1998d). The regulator has allowed these payments, but only for eight years.

18. Green (1998) tabulates the offers by each REC in each area for a 3,300 kWh customer and shows that in most cases the incumbent REC charges the highest price in its own region and undercuts incumbents in other regions.

19. The limits, set in MW of capacity, were based on 15 percent of the maximum demand in each REC's area. The limits were based on the REC's share of the equity in a station, rather than their purchases, and so the limit could allow a REC to buy more than half the energy it needs for the franchise market. By 1998 the actual share was 21 percent.

20. The first figure is the amount needed to justify FGD (Newbery 1994a), comparable to the values revealed in U.S. sulfur auctions (but lower than some estimates of the damage), while the second figure is a rough estimate of the possible externality cost of global warming (Pearce 1993) of $2/barrel oil. Note this is below the proposed EC carbon component of the carbon-energy tax at its final full rate of $5/barrel oil equivalent in 1992 prices (and the total tax would be $10/barrel, but of that $5 would be for energy and hence identical for all fuels if measured on electricity output).

21. Turnover was used by Galal et al. (1994) as the scaling factor, though it makes the ratios of present discounted gains to annual turnovers tend to be rather large. At 6 percent discount rate, the ratio of the present discounted benefits to turnover can be multiplied by 0.06 to give a comparison of annualized gains to annual turnover. The turnover of the ESI (including distribution) of England and Wales was £16 billion, while that of Scotland was £1.9 billion and of NIE was about £0.5 billion. There is an obvious problem in making comparisons across the three cases as Scotland and NIE are vertically integrated, while the case study of the CEGB excludes the RECs. The approach taken is to relate the CEGB to total ESI turnover and ignore any REC improvements, which understates its performance.

22. For example, see the evidence of Sir Alastair Frame and Michael Prior to the Sizewell Inquiry (Layfield 1987; Prior 1983). Thus the CEGB estimated that the cost of a coal alternative to Sizewell would be £664/kw (£1982) compared with an average for U.S. and European plants of £490/kw, or 136 percent of this average. But the CEGB's average cost overrun on coal-fired plant was 18 percent in real terms at this date, bringing the costs to more than 50 percent that of the average elsewhere (cited in Henney 1991, p. 119).

23. From 1996 to 1998 Norway allowed regional prices to differ, but Sweden maintained a single price, rather like England and Wales. The systems operators collected the revenue from trade between zones of different price and used them to lower transmission charges. In 1997 there was a single price for 5,200 hours out of the 8,760.

24. Data can be conveniently downloaded from http://www.nordpool.no/

25. The spot and futures prices can be downloaded from the web site.

26. ENDESA spun off the transmission assets into Transelec in 1993, though it is not clear whether this will solve the problem of preferential access.

27. Originally SMP was set by the most expensive thermal set called on, though this restriction has been lifted and the SMP can be set either by thermal or hydro plant.

28. Market reports can be downloaded from http://www.neca.com.au/links.

29. Kahn, Bailey, and Pando (1997) also modeled the gains from pooling over a wider area including California, and their estimates, which use a more satisfactory methodology, are only about one-tenth those of White. Their claims are discussed further below.

30. Prices and other information can be viewed on the web sites http://www.caiso.com and http://www.capx.com.

31. Though at each periodic review, the allowable revenue is related to the capital base, which would be increased and take the form of higher systems charges for remaining users.

32. The early capacity charges were supplemented with kWh charges which were ended after the review. Generators facing negative payments are paid on the lower of their registered capacity and the average of their generation on the highest three half-hours each separated by ten days. Consumers have to pay according to their demand on the three half-hours of system maximum demand that are 10 days apart, and their charges are almost a mirror image, being £0.88/kW in the north and £16.26/kW in Peninsular in 1997–98.

33. The average marginal loss between North and Peninsular is 12 percent, so if the load factor is 66 percent and half the costs are variable, the variable loss is $12 \times \frac{2}{3} \times \frac{1}{2} = 4$ percent.

34. The zonal differential between the north and Peninsula is £18/kW annually, which is about half the annual interest and depreciation on the capital cost of CCGT, while annual cost differences are only 12 percent, suggesting that the zonal prices signals are very strong.

35. The DGES also published a set of objectives that were similar to but rather less precise than these (Newbery 1998a).

36. There are additional complications caused by the unreasonable behavior of the Environment Agency in imposing site-specific sulfur emissions, and requiring new owners to meet tighter standards, discussed in Newbery (1998a).

37. This is taken from Newbery (1998b), which in turn builds on Green and Newbery (1992).

38. Wolfram (1997) shows that many of the predictions of the two approaches are the same, as well as testing them empirically using English pool data.

39. Consumers suffer from increasing price variability about an unchanged average as they buy more at higher (peak demand) prices than at lower prices.

Chapter 7

1. Thus GTE has recently bid U.S.$1.8 billion for 56 percent of Puerto Rico Telephone, which has 1.5 million lines, while Tisa bid $1.925 billion, suggesting a price of nearly $2,300/line (FT, 15/7/98). Wellenius (1994) reports bids varying from U.S.$700/line for

the earlier Chile privatizations, up to $3,300/line for Venezuela in 1991, compared with the cost of building a network of perhaps $1,000 to $1,500 per line. Bids for mobile telephone companies may be three times asset value, reflecting the value of the customer base and its associated profit stream.

2. If the price were the unconstrained monopoly price, the implied demand elasticity would be given by $p/(p - m)$, where p is the price, 55 cents, and m is the marginal cost (8.57 cents), and would be 1.18. However, the vagaries of the international settlement system (described in the next section) and the presence of some competition rule out such a simple deduction.

3. At an elasticity of 2, calling would have increased to 13 hours per head and the deadweight loss would have been $2,500 million.

4. The U.S. Federal Communications Commission announced on August 7, 1997 (IB Docket 96–261), that it would significantly lower international settlement rates. U.S. consumers paid on average 88¢/min for international calls compared to 13¢/min U.S. long-distance calls, and proposed establishing benchmark rates of 15¢/min for high-income countries—about one-sixth the average prevailing rate.

5. In late 1998 one company was offering calls from the United Kingdom to the United States at 3p or 4.5¢/min, which rivals claimed had to be below cost, meaning the cost of the interconnection at each end.

6. The regression of revenue per line against GNP per capita fits slightly better, with an R^2 of 0.3, and a slope coefficient of 0.024, so an increase in per capita income of $1,000 might be expected to increase line revenue by $24.

7. A regression of $\ln Q$ on $\ln P$, where Q is the penetration rate and P is the effective cost, has a slope (i.e., a price elasticity) of -1.089 with a standard error of 0.04, which is significantly greater than unity in absolute value ($R^2 = 0.93$).

8. In most, but not all, cases all operators have the same accounting rates.

9. OECD (1997, tab. 6) compares its estimate of the termination rate with the settlement rate, taking the former as the cost of a rather inefficient 64 kb/s leased line and any local charges. The average termination charge is 10¢/min with a range from 6¢ to 17¢/min, but since it is also based on charges, it overstates the true cost.

10. Both WTO and FCC current information is readily accessed via the web at http://www.fcc.gov and http://www.wto.org/services/ (as is OECD and Oftel information).

11. Mason (1996) compares PSTN, Analogue Mobile, Digital Mobile, Private Circuits, Virtual Private Networks, High Speed Data Services, and Specially Tariffed Services, as well as calling cards.

12. The simplest form of compression is to indicate only when the image changes—perhaps from a blank to a letter in a fax, or to indicate which parts in a sequence of moving images need to be updated.

13. A modem converts the digital signals from the computer or fax machine into analogue signals to send over the twisted copper pair to the local switch (where it may be converted back into a digital signal). The modem creates a carrier wave which it *modulates* with the digital signal, and *demodulates* the incoming carrier wave to recover the

digital information—hence *modem*. Different frequencies and forms of modulation (amplitude, or phase, or both) allow increasing amounts of information to be sent over the same wire.

14. Claims that inappropriate equipment might damage the network have always seemed suspect, and might better have been met by allowing the telephone company to sue for damage and the equipment provider to provide guaranteed quality.

15. Gross output, including materials, Tornquist-weighted 3-factor total factor productivity.

16. On September 4, 1998, the Fifth Circuit Court of Appeals in New Orleans reversed the lower court judgment that key sections of the 1996 Telecommunications Act were unconstitutional for unfairly singling out the RBOCs, though the plaintiffs are expected to appeal to the Supreme Court, which must also adjudicate on the pricing conditions imposed on the unbundled parts of the network. Litigation continues to plague the process of liberalizing the local markets.

17. BT's productivity is measured as real turnover per person employed, deflating the value of turnover given in Armstrong, Cowan, and Vickers (1994) by the index of retail prices of domestic telephones from the CSO *Monthly Digest of Statistics*. CEGB productivity is an index of kWh per person employed in the CEGB or successor companies from Newbery and Pollitt (1997). Industrial productivity is manufacturing output per person employed, also from the CSO *Monthly Digest of Statistics*. The graphs are of the ratios of the labor productivity of each industry to the index of industrial productivity.

18. Comparing lines per employee across countries and over time runs into problems if different telecoms companies have different policies on subcontracting, though the productivity trends are less prone to these difficulties.

19. The average cost per customer per year including line rentals for a six-line business customer.

20. They have the additional advantage for potential entrants that the initial investment in transmitters is low, with most of the cost embodied in the receiver station on the house, which is proportional to the number of subscribers (and hence revenue) and can be relocated at negligible cost if the subscriber discontinues service—unlike cable and traditional local loops.

21. The German regulator shocked Deutsche Telecom by imposing an access charge of 2.7 pfennig/min (1.5¢/min) in 1998.

22. There are several options for CPS—either a choice of carrier for each of long-distance and international, *or* a choice of a single carrier for all calls (local, mobile, L-D, and international).

23. There are several solutions to giving equal access to different carriers, though it seems preferable for the customer to choose which one is simplest to dial, rather than giving that right to the incumbent.

24. It is normally claimed that the line rental is too low compared to the fixed costs; on the other hand, there are subsidies from long-distance, so the variable element may still be calculable as before.

25. Modern equivalent asset costs for local loops were estimated at $700 on average in 1992.

Chapter 8

1. If the spot price of gas is p_g, that of electricity is p_e, and the thermal efficiency (GCV, as a percentage) is e, then gas should be sold in the spot market rather than being turned into electricity if $ep_e < 100 p_g$. Thus, if $e = 50$ percent, and $p_g = 0.5$ p/kWh (14.65 p/therm, £1.465/MBTU (million British thermal units, about $2.4/MBTU), the fuel cost of generation is 1 p/kWh or £10/MWh. Other use-related costs should be included in deciding whether to bid into the electricity pool, such as start-up costs and those maintenance costs related to operation.

2. The ratio of electricity to gas costs per kWh (excluding all standing charges for both fuels and taking the Economy 7 electricity tariff) has varied from 2.92 to 3.14 with an average of 3.01 from 1993 to 1997. The average ratio of electricity to gas prices for very large industrial users has varied from 4.6 to 7 in the United Kingdom but is considerably lower in some continental countries.

3. The load factor is the inverse of the swing. These and other technical details are available in MMC (1993) and refer to 1992.

4. Gas units are more than usually complicated, as gas is variously measured by volume or heat content (usually gross calorific value but sometimes net, meaning net calorific value = 0.9 GCV). Heat content in Britain was measured in therms (100,000 BTU) until recently, but it is now usually measured in kWh (29.27 kWh/therm), though MJ and kilocalories and tonnes oil equivalent are variously used. Volume is measured either in cubic feet (cf) (in the United States and in the United Kingdom until recently) or cubic meters (cm). One cubic meter of gas has a calorific value of approximately 10 kWh (10.68), so 1 million cm (Mcm) is about 10 GWh. 1 million cf (Mcf) is roughly 1,000 million BTU (so 1,000 cf = 1 MBTU, the standard U.S. measure). Life is further complicated by the use of m for thousands and mm for millions (as in mmBTU), though usually M (for mega) means million.

5. At a price of 30 p/therm, the annual bill for 25,000 therms is £7,500 or U.S.$12,000.

6. The modern theory of regulation arguably places too much weight on the asymmetry of information, which overlooks the risk that information, once available, tends to leak out or be the subject of requests for disclosure.

7. CCA revalues assets in line with price movements, allowing for depreciation, and was the required form of accounting in the public sector, and for most regulated utilities except BT. It has the attraction to the utility of increasing the money value of the asset base, though the rate of return allowed on this has to be a real rate of return, not the nominal rate of return that could be defended in the case of historic cost accounting.

8. At $1.60 = £1, 10 p/therm = $1.60/million BTU. European border prices in September 1995 were about $2.80/MBTU when the spot price had fallen to 9 p/therm, and the forward priced for April 1996 was 8 p/therm. Spot prices at Bacton are quoted in the *Financial Times*.

9. The United Kingdom has a 30 bcm/yr link from Bacton on the East Coast to Zeebrugge in Belgium which opened on October 1, 1998, with contracts then signed for 8 bcm/yr exports to the continent. The spare capacity is available for opportunistic trading in either direction, though imports would effectively be managed as reduced exports. The contracting parties share capacity rights in proportion to their ownership, and can subcontract this to other parties.

10. The LRMCs and derived entry and exit charges are published annually by Transco, who have now made available a computer program, Transcost, which can compute LRMCs for various assumptions about forecast demand and supply (and specify the required investments, their costs and timing).

Chapter 9

1. This claim was made in a book review of Vickers and Yarrow (1988), who were critical of the approach of transforming public monopolies into unreconstructed private monopolies.

2. This argument is in any case flawed, since it would be more efficient to tax a competitive industry's output to create revenue for the exchequer than to capitalize the monopoly tax into a present value which shareholders will heavily discount as unlikely to persist.

3. Newbery (1989) notes a similar device used in sharecropping in the United States. Share tenants receive only a fraction of any increase in gross output, reducing their risk but also their incentives. By making the rent they pay equal to a specified share of the average yield in the locality, risk sharing is provided without any diminution of incentives.

4. Provided the demand schedule in the final market is convex, as normal.

5. The reasoning is that if there are constant returns to scale in generation (above the minimum scale) then new plant will be justified when its average total cost is less than the avoidable cost of the marginal plant. Since the marginal plant sets the SMP and hence determines the revenue from spot and contract sales, the extra revenue from selling the output of the new investment will cover its total cost. The dynamic counterpart to this is that new investment is justified if it lowers the present discounted value of total system costs, in which case the present value of the SMP will cover the total cost of the new plant. If there are economies of scale, as there are in transmission, marginal prices will not cover average costs, and additional fixed charges will be needed.

6. Before 1990 this involvement was restricted to Chile and a few small-scale examples elsewhere.

7. Some of the early projects were modest-sized barge-mounted diesel generators, which could be moved in rapidly and which, being mobile, were not as vulnerable to contract failure or renegotiation. Such plant inevitably has higher operating costs (and short-term scarcity value) and may have helped subsequent investors to assess the credibility of the power company and the regulatory agencies. The high costs may therefore have had off-setting benefits.

References

Armstrong, M. 1996. Network interconnection. Discussion paper 9625, Southampton.

Armstrong, M. 1998. Network interconnection in telecommunications. *Economic Journal* 108: 545–64.

Armstrong, M., S. Cowan, and J. Vickers. 1994. *Regulatory Reform: Economic Analysis and British Experience.* Cambridge: MIT Press.

Armstrong, M., C. Doyle, and J. Vickers. 1996. The access pricing problem: a synthesis. *Journal of Industrial Economics* 44: 131–50.

Atkinson, A. B., and J. E. Stiglitz. 1980. *Lectures on Public Economics.* New York: McGraw-Hill.

Atkinson, A. B. 1970. On the measurement of inequality. *Journal of Economic Theory* 2: 244–63.

Atkinson, S. E., and R. Halvorsen. 1986. The relative efficiency of public and private firms in a regulated environment: the case of U.S. electric utilities. *Journal of Public Economics* 29: 281–94.

Averch, H., and L. L. Johnson. 1962. Behavior of the firm under regulatory constraint. *American Economic Review* 52: 1053–69.

Baker, C. A. 1913. *Private versus Public Electricity Supply.* Fabian Tract 173.

Baker, C. A. 1915. Load factor, output and cost. *Electrical Review* 11: 841–3.

Baltagi, B. H., J. M. Griffin, and D. P. Rich. 1993. Airline deregulation: The cost pieces of the puzzle. *International Economic Review* 36: 245–60.

Barker, J., B. Tenenbaum, and F. Woolf. 1997. Governance and regulation of power pools and systems operators: An international comparison. Washington, DC: World Bank Technical Paper 382.

Barnes, F. 1998. Regulating telecommunications. In *Competition in Regulated Industries*, D. Helm and T. Jenkinson, eds. Oxford: Oxford University Press, pp. 213–33.

Baron, B. 1998. No licenses, no regulators: an overview of New Zealand's reforms. IAEE Conference Proceedings, Quebec, vol. 1. Cleveland, OH: International Association for Energy Economics, pp. 299–308. May.

Baron, D. P. 1989. Design of regulatory mechanisms and institutions. ch. 24, In *Handbook of Industrial Organization*, vol. 2, R. Schmalensee and R. Willig, eds. Amsterdam: Elsevier.

Baumol, W. J., and A. K. Klevorick. 1970. Input choices and rate-of-return regulation: An overview and discussion. *Bell Journal of Economics* 1: 162–90.

Baumol, W. J., J. C. Panzar, and R. D. Willig. 1982. *Contestable Markets and the Theory of Industry Structure*. San Diego, CA: Harcourt Brace Jovanovich/Academic Press.

Bell, A. 1995. The Telecommunications Industry 1994–95, In *CRI Regulatory Review 1995*, P. Vass, ed. London: CIPFA, pp. 93–104.

Berg, S. V., and J. Tschirhart. 1988. *Natural Monopoly Regulation*. Cambridge: Cambridge University Press.

Bergman, L., C. Doyle, J. Gual, L. Hultkrantz, D. Neven, L.-H. Röller, and L. Waverman. 1998. *Europe's Network Industries: Conflicting Priorities*. London: Centre for Economic Policy Research.

Bernard, J.-T., and M. Roland. 1995. Rent dissipation through electricity prices of publicly-owned utilities. Quebec: Université Laval, cahier 9512.

Besant-Jones, J. E., ed. 1993. Reforming the policies for electric power in developing countries. Washington, DC: World Bank, Industry and Energy Department.

Bishop, M., and M. Green. 1995. Privatisation and Recession: The Miracle Tested. CRI Discussion Paper 10.

Blumstein, C., and J. Bushnell. 1994. A readers guide to the Bluebook: Issues in California's electric industry restructuring and reform. Berkeley: University of California Energy Institute, June 2.

Bohn, R. E., A. K. Klevorick, and C. G. Stalon. 1998. *Report on Market Issues in the California Power Exchange*. Pasadena: California Power Exchange Market Monitoring Committee (at URL http://www.calpx.com/).

Brock, G. W. 1994. *Telecommunication Policy for the Information Age: From Monopoly to Competition*. Cambridge: Harvard University Press.

Bushnell, J., and Stoft, S. 1995. Electric grid investment under a contract network regime. Berkeley: University of California Energy Institute PWP–034.

Caudill, S. B., B.-G. Im, and D. L. Kaserman. 1993. Modelling regulatory behavior: The economic theory of regulation versus alternative theories and simple rules of thumb. *Journal of Regulatory Economics* 5: 251–62.

Cleevely, D. 1997. The U.K. market: First economic lessons from liberalization. Presentation to the 1997 Telecom Convention at Geneva (at URL http://www.analysys.co.uk/news/1998).

Coase, R. 1964. The regulated industries: Discussion. *American Economic Review* 54 (May): 194–8.

Covarrubias, A. J., and S. B. Maia. 1994. Reforms and private participation in the power sector of selected Latin American and Caribbean and industrialized countries, vol. 2. Washington, DC: World Bank Latin American and Caribbean Technical Department, Report 33.

Crandall, R. W. 1983. *Controlling Industrial Pollution: The Economics and Politics of Clean Air*. Washington, DC: Brookings Institution.

Crandall, R. W. 1991. *After the Breakup: U.S. Telecommunications in a More Competitive Era*. Washington, DC: Brookings Institution.

Crandall, R. W., and L. Waverman. 1995. *Talk Is Cheap: The Promise of Regulatory Reform in North American Telecommunications*. Washington, DC: Brookings Institution.

Crandall, R. W., and L. Waverman. 1999. *Universal Service: For Whom the Bell Used to Toll*. Washington, DC: Brookings Institution.

CSO. 1996. *UK National Accounts (the "Blue Book")*. Central Statistical Office. London: HMSO.

CSO. 1997. *Annual Abstract of Statistics 1997 Edition*. Central Statistical Office. London: HMSO.

Culy, J .G., G. Read, and B. D. Wright. 1996. The evolution of New Zealand's electricity supply structure. In Gilbert and Kahn 1996, pp. 312–65.

Dasgupta, P. S., S. A. Marglin, and A. K. Sen. 1974. *Guidelines for Project Evaluation*. New York: UNIDO.

Deaton, A., and N. Stern. 1986. Optimally uniform commodity taxes, taste differences, and lump-sum grants. *Journal of Public Economics* 20: 333–46.

Deaton, A. 1987. Econometric issues for tax design in developing countries. In Newbery and Stern (1987), pp. 92–113.

Department of Energy. 1988. *Privatizing Electricity: The Government's Proposals for the Privatization of the Electricity Supply Industry in England and Wales*. London: HMSO.

Dobozi, I. 1995. Electricity consumption and output decline: An update. *Transition* 6: 19–20.

DTI. 1993. *The Prospects for Coal: Conclusions of the Government's Coal Review*. Department of Trade and Industry, CM 2235. London: HMSO.

DTI. 1995. *The Prospects for Nuclear Power in the U.K.: Conclusions of the Government's Nuclear Review*. CM 2860. London: HMSO.

DTI. 1996. Press Release P/96/329 on May 2 (at URL http://www.coi.gov.uk/depts/GTI/GTI96Q2.html).

DTI. 1998a. *A Fair Deal for Consumers: Modernising the Framework for Utility Regulation*. Department of Trade and Industry. CM 3898. London: HMSO.

DTI. 1998b. *Review of Energy Sources for Power Generation: Consultation Document*. London: Department of Trade and Industry.

DTI. 1998c. *A Fair Deal for Consumers: Modernising the Framework for Utility Regulation: The Response to Consultation*. London: Department of Trade and Industry.

DTI. 1999. *The Digest of UK Energy Statistics 1999*. London: The Stationary Office.

EC. 1992. *Proposal for a Council Directive Concerning Common Rules for the Internal Market in Natural Gas*. Com(91) 548 Final-SYN 385, Brussels, February 21, 1992.

EC. 1997. Directive 96/92/EC of the European Parliament: Official Journal No. L 027. 30/01/97 P.0020.

Electricity Council. 1990. *Handbook of Electricity Supply Statistics 1989*. London: The Electricity Council.

Electricity Pool. 1998. *Pool Review Steering Group Response to Offer's Interim Conclusions of June 1998*. London: Electricity Pool.

Ellig, J. 1991. Endogenous change and the economic theory of regulation. *Journal of Regulatory Economics* 3: 265–85.

Emmons, W. M. 1991. Private and public responses to market failures in the United States electric power industry, 1882–1942. *Journal of Economic History* 51: 452–54.

Erbenovà, M., and Z. Hruby. 1995. Regulation and tariffs in the telecommunication sector: the case of the Czech Republic. Prague: Academy of Sciences.

Evans, W. N., and I. Kessides. 1993. Structure, conduct, and performance in the deregulated airline industry. *Southern Economic Journal* (January) 59(3): 450–67.

Fare, R., S. Grosskopf, and J. Logan. 1985. The relative performance of publicly owned and privately owned electric utilities. *Journal of Public Economics* 26: 89–106.

Farrell, J. 1997. Prospects for deregulation in telecommunications. Speech given on May 9. http://www.fcc.gov/Bureaus/OPP/Speeches/jf050997.html.

Farrell, M. J. 1957. The measurement of productive efficiency. *Journal of the Royal Statistical Society* A125: 252–67.

Farrer, T. H. 1902. *The State in its relation to Trade*. London: Macmillan.

FCC. 1997. *Pricing of Interconnection and unbundled elements*. Available at URL http://www.fcc.gov/ccb/universal_service/.

Federal Power Commission v. Hope Natural Gas Co. 1944. 320 U.S. 591, 601.

Feldstein, M. S. 1972. Distributional equity and the optimal structure of public prices. *American Economic Review* 62: 32–36.

FERC. 1994. *Recovery of stranded costs by public utilities and transmitting utilities*. Docket number RM94-8-001. *Notice of proposed rule making and supplemental of proposed rule making*. March 29.

FERC. 1995. *Promoting wholesale competition through open access non-discriminatory transmission services by public utilities*. Docket number RM95-8-000.

Foreman-Peck, J., and R. Millward. 1994. *Public and Private Ownership of British Industry 1820–1990*. Oxford: Clarendon Press.

Foster, C. D. 1993. *Privatization, Public Ownership and the Regulation of Natural Monopoly*. Oxford: Basil Blackwell.

Frantz, R. S. 1988. *X-efficiency: Theory, Evidence and Applications*, Norwell, MA: Kluwer.

Galal, A., and C. Torres. 1994. Compaña de Teléfonos de Chile. In Galal, Jones, Tandon, and Vogelsang (1994).

Galal, A., L. Jones, P. Tandon, and I. Vogelsang. 1994. *Welfare Consequences of Selling Public Enterprises: An Empirical Analysis*. Oxford: Oxford University Press.

Galal, A. 1994a. CHILGENER. In Galal, Jones, Tandon, and Vogelsang (1994), ch. 9.

Galal, A. 1994b. ENERSIS. In Galal, Jones, Tandon, and Vogelsang (1994), ch. 10.

Galal, A. 1996. Chile: Regulatory specificity, credibility of commitment and distributional demands. In Levy and Spiller (1996), pp. 121–46.

Gibbons, R. 1997. An introduction to applicable game theory. *Journal of Economic Perspectives* 11: 127–49.

Gilbert, R. J., and J. Henly. 1991. The value of rate reform in a competitive electric power market. In *Regulatory Choices: A Perspective on Developments in Energy Policy*, R. Gilbert, ed. Berkeley: University of California Press.

Gilbert, R. J., and E. P. Kahn. 1996. Competition and industrial change in U.S. electric power regulation. In Gilbert and Kahn (1996), ch. 5.

Gilbert, R. J., and E. P. Kahn, eds. 1996. *International Comparisons of Electricity Regulation*. New York: Cambridge University Press.

Gilbert, R. J., and D. M. Newbery. 1988. Regulation games. CEPR Discussion Paper 267.

Gilbert, R. J., and D. M. Newbery. 1994. The dynamic efficiency of regulatory constitutions. *Rand Journal* 25(4): 538–54.

Green, R. J. 1998. Can competition replace regulation for small utility customers? Mimeo. Cambridge University. Department of Applied Economics.

Green, R. J. 1999. The electricity contract market in England and Wales. *Journal of Industrial Economics* 47(1): 107–23.

Green, R. J., and D. M. Newbery. 1992. Competition in the British electricity spot market. *Journal of Political Economy* 100: 929–53.

Greenwald, B. C. 1984. Rate base selection and the structure of regulation. *Rand Journal of Economics* 15: 85–95.

Hadley, S., and E. Hirst. 1998. Will competition hurt electricity consumers in the Pacific Northwest? *IAEE Conference Proceedings*, Quebec, vol. 2. Cleveland, OH: International Association for Energy Economics, pp. 223–32.

Hannah, L. 1979. *Electricity before Nationalisation*. London: Macmillan.

Hannah, L. 1982. *Engineers, Managers and Politicians: The First Fifteen Years of Nationalised Electricity Supply in Britain*. London: Macmillan.

Harris, R. G., and C. J. Kraft. 1997. Meddling through: Regulating local telephone competition in the United States. *Journal of Economic Perspectives* 11: 93–112.

Harsanyi, J. C. 1955. Cardinal welfare, individualistic ethics and interpersonal comparisons of utility. *Journal of Political Economy* 73: 309–21.

Hausman, J. A. 1997. Valuing the effect of regulation on new services in telecommunications. *Brookings Papers: Microeconomics*: 1–38.

Hausman, J. A. 1998. Taxation by telecommunications regulation. Cambridge, MA: NBER Working Paper 6260.

Hausman, J. A, T. Tardiff, and A. Belinfante. 1993. The effects of the breakup of AT&T on telephone penetration in the United States. *American Economic Review* 83: 178–84.

Hausman, W. J., and J. L. Neufeld. 1991. Property rights versus public spirit: Ownership and efficiency of U.S. electric utilities prior to rate-of-return regulation. *Review of Economics and Statistics* 73: 414 23.

Heady, C., and S. Smith. 1995. Tax and benefit reform in the Czech and Slovak Republics. In Newbery (1995c), ch. 2.

Henck, F. W., and B. Strassburg. 1988. *A Slippery Slope: The Long Road to the Breakup of AT&T*. Westport, CT: Greenwood Press.

Henney, A. 1991. *The Economic Failure of Nuclear Power in Britain*. London: Greenpeace.

Hirschman, A. O. 1970. *Exit, Voice, and Loyalty*. Cambridge: Harvard University Press.

Hjalmarsson, L., and A. Veiderpass. 1992a. Efficiency and ownership in Swedish electricity retail distribution. *Journal of Productivity Analysis* 3: 7–23.

Hjalmarsson, L., and A. Veiderpass. 1992b. Productivity in Swedish electricity retail distribution. *Scandinavian Journal of Economics* 94: S193–205.

Hogan, W. 1992. Contract networks for electric power transmission. *Journal of Regulatory Economics* 4: 211–42.

Hogan, W. 1994. An efficient bilateral market needs a pool. CPUC Hearings August 4, Harvard Electricity Policy Group, Harvard University.

Hogan, W. 1998. Getting the prices right in PJM: What the data teaches us. *Electricity Journal* 11: 61–67.

House of Commons. 1993. *British Energy Policy and the Market for Coal*. Report HC 237. London: HMSO.

House of Commons. 1995a. *Aspects of the Electricity Supply Industry—Report*. Trade and Industry Committee Eleventh Report, HC 481-1. London: HMSO.

House of Commons. 1995b. *Aspects of the Electricity Supply Industry*, vol 2, Memo. Trade and Industry Committee Eleventh Report, HC 481-II. London: HMSO.

House of Commons. 1998a. *Trade and Industry Fourth Report: Coal*. HC 401. London: HMSO.

House of Commons. 1998b. *Trade and Industry Tenth Report: Developments in the Liberalisation of the Domestic Electricity Market*. London: HMSO.

IEA. 1994. *Natural Gas Transportation: Organization and Regulation*. Paris: IEA/OECD.

IEA. 1997. *Energy Prices and Taxes 1997*. Paris: IEA/OECD.

ITU. 1998. *World Telecommunications Development Report 1997*. Geneva: ITU.

Izaguirre, A. K. 1998. Private participation in the electricity sector—Recent trends. *Private Sector*, December (also at http://www.worldbank.org/html/fpd/notes/).

Járai, Z. 1993. 10 percent already sold: Privatisation in Hungary. In *Hungary: An Economy in Transition*, D. M. Newbery and I. P. Székely, eds. Cambridge: Cambridge University Press.

Joskow, P. L., and N. L. Rose. 1989. Effects of economic regulation. In *Handbook of Industrial Organization*, vol. 2, R. Schmalensee and R. Willig, eds. Amsterdam: Elsevier.

Jones, L., P. Tandon, and I. Vogelsang. 1990. *Selling Public Enterprises: A Cost–Benefit Methodology*. Cambridge: MIT Press.

Kahn, E. 1991. Risks in Independent Power Contracts: An Empirical Survey. *Electricity Journal* 4: 30–45.

Kahn, E., S. Bailey, and L. Pando. 1997. Simulating electricity restructuring in California: Interactions with the regional market. *Resource and Energy Economics* 19: 3–28.

Kaestner, R., and B. Kahn. 1990. The effects of regulation and competition on the price of AT&T intrastate telephone service. *Journal of Regulatory Economics* 2: 363–87.

Kaserman, D. L, J. W. Mayo, and P. L. Pacey. 1993. The political economy of deregulation: The case of intrastate long distance. *Journal of Regulatory Economics* 5: 49–63.

Kelly, F. P. 1991. Network routing. *Philosophical Transactions of the Royal Society* A337: 343–67.

Klein, M. 1998. Infrastructure concession—to auction or negotiate? *Private Sector*, December (also at http://www.worldbank.org/html/fpd/notes/).

Kleinwort Benson. 1995. *The Argentine Power Book*. London: Kleinwort Benson Securities, Ltd.

Klemperer, P. D., and M. A. Meyer. 1989. Supply function equilibria in oligopoly under uncertainty. *Econometrica* 57: 1243–77.

Kreps, D. 1990. *Game Theory and Economic Modelling*. Oxford: Clarendon Press.

Kwoka, J. E. 1995. Public vs. private ownership and economic performance: Evidence from the U.S. electric power industry. Discussion Paper 1712. Harvard Institute of Economic Research.

Kwoka, J. E. 1996. *Power Production: Ownership, Integration and Competition in the United States Electricity Industry*. Boston: Kluwer.

Laffont, J.-J. 1994. The new economics of regulation ten years after. *Econometrica* 62: 507–38.

Laffont, J.-J., and J. Tirole. 1993. *A Theory of Incentives in Procurement and Regulation*. Cambridge: MIT Press.

Laffont, J.-J., P. Rey, and J. Tirole. 1998a. Network competition: i. Overview and nondiscriminatory pricing. *Rand Journal of Economics* 29(1): 1–37.

Laffont, J.-J., P. Rey, and J. Tirole. 1998b. Network competition: ii. Price discrimination. *Rand Journal of Economics* 29(1): 38–56.

Layfield, F. 1987. *Sizewell B Public Inquiry*. Report by Sir Frank Layfield, Department of Energy. London: HMSO.

Levy, B., and P. Spiller, eds. 1996. *Regulations, Institutions and Commitment*. Cambridge: Cambridge University Press.

Little, I. M. D., and J. A. Mirrlees. 1969. *Manual of Industrial Project Analysis in Developing Countries*, vol 2. Paris: OECD.

Little, I. M .D., and J. A. Mirrlees. 1974. *Project Appraisal and Planning for Developing Countries*. New York: Basic Books.

Littlechild, S. 1983. *Regulation of British Telecommunications profitability*. London: HMSO.

Lowry, E. D. 1973. Justifications of regulation: The case for natural monopoly. *Public Utilities Fortnightly* (November 8): 1–8.

Mason, R. 1998. Internet telephony and the international accounting rate system. Mimeo. Cambridge, England: Centre for Communications Systems Research.

Mason. 1996. *Benchmarking Studies for Oftel: Comparison of U.K. Telecoms with Other Leading Countries*. Mason Communications; http://www.masoncom.co.uk/masoncom/.

Mcafee, R. P., and J. McMillan. 1987. Auctions and bidding. *Journal of Economic Literature* 25: 699–838.

Mathios, A. D., and R. P. Rogers. 1989. The impact of alternative forms of state regulation of AT&T on direct-dial, long-distance telephone rates. *Rand Journal of Economics* 20: 437–53.

Mejstřík, M., ed. 1997. *The Privatization Process in East-Central Europe*. Dordrecht: Kluwer.

Mihályi, P. 1993. Hungary: A unique approach to privatisation—past, present and future. In *Hungary: An Economy in Transition*, I. P. Székely and D. M. G. Newbery, eds. Cambridge: Cambridge University Press, ch. 6.

Mihályi, P. 1995. Privatisation in Hungary: Now comes the "hard core." Mimeo. Budapest, APV Rt.

Mitchell, B. M., and I. Vogelsang. 1991. *Telecommunications Pricing: Theory and Practice*. Cambridge: Cambridge University Press.

MMC (Monopolies and Mergers Commission). 1981. *Central Electricity Generating Board: A Report on the Operation by the Board of Its System for the Generation and Supply of Electricity in Bulk*. HC 315. London: HMSO.

MMC. 1988. *Gas: A Report on the matter of the existence or possible existence of a monopoly situation in relation to the supply in Great Britain of gas through pipes to persons other than tariff customers*. CM 500. London: HMSO.

MMC. 1993a. *British Gas Plc*. CM 2315. London: HMSO.

MMC. 1993b. *Gas*. CM 2314. London: HMSO.

MMC. 1993c. *Gas and British Gas plc*, vol 2. CM 2316. London: HMSO.

MMC. 1997. *BG Plc*. CM 2316. London: HMSO.

Moen, J. 1995. *Electricity Utility Regulation, Structure and Competition: Experiences from the Norwegian Electric Supply Industry*. Oslo: Norwegian Water Resources and Energy Administration.

Morrison, S. A., and C. Winston. 1995. *The Evolution of the Airline Industry*. Washington, DC: Brookings Institution.

Morrison, S. A., and C. Winston. 1996. Causes and consequences of airline fare wars. *Brookings Papers on Economic Activity: Microeconomics*: 85–123.

Müller, J., and K. Stahl. 1996. Regulation of the market for electricity in the Federal Republic of Germany. In Kahn and Gilbert (1996), pp. 277–311.

Newbery, D. M. 1989. Missing markets: Consequences and remedies. In *Economics of Missing Markets, Information, and Games*, F. H. Hahn, ed. Oxford: Clarendon Press, pp. 211–42.

Newbery, D. M. 1992a. The role of public enterprises in the national economy. *Asian Economic Review* 10: 1–34.

Newbery, D. M. 1992b. Supply function equilibria: Mixed strategy step functions and continuous representations. Mimeo. Department of Applied Economics, Cambridge University.

Newbery, D. M. 1994a. Restructuring and privatising electric utilities in Eastern Europe. *Economics of Transition* 2: 291–316.

Newbery, D. M. 1994b. The impact of sulfur limits on fuel demand and electricity prices in Britain. *Energy Journal* 15: 19–41.

Newbery, D. M. 1995a. Power markets and market power. *Energy Journal* 16: 41–66.

Newbery, D. M. 1995b. The distributional impact of price changes in Hungary and the U.K. *Economic Journal* 105(July): 847–63.

Newbery, D. M., ed. 1995c. *Tax and Benefit Reform in Central and Eastern Europe*. London: Centre for Economic Policy Research.

Newbery, D. M. 1996. The budgetary impact of privatization. In *Fiscal Policy and Economic Reforms*, by M. I. Blejer and T. Ter-Minassian, eds. London: Rutledge.

Newbery, D. M. 1997. Determining the regulatory asset base for utility price regulation. *Utilities Policy* 6: 1–8.

Newbery, D. M. 1998a. The regulator's review of the English Electricity Pool. *Utilities Policy* 7: 129–41.

Newbery, D. M. 1998b. Competition, contracts and entry in the electricity spot market. *Rand Journal of Economics* 29: 726–49.

Newbery, D. M. 1998c. Pool reform and competition in electricity. In *Regulating Utilities: Understanding the Issues*, M. Beesley, ed. London: Institute of Economic Affairs, pp. 117–66.

Newbery, D. M. 1998d. Rate-of-return regulation versus price regulation for public utilities. Contribution to *The New Palgrave Dictionary of Economics and the Law*. London: MacMillan.

Newbery, D. M., and N. H. Stern, eds. 1987. *The Theory of Taxation for Developing Countries*. New York: Oxford University Press.

Newbery, D. M., and M. G. Pollitt. 1997. The restructuring and privatisation of the CEGB—Was it worth it. *Journal of Industrial Economics* 45: 269–303.

Newbery, D. M., and R. Green. 1996. Regulation, public ownership and privatisation of the English electricity industry. In Gilbert and Kahn (1996b), pp. 25–81.

NGC. 1993. *Seven Year Statement for the Years 1993/4 to 1999/2000*. Coventry: National Grid Company plc.

NGC. 1995. *Seven Year Statement for the Years 1995/6 to 2001/2.* Coventry: National Grid Company plc.

Noam, E. M. 1993. Assessing the Impacts of Divestiture and Deregulation in Telecommunications. *Southern Economic Journal* 59: 438–49.

Noll, R. G. 1989. The Politics of Regulation. In *Handbook of Industrial Organization,* vol. 2, R. Schmalensee and R. Willig, eds. Amsterdam: Elsevier.

North, D. C. 1991. Institutions. *Journal of Economic Perspectives* 5: 97–112.

North, D. C., and B. R. Weingast. 1989. Constitutions and commitment: The evolution of institutions governing public choice in seventeenth-century England. *Journal of Economic History* 49: 803–32.

OECD. 1995. *Communications Outlook 1995.* Paris: OECD.

OECD. 1996a. *Historical Statistics 1960–94.* Paris: OECD.

OECD. 1996b. *National Accounts.* Paris: OECD.

OECD. 1997. *New Technologies and Their Impact on the Accounting Rate System.* Paris: OECD, OCDE/GD(97)14.

Offer. 1992a. *Report on Constrained-on Plant.* Birmingham: Office of Electricity Regulation. October.

Offer. 1992b. *Review of Pool Prices.* Birmingham: Office of Electricity Regulation. December.

Offer. 1992c. *Review of Economic Purchasing.* Birmingham: Office of Electricity Regulation. December.

Offer. 1994a. *Decision on a Monopolies and Mergers Commission Reference.* Birmingham: Office of Electricity Regulation. February.

Offer. 1994b. *Submission to the Nuclear Review.* Birmingham: Office of Electricity Regulation. October.

Offer. 1994c. *Trading outside the Pool.* Birmingham: Office of Electricity Regulation. July.

Offer. 1997. *The Competitive Electricity Market from 1998: Price Restraints, Proposals October 1997.* Birmingham: Office of Electricity Regulation.

Offer. 1998a. *Reviews of Public Electricity Suppliers 1998 to 2000: Separation of Businesses Consultation Paper.* Birmingham: Office of Electricity Regulation. May.

Offer. 1998b. *Review of Electricity Trading Arrangements—Interim Conclusions.* Birmingham: Office of Electricity Regulation. June.

Offer. 1998c. *Review of Electricity Trading Arrangements.* Birmingham: Office of Electricity Regulation. July.

Offer. 1998d. *Report on Pool Price Increases in Winter 1997/98.* Birmingham: Office of Electricity Regulation. June.

Oftel. 1997a. *Network charges from 1997—Consultation Document,* Oftel (at URL http://www.oftel.gov.uk/feedback/interac1.htm).

Oftel. 1997b. *An Assessment of the Interim 1996/7 Top Down Model,* Oftel, July (at URL http://www.oftel.gov.uk/pricing/td797.htm).

Oftel. 1997c. *Toward better Telecoms for Customers*. London: Office of Telecommunications, June.

Oftel. 1998a. *Oftel's submission to the Monopolies and Mergers Commission inquiry into the prices of calls to mobile phones*, May (at URL http://www.oftel.gov.uk/pricing/mmc0598.htm).

Oftel. 1998b. *Carrier Pre-selection in the U.K.*, Oftel, July (at URL http://www.oftel.gov.uk/competition/cps798.htm).

Oftel. 1999. *Toward Better Telecoms for Customers—1998 Progress Report*, February (at URL http://www.oftel.gov.uk/consumer/tbt0299.htm).

ONS. 1999. *Monthly Digest of Statistics*. Office of National Statistics (previously Central Statistical Office). London: The Stationary Office.

Parker, P. M., and L.-H. Röller. 1997. Collusive conduct in duopolies: Multimarket contact and cross-ownership in the mobile telephone industry. *Rand Journal of Economics* 28(2): 304–22.

Peltzman, S. 1976. Toward a more general theory of regulation. *Journal of Law and Economics* 19: 211–40.

Perez-Arriaga, I. 1994. *The Organization and Operation of the Electricity Supply Industry in Argentina*. London: Energy Economic Engineering Ltd.

Pierce, R. J. 1988. Reconstituting the natural gas industry from well head to burnertip. *Energy Law Journal* 9: 11–57.

Pierce, R. J. 1994. The state of the transition to competitive markets in natural gas and electricity. *Energy Law Journal* 15: 323–50.

Pollitt, M. G. 1993. The Relative Performance of Publicly Owned and Privately Owned Electric Utilities: International Evidence. PhD thesis. Oxford University.

Pollitt, M. G. 1994. Technical efficiency in electric power plants. Cambridge University. DAE Working Paper 9422.

Pollitt, M. G. 1995. *Ownership and Performance in Electric Utilities*. Oxford: Oxford University Press.

Pollitt, M. G. 1997. The restructuring and privatization of the electricity supply industry in Northern Ireland—Will it be worth it? Mimeo. Cambridge University. February.

Pollitt, M. G. 1998. The restructuring and privatization of the electricity supply industry in Scotland. Mimeo. Cambridge University. June.

Posner, R. A. 1971. Taxation by regulation. *Bell Journal of Economics* 2: 22–50.

Powell, A. 1993. Trading forward in an imperfect market: The case of electricity in Britain. *Economic Journal* 103: 444–53.

Priest, G. L. 1993. The origins of utility regulation and the "Theories of Regulation" Debate. *Journal of Law and Economics*, pt. 2, 36(1): 289–323.

Primeaux, W. J. 1977. An assessment of X-efficiency gained through competition. *Review of Economics and Statistics* 59: 105–108.

Primeaux, W. J. 1978. The effect of competition on capacity utilization in the electric utility industry. *Economic Inquiry* 16 (April): 237–48.

Prior, M. 1983. *Sizewell B Power Station Public Inquiry, Aspects Concerning Fossil Fuels, Proof of Evidence*. London: Town and Country Planning Association, September.

Ray, A. 1984. *Cost-Benefit Analysis*. Baltimore: Johns Hopkins for World Bank.

Rawls, J. 1971. *A Theory of Justice*. Cambridge: Harvard University Press.

Riordan, M. 1998. Conundrums for telecommunications policy. Washington, DC: FCC (at URL http://www.fcc.gov/Bureaus/OPP/Speeches).

Salop, S. C., and D. T. Scheffman. 1983. Raising rivals' costs. *American Economic Review* 73: 261–81.

Schecter, P. B. 1996. Customer ownership of the local loop. *Telecommunications Policy* 20: 573–84.

Schweppe, F., M. Caramanis, R. Tabors, and R. Bohn. 1988. *Spot Pricing of Electricity*, Dordrecht: Kluwer.

Seda, R., and Z. Hruby. 1995. Czech telecommunications: Financing of network expansion and the choice of strategic partner. Prague: Academy of Sciences.

Selten, R. (1965) Spieltheoretische Behandlung eines Oligopolmodels mit Nachfragtragheit, *Zeitschrift fuer die Gesamte Staatswirtschaft* 121: 301–24, 667–89.

Sharkey, W. W. 1982. *The Theory of Natural Monopoly*. Cambridge: Cambridge University Press.

Sherman, R. 1989. *The Regulation of Monopoly*. Cambridge: Cambridge University Press.

Shin, R. T., and J. S. Ying. 1992. Unnatural monopolies in local telephone. *Rand Journal of Economics* 23: 171–83.

Shleifer, A. 1985. A theory of yardstick competition. *Rand Journal of Economics* 16: 319–27.

Smith, V. 1996. Deregulation of natural monopoly industries. Paper presented to International Conference in Industrial Economics, Madrid, July 3–5.

Smythe vs. Ames. 1898. 169 U. S. 466, 546–48.

Spiller, P. 1993. Institutions and regulatory commitment in utilities' privatization. *Industrial and Corporate Change* 2: 317–80.

Spiller, P. 1994. Contracts, administrative law or regulatory specificity: Workable regulatory frameworks for developing economies. Washington, DC: Institute for Policy Reform, Working Paper IPR97.

Spiller, P. T., and C. G. Cardilli. 1997. The frontier of telecommunication deregulation: Small countries leading the pack. *Journal of Economic Perspectives* 11: 127–38.

Spiller, P. T., and L. V. Martorell. 1992. How should it be done? Electricity regulation in Argentina, Brazil, Uruguay and Chile. In Gilbert and Kahn (1996), pp. 82–125.

Spring, P. 1995. The restructured gas industry 1994/95. In *Regulatory Review 1995*. London: Centre for the Study of Regulated Industries, ch. 3.

Squire, L., and H. van der Tak. 1975. *Economic Analysis of Projects*. Baltimore: Johns Hopkins for the World Bank.

Stern, J. P. 1993. *Third Party Access in European Gas Industries: Regulation-Driven or Market-Led?* London: Royal Institution of International Affairs.

Stern, J. P. 1994. Gas regulation and the MMC Review 1993. In *Regulatory Review 1994*. London: Centre for the Study of Regulated Industries, ch. 2.

Stern, J. P. 1998. *Competition and Liberalization in European Gas Markets: A Diversity of Models*. London: Royal Institution of International Affairs.

Stevenson, R. E. 1982. X-inefficiency and interfirm rivalry: Evidence from the electric utility industry. *Land Economics* 58(February): 52–66.

Stigler, G. J. 1971. The theory of economic regulation. *Bell Journal of Economic and Management Science* 2: 3–21.

Stoft, S. 1997. What should a power market want? *Electricity Journal* 10(5): 34–45.

Tabors, R. D., and L. P. Galindo. 1999. *Transmission Pricing in PJM: Allowing the Economics of the Market to Work*. Cambridge, MA: Tabors Caramanis and Associates.

Tandon, P., and M. Abdala. 1994. Teléfonos de México. In Galal, Jones, Tandon, and Vogelsang (1994), pp. 417–56.

Taylor, W. E., and L. D. Taylor. 1993. Postdivestiture long-distance competition in the United States. *American Economic Review* 83(May): 184–90.

Temin, P., with L. Galambos. 1987. *The fall of the Bell system: A study in prices and politics*. Cambridge: Cambridge University Press.

Thatcher, M. 1993. *The Downing Street Years*. London: HarperCollins.

Vass, P., ed. 1996. *Regulatory Review 1996*. London: Chartered Institute of Public Finance and Accountancy.

Vickers, J., and G. Yarrow. 1988. *Privatization: An Economic Analysis*. Cambridge: MIT Press.

Vogelsang, I. 1990. *Public Enterprise in Monopolistic and Oligopolistic Industries*. Chur: Harwood.

Vogelsang, I., L. Jones, P. Tandon, M. Abdala, and C. Doyle. 1994. British Telecom. In Galal, Jones, Tandon, and Vogelsang. (1994), pp. 51–106.

Wallace, R. L., and P. L. Junk. 1970. Economic inefficiency in small municipal electric generating systems. *Land Economics* 46: 98–104.

Ware, R. 1986. A model of public enterprise with entry. *Canadian Journal of Economics* 19: 642–55.

Wellenius, B. 1994. Telecommunications restructuring in Latin America: An overview. In Wellenius and Stern (1994), 113–44.

Wellenius, B., and P. A. Stern. 1994. *Implementing Reforms in the Telecommunications Sector*. Washington, DC: World Bank.

Whish, R. 1995. Regulatory Processes and the Law. In *Regulatory Review 1995*, P. Vass, ed. London: Chartered Institute of Public Finance and Accountancy.

Williamson, O. E. 1985. *The Economic Institutions of Capitalism*. New York: Free Press.

Winsor, T. 1996. Rail Regulation 1995/96. In Vass (1996), pp. 73–86.

White, M. W. 1995. Valuing market trading mechanisms: Evidence from electricity markets. Berkeley: University of California Energy Institute PWP–033.

Wolak, F. A. 1996. The welfare impacts of competitive telecommunications supply: A household-level analysis. *Brookings Papers on Economic Activity: Microeconomics*: 269 350.

Wolak, F. A. 1998. Market design and price behaviour in restructured electricity markets: An international comparison. Paper presented before Conference on Electricity Industry Restructuring, Berkeley, March 20.

Wolak, F., R. Nordhaus, and C. Shapiro. 1998. Preliminary Report on the operation of the ancillary services market of the California Independent Systems Operator (ISO). California ISO Market Surveillance Committee (http://www.caiso.com/).

World Bank. 1993. *The World Bank's Role in the Electric Power Sector*. Washington DC: World Bank.

World Bank. 1994. *World Development Report 1994*. New York: Oxford University Press for World Bank.

World Bank. 1995. *Bureaucrats in Business*. Oxford: Oxford University Press for World Bank.

WTO. 1998. *Data on Telecommunications Markets Covered by WTO Negotiations on Basic Telecommunications* (at URL http://www.wto.org/press/data3.htm).

Yarrow, G. 1988. The price of nuclear power. *Economic Policy* 6: 81–132.

Yarrow, G. 1991. Vertical supply arrangements: Issues and applications in the energy industries. *Oxford Review of Economic Policy* 7: 35–53.

Yergin, D. 1992. *The Prize: The Epic Quest for Oil, Money and Power*. New York: Simon and Schuster.

Index